How Russia Loses
Hubris and Miscalculation in Putin's Kremlin

Washington, DC
October 2023

THE JAMESTOWN FOUNDATION

1310 L Street NW
Suite 810
Washington, DC 20005
http://www.jamestown.org

Copyright © 2023 The Jamestown Foundation

All rights reserved. Printed in the United States of America. No part of this book may be reproduced in any manner whatsoever without written consent.

For copyright and permissions information, contact The Jamestown Foundation, 1310 L Street NW, Suite 810, Washington, DC 20005.

The views expressed in the book are those of the contributors and not necessarily those of The Jamestown Foundation or any other organization or government.

For more information on this book, email pubs@jamestown.org.

ISBN: 979-8-9874519-3-9

Cover art provided by Peggy Archambault of Peggy Archambault Design, archdesign1.com.

For Sophie Arielle Kent

my muse and counselor

Jamestown's Mission

The Jamestown Foundation's mission is to inform and educate policymakers and the broader community about events and trends in those societies that are strategically or tactically important to the United States but that frequently restrict access to such information.

Using indigenous and primary sources, Jamestown's material is delivered without political bias, filter, or agenda. It is often the only source of information that should be, but is not always, available through official or intelligence channels, especially in regard to Eurasia and terrorism.

Origins

Founded in 1984 by William Geimer, The Jamestown Foundation made a direct contribution to the downfall of Communism through its dissemination of information about the closed totalitarian societies of Eastern Europe and the Soviet Union.

William Geimer worked with Arkady Shevchenko, the highest-ranking Soviet official ever to defect when he left his position as undersecretary general of the United Nations. Shevchenko's memoir *Breaking With Moscow* revealed the details of Soviet superpower diplomacy, arms control strategy, and tactics in the Third World at the height of the Cold War. Through its work with Shevchenko, Jamestown rapidly became the leading source of information about the inner workings of the captive nations of the former Communist Bloc.

In addition to Shevchenko, Jamestown assisted former top Romanian intelligence officer Ion Pacepa in writing his memoirs. Jamestown ensured that both men published their insights and experience in what became bestselling books. Even today, several decades later, some credit Pacepa's revelations about Nicolae Ceausescu's regime in his book *Red Horizons* with the fall of that government and the freeing of Romania.

The Jamestown Foundation has emerged as a leading provider of information about Eurasia. Our research and analysis on conflict and instability in Eurasia enabled Jamestown to become one of the most reliable sources of information on the post-Soviet space, China, the Caucasus, and Central Asia. Furthermore, since 9/11, Jamestown has used its network of indigenous experts in more than 50 different countries to conduct research and analysis on terrorism and the growth of al-Qaeda and its offshoots throughout the globe.

By drawing on our ever-growing global network of experts, Jamestown has become a vital source of unfiltered, open-source information about major conflict zones around the world—from the Black Sea and Siberia to the Persian Gulf, Latin America, and the Pacific. Our core of intellectual talent includes former high-ranking government officials and military officers, political scientists, journalists, scholars, and economists. Their insights contribute significantly to policymakers engaged in addressing today's newly emerging global threats in the post-9/11 world.

Table of Contents

Introduction 1

Chapter 1: Ukraine: From Obsession to Catastrophe 11
Ukraine and Muscovy 12
An Independent Ukraine 20
'George, Ukraine Is Not Even a State!' 27
Russian Pressure Fails 37
Miscalculations and War 46
Epilogue: After February 2022 65

Chapter 2: South Africa: The Deal Too Big to Succeed 67
The Soviet Union and the Struggle Against Apartheid 69
Russia and the New South Africa 77
'A Scarcely Believable Picture of Rampant Corruption' 83
The Nuclear Deal 92
The Cost of Overreach 106
Epilogue: South Africa After Zuma 111

**Chapter 3: The Sputnik Vaccine: From Breakthrough to
Footnote** 119
'The World's First Vaccine' 121
Vaccines Roll Out 134
Trouble for Sputnik 141
The Information Struggle 150
'A Flawed and Irredeemable Venture' 159
Epilogue: Variants, Sanctions, and War 169

Chapter 4: Nord Stream 2: So Near and Yet So Far 173
Russia's Blue Gold 174
Nord Stream 1: 'A Secure, Resilient Partnership' 178
Nord Stream 2: Security or Vulnerability? 182
Money and Influence 209
Dead in the Water 214
Epilogue: Nord Stream 2 After the Invasion of Ukraine 222

iii

iv | HOW RUSSIA LOSES

Chapter 5: Macedonia: The Tank and the Lada **227**
Betrayal in Bucharest *228*
The Paint and Bubblebath Revolt *234*
Russia and Its Allies: Threats, Bots, and Motorcycles *243*
The West's Campaign: Star Power and the Team From DC *253*
Referendum Day and the Constitution *259*
Russia's Loss in Macedonia *268*
Epilogue: A Frustrated North Macedonia *275*

Chapter 6: Ecuador: Who Played Whom? **279**
La Revolución Ciudadana *281*
Correa and the United States *283*
Correa at Home *290*
Correa and Russia *299*
Ecuador Reverses Course *306*
Moscow and Quito: The Limits of Solidarity *313*
Epilogue: New Crises for Ecuador *326*

Chapter 7: How Russia Loses **331**

Chapter 8: Strategies for the West **349**

Chronology **373**

Acknowledgments **378**

About the Author **379**

Introduction

Vladimir Putin's Russia is weak in the traditional sources of geopolitical power. Its gross domestic product (GDP) barely beats out those of Canada and Italy. It maintains strong nuclear forces but struggles to combat a well-armed conventional opponent. It has no military ally pledged to its defense.

Unlike its Soviet predecessor, the Russian Federation proposes no coherent ideology for others to adopt. Its belief system at home is essentially the inward-facing Tsarist creed of "orthodoxy, autocracy, and nationality." Abroad, it derides the supposed corruption of the West while offering no model of a more just or prosperous society. Its international ventures offer little to impoverished peoples, focusing mainly on building geopolitical advantage for Russia and wealth for local and Russian elites.

All that said, the Kremlin has scored many successes abroad. Putin has seized territory from Georgia and Ukraine, deepened ties with authoritarian and conservative governments worldwide, and built a disinformation empire that threatens to undermine the very foundations of democratic states. His loyalists have penetrated deeply into the West's political, financial, and cultural worlds, reaping financial windfalls while neutralizing politicians and institutions that might oppose Russian influence. At least until his full-scale invasion of Ukraine in 2022, common wisdom held that Putin was a master tactician, armed with a vast array of influence tools that would more than compensate for Russia's weaknesses.

This book takes a more skeptical view. While acknowledging Putin's successes, I argue that Russian influence operations during his rule have also been plagued by a non-trivial set of failings—and that these failings repeat themselves in case after case. The book offers six case studies in which hubris and miscalculation by Putin and his lieutenants led to either temporary reversals or lasting defeat. The purpose of the book is

2 | HOW RUSSIA LOSES

to study these common failings so the West can be prepared to exploit them in future contests with the Kremlin.

The six studies describe cases in which Russia has seen its tactics exposed and resisted, its allies defeated, its power insufficient, and its political calculations upended. Key roles have been played by Western governments that acted vigorously at critical moments, journalists and civil society activists who took action against corruption and violence, Russian economic weakness, and Russia's own conflicting goals.

The case studies begin with Russian activity in Ukraine from that state's independence in 1991 to the Russian invasion in 2022, with the emphasis on Putin's time in power. Over more than two decades, Putin transformed a country where he was initially highly popular into an implacable enemy, repeatedly alienating Ukrainians through clumsy attempts to dominate them rather than working to build mutually beneficial relations. Putin, of course, claimed that years of skilled Western machinations turned Ukraine against Russia. Some factors did inevitably pull Ukraine toward the West. But given Russia's deep history and experience with its neighbor, the country was Putin's to lose—and he lost it.

The second case study is South Africa from 2009 to 2018. Putin worked hard to become that nation's essential ally, aided by a strongly pro-Russian president, Jacob Zuma. The Soviet Union's unwavering support for South Africa's Black population through decades of apartheid rule left Russia a deep reservoir of goodwill in a country that is strategically located and rich in critical materials. Relations between the two countries deteriorated under Mikhail Gorbachev and Boris Yeltsin but surged again under Putin, who saw South Africa as a political and economic springboard to the rest of the continent. However, the Russian president overreached, trying with Zuma to ram through a nuclear power deal so massive that it could have made the country an economic vassal of Moscow for decades. Strongly resisted by civil society and the courts, the deal collapsed and was a major reason for Zuma's forced resignation.

Introduction | 3

In Ukraine and South Africa, Russian efforts were aimed at cultivating broad, long-term influence. The case studies also include three Russian campaigns aimed at very specific shorter-term goals.

In August 2020, Putin announced that Russia had become the first country to register a COVID-19 vaccine. With nearly a million people already dead from the virus, and Western scientists warning that a vaccine could be at least a year away, the sudden appearance of Russia's Sputnik vaccine could have become an even more spectacular success than the Soviet satellite of the same name launched in 1957. Putin's Russia looked set to save millions of lives, rack up billions in sales, and once again humble the West's best scientists. Yet, within a couple of years, Sputnik was barely a footnote in the global vaccine race. It fell victim to Russian overconfidence; economic weakness; a tidal wave of Chinese vaccines; and eventually an even bigger wave of Western vaccines that became the world standard.

Russia made an enormous political, financial and influence investment in the Nord Stream 2 gas pipeline from Russia to Germany. The Kremlin cultivated top European politicians and industrialists, battled environmentalists, dispatched lobbyists to fight legal obstacles, and ridiculed Western worries about Russian energy blackmail. The project failed completely with Russia's invasion of Ukraine. But even before that it was hamstrung by US sanctions, a change of government in Germany, and even a critically important delay imposed by Denmark. Some believe that, even without the invasion, Nord Stream 2 might never have opened. The project suffered from Russia's own clashing priorities; its contempt for regulators and legal processes; a declining demand for gas; and nimble obstructive tactics by the United States, Poland, and others.

In Macedonia,[1] Russia and its allies failed in a hard-fought effort in 2018–19 to block the country from changing its name—an

---

[1] Macedonia changed its name to North Macedonia on February 1, 2019. Both names are used in this book, depending on the period referenced.

essential step for it to become eligible to join the North Atlantic Treaty Organization (NATO) and the European Union (EU). From 2008 to 2016, the Western-leaning Balkan nation had begun to swing strongly toward authoritarianism and friendship with Russia under Prime Minister Nikola Gruevski. Civil society actors, many of them funded by Western governments and foundations, joined with opposition politicians to force Gruevski from power. In a surprisingly intense battle of influence, Russia and the West deployed their best capabilities to affect the outcome of a national referendum and two parliamentary votes on the name change. The West won. Moscow's defeat reflected its tendency to ally itself with top powerbrokers failing to project Russia as a country that could help Macedonia; the failure of its overt threats; the economic allure of the EU; and the willingness of Western nations to make an all-out effort where Russia might not have anticipated such vigor.

The final case study examines Russian influence in Ecuador during the presidency of Rafael Correa, who ruled from 2007 to 2017. Correa, an outspoken leftist who accused the United States and international financial institutions of dominating and exploiting Latin America, expelled the US ambassador, shut down a base for US anti-drug flights, and gave WikiLeaks founder Julian Assange refuge in Ecuador's London Embassy. Correa visited Moscow twice, and some in Russia saw him as the ideological heir of Venezuela's Hugo Chávez.

Yet, Correa never fully requited Moscow's hopes for his regime. When he fell from power and his chosen successor turned Ecuador sharply back toward Washington, Russia's position in the country evaporated. The Kremlin's loss stemmed from putting all its chips on Correa, not creating a public image that could survive a new government, and economic weakness that left Russia a poor third to US and Chinese influence. Correa made his relationship with Moscow largely transactional; he took what the Kremlin offered but felt no obligation to follow its lead on every issue. One wondered, in the end, who had been playing whom.

As these brief summaries suggest, several weaknesses repeat themselves in Russian influence operations. Russia yokes its

Introduction | 5

fortunes to the strength and durability of top personalities in areas it seeks to influence. It pays little attention to foreign aid. It overestimates its own capabilities and underestimates the strength of democratic institutions and civil society. While Russian propaganda routinely paints Western countries as constantly on the verge of attacking Russia, Kremlin policymaking often seems to work from a contradictory narrative: that the West is weak, confused, and can easily be bested in any contest. Thus, Russia underestimates the capabilities of Western nations and can be surprised when the West resolves to use them.

The case studies also demonstrate that Russia is contemptuous of international organizations, independent regulators, and legal processes, unless it can fully control them. Russia's influence and business ventures are low on altruism, focusing mainly on benefits for Moscow. In addition, Moscow's goals often conflict, blunting its ability to focus whatever power it has on a primary aim. Clashes between powerful Russian actors can even threaten the security of the state, as demonstrated by Yevgeny Prigozhin's rebellion in June 2023. Finally, Russian policy options are constricted by a new wave of ideology, closely linked to Putin's personal beliefs and his intolerance for other views.

Each case study in this book begins with historical background on the country or issue involved to establish the context for what Russia hoped to accomplish. The Russian effort is then described, along with the outcome. This is followed by an analysis of the Kremlin's strategy, with special attention to behavior that repeats itself in other situations. Each study ends with an epilogue that brings the story up to the present day.

The case studies are followed by a chapter that synthesizes Russian failings across all six case studies, pulling in examples from Russian misadventures elsewhere as well.

A final chapter offers recommendations as to how the West can benefit from being aware of Russia's weaknesses.

These recommendations begin with judiciously assessing the alliances the Kremlin tends to make with top power brokers in areas it seeks influence. Do these alliances pose a real danger to Western security that must be actively opposed? Or is the threat they present mainly one of rhetoric or propaganda, meaning they perhaps can be waited out?

Hopeful waiting, however, can sometimes turn into dangerous complacency. The recommendations therefore also include taking aggressive action where warranted. In the cases in this book, the West and its allies countered Russian influence by means including information tactics (some overt and others less so); direct pressure on governments and parliament members; the use of a wiretap for political advantage; sanctions at key moments; the deployment of arms and military trainers; and by entangling Russian projects in lawsuits, bureaucratic red tape, and administrative processes.

Some of these Western actions were last-minute decisions or resulted from luck or coincidence. Still, they stymied Russian efforts that might otherwise have succeeded.

The recommendations emphasize the importance of aid, trade, and public diplomacy, which can make populations less hospitable to Russian influence. I pay special attention to shaky democracies in Eastern Europe and the Global South, where the West's concept of "exporting" democracy and human rights may be viewed with suspicion.[2] The recommendations suggest maximizing the role of local pro-democracy actors and independent journalists, who benefit from organic credibility and authenticity.

The recommendations also call for leveraging the power of courts, legislative bodies, and international organizations. Russia has particular trouble prevailing in these bodies because of its disdain for laws and procedures. I recommend, as well, ways to profit from Moscow's conflicting goals.

---

[2] A better concept, I argue later in the book, is that democracy is not a Western product but the natural right of people in all countries.

Introduction | 7

Finally, the recommendations note the power that Russia derives from the myth that its influence operations are always successful. In fact, they do not always succeed. Nevertheless, the myth is a Russian asset in itself.

Several other case studies could have been chosen for this book. One would be Kosovo. Ever since the end of the Yugoslav wars, Russia and its Serbian ally have made constant efforts to delegitimize the tiny Balkan state. Kosovo, however, has survived despite intense, continuing pressure, and has won recognition from more than 100 countries and international organizations.

Another example of the failure of Russian influence might have been the Kremlin's long struggle to reverse the US and European economic sanctions imposed after its seizure of Ukrainian territory in 2014. At many points, it seemed possible that European nations might drop them because they hurt European businesses and were not changing Russian behavior. However, despite Russian efforts, the sanctions held.

Russia failed, too, in Montenegro, whose aspiration to join NATO and the EU was fiercely opposed by Moscow and its proxies. Russia had deep historical and business ties to Montenegro, and though the nation is tiny, its entry into NATO would complete the alliance's control of the Adriatic Sea. Prosecutors implicated Russian agents in a desperate, unsuccessful coup attempt against the country's pro-Western leadership in 2016. Montenegro is now a NATO member and candidate EU member.

Other case studies could have included Central Asia, where much of Russia's influence is being replaced by Turkey and China, or Azerbaijan, whose oil and gas wealth, as well as Turkish and European connections, have eroded the Kremlin's importance.

I chose the six case studies in the book because of their geographical spread and the variety of challenges to Russian influence that they illustrate. Russian economic weakness figures particularly in the Sputnik and Ecuador cases; Moscow's disregard for legal and regulatory procedures in the cases of Sputnik and Nord Stream 2; vigorous pushback by Western

8 | HOW RUSSIA LOSES

nations and pro-democracy forces in the cases of Nord Stream 2, Macedonia, and South Africa; and the dangers of relying on one powerful leader in the cases of Macedonia, South Africa, Ecuador, and Ukraine. The limits of Russian threats and bullying are evident in the Ukraine and Macedonia chapters, while the Ecuador chapter underlines the transactional nature of some leaders' relationships with Moscow.

The South African case adds additional value because it demonstrates that Russian losses are not necessarily forever. Moscow's influence there has grown again since Zuma's downfall. Russia failed to secure a victory for its favored candidate in Madagascar's 2018 election but switched to backing another before election day and still enjoyed an outcome satisfactory to its interests. In Sudan, Russian influence continued despite the overthrow of Kremlin ally Omar al-Bashir in 2019, though renewed chaos in 2023 threatened Moscow's position anew.

While the studies in this book cover vastly different geographies and subject matter, some cases overlap interestingly. The stories of Gruevski, Correa, and Zuma are nearly contemporaneous; they all rose to power within less than three years of each other, and all lost power within a period of 13 months. Among the few foreign dignitaries who attended Russia's 2015 World War II Victory Day ceremonies, boycotted by most Western leaders, were both Zuma and the president of Macedonia, Gjorge Ivanov, an ally of Gruevski. When Western nations sanctioned Russia after it invaded Ukraine in 2014, South Africa, Ecuador, and Macedonia all ignored the trade ban. The 2008 NATO summit in Bucharest was fateful both for Ukraine and Macedonia. The years 2021 and 2022 were critical to Russia's struggles with both the Sputnik vaccine and the Nord Stream 2 pipeline. A chronology at the end of the book shows how events in the six case studies interlace with one another.

US presidents and members of Congress play roles in all of the studies. Donald Trump was contemptuous of Ukraine, undermining its credibility when it needed all the support it could get against Russia. However, he spoke out sharply, at least sometimes, against Nord Stream 2 and signed the sanctions

Introduction | 9

legislation that stopped it. In Macedonia, Republican Senator Ted Cruz's ideological convictions threatened to undercut a successful Western effort against Russian influence. In the case of Nord Stream 2, however, Cruz was key in promoting the US sanctions that stopped the project.

Some may argue that none of the Russian setbacks in these studies represented a total loss for the Kremlin, or that Russia's successes elsewhere far outweigh its losses in these instances. Ecuador and Macedonia probably never ranked as towering issues in the Kremlin. As noted, Russia appeared to recover from its loss in South Africa. The Sputnik vaccine, though it never gained worldwide traction, undoubtedly saved many lives. The Nord Stream 2 pipeline might have opened. As for Putin's Ukraine policy, its ultimate fate has not yet been written.

In recognition of these arguments, each case study includes alternative interpretations of the events described, acknowledging the view that the Kremlin did not suffer a significant defeat, or that the loss was of little consequence to Moscow. However, the failure of Russian tactics—at least at some point—is a fact in each case, and, in the aggregate, the cases show a pattern of Russian hubris and miscalculation. To assert, as some do, that even Russian failures are a success because the Kremlin learns not to repeat its missteps is not justified by this examination's findings.

To be sure, the Kremlin has sometimes triumphed over these failings as it has built its power from region to region. Russia's tight relations with top elites can pay off if those elites manage stay in power. Though economically weak overall, Russia still has enough financial throwweight to make an impact in some struggling countries. Although Russia offers other nations no coherent prescription to make them more prosperous, its pan-Slavist and anti-colonialist slogans resonate with some populations. Sometimes different Russian interest groups do work together, significantly increasing Moscow's influence. However, the failings described in this study are frequent and significant enough that they can create opportunities for astute Western statecraft.

10 | HOW RUSSIA LOSES

This book will attain its goal if it demonstrates that many Russian influence operations contain the seeds of their own destruction—if Russia's adversaries can anticipate, detect, and exploit them. By recognizing the patterns in the Kremlin's setbacks of the past, pro-democracy forces can learn to counter Russian adventurism in the future.

One note on terminology. The term "Russian" is usually used in this book to refer to Kremlin activities or policy under Vladimir Putin. It is not meant as a generalized comment about the Russian people.

1.

Ukraine: From Obsession to Catastrophe

Russia handled few issues so badly, over such a long period, as its relationship with Ukraine. When Ukraine became independent in 1991 after the collapse of the Soviet Union, its ties to Russia could not have been tighter—the fruit of centuries of political and social integration. Ukraine was an ideal partner for Moscow in a market-driven world: it is the largest country in Europe after Russia itself, strong in agriculture and high-tech, with an economy that was deeply interdependent with Russia's.

Yet, again and again, Russia missed or ignored opportunities to build a good-neighbor relationship with the critically important country next door. Misunderstandings, Russian arrogance, trade disputes, and political confrontations began under Boris Yeltsin and crested under Vladimir Putin. After winning independence, Ukraine did build bridges to the West—but fitfully, and always aware of Russia's importance and power. Putin, however, saw any movement westward as a threat to Russia. He also feared that for all the chaos of Ukraine's democracy, his own citizens might find Ukrainian freedoms a better model than his oppressive rule. The Russian president saw Ukraine as a reverse image of his state, a parallel-universe Russia with people who were almost identical but free. For Putin, such a Ukraine was like antimatter—an "anti-Russia," he called it—that could destroy his system just by contact.

Defenders of Russian policy argue that Putin never had a choice— that the relentless expansion of Western ties with Ukraine created

12 | HOW RUSSIA LOSES

a security crisis that eventually forced him to invade in 2022. But throughout the period of its independence, provocations against Ukraine by Russia and its allies abetted its Western movement. A pro-Russian candidate rigged a presidential election in 2004, triggering a national rebellion. Ukrainians turned sharply against Russia again after the 2014 Maidan revolution, when Russia annexed Crimea and, through proxies, took control of much of Ukraine's Donbas. Russia frequently clashed with Ukraine over energy supplies and trade. Putin had many opportunities to build a relationship of trust with Kyiv. However, he let himself be guided by other priorities: the re-establishment of Russian suzerainty over the "near-abroad," the preservation of his repression at home, and his broader conflict with the West—all of which raised Ukraine's importance to Western countries as a counterweight to Russia.

Yet, however the West involved itself in Ukraine—and it did— Ukraine was still Russia's to lose. Over three decades of opportunities, how might Moscow have built positive relations, or at least a stable modus vivendi, with Kyiv? How might Putin, who ruled Russia for two of those decades, have managed matters so that he would never had had to think of invading?

Ukraine and Muscovy

Many Russians consider Ukraine an inalienable part of their identity. Family and economic connections between Russia and Ukraine are deep. Nikita Khrushchev and Leonid Brezhnev were born there. Mikhail Gorbachev had a Ukrainian mother and wife. Some of the most important battles of World War II were fought on Ukrainian soil. Generations of Russian intellectuals saw "Little Russians" (Ukrainians) and "White Russians" (Belarusians) as integral parts of a single Russian fraternity. Nikolai Gogol and Mikhail Bulgakov were born in Ukraine. Pushkin, Tolstoy, and Chekhov set literary works in Crimea, the summer playground of Tsarist Russia's elite. Major Russian and Soviet figures as different as Vladimir Lenin, Mikhail Gorbachev, Alexander Solzhenitsyn,

Ukraine: From Obsession to Catastrophe | 13

and Joseph Brodsky all believed Ukraine was a natural part of a Moscow-ruled state.[1]

Yet, Russia and Ukraine are neither congruent in history nor psychological experience.

The rich lands that make up present-day Ukraine were crisscrossed by Scythians, Khazars, Vikings, Greeks, Romans, Byzantines, Poles, Lithuanians, Jews, Venetians, Genoans, Habsburgs, Romanovs, Ottomans, Hungarians, Mongols, and Crimean Tatars. Each of these peoples brought their own social and political influence. Roman and Greek Catholicism, Orthodox Christianity, Protestantism, Judaism, and Islam all contributed to Ukraine's religious heritage.

By comparison to all the cultures that touched Ukraine, Muscovite Russia developed as a far more isolated entity. The Orthodox church was the state religion, the government always authoritarian. The biggest foreign influence on Muscovy was from the Mongol invaders.

Although Putin built his Ukraine policy on the claim that Ukrainians and Russians are the same people, a review of Ukraine's history brings that assertion very much into question.

Distinct Eastern Slavic peoples first appeared in the area now occupied by Ukraine in the 5th century. The city of Kyiv, by varying accounts, has existed since the 5th, 6th, or 7th centuries. By the 9th century, rival groups of Vikings entered the region in search of trade and slaves. The dominion they created came to be known as "Rus," a Norse word believed to refer to a trading company or to "those who row."

Beginning with the reign of Volodymyr the Great, a prince of Nordic descent who would have been known at the time as

---

[1] Solzhenitsyn believed "local populations" in Ukraine should be able to determine their own destinies, such as western regions becoming independent or eastern regions joining Russia, but that no decision could be made for Ukraine as a whole.

14 | HOW RUSSIA LOSES

"Waldemar," the Rus state expanded dramatically in the 10th and 11th centuries. Rus, ruled from Kyiv, became the largest state in Europe, dominating most of present-day western Russia and Belarus. At the time, Moscow was a minor trading town.

Despite their Nordic roots, Rus's rulers increasingly assimilated into the Slavic population. Volodymyr was baptized into Byzantine Christianity in 988 in return for the hand of a sister of two Byzantine emperors. Slavic landowners were granted rights and became a semi-aristocratic class of warriors and administrators. Urban tradesmen and skilled artisans also enjoyed some authority in local matters. Peasants had no rights.

Rus disintegrated into rival dominions in the 12th century, and the Mongols conquered and pillaged Kyiv in 1240. The conquest ended, for four centuries, Kyiv's place as the region's most important center. In place of a Kyiv-centered entity, the Mongols recognized two successor dominions: an eastern principality in Vladimir and Suzdal, which evolved into modern Russia, and a western one, Galicia-Volhynia, which included much of modern central and western Ukraine.

Very different histories and conceptions of state power evolved in the two entities. The Mongols remained in Vladimir-Suzdal for two centuries, which Russian historiography remembers as the brutal era of the "Tatar yoke." Vladimir-Suzdal became the Grand Duchy of Moscow in the 13th century but still under Mongol control. The descendants of its princes became the Tsars of Russia.

In Galicia-Volhynia, the Mongols were less visible, letting local rulers run their own affairs in return for tribute. Their presence lasted half the time it did in Vladimir-Suzdal. Galicia-Volhynia later collapsed in a succession struggle. In the 14th century, its territory was divided between Poland and Lithuania. The Polish state assimilated Rus nobles into its system, reducing their independence while still recognizing their status. Lithuanian nobility assimilated quickly into Rus life and culture. In both dominions, the Rus nobility retained rights; neither territory had the features of absolute monarchy that became Russia's lot.

The treaty of Lublin in 1569 created the Polish-Lithuanian Commonwealth. Under it, most of the land of present-day Ukraine was transferred to Poland and most of modern Belarus to Lithuania, thereby roughly defining Ukraine's northern borders. The region Poland controlled became known as "Polish Rus," distinct from Roman Catholic Poland. Within a century after Lublin, a distinct Ukrainian language became widely spoken among the common people, and the term "Ukraine" began to be used as a geographical term for the region.

Ukraine was not easy for Poland to rule. In particular, Poland struggled to control and appease large armies of independent-minded Cossacks. These Ukrainian warriors, who chose their rulers by democratic means, alternately fought for and rebelled against the Polish state, Russia, and the Crimean Tatars.[2] Their ranks were swelled by peasants fleeing forced servitude on Polish landlords' estates. Poland also faced resistance in Ukraine to the 1596 Union of Brest, an agreement with the pope by Poland and some Ukrainian Orthodox churchmen that put Orthodox believers under the authority of Rome instead of Constantinople. (Ultimately, many Uniate churches appeared in Ukraine with Eastern rites but subordinate to the pope.) The power of the Cossacks and the resistance to Brest were quite different issues but had a common effect: both helped to further solidify the idea of a Ukraine that was not simply part of Poland but had an identity of its own.

In 1610, the Cossacks joined with the Poles to capture and occupy Moscow. But in 1648, headed by Bohdan Khmelnytsky, they staged their Great Revolt against Poland. They won from Poland the right to establish a nearly independent state. The "Cossack Hetmanate" encompassed much of present-day central Ukraine. Fighting continued between the Hetmanate and Poland, however, and after several defeats, the Hetmanate was forced to look for new allies. In 1654, in a fateful decision for the future of Ukraine,

---

[2] The Tatars, descendants of indigenous Crimean people and the Mongols, became a vassal state of the Ottoman Empire at the end of the 16th century.

16 | HOW RUSSIA LOSES

Khmelnytsky and his officers swore allegiance to Tsar Alexei Romanov of Muscovy.

The 1654 agreement was hardly a re-unification of two brotherly realms, as often claimed by Soviet and Russian historians.[3] Khmelnytsky came to Muscovy not out of fraternal affection born of a common Kievan Rus past, but out of military necessity. He had even warned that, if an alliance with Muscovy was not reached, he could turn to the Ottomans. Ukraine and Russia had developed very differently from each other over four centuries. As one example, their languages had diverged so much that interpreters were needed at the negotiations.

Built as it was on convenience, the alliance between Muscovy and the Cossacks soon collapsed after Muscovy made a separate peace with Poland, the Cossacks' archenemy. Khmelnytsky died, and a succession struggle undermined the Cossack state. After more years of war and attempted deals with Russia and Poland, the Cossacks became divided in 1667 into two hetmanates split by the Dnipro River: a western one subordinate to Poland and an eastern one allied with Moscow.

The state of Moscovy formally became the Russian Empire under Peter the Great (known in Ukraine by the modest name Peter I). Neither Peter nor Catherine the Great, whose reign began three decades after Peter's death, believed the hetmanate under their control was entitled to any special status. The lands of the eastern hetmanate became provinces of Russia, serfdom and imperial taxation were established there, and the Cossack military was absorbed into the Russian army.[4] With the weakening of Poland

---

[3] For a more detailed discussion of the historical differences between Russia and Ukraine—despite Putin's efforts to deny them—see Arnold, Katherine, " 'There is no Ukraine': Fact-Checking the Kremlin's Version of Ukrainian History," London School of Economics, https://blogs.lse. ac.uk/lseih/2020/07/01/there-is-no-ukraine-fact-checking-the-kremlins-version-of-ukrainian-history

[4] Serfdom was far less part of the Ukrainian psychological experience than it was for Russians. Serfdom reigned in Russia from the 16th century until Alexander II abolished it in 1861. In Ukraine, large numbers of peasants avoided serfdom by fleeing to Cossack lands

and its eventual partition, Russian forces moved far west of the Dnipro. By the end of the 18th century, Moscow controlled almost all of present-day Ukraine except Galicia in the southwest, which became part of the Austrian Empire. Constantinople lost all its territory in southern Ukraine and Crimea.

Possession of Ukraine gave Russia a new window on the West, but it was perpetually concerned that Ukrainian nationalism could threaten its grip. Starting in the late 18th century, local people increasingly began to call themselves "Ukrainians" instead of "Little Russians." Tsarist authorities moved quickly to stamp out the growing Ukrainian identity through an intense Russification campaign. Arrests and exile choked off a blossoming Ukrainian cultural movement among intellectuals. The great Ukrainian writer Taras Shevchenko was exiled and banned from artistic work. Ukrainian schools closed. A decree stated that "a separate Little Russian language has never existed, does not exist and cannot exist." Moscow ordered the restoration of full Orthodoxy to Uniate churches. Alexander II forbade all Ukrainian-language publications in 1876. However, Ukrainian cultural and political life flourished in neighboring Galicia, helping feed Ukrainian consciousness in Russian-ruled lands. Only after the 1905 revolution did Russia allow Ukrainian publishing again.

In World War I, some Ukrainians fought for the Russian Empire, and others for the Central Powers that included Germany, Austria, and the Ottomans. Those who fought against Russia focused mainly on the hope that the war would yield an independent Ukrainian state. Two such states were attempted in the chaos following the war and the 1917 Bolshevik Revolution. The period saw widespread fighting in Ukraine among the Polish and Bolshevik armies, anti-Bolshevik Whites seeking a return to the pre-revolutionary Tsarist order, and troops loyal to the short-lived Ukrainian states.

---

during Polish and Lithuanian rule. Under Russian control, the oppressive institution lasted only a couple of generations before abolition.

18 | HOW RUSSIA LOSES

The most effective fighters were the Bolsheviks, who captured major cities but failed to control the countryside. Peasants rebelled against them when they tried to seize grain. The Bolsheviks were forced out but returned under a new guise after Lenin decided the Bolsheviks had mishandled the "nationality question." This time, the Bolsheviks came to establish the "Ukrainian Socialist Soviet Republic,"[5] a state that, in a bow to Ukrainian nationalism, would be nominally independent in association with Soviet Russia. The Bolsheviks allowed Ukrainian leftists to join their party and let peasants split up land they had formerly worked. With those inducements, all of modern-day Ukraine was soon under Soviet control except the west—now transferred, after the war, from Austria back to Poland.

Lenin's Bolsheviks included in the new Ukrainian republic the Donbas region in the east. In the lead-up to his 2022 invasion of Ukraine, Putin said Lenin had no right to include those territories in Ukraine. But the Bolsheviks had their reasons. First, the Ukrainian elites, to whom the Bolsheviks were trying to appeal, had long seen Donbas as Ukrainian territory. (It was claimed by both of the failed Ukrainian states at the end of the war). Second, Donbas cities, many of them originally settled by Cossacks, became crowded with Russian peasants who migrated there for higher pay. The Bolsheviks believed their power would be strong among those "working-class" citizens. They could serve as a counterweight to Ukrainian peasants in the countryside, whose loyalty they still considered uncertain.

The nominal independence of the Ukrainian republic soon proved to be worth nothing. Soviet forces violently imposed collectivization on Ukraine's agriculture and seized food for desperate Soviet cities. Raiding parties even took precious seed stocks set aside for future planting. Millions of Ukrainians starved to death or were murdered by Soviet police and troops in the Great Famine of 1932–1933, known to Ukrainians as the Holodomor ("death by hunger"). More died in Stalin's murderous purges throughout the 1930s. The deaths of so many Ukrainian

---

[5] The name was changed in 1936 to the Ukrainian Soviet Socialist Republic as part of a nationwide modification of republic names.

speakers from starvation and execution, as well as a renewed official campaign of Russification, contributed to the number of people in Ukraine today who list Russian as their first language.

In World War II, most Ukrainians fought with the Red Army against Nazi Germany. An estimated six million Ukrainians died. Some initially fought on the side of the German forces, hoping the war would push back the Soviets and allow for the creation of an independent Ukraine. As Germany's occupation of Ukraine became increasingly murderous, Ukrainians began to form armed anti-Nazi undergrounds. Remnants of these fighters clashed with Soviet security forces into the 1950s.

With Germany's defeat, Stalin deported to other parts of the country hundreds of thousands of Ukraine residents whose loyalty he questioned, including Russians, Ukrainians, ethnic Germans, and the republic's entire population of Crimean Tatars. As part of the postwar settlement, Stalin won Galicia and Volhynia for Ukraine, as well as Czechoslovakia's territory of Carpathian Ruthenia.

Khrushchev, who succeeded Stalin as Soviet leader in 1953, had a long political history in the Communist Party of Ukraine. He poured funds into Ukraine's economic development and made it a center for the Soviet Union's metallurgical, defense, and high-tech industries. He also allowed some revival of Ukrainian national consciousness, which was repressed again under Brezhnev.

In 1954, Khrushchev transferred Crimea from the Russian Soviet Federated Socialist Republic to Ukraine. Speculation remains rife over Khrushchev's motive. The gesture was variously understood as an effort to appease Ukrainians still resistant to Russian domination or to gain Ukrainian party support for Khrushchev's political battles in Moscow. Other reputed motives were a desire to increase the number of ethnic Russians in Ukraine (since Crimea had many such inhabitants) or because of Crimea's dense

20 | HOW RUSSIA LOSES

transport, water, and energy connections to Ukraine.[6] In any case, the transfer was simply a technicality within the Soviet Union, where everything was controlled from Moscow. Khrushchev could not have known that his decision would, by 1991, make Crimea the property of an independent Ukraine. Today, many Russians believe Khrushchev's transfer of the territory should carry no more weight than any other misguided decision by the Soviet government.

An Independent Ukraine

Ukraine played an essential role in the death of the Soviet Union. Gorbachev's policy of *glasnost*, which encouraged discussion of once-taboo topics, was at first approached gingerly by Ukrainian Soviet media and politicians. Soon, however, it led to a torrent of Ukrainian patriotic fervor and pressure for democratic institutions. Ukrainian elites buzzed with discussions of the Holodomor and Stalin's repressions, how the Ukrainian language might be advanced, and environmental destruction that had been covered up by the Soviets—including the April 1986 disaster at Chornobyl.

The waves of Ukrainian consciousness united citizens who previously had little in common. Russian-speaking miners in Donbas, angry over dangerous working conditions, joined with cultural elites in the West. Communist officials reinvented themselves as Ukrainian patriots. Political dissidents, who under the Soviets had clandestinely circulated *samizdat* appeals for human rights, openly demanded that Ukraine become a sovereign nation. Elections in 1989 sent many non-communist Ukrainians to the national parliament in Moscow, putting additional pressure on Gorbachev. After elections to the Verkhovna Rada (Ukraine's parliament) in March 1990, a third of its officials were members of democratic movements.

---

[6] For more detail, see "The transfer of the Crimea to the Ukraine," Bulletin of the Institute for the Study of the History and Culture of the USSR," Vol. 1, No. 2 (April 1954), reposted at https://iccrimea.org/historical/crimeatransfer.html.

Ukraine: From Obsession to Catastrophe | 21

In July, the Rada passed the "Declaration of State Sovereignty of Ukraine." The document stopped short of proclaiming full independence but declared the supremacy of Ukrainian laws over Soviet ones, as well as Ukraine's right to create its own armed forces. There was even an early version of the mass demonstrations that would be so important to Ukraine in 2004 and 2014. More than 100,000 students converged on Kyiv in the "Revolution on Granite" in October 1990. The demonstration on the capital's central square, known as the Maidan, included demands that Ukraine not enter a proposed "union treaty" to replace the Soviet Union, even if it were styled as a union of sovereign states.

Kyiv's defiance toward Moscow made it a key ally for Russian President Boris Yeltsin. He was bent on removing Gorbachev from power by dissolving the Soviet Union that Gorbachev reigned over. In November 1990, Yeltsin and Leonid Kravchuk, chairman of the Rada, signed a treaty between their republics stating that each was a sovereign entity, that neither would interfere in the other's internal affairs, and that they recognized each other's existing borders. Yeltsin did Ukraine the honor of signing the agreement in Kyiv, where he told the Rada:

> Russia does not aspire to become the center of some sort of new empire. It does not want to have an advantage over other republics. Russia understands better than others the perniciousness of that role, inasmuch as it was Russia that performed precisely that role for a long time. What did it gain from this? Did Russians become freer as a result? Wealthier? Happier? You yourselves know the truth; history has taught us that a people that rules over others cannot be fortunate.[7]

---

[7] *Molod' Ukrainy*, December 2, 1990, cited in Solchanyk, Roman, "Ukraine, Russia and the CIS," Harvard Ukrainian Studies, 1996, Vol. 20, https://www.jstor.org/stable/41036683

22 | HOW RUSSIA LOSES

The prospect of the disintegration of the Soviet Union into independent states caused alarm in the West. Officials there feared chaos, conflict, and—particularly—loss of control over Soviet nuclear weapons. They believed Gorbachev's vision of a "Soviet-Union-with-freedom" was still sustainable if the Soviet republics would support it. In what became known as his "Chicken Kiev" speech, US President George H. W. Bush warned the Rada on August 1, 1991, against "suicidal nationalism."

Such warnings had little effect on the rocketing support for Ukrainian independence. The coup attempt against Gorbachev just 18 days after Bush's speech only reinforced Ukrainians' conviction that their country needed to insulate itself from unpredictable events in Moscow. On August 24, the Rada declared Ukraine an independent state, with the decision to be confirmed by a referendum on December 1. The voters ratified independence by nearly 93 percent.

In the referendum, it was clearer what Ukrainians were voting against—Moscow's domination of Ukraine, chaos in the Kremlin, and Soviet-era atrocities—than what they were voting for. Ukraine had almost never been free from outside domination; its national project was only beginning. "The Ukrainians got a state but not a nation," said Serhii Plokhy, a leading historian of Ukraine. "This has been the project of the past 30 years: determining what it means to be a Ukrainian. It was a guessing game. No one knew what would happen. The moments of truth came in 2014 and 2022."[8]

Although the Baltic states and Georgia had declared independence ahead of Ukraine, the loss of Ukraine's vast territory made clear that Gorbachev and the Soviet Union could not survive. On December 8, Yeltsin, Kravchuk, and Stanislav Shushkevich, chairman of the Belarusian parliament, signed the Belovezh Accords, proclaiming the end of the Soviet Union and the beginning of the Commonwealth of Independent States (CIS). Gorbachev resigned on December 25, 1991, and Yeltsin became Russia's leader.

---

[8] Serhii Plokhy, interview with author, October 20, 2022.

Ukraine: From Obsession to Catastrophe | 23

Yeltsin expected that Ukraine and Russia, sovereign as they might be, would still be united through the CIS. Yeltsin had spoken in September 1991 of a new voluntary economic alliance of Soviet republics in which Russia would be "an equal among equals."[9] Ukrainian independence threw such concepts into doubt. Russian politicians began to insist that the December 1 referendum had been illegal, that issues like Crimea still needed to be resolved, and that Russia had a duty to protect Russian-speakers in Ukraine.

Kravchuk, who became Ukraine's president in a vote simultaneous with the independence referendum, had been clear in the Belovezh talks that Ukraine did not intend the CIS to be a Russian-dominated replacement for the Soviet Union. The Rada ratified Ukraine's CIS membership but insisted on the inviolability of its borders and right to have its own armed forces.

Yeltsin soon began to turn away from his "equal among equals" rhetoric and the modest role for Russia that he had expressed in his 1990 Rada speech. By 1994, he was saying Russia should be "first among equals" within the CIS. He told the UN General Assembly that this extended to security matters, saying "the main peacekeeping burden in the territory of the former Soviet Union lies today on the shoulders of the Russian Federation." Yeltsin said Russia had a responsibility to protect millions of Russians in the newly independent states: "Once they were at home, then they became guests—and not always welcome ones."[10] However, unlike his successor Putin, he never suggested Ukraine had no right to exist as a sovereign state.

Ukraine did not join other CIS members in collective political activities, nor did it sign the CIS joint security treaty in 1992.[11] Like some other Soviet republics, it was suspicious of Russia's

---

[9] Audio of September 3, 1991, speech at https://yeltsin.ru/archive/audio/8976.

[10] Audio of September 26, 1994, speech at https://yeltsin.ru/archive/audio/9033.

[11] The treaty laid the groundwork for today's Moscow-led Collective Security Treaty Organization (CSTO).

eagerness to dispatch "peacekeepers" to Moldova's Transnistria region and Georgia's Abkhazia. The Kremlin had been stirring up separatist sentiment among Russian speakers in both places, and Kyiv could easily imagine the same scenario recurring in its own Russian-speaking regions. In 1994, Russia launched its war against separatists in Chechnya, a brutal conflict in which indiscriminate Russian air strikes and artillery barrages killed tens of thousands of civilians. To Ukraine and the other former Soviet republics, it was clear that when Russia felt its interests threatened, it would be a force to reckon with.

Still, Ukraine realized its enormous economic dependence on Russia. It needed Moscow for oil, natural gas, and fuel for its nuclear reactors. At the same time, the Russian authorities were angered by Ukraine's liberal monetary policy and state subsidies to industry. (This clashed with Russia's "shock therapy" austerity and fueled inflation in both countries.) Leonid Kuchma, a former industrial official, succeeded Kravchuk as president in 1994 with a program that included building stronger economic ties with Russia and restoring the status of Russian as an official language in Ukraine. He signed an agreement aimed at coordinating economic activity with Russia and the other CIS nations, and in return won oil and gas from Russia at reduced prices.

Kuchma made clear, however, that Ukraine would not be ruled politically by Moscow. Seeking to balance relations between East and West, he proclaimed a "multi-vector" foreign policy anchored in Moscow, Brussels, and Washington. Although Ukraine's 1990 Declaration of State Sovereignty said the country would be neutral and belong to no military bloc, the Rada stated in 1993 that this would not prevent the country from joining "a pan-European security structure." The Rada also set a long-term goal of joining the EU.[12] In 1994, Ukraine became the first CIS nation to join NATO's Partnership for Peace—a program that could serve as a track to NATO membership.

---

[12] Rada statement at https://zakon.rada.gov.ua/laws/show/3360-12#Text

Two major issues beyond economic questions complicated Ukrainian-Russian relations in the 1990s: the presence of Soviet nuclear weapons in Ukraine, which Western officials had already worried about, and the future of Crimea and the Black Sea Fleet.

When Ukraine became independent, it asserted ownership of all Soviet weaponry on its territory. This included more than 4,000 strategic and tactical nuclear warheads, 176 intercontinental ballistic missiles, and 44 TU-160 strategic bombers. Questions abounded about whether the warheads were even usable without codes and keys held by Moscow, but some Ukrainian politicians believed their very presence could help ensure Ukraine's security against Russia. However, the United States was concerned about Ukraine's ability to manage and protect the warheads. It also feared that the appearance of new nuclear states—Belarus and Kazakhstan had inherited nuclear weapons as well—could threaten existing nuclear treaties with Moscow. Thus, Washington demanded that Ukraine's warheads be turned over to Russia.

Ukraine held out for security guarantees and financial compensation. Russia initially agreed to recognize Ukraine's territorial integrity "within the borders of the CIS." Kyiv rejected this phrasing because the guarantee would apply only if it remained a CIS member. The nuclear issue was finally solved—quite imperfectly, as later events would demonstrate—with the 1994 Budapest Memorandum. In it, the US, Russia, and the UK all recognized an obligation to respect Ukraine's sovereignty and territorial integrity. The wording of the memorandum was hardly airtight. There was no enforcement mechanism, other than a promise that the three countries would consult if questions about their commitments arose.[13]

---

[13] The three parties agreed to not use force or the threat of force against the territorial integrity or political independence of Ukraine "except in self-defense." After the 2014 invasion of Ukraine, Russia claimed that it was not bound by the memorandum since the government it had signed the document with had been, in Moscow's view, overthrown by a coup at Maidan. Putin also asserted the 2022 invasion was justified by self-defense. For the text of the memorandum,

26 | HOW RUSSIA LOSES

The memorandum was the best deal Ukraine could get. Upon its signing, the nuclear arms were transferred to Russia. The other permanent UN Security Council members, China and France, delivered separate statements to Ukraine about respecting its territorial integrity but without any language about what would happen if it were violated. (Bill Clinton, the US president at the time, said in 2023 that he regretted the Budapest deal and believed Russia would not have invaded if Ukraine still had nuclear weapons.[14])

As for Crimea, the peninsula had been part of the Russian Empire since 1783. When Ukraine became independent nearly 67 percent of Crimeans were ethnic Russians. Crimea was also geopolitically crucial to the Soviet Union as the headquarters of its Black Sea Fleet, based at Sevastopol.

Russia and Ukraine engaged in a series of threats, negotiations, and decrees, often conflating questions of Crimea's political future with the issue of the fleet. Russia cut off the flow of gas to Ukraine in 1993 as a bargaining tactic over control of the fleet and Sevastopol. The Crimean parliament declared independence in 1992, apparently in a step toward joining Russia. Ukraine put down the effort and deported Crimea's pro-Russian president, Yuri Meshkov, to Russia in 1995.

The disputes between Moscow and Kyiv over Crimea and the fleet had the potential to cause a true crisis. Each nation, however, was distracted by other issues. Both Russia and Ukraine were struggling with political and economic turbulence at home, and the Kremlin was enmeshed in its Chechen wars. In 1997, Yeltsin and Kuchma signed a Treaty on Friendship, Cooperation, and

---

see https://treaties.un.org/doc/Publication/UNTS/Volume% 203007/Part/volume-3007-I-52241.pdf. Similar agreements were signed in Budapest regarding the sovereignty of Belarus and Kazakhstan.

[14] O'Callaghan, Miriam, "Clinton regrets persuading Ukraine to give up nuclear weapons," *RTÉ*, April 4, 2023, https://www.rte.ie/news/ primetime/2023/0404/1374162-clinton-ukraine

Partnership that recognized each state's borders and territorial integrity.

With that agreement, each side retreated on critical issues. Ukraine ceded 80 percent of the fleet to Russia and gave it a 20-year lease on its Sevastopol base, despite a provision in its constitution prohibiting foreign military bases. Russia's recognition of Ukraine's borders implicitly confirmed that Crimea belonged to Ukraine. Many high-profile Russians, including Moscow Mayor Yuri Luzhkov, complained that Yeltsin had conceded too much. The Russian parliament delayed ratifying the accord until 1999.

'George, Ukraine Is Not Even a State!'

The 1997 treaty only papered over the deep divisions between Ukraine and Russia. When Vladimir Putin took power in Russia in the first moments of the 21st century, he faced a series of issues much broader than Ukraine. Yet almost every major issue he dealt with in his first years would eventually bear on Ukraine in some way. Especially important in this regard were his gradual transformation of Russia into an authoritarian state and the decline in relations between Russia and the West.

Putin's first concerns were saving Russia from collapsing into a patchwork of regional power centers, defeating Chechen separatists, and reversing the economic disaster of the Yeltsin years. "We want our Russia to be a free, prosperous, rich, strong and civilized country, a country of which its citizens are proud and which is respected in the world," said Putin in his inaugural address after his formal election in March 2000.[15]

As president, he moved quickly to rein in oligarchs who used their ill-gotten fortunes to build political power, and regional governors who behaved like feudal lords and blocked tax revenues from Moscow. It soon became obvious, however, that

---

[15] Text at http://www.kremlin.ru/events/president/transcripts/21399

Putin's restoration of internal order would include a sharp curtailment of political and media freedom—as well as neutralization of anyone who could challenge his personal authority. Uncooperative oligarchs, such as media moguls Boris Berezovsky and Vladimir Gusinsky, were forced to leave the country; oil tycoon Mikhail Khodorkovsky was jailed, and his Yukos company dismantled. By mid-2003, all major television networks and most national radio outlets were controlled by the government or Putin allies.

In 2004, Chechen militants shocked Russia with an attack on a school in Beslan in Russia's North Caucasus region. More than 300 people died during the attack and subsequent response by security forces. Putin took the opportunity to push through new laws that tightened his control over Russian society as a whole. Regional governors would no longer be popularly elected, but nominated by Putin and approved by regional legislators. Changes in the electoral system would sharply limit the opportunity for opposition parties to win seats in the Duma. Authorities stepped up control of the judiciary. By 2005, human rights groups found that, in cases with high political stakes, Kremlin pressure on judges dictated the verdicts.

In foreign affairs, Putin moved initially to improve relations with Western nations. After the September 11, 2001, attacks in the United States, he offered Washington help in its military campaign against Afghanistan. At a meeting with Putin in 2003, President George W. Bush said, "I respect President Putin's vision for Russia: a country at peace within its borders, with its neighbors, and with the world, a country in which democracy and freedom and rule of law thrive."[16]

However, the two countries had much to overcome. The West was alarmed by Russia's democratic backsliding and its brutality in Chechnya. Putin suggested that the US had aided the Chechen separatist movement and thereby bore part of the blame for

---

[16] Text at https://georgewbush-whitehouse.archives.gov/news/releases/2003/09/20030927-2.html

Beslan.[17] Russia had been angered by the expansion of NATO, starting in 1999, and was still smoldering over events in Serbia and Kosovo that year: the alliance had bombed Serbia, and NATO and Russian forces nearly opened fire on each other in June 1999 at Kosovo's airport. Putin said later that he had been involved in Russian decision-making during the Kosovo crisis.

Arms control, traditionally one of the few bright areas in Washington-Moscow relations, began to unravel. In 2001, the United States withdrew from the Anti-Ballistic Missile Treaty.[18] The two countries also failed to reach a START II agreement.

Soon Putin began denouncing US policy in Afghanistan, Iraq, and Guantanamo Bay. At the 2007 Munich Security Conference, he accused Washington of using force to dominate the world. Putin's allies encouraged a wave of nationalism in Russia, fueled by nostalgia for the Soviet Union, the resurgence of the Russian Orthodox Church, and visions of a new pan-Eurasian civilization led by Moscow.

It will long be disputed whether Putin stoked nationalism and exaggerated a Western threat as a pretext for establishing autocracy at home, or if he believed there was a genuine foreign menace that only an authoritarian state could repulse. A parallel question was whether Western actions needlessly torpedoed what could have been real Russian friendship with the West, or were a reasonable response to Putin's growing authoritarianism and hostility.

---

[17] See Ignatius, David, "The moment when Putin turned away from the West," *The Washington Post*, March 9, 2023, https://www.washington post.com/opinions/2023/03/09/putin-bush-chechnya-ukraine-war

[18] President George W. Bush argued that war between the US and Russia was out of the question and that the US needed more flexibility on missile defense to counter countries such as North Korea. Russia, however, believed the US still had a goal of making itself invulnerable to any Russian attack.

30 | HOW RUSSIA LOSES

NATO expansion was not something the West forced on the Central and East European nations. They sought it—and if NATO had denied them membership, it would have given license to Russia to dominate those countries again. Yet NATO might also have extended Russia some security guarantees, or taken other measures to compensate Moscow for losing its entire Warsaw Pact defensive shield. From another perspective, one could argue that Putin chose to portray NATO's expansion as more momentous than it was, to encourage the West to flagellate itself for its insensitivity rather than focus on Russia's behavior.

Ukraine had to navigate carefully amid all these developments. Kuchma veered between pro-Western and pro-Russian positions. Ukrainian forces exercised with NATO armies, and a series of cooperation agreements were signed between Kyiv and the alliance. In 2003, the Rada proclaimed an intent to join NATO,[19] and Kuchma dispatched 1,700 soldiers to aid the US-led Operation Iraqi Freedom. In yet another twist, responsibility for security policy was then moved from the Rada to the president, whereupon Kuchma nullified the Rada's statement about joining the Western alliance.

Meanwhile, overall Western support for Kuchma slipped. Many of his actions suggested a taste for authoritarian rule; recordings surfaced suggesting he had been involved in the kidnapping and murder in 2000 of Georgiy Gongadze, an investigative journalist. There were also unconfirmed reports that Kuchma's government had sold anti-aircraft radar to Iraq. The US House of Representatives passed a resolution warning that Ukraine's 2002 parliamentary elections must be conducted fairly and transparently.

Kuchma looked to Russia for support. But Moscow had its price. Putin's officials said relations with Ukraine could depend on whether anti-Russian "nationalists" were elected in large

---

[19] Rada statement at https://zakon.rada.gov.ua/cgibin/laws/main.cgi?nreg=964-15#Text

numbers to the Rada.[20] Moscow also pressed Ukraine to become more active in the CIS. Russian-Ukrainian trade fell precipitously from the middle of the Yeltsin period to the early Putin years amid a series of economic disputes. Kuchma agreed in 2003 to become the largely ceremonial head of the CIS, even though Ukraine had declined to be a full member and to create a "joint economic space" with Russia, Belarus, and Kazakhstan. Kuchma also declared 2003 a cultural "Year of Russia" in Ukraine, winning a visit by Putin to kick off the event.

Political tensions, however, continued. As a hint of its power, Russia began in 2003 to build, with no warning to Ukraine, a dam from its side of the Kerch Strait to Ukraine's Tuzla Island in the center of the strait. The project threatened to make the island part of Russia, giving Moscow control of all traffic transiting the strait on its way to Ukraine's Azov Sea ports. Ukraine sent troops to the island, and Russia halted the project. But the Kremlin had demonstrated its capabilities.

Meanwhile, Kuchma maintained a dialogue with Brussels about joining the EU. (Association with the EU served the interests of some of the new Ukrainian oligarchs, who feared being dominated at home by even wealthier Russian tycoons.)

Kuchma was barred by term limits from running again in 2004 and threw his support behind Viktor Yanukovych. Arrested in his youth for robbery and assault, Yanukovych had become a regional transport manager in Donbas before rising in the local political structure. Kuchma named him prime minister in 2002. Like many in Donbas, he was believed to have strong pro-Russian sympathies.

Yanukovych's opponent was Viktor Yushchenko, a government finance official and former prime minister who envisaged Ukraine becoming a full member of both the EU and NATO. It appeared as if Kuchma's "multi-vector" foreign policy would soon give way to

---

[20] Maksymiuk, Jan, "Ukrainian election as 'strategic football'," *RFE/RL Newsline*, April 2002, http://ukrweekly.com/archive/pdf3/2002/ The_Ukrainian_Weekly_2002-14.pdf

32 | HOW RUSSIA LOSES

a much more one-sided orientation toward either Moscow or the West.

Putin's government leapt to support Yanukovych. Russian consultants filled his campaign team, and Russian media—widely watched in Ukraine—strongly endorsed him. Putin visited Ukraine twice in one month to back Yanukovych, appearing with him at parades and on TV. Putin personally introduced Yanukovych to US Secretary of State Condoleezza Rice in Moscow before the election, underlining the Kremlin's support. Yanukovych campaigners smeared Yushchenko's supporters with claims that they were pro-Nazi and agents of the West—assertions Putin would use against his Ukrainian enemies two decades later. Shortly before voting began, Yushchenko was poisoned with dioxin that, researchers said, was in such concentrated form that it must have been produced in a laboratory.

Yanukovych won the 2004 election by a margin of 49-47, according to results issued by the government. Putin congratulated Yanukovych on his victory. However, widespread claims of voter intimidation and ballot-rigging touched off the Orange Revolution, a string of protests and strikes. Some 500,000 demonstrators massed on the Maidan to demand a rerun of the second round of voting. In eastern Ukraine, where Yanukovych's power base was largely situated, demonstrations broke out in his support. A re-vote was held under the eyes of international monitors and resulted in a victory for Yushchenko by a margin of 52-45.

Moscow was dismayed by Yanukovych's loss, but even more by the process that led to it. To Putin, the Orange Revolution was another alarming instance of popular protests deciding a country's leadership. Public demonstrations, some by groups that received American support, had forced Serbia's Slobodan Milošević from power in 2000. The Rose Revolution toppled Eduard Shevardnadze in Georgia in 2003, and the Tulip Revolution ousted Kyrgyzstan's Russian-advised president in 2005.

Ukraine: From Obsession to Catastrophe | 33

Some civil society organizations involved in the Orange Revolution protests received funding from the United States and other Western sources. It would have been easy for Putin to imagine that the West's strategy was to hold off Russia militarily through NATO while funding "pro-democracy" movements to topple regimes in Moscow's neighborhood and perhaps eventually his own. (Later, after the Arab Spring protests in 2010 and pro-democracy demonstrations in Moscow in 2011, Putin became even more repressive at home, with renewed crackdowns on both political and media opponents.)

As president, Yushchenko switched Ukraine's security policy once again, restoring the official intent to join NATO. He promoted the use of the Ukrainian language over Russian and launched an international campaign to have the Holodomor declared as a genocide. Yet his administration neither swung Ukraine into full alignment with the West, nor addressed the nation's economic problems. Infighting among politicians blocked significant reforms. Many voters soon decided that the government they had elected with such high hopes had become dysfunctional.

After a rush of enthusiasm and aid at the start of Yushchenko's term, the West settled into what became known as "Ukraine fatigue." Ukrainian politics were so chaotic that Yanukovych was rehabilitated, becoming Yushchenko's prime minister in 2006. Splitting with Yushchenko, Yanukovych called for a delay in joining NATO due to a lack of public support.

By the April 2008 NATO summit in Bucharest, Yushchenko had yet another prime minister, Yulia Tymoshenko, and was strongly pushing for membership in the alliance. Some NATO members, especially Germany and France, opposed it, and Putin was vehemently against the idea. At a news conference with Yushchenko just before the summit, Putin raised the prospect of "retaliatory actions" against Ukraine if NATO set up bases on its territory:

> It is frightening not just to say, but even to think that Russia, in response to such a deployment, the possibility of such a deployment—and

theoretically one cannot exclude such a deployment there—that Russia will target its nuclear strike systems at Ukraine. Just imagine that for a second! This is what worries us.[21]

Putin told the Bucharest meeting: "We do not have any right to veto, and cannot have that, and we aren't claiming that. But I want for all of us, when we are deciding such issues, to understand that we, too, have our interests. Well, 17 million Russians live in Ukraine. Who can tell us that we have no interests there? In the south, the whole south of Ukraine, there are only Russians."[22] He reportedly told Bush at the session, "Understand, George, that Ukraine is not even a state! What's Ukraine? Part of its territory is Eastern Europe and part—the main part—was a gift from us!"[23]

Ultimately, the alliance procrastinated the question of Ukrainian membership. Distracted by a recession at home and wars in Iraq and Afghanistan (where NATO needed Russian help), the alliance decided to delay embarking on a Membership Action Plan for Ukraine or Georgia. However, the summit communiqué stated that both countries "will become" NATO members. Four months after Bucharest, Russia invaded Georgia.

Yushchenko condemned the invasion. At the end of 2008, the United States and Ukraine signed a Charter on Strategic Partnership. It fell far short of a security alliance but, among other things, called for increasing the "interoperability and coordination of capabilities between NATO and Ukraine."

---

[21] Text at http://www.kremlin.ru/events/president/transcripts/24833

[22] Text at https://www.unian.info/world/111033-text-of-putin-s-speech-at-nato-summit-bucharest-april-2-2008.html. Putin exaggerated his figures. According to the 2001 census, about 8.3 million of Ukraine's 48.4 million people identified as ethnically Russian. See http://2001.ukrcensus.gov.ua/eng/results/general/nationality

[23] *Kommersant*, "Блок НАТО разошелся на блокпакеты [NATO bloc divided into little blockages]," April 7, 2008, https://www.kommersant.ru/doc/877224

Ukraine: From Obsession to Catastrophe | 35

Russian talk about Ukraine began to take on an increasingly ominous tone. Ukrainians took as practically an ultimatum a speech in May 2009 by Konstantin Zatulin, a Russian member of parliament who specialized in relations with post-Soviet states. Zatulin warned that most of Ukraine's elites were "oriented toward the so-called European choice" and that Ukraine was claiming to be "an alternative center of gravity in the post-Soviet space." Ukraine, he said, must declare neutrality; establish a federal system to guarantee the rights of Crimea and the Donbas region; guarantee the dominance in Ukraine of the Moscow Patriarchate of the Russian Orthodox Church; oust "openly anti-Russian" elements from state institutions; and enter a "military-political alliance" and "monetary and customs union" with Russia. If Ukraine failed to accept such conditions, he said, any Russian government would inevitably conclude "that it is not at all necessary that Ukraine be preserved as a state in the interests of Russian politics."[24]

Yushchenko's popularity fell precipitously amid the administrative chaos and infighting of his administration. He faced claims that he was corrupt and constantly battled the Rada and the Constitutional Court. Yanukovych reentered the electoral arena, running for president in 2010 with the help of a passel of American consultants—who later worked for Donald Trump, Bernie Sanders, and John Kerry. Yushchenko managed to win less than 6 percent of the vote and was eliminated in the first round; Yanukovych won the second round, defeating Tymoshenko.

---

[24] Text at https://zatulin.ru/vystuplenie-k-f-zatulina-na-konferencii-russkoyazychnaya-ukraina-vozmozhnosti-i-problemy-konsolidacii. With tortured logic, Zatulin explained that Moscow was seeking only neutrality, not a military alliance, from Ukraine, but that a military alliance was essential to make sure that neutrality was not being used as a smokescreen to conceal NATO arms and training. For the alarm Zatulin's speech caused in Ukraine, see Litvinenko, Alexander, et al., "Большой сосед определился. Что Украине делать дальше? [The big neighbor has made up his mind. What does Ukraine do now?]," *ZN.UA*, September 18, 2009, https://zn.ua/international/bolshoy_sosed_opredelilsya_chto_ukraine_delat_dalshe.html

36 | HOW RUSSIA LOSES

Yanukovych came to power on February 10, 2010, with his own version of Kuchma's three-vector policy. He insisted that Ukraine could live securely as a "bridge" between East and West. He wrote optimistically for *The Wall Street Journal*:

> We should not be forced to make the false choice between the benefits of the East and those of the West. As president I will endeavor to build a bridge between both, not a one-way street in either direction. We are a nation with a European identity, but we have historic cultural and economic ties to Russia as well. The re-establishment of relations with the Russian Federation is consistent with our European ambitions. We will rebuild relations with Moscow as a strategic economic partner. There is no reason that good relations with all of our neighbors cannot be achieved.[25]

Yanukovych quickly improved relations with Russia with another turnabout regarding NATO, declaring once again that Ukraine did not intend to join the alliance. He also agreed to a 25-year extension of Russia's lease on the Black Sea Fleet's Sevastopol base. However, he continued exercises between Ukrainian forces and NATO and contributed ships to the alliance's anti-piracy and anti-terrorism operations.

Overall, economic issues were the main preoccupation of Yanukovych's time in office—and the cause of his downfall. Trade relations between Moscow and Kyiv had been poor under Yushchenko, involving, in particular, a series of disputes between 2005 and 2009 over natural gas supplies from Russia. In 2009, the European Union established its Eastern Partnership, a wide-ranging program to build economic and other ties with Ukraine and five other post-Soviet nations.[26] (Russia was not included.) Particularly alluring to the post-Soviet states was the Deep and

---

[25] Text at https://www.wsj.com/articles/
SB10001424052748704804204575069251843839386
[26] The others were Armenia, Azerbaijan, Belarus, Georgia, and Moldova.

Comprehensive Free Trade Agreement, a customs union with the EU. To compete, Russia, Belarus, and Kazakhstan launched the Eurasian Customs Union and called on Ukraine to join. Since a country cannot belong to two customs unions, Ukraine faced a fateful choice, one that could not be finessed by Yanukovych's proclaimed desire to balance relations with Brussels and Moscow. Joining one customs union or another would tie the Ukrainian economy for the long term to one side or the other, though Brussels offered to negotiate ways to maintain some trade advantages for Moscow.

Russia poured on the pressure. Putin was widely reported to be contemptuous of Yanukovych for what he saw as his indecisiveness, his attempts to play off the EU against Russia, and overwhelming interest in his own personal enrichment. In the summer of 2013, Russian customs officials started blocking Ukrainian exports. The heavy-handed tactics angered Ukrainians, and the Rada supported taking the European offer.

Yanukovych looked ready to sign the EU deal and a signing ceremony was set for Vilnius in late November 2013. But a week beforehand, after a meeting with Putin, Yanukovych suddenly decided to suspend the EU process, receiving from Russia a break on gas prices and a $15 billion credit line.

Russian Pressure Fails

It had been clear since the Orange Revolution that the Ukrainian people would have their own say on key events affecting their country's future. While the customs union itself was a rather esoteric subject, many Ukrainians saw the deal as opening the door to full EU membership—and all the travel, study, and business opportunities that offered. Thousands of Ukrainians, many shouting "Ukraine is Europe," launched demonstrations in Kyiv against Yanukovych's decision and set up a permanent occupation of the Maidan. Students led the protests at first, but the crowds grew rapidly after police began beating protesters. Demonstrators soon occupied government buildings throughout the country, demanding Yanukovych's resignation. In mid-

38 | HOW RUSSIA LOSES

February, the demonstrations peaked with police firing on the crowds and demonstrators fighting back with Molotov cocktails and, the government claimed, firearms of their own. More than 100 demonstrators and a dozen police officers were killed.

The Barack Obama administration sided strongly and visibly with the protesters. Assistant Secretary of State Victoria Nuland mingled with them on the Maidan. Senator John McCain shouted, "America is with you!" International mediators patched together an agreement for early elections with Yanukovych remaining president in the interim. The demonstrators would not hear of it. Yanukovych fled Kyiv for Russia on February 22, 2014, a resounding defeat for Russian influence that upstaged the last days of Putin's Sochi Olympics showcase. The Rada installed a caretaker government led by Oleksandr Turchynov, and Petro Poroshenko was elected president in May.

Western governments rushed to give the new government financial aid. They also froze the assets of Yanukovych, whose enormous residential compound was discovered to contain luxurious homes, an artificial lake, an automobile museum, and a private zoo.

Even before Yanukovych's ousting, Russia had prepared to intervene in Ukraine. As soon as the Maidan protests began, Russian assets began stirring up fears in Crimea and Donbas that Russian-speakers faced imminent peril from Kyiv. By January 2014, pro-Russian activists in Crimea were burning EU flags, blaming the West for the crisis and calling for Crimea to secede from Ukraine. Immediately after Yanukovych fled, Putin held an all-night meeting with his security chiefs and told them, "We must start working on returning Crimea to Russia."[27] On February 27, armed men took over the Crimean parliament. Although it was not clear what exactly had happened inside, it was announced that the body had decided to hold a referendum on greater autonomy for the peninsula.

---

[27] *Agence France-Presse*, "Putin describes secret operation to seize Crimea," March 8, 2015, https://news.yahoo.com/putin-describes-secret-operation-seize-crimea-212858356.html

Ukraine: From Obsession to Catastrophe | 39

Pro-Russian militants took over government bodies throughout Crimea. Russian troops without insignia, commonly referred to as "little green men," appeared on the streets, and Ukraine's few forces found themselves surrounded. On March 16, a referendum was held on uniting Crimea with Russia. According to the pro-union officials who ran the vote, 95.5 percent of voters approved. The foreign ministers of the United States, the UK and Ukraine convened in Paris on March 5 to underline the importance of the Budapest Memorandum; Russia was invited but did not show up. On March 18, 2014, Russia formally annexed Crimea. The Kremlin also expropriated the Sevastopol headquarters, fleet, and drilling rigs of Ukraine's national gas company. Ukraine lost control of 80 percent of its known Black Sea oil and gas deposits.

Russia intervened next in Donbas, a region of many Russian-speakers with a history of suspicion toward the central government. Many there had been shocked by the fall of Yanukovych, whom they had seen as their protector in Kyiv. Local business interests demanded the new Kyiv government grant special economic privileges to the region of three million people. Others in Donbas called for the territory to be granted full autonomy within Ukraine, or even for secession from the Ukrainian state.

The new Ukrainian government engaged in a series of actions that made the Donbas situation worse. It marginalized Donbas politicians in Kyiv who had long played an influential role in Ukrainian politics. It also failed to secure the border between Donbas and Russia. Separatists took up weapons and seized buildings in Donetsk and Luhansk, claiming they were threatened by local Ukrainian nationalists supported by Kyiv.

In April 2014, the United States, European Union, Ukraine, and Russia reached a deal in Geneva that called for disarming all illegal groups in Donbas and opened the way for talks on some form of autonomy for the territory. Almost simultaneously, heavily armed Russians, officially described as volunteers and vacationers, entered Donbas. Along with local formations rebelling against Kyiv, they engaged Ukrainian forces. By summer, Ukrainian troops were fighting back with artillery and air power,

40 | HOW RUSSIA LOSES

leading to an invasion by regular Russian troops in August. The Russian forces inflicted heavy casualties on the Ukrainians, leaving the rebels in control of large parts of the Donetsk and Luhansk provinces.

From that time on, Ukraine blocked all commerce with Crimea and rebel-held Donbas. In December, the Rada voted 303-8 to rescind Ukraine's official policy of nonalignment with any military bloc, a principle dating to its 1990 declaration of sovereignty. In 2017, Ukraine further amended its laws to make NATO membership a national strategic priority. International negotiations to resolve the Donbas situation, based on the Minsk cease-fire agreements and the so-called Normandy Format, went nowhere.

Moscow's seizure of Ukrainian territory had effects far beyond the political and military realms. When Ukraine's trade accord with the EU went into effect on January 1, 2016, Russia unilaterally canceled its free-trade agreement with Kyiv. If Moscow felt this would cripple Ukraine, it was wrong. Ukrainian exports to the EU had begun to narrowly exceed those to Russia starting in 2013; the difference grew rapidly after the Maidan and the start of the EU accord. By 2018, 43 percent of Ukraine's exports went to the EU and 8 percent to Russia. Imports declined similarly, aided by the replacement of gas imported from Russia by reverse-flow gas (some of it of Russian origin) from the EU.[28] China became a key partner for Ukraine for trade and infrastructure projects, further shrinking Russia's economic footprint. Ukrainians gained the right to travel to the European Union without visas. Ukrainian migrant workers, who had helped relieve labor shortages in Russia, started switching to jobs in the West.

In 2019, Bartholomew I, the ecumenical patriarch of Constantinople, accorded autocephaly (i.e., self-government) to the Orthodox Church of Ukraine. This was a major blow to the Russian Orthodox Church, which for three centuries had

---

[28] World Bank statistics cited in https://www.bruegel.org/blog-post/ukraine-trade-reorientation-russia-eu

controlled half the Orthodox churches in the country and been a key vector of Russian influence.

Putin was infuriated by Bartholomew's decision. In his view, Orthodox Christianity under the Moscow-led church was the fundamental factor that tied the Russian and Ukrainian people together. Rubbing salt in the wound, Bartholomew used a meeting with Russian Patriarch Kirill, a close Putin ally, to question the religious devotion of Russia's own Orthodox flock. He asked Kirill how many of his adherents were actually baptized and attended church.[29] Moscow was outraged by the patriarch and his piety getting involved in Russia's relationship with Ukraine. "Putin's attitude was 'how dare he drag God into this!' " said Andrew Wilson of the European Council on Foreign Relations.[30]

Russia's control of Donbas proved to be a poisoned chalice economically. The region's failing rust-belt industries spawned constant strikes and demands for economic aid. The thousands of residents who accepted Russian passports expected Russia to look after them. In most cases, Russia did not. Well-connected Russian business interests stripped factories of their assets, leaving skilled workers unemployed.

Meanwhile, Moscow's local allies turned the Donbas territories into police states. Under such circumstances, Ukraine and its Western partners could hardly support a proposal that Russia avidly promoted: the reintegration of Donbas into Ukraine with constitutional changes that would create a federal system. Such a deal would leave pro-Russian actors running Donbas, shift the economic burden of the territories back onto Ukraine, and restore Donbas politicians' lever on policy in Kyiv.

---

[29] Loudaros, Andreas, "Exclusive: The dialogue between the Patriarchs of Constantinople and Moscow during their meeting at the Phanar," *Orthodoxia Info*, October 1, 2018, https://orthodoxia.info/news/exclusive-the-dialogue-between-the-patriarchs-of-constantinople-and-moscow-during-their-meeting-at-the-phanar
[30] Andrew Wilson, interview with author, November 10, 2022.

42 | HOW RUSSIA LOSES

The Ukrainian army and pro-Russian forces in Donbas continued artillery duels that left some 14,000 people dead and two million displaced. Russia ran intense information operations to undermine Ukrainian unity and morale, barraged Ukrainian institutions and power grids with cyberattacks, and fortified Crimea to the point that it could support long-range offensive operations against Ukraine.

In 2016, Putin dedicated a statue just outside the Kremlin walls to Volodymyr the Great (St. Vladimir to Russians), suggesting that Ukrainians and Russians had been immutably linked since the Middle Ages. Such claims, Owen Matthews has noted, would be the equivalent of Germans saying they were the same people as the French because in medieval times both of their lands belonged to Charlemagne (a close contemporary of Volodymyr).[31] In May 2018, Russia opened a 12-mile bridge from the Russian mainland to Crimea. The bridge limited the size of ships traveling to Ukrainian ports on the Azov Sea. Russia claimed the right to inspect those ships to assure the security of the bridge. At the end of 2018, Russian forces fired on and seized three Ukrainian naval vessels.

Ukraine became a key element of a broad deterioration of relations between Russia and the West, already strained by Russian adventurism in Syria, Libya, Venezuela, and Sub-Saharan Africa; assassinations in the UK and Germany; Russia's internal repression; and its attempts to interfere in Western elections. (For its part, Moscow accused the West of trying to impoverish Russia through sanctions and build a fifth column of anti-Putin Russian citizens.)

In 2019, Volodymyr Zelenskyy, a comedian best known for his television shows mocking corrupt officials, defeated Poroshenko for the Ukrainian presidency. The key planks of his election platform were fighting corruption and ending the war in Donbas. Zelenskyy, a native Russian speaker, was a well-known personality in Russia, even co-hosting a Russian New Year's

---

[31] Matthews, Owen, *Overreach: The Inside Story of Putin and Russia's War Against Ukraine* (London: Mudlark, 2022).

telecast to mark the start of 2014. Zelenskyy talked with Putin by phone and in person, avoided (for a time) referring to Russia as the aggressor in Donbas, and struggled to implement a referendum there that would hopefully return the territory to full Ukrainian control.

Zelenskyy and Putin met in Paris in December. Zelenskyy sought to reassert Ukrainian control over the border between Donbas and Russia before a referendum; Russia wanted the referendum to take place while it still had unfettered access to Ukraine. The only progress from the talks was a Donbas cease-fire, which later collapsed.

With no cooperation from Putin and heavy pressure from Ukrainians mistrustful of Moscow, Zelenskyy became increasingly anti-Kremlin in his public remarks. In a particular provocation to Moscow, in February 2021, his government shut down three television stations believed to be controlled by Ukrainian oligarch Viktor Medvedchuk, a personal friend of Putin who had thrived untouched through all the previous Ukrainian power shifts. The government also froze his assets, and in May charged him with treason. Russia was further infuriated by Ukrainian policies (some begun under Poroshenko) that banned television networks based in Russia, limited Russian-language content on Ukrainian TV channels, and restricted Russian-language schools. Russian propagandists improvised on such measures to accuse Ukraine of "genocide" against the country's Russian-speakers—who, Russian officials said, were entitled to protection from the Kremlin.

While insisting that Ukrainians were on the verge of liquidating the Russian-speaking population, the Kremlin simultaneously held to its claim that Ukrainians and Russians were, and had always been, a single people. Russia stepped up its claims that the whole idea of a border between Ukraine and Russia was an artificial creation, based on Lenin's whim. Ukraine's anti-Kremlin policy, in Moscow's view, was driven entirely by a clique of "fascists" under the control of the United States. Their ultimate goal was to bring Ukraine into NATO, which potentially could put US troops within 300 miles of Moscow. Putin wove all these claims—Ukraine's illegitimacy as a country, its fascist rulers, the danger to Russian-speakers, and the NATO threat—into a tissue of grievance that became the basis of Russia's 2022 full-scale invasion. Putin occasionally acknowledged as a technical point that Ukraine was a separate state. But in his view that fact ranked far behind matters of kinship, history, and Russia's national security.

In March and April 2021, Russia massed some 100,000 troops near its borders with Ukraine. The troops were pulled back but began returning in September. Putin made clear that he considered Ukraine an enduring threat from Western powers. He said it was being transformed "slowly but surely" into a platform that would permanently challenge Russian security.[32]

None of Moscow's threats or actions seemed to intimidate the West or Ukraine. In fact, the very ferocity of the Kremlin led Western leaders to speak and act with increasing vigor in Ukraine's defense. From March to June, NATO staged the "Steadfast Defender" and "Defender Europe" exercises, involving forces from more than 20 allies and partners, including all East European members of the alliance. In June and July, the US and Ukraine held the largest of their regular "Sea Breeze" exercises in the Black Sea. In November, Washington and Kyiv signed a new Charter on Strategic Partnership. The document endorsed Ukraine's right to seek NATO membership and promised a range of continued efforts to "prevent external direct and hybrid aggression against Ukraine."

Both the West and Moscow could see in these events what they wanted. NATO saw a growing Russian threat that it had no choice but to challenge with its own deployments. Russia saw a display of NATO military might that was capable of doing much more than defending Ukraine; hawks in Moscow could conclude that NATO was preparing actions against Russia itself.

---

[32] *TASS*, "Путин считает, что Украину превращают в 'антипод' России [Putin thinks Ukraine is being transformed into an antipode of Russia]," May 14, 2021, https://tass.ru/politika/11374643

Ukraine: From Obsession to Catastrophe | 45

In December 2021, Russia issued a set of stunning proposals designed to counter the whole breadth of the threat it claimed to feel from NATO. The proposals—which were presented essentially as an ultimatum—would have banned any future expansion of NATO (precluding the incorporation of Ukraine, Georgia, or any other state); the basing of any additional troops or armaments in NATO countries in Eastern Europe; and any NATO "military operations" in the Caucasus, Central Asia, or Eastern Europe. The provision on Eastern Europe would have essentially banned any NATO activities in any of the countries that joined the alliance after the Soviet Union's collapse. The proposals also would have barred Russia and the United States from deploying short- and medium-range missiles in places where they could strike each other's territory—a provision that would block US missile systems in Central and Eastern Europe, while allowing Russia to maintain its ability to hit targets there.[33]

On February 21, 2022, three days before his invasion, Putin made a lengthy speech that reiterated all his past grievances about Ukraine. Kyiv, he asserted, was based on an ideology of "Neanderthal and aggressive nationalism and neo-Nazism." He said Ukraine intended to develop its own nuclear weapons and that it was plotting with NATO to attack Crimea, Donbas, and ultimately Russia.[34] He then declared Russia was recognizing the independence of the so-called Donetsk and Luhansk "people's republics," its two client regimes in Donbas.

On February 24, as he launched his invasion, Putin declared his intent to "demilitarize and de-nazify" Ukraine. He claimed he respected the freedom of the Ukrainian people to make their own choices. However, he said, they were being held hostage by Western and Nazi forces. The "special military operation," Putin said, would enable Ukrainians and Russians to work together "to

---

[33] Demands at https://ria.ru/20211217/bezopasnost-1764226189.html
[34] Text at http://www.kremlin.ru/events/president/transcripts/speeches/67828

46 | HOW RUSSIA LOSES

strengthen us from within as a single whole, despite the existence of state borders."[35]

As the invasion started, a Kremlin envoy, Dmitry Kozak, reportedly secured from Ukraine a promise not to join NATO.[36] But Putin's demands had now gone far beyond that one issue, and the invasion continued.

Miscalculations and War

Not since the Tsars had a Russian leader enjoyed such freedom to chart his country's course as Vladimir Putin when he came to power in 2000. Soviet Communism had failed. So had Boris Yeltsin's clumsy effort at a market economy. Russians were desperate for any new formula that might work. Putin could choose between a free economy or one ruled by ideology and bureaucracy; democratic freedoms or repression; collective leadership or one-man rule.

As for the former Soviet republics, including Ukraine, the Russian president also had a choice: an irredentist course, aimed at forcing them back into union with Russia by whatever means it took, or a good-neighbor strategy, recognizing the republics' sovereignty and building a relationship based on confidence and trust.

In the case of Ukraine, Putin appeared to firmly believe that Russia could be safe only if it totally dominated Ukraine, and Ukrainians understood their future lay with Russia. That belief underlay a cascading series of miscalculations that dogged Putin's Ukraine policy from its earliest days until the 2022 invasion:

---

[35] Text at http://www.kremlin.ru/events/president/news/67843

[36] Kremlin spokesman Dmitry Peskov said the report had "absolutely no relation to reality." See "Exclusive – As war began, Putin rejected a Ukraine peace deal recommended by his aide: sources," *Reuters*, September 14, 2022, https://www.reuters.com/article/ukraine-crisis-kremlin-deal-exclusive-idAFKBN2QF0CH

Ukraine: From Obsession to Catastrophe | 47

• **Putin never came to terms with the idea that Ukrainians and Russians are different peoples.** Certainly, Russia had controlled almost all of Ukrainian territory from the end of the 18th century until the Soviet collapse—a huge stretch of history, as long as the entire existence of the United States. However, Ukrainians and Russians had vastly different historical experiences and views of themselves. Ukraine's culture was far more cosmopolitan than Russia's, touched by a broad variety of foreign influences, including three religious traditions. Rather than enduring oppression, Ukrainians had a long history of rebelling against unjust rulers, or simply running away to the unruly Cossack lands. None of this mattered to Putin, who reportedly spent years brooding over revanchist literature about Russia's right to rule Ukraine. Seizing on the heritage of Kievan Rus, the Cossacks' submission to Muscovy in 1654, and World War II, he asserted in a 5,000-word essay in July 2021:

> I am convinced that the true sovereignty of Ukraine is possible precisely in partnership with Russia. Our spiritual, human, and civilizational ties have been formed by the centuries and go back to the same sources, tempered by common trials, achievements, and victories. Our kinship is passed down from generation to generation. It is in the hearts and memory of people living in modern Russia and Ukraine, and in the blood ties that unite millions of our families. Together we have always been and will be many times stronger and more successful. For we are one people.[37]

Unfortunately for Putin, Ukraine's independence only reinforced Ukrainians' sense of separateness from Russians. The time from 1991 until Russia invaded in 2022 was about the same as the period from America's War of Independence to the War of 1812. In that brief time, the United States forged a strong enough national identity to fiercely defend it in a new confrontation with

---

[37] Text at http://www.kremlin.ru/events/president/transcripts/66181

48 | HOW RUSSIA LOSES

Britain. It was no surprise that Ukrainians could come to revere their independence in the same amount of time.

Since Ukrainians were not a separate people in Putin's view, he and his proxies saw no need to show respect for their distinct historical memories. Asked in 2003 about his view of the Holodomor, Russian Ambassador Viktor Chernomyrdin declared, "We are not going to apologize to anyone." There was famine at the time across the Soviet Union, Chernomyrdin said, and suggested Ukrainians might as well blame Georgia, Stalin's home, as blame Russia.[38] In other situations, Putin had no problem criticizing his Soviet predecessors; he had no trouble vilifying Lenin over the borders he created for Ukraine. But Putin's regime was so oblivious to Ukrainians' feelings that it would not even partially acknowledge the starvation, deportations, pillage, torture, and summary killings under Soviet power that were so deeply woven into Ukraine's national story.

Such arrogance appeared repeatedly, as when Putin told Ukrainians to vote for Yanukovych in the 2004 elections; when he declared during a 2009 visit that Ukraine and Russia were indivisible; and when in 2016 he hijacked Ukrainians' identification with the heritage of Kievan Rus by unveiling the Volodymyr the Great statue in Moscow.

• **Putin never appeared to consider that Ukraine, if treated with respect, might become a model buffer state between Russia and the West.** The preconditions for such an outcome were there from the beginning of his rule. The nations' economies were closely interlaced. The Russian and Ukrainian elites were intimately familiar with each other's thinking and concerns—including oligarchs who freely did deals across the two countries' borders.

---

[38] "Черномырдин: Мы не извинимся перед Украиной за события 1932-33. Это нам нужно 'в ноги поклониться' [Chernomyrdin: We will not apologize to Ukraine for the events of 1932-33. We should be 'knelt to']," *Ukrainskaya Pravda*, August 6, 2023, https://www.pravda.com.ua/rus/news/2003/08/6/4373805

Russian television stations were popular throughout Ukraine, and the Moscow Patriarchate of the Russian Orthodox Church had strong influence. Ukraine's independence had brought no immediate push to discourage the use of the Russian language, or any other anti-Russian "Ukrainization." John Herbst recalls that, when he was accredited in Kyiv in 2003 as US ambassador, "Putin was the most popular politician in the country."[39] (Even in 2007, two years after the Orange Revolution, 81 percent of Ukrainians had a favorable view of Russia and 56 percent felt positively about Putin.[40]) Ukraine and Russia had even resolved the issue of Sevastopol and the Black Sea Fleet, a highly charged issue for both nations.

In a gentler universe, one might have imagined Ukraine and Russia becoming something akin to the Czech Republic and Slovakia: countries similar in language and culture, once part of one nation but now interlinked closely as separate ones. Or, taking into account the differential in strength between Moscow and Kyiv, the relationship might have been more like that of the Soviet Union and Finland during the Cold War. Finland had a capitalist economy and strong cultural ties to the West but was firmly neutral and respectful of Moscow's power and interests. Even Ukrainian integration into the EU did not have to be a deal-breaker. In the words of Steven Pifer of the Brookings Institution in 2014:

> Seen objectively, a Ukraine that is integrating with the European Union and at the same time maintaining a full range of political, economic, and commercial relations with Russia should not pose a threat to Moscow. The European Union is not NATO. But Putin views this through his own prism and seems to regard it as a menace.[41]

---

[39] John Herbst, interview with author, September 16, 2022.
[40] See https://www.pewresearch.org/fact-tank/2020/02/07/russia-and-putin-receive-low-ratings-globally
[41] Pifer, Steven, "Ukraine's Perpetual East-West Balancing Act," Brookings Institution, February 28, 2014, https://www.brookings.

50 | HOW RUSSIA LOSES

Putin certainly was aware of the concept of good-neighbor relations. In his long 2022 essay, he seemed wistful about what Russian-Ukrainian ties could have been. Reflecting on the close links between Austria and Germany and the United States and Canada, he said:

> Close in ethnic composition, culture, in fact sharing one language, they remain sovereign states with their own interests, with their own foreign policy. But this does not prevent them from the closest integration or allied relations. They have very conditional, transparent borders. And when crossing them the citizens feel at home. They create families, study, work, do business. Incidentally, so do millions of those born in Ukraine who now live in Russia. We see them as our own close people.[42]

Putin never acted, however, in a way that might bring about such a good-neighbor outcome. As James Sherr and Igor Gretskiy put it in an analysis of the 2022 war:

> Russia has little experience of living with neighbours who are both friendly and independent. When Muscovy emerged from the Mongol conquest, it did so as a multinational entity with few natural frontiers. As these frontiers expanded, threats expanded with them, to Russia and to others. The classic responses to this state of affairs have been 'coercion into friendship' and further expansion. On Russia's periphery, the distinction between foreign and internal affairs was nebulous.[43]

---

edu/blog/up-front/2014/02/28/ukraines-perpetual-east-west-balancing-act

[42] Text at http://www.kremlin.ru/events/president/news/66181

[43] Sherr, James, et al., "Why Russia Went to War," International Centre for Defence and Security, January 2023, https://icds.ee/en/why-russia-went-to-war-a-three-dimensional-perspective

Ukraine: From Obsession to Catastrophe | 51

"The Kremlin could have produced a much calmer relationship and slowed [Ukraine's] trajectory toward the West," Herbst said. "If Putin had had a better sense of what could be done in Ukraine, he would have had more success." Russia could have more clearly acknowledged Ukraine's sovereignty and business interests, grown its influence through strategic investments, and rewarded favorable policies from Kyiv with advantageous deals on energy. (Russia cut its gas price after Yanukovych agreed to extend Russia's lease on Sevastopol.) Moscow could have adopted more broadly the calm economic view of its ambassador Chernomyrdin. He told a conference in 2007 that Ukraine's course toward economic integration with Europe would have no effect on its booming relations with Russia.[44]

The Kremlin had time enough to take such an approach. Neither the EU nor NATO was rushing to embrace Ukraine, with its history of corruption and chaotic politics. Despite inviting Ukraine to join its customs union in 2007, the EU did not extend it candidate membership until 2022, four months after Russia's invasion.

Instead of building good-neighbor relations, Moscow's approach to Ukraine was based largely on pressure and threats. Russia's gas cutoffs in 2006 and 2009, its attempt to circumvent Ukraine's natural gas pipeline business through projects like Nord Stream, its blockade of imports from Ukraine as it pressured Yanukovych to sign the Eurasian Customs Union deal—these and other provocations had their effect on the Ukrainian population. After the initial gas price cut given to Yanukovych, Moscow refused to grant additional discounts, although they would have been appropriate based on global prices.

---

[44] *RIA Novosti*, "Виктор Черномырдин призывает ЕС выработать единую позицию по поводу вступления Украины в Евросоюз [Victor Chernomyrdin calls on the EU to form a united position on the entry of Ukraine into the European Union]," June 29, 2007, http://viperson.ru/articles/viktor-chernomyrdin-prizyvaet-es-vyrabotat-edinuyu-pozitsiyu-po-povodu-vstupleniya-ukrainy-v-evrosoyuz

52 | HOW RUSSIA LOSES

The Ukrainians also were well aware of Russia's slide toward authoritarianism under Putin. In the words of a statement in January 2022 by discontented Russian military officers and signed by retired Colonel-General Leonid Ivashov:

> Naturally, for Ukraine to remain a friendly neighbor to Russia, it [Russia] needed to demonstrate the attractiveness of the Russian state model and system of power. But the Russian Federation has not done that; its model of development and its foreign policy mechanism for international cooperation alienate almost all of its neighbors, and not only those.[45]

Against the background of Moscow's behavior, Ukrainian attitudes toward their country's economic orientation changed dramatically. In a 2009 poll, in which respondents had to choose among the economic blocs Ukraine should join, 52 percent favored integration with the CIS and 24 percent with the EU; by 2013, Ukrainians favored the EU over the CIS by a margin of 43 to 33 percent.[46]

A more balanced Russian attitude toward Ukraine might have removed any prospect of Ukraine joining NATO. Successive governments in Kyiv sought relationships with the alliance, then reversed course. Between 2002 and 2009, public support for joining NATO ranged only between 15 and 32 percent. Even in 2013, the summer before the Maidan and Russia's first invasion, more Ukrainians considered NATO a threat to peace than a source of protection.[47] NATO's view was that "Ukraine was 'in the

---

[45] "Обращение Общероссийского офицерского собрания к президенту и гражданам Российской Федерации [Appeal of the All-Russian Assembly of Officers to the president and citizens of the Russian Federation]," Jan. 28, 2022, http://www.ooc.su/news/obrashhenie_obshherossijskogo_oficerskogo_sobranija_k_prezidentu_i_grazhdanam_rossijskoj_federacii/2022-01-31-79
[46] See https://razumkov.org.ua/uploads/2021-independence-30.pdf, p. 363.
[47] See https://web.archive.org/web/20140502193915/http://www.razumkov.org.ua/eng/poll.php?poll_id=46 and

middle,' in no-man's land," said Plokhy. "It was messy, not committed either way, and Russia opposed NATO membership. So why antagonize them?" At the time of the Bucharest summit, six NATO countries already bordered Russia and Ukraine; this was already a commanding forward position for the alliance, without the problems of integrating Ukraine itself. Ukrainians began to strongly favor NATO membership only after the 2014 invasion.

All this suggests that, properly managed, there was a possibility for Ukraine to become a buffer country for both Russia and the West, unlikely to swing in one direction so sharply that it threatened the other's interests. As Sean Mirsky wrote in *The National Interest* in 2015:

> The swing of the electoral pendulum was bounded. So long as Ukraine remained a democracy, there was never any serious risk that the country would become permanently ensconced in either the Western orbit or the Russian constellation. To do so would risk alienating half the country. Thus, by default, Ukraine adopted a self-correcting policy of nonalignment. Kiev would sometimes lean toward the West, and other times toward Russia, but there was always an electoral check on permanent alignment with either geopolitical pole.[48]

Elise Giuliano of Columbia University adds to this picture that many public attitude surveys offered Ukrainians only binary choices between joining Western or Kremlin-controlled military and economic blocs, leaving no option for citizens to say they

---

https://news.gallup.com/poll/167927/crisis-ukrainians-likely-nato-threat.aspx

[48] Mirski, Sean, "Russia's Misstep: How Putin's Ukraine Adventure Backfired," *The National Interest*, March 11, 2015, https://nationalinterest.org/feature/russias-misstep-how-putins-ukraine-adventure-backfired-12394

54 | HOW RUSSIA LOSES

wanted their country to remain neutral or maintain good relations with all sides. Polls that offered more options revealed a good deal of nuance, she noted, and, before February 2022, "considerable numbers of Ukrainians did not conceptualize Ukraine's foreign policy in zero sum terms in the manner of many political and civic leaders."[49] For instance, even amid the sharp rise in anti-Kremlin feeling after Russia's 2014 invasion, a poll that offered several options found that a plurality of those who voted for Zelenskyy in 2019 favored Ukrainian neutrality (42.7 percent) over NATO membership (36.5 percent).[50]

Putin, however, seemed to have little interest in Ukraine as a neutral, good-neighbor state. In a 2018 interview, he was asked if neutrality similar to Sweden's or Austria's would solve the Ukraine problem. Busy reciting complaints about Ukraine, he brushed past the question.[51] His reference in 2021 to the genial relations between the US and Canada, and Germany and Austria, came only after he had massed a force to invade Ukraine. Putin saw former Soviet republics less as sovereign states deserving respect for their borders, and more as renegade fragments of the Soviet Union. "Putin's project was dominance over all the post-Soviet states," Plokhy said. Putin felt Russia was not complete without the symbolism of owning Kyiv, said Orysia Lutsevych of Chatham House in London. "Just having acceptable political and economic relations with Ukraine was not enough."[52]

Putin, of course, may also have felt that Ukrainian neutrality, even if established, could not be guaranteed. As its governments changed, Ukraine's laws regarding neutrality and foreign alliances had been constantly rewritten. No cosmic mechanism guaranteed that the Ukrainian pendulum would always swing back to the center. The decisions by Sweden and Finland to join

---

[49] Giuliano, Elise, "Ukrainian Public Opinion and Foreign Policy" (paper presented at the 2021 Association for the Study of Nationalities World Convention, May 5–8, 2021).
[50] Survey at https://kiis.com.ua/materials/pr/20201011_soc-politic/polit_orient_oct%202020.pdf
[51] http://www.kremlin.ru/events/president/news/57675
[52] Orysia Lutsevych, interview with author, November 9, 2022.

Ukraine: From Obsession to Catastrophe | 55

NATO after Putin's 2022 invasion showed that any country can review its neutrality. However, Putin seemed to have made little attempt at all to create an atmosphere of mutual respect between Kyiv and Moscow.

- **Putin consistently misjudged Ukraine's internal politics.** Regarding the choice between the European Union or the Eurasian Customs Union, "the Russians thought that if they had Yanukovych, they'd have Ukraine," said Plokhy. As in the case of other countries where Russia has sought influence, Putin vastly underestimated the power of ordinary citizens. The Revolution on Granite, Orange Revolution, and Maidan uprising were all the work of regular citizens who believed their opinions mattered. Whether they were channeling the spirit of Western democracy or their own history of rebellious Cossacks, Ukrainians expected to have a say in their own future. In Putin's view, citizen involvement in government decisions is dangerous, unnatural, and usually the result of foreign agitation.

Putin had little patience for Ukraine's back-and-forth political pendulum, even when it swung back to Russia's advantage. His government, for instance, saw the Orange Revolution as a blow to Russian influence in Ukraine. Ultimately, however, its impact on Ukrainian politics was slight, and within five years, Moscow's choice, Yanukovych, had been legitimately elected president.

The Maidan revolution might also have had a limited effect on Ukrainian internal politics. As soon as the immediate excitement had passed, Ukrainians began complaining bitterly that the new authorities were nearly as corrupt and incompetent as the former regime. Civil society activists who had led the struggle against Yanukovych began to accuse Poroshenko, and then Zelenskyy, of trying to become dictators themselves. Pro-Russian and Euroskeptic politicians renewed their activity, winning in six out of 25 regions in the October 2020 regional elections.

The actor who contributed the most to the solidarity of post-Maidan Ukraine was Putin himself. His backing of the brutal Yanukovych and his seizure of Ukrainian territory in 2014 enraged not only traditionally pro-Western Ukrainians but also

56 | HOW RUSSIA LOSES

many others who had previously favored closer relations with Russia. "He only killed his reputation after Maidan," said Herbst. By April 2014, 71 percent of Ukrainians felt negatively about Putin.[53] Crimean and Donbas residents had been some of the most pro-Russian voters in the country. By removing these citizens from Ukraine's voter rolls, Putin decisively reduced Russian influence in Ukrainian politics.

Ukrainians' perpetual discontent with their political leaders may also have fueled Putin's skewed vision of the Ukrainian state. Donald Trump's comment in 2019 that Ukraine was "a very corrupt country," impolitic as it may have been, hardly contradicted the opinions of most Ukrainians. For almost the entire time from 2004 to 2021, a majority of Ukrainians believed events in their nation were moving in the wrong direction.[54] Such public discontent may well have encouraged the feeling, apparently widespread within Putin's top circle, that the Ukrainian state was so hollow and unloved that the disgusted population would hardly fight for it.

A December 2021 survey found half of Ukrainians were ready to resist a Russian invasion by taking up arms, joining protests, or engaging in civil disobedience[55]—a finding which the Kremlin could have chosen to view as an encouraging sign that at least the other half would not resist.

Russia's intelligence services, so expert in parsing the internal workings of Western societies, seemed to fail entirely in judging Ukraine—unless Putin received accurate advice but ignored it.[56]

---

[53] https://razumkov.org.ua/uploads/2021-independence-30.pdf, p. 131.
[54] https://razumkov.org.ua/uploads/2021-independence-30.pdf, pp. 341 and 349.
[55] See https://www.kiis.com.ua/
?lang=ukr&cat=reports&id=1079&page=1
[56] Such advice was readily available, even from Russian public sources. Just two weeks before the invasion, a retired Russian colonel wrote in *Nezavisimaya Gazeta* that "to assert that no one in Ukraine will defend the regime means, in practice, complete ignorance of the military-political situation and the mood of the broad masses of the people in

He may have preferred information from a series of figures who stood to gain if an invasion had quickly attained its goals: Donbas politicians, Russian military officers eager for glory and promotions, and Ukrainian oligarchs like Medvedchuk.[57] Alternatively, Russian information operators may have puffed up for Putin tales of their own success in undermining Ukrainian unity. By one account, the Russian Foreign Ministry routinely engages in a practice known as "executive discipline," in which reports of what it has accomplished are written in almost identical wording to what the ministry was ordered to do.

Many analysts believe that because of COVID, Putin sharply limited his circle of advisors. Members of such an exclusive group would put a premium on not disagreeing too much with their boss. Reportedly, the Russian president is not a frequent internet user, which further limits his sources of information to those around him.[58]

- **Putin would not take "yes" for an answer.** For years he ignored opportunities that could have led to far better relations with Kyiv. If, as he constantly emphasized, his greatest concern about Ukraine was that it would join NATO, the alliance had

---

the neighboring state. Moreover, the degree of hatred (which, as is known, is the most effective fuel for armed struggle) in the neighboring republic in relation to Moscow is frankly underestimated. No one will meet the Russian army with bread, salt, and flowers in Ukraine." Khodarenok, Mikhail, "Прогнозы кровожадных политологов [Predictions of bloodthirsty politicians]," *Nezavisimaya Gazeta*, February 3, 2022, https://nvo.ng.ru/realty/2022-02-03/3_1175_donbass.html

[57] Medvedchuk reportedly assured Putin that Ukrainians saw themselves as Russians and would welcome the invading Russian army. See Gershkovich, Evan, et al., "Putin, Isolated and Distrustful, Leans on Handful of Hard-Line Advisers," *The Wall Street Journal*, December 23, 2022, https://www.wsj.com/articles/putin-russia-ukraine-war-advisers-11671815184

[58] Kinetz, Erika, " "He's a war criminal': Elite Putin security officer defects," *The Associated Press*, April 5, 2023, https://apnews.com/article/russia-putin-defector-war-crimes-khodorkovsky-karakulov-dossier-845421fe06ed9cfa1962ad4f98a2e413

58 | HOW RUSSIA LOSES

shown no interest in full Ukrainian membership since 2008. Yanukovych had ended any interest from the Ukrainian side. Russia's logical move would been to celebrate that situation and provide visible favors to Ukraine in return. Instead, Moscow overreached, leaping beyond the NATO issue and trying to force Ukraine under Russia's economic umbrella as well. That was the spark that touched off Maidan and forced Yanukovych from power.

Putin had another opportunity to normalize relations when Zelenskyy was elected. One of Zelenskyy's main promises was to end the fighting in Donbas and improve relations with Moscow. The new president knew that many of his voters were not wedded to a hard anti-Russian position; he demonstrated his commitment to improving relations by facing down opposition from thousands of Ukrainian demonstrators who demanded "no capitulation" to Moscow. Putin could have seized the moment of his December 2019 meeting with Zelenskyy by turning it into an occasion to show mutual respect and agree on confidence-building measures that Russia would actually implement. As late as December 2021, as Russian troops were lining up to invade his country, Zelenskyy held open the possibility of holding referendums in Crimea and Donbas on those territories' statuses[59]—a vote that might very well have sealed their future as Russian territories.

In his relations with the West, Putin began to make clear soon after Maidan that NATO must take significant steps to ease Russia's security concerns. Past Russian verbiage about mutual measures to improve European security gave way increasingly to demands for unilateral Western and Ukrainian concessions, even as Moscow deepened its control and militarization of Crimea and Donbas. After his December 2021 demands to the US and NATO, Putin chose not to capitalize on a flurry of Western diplomatic feelers. While the demands were clearly unacceptable, some in

---

[59] Zinets, Natalia, "Ukrainian president does not exclude referendum on Crimea and Donbass," *Reuters*, December 10, 2021, https://www.reuters.com/world/europe/ukrainian-president-does-not-exclude-holding-referendum-crimea-donbass-2021-12-10

the West felt that they could open the way to some form of confidence-building measures that could reduce the risk of war.

US Deputy Secretary of State Wendy Sherman reportedly offered to talk about such matters in a January meeting with her Russian counterpart; however, US diplomats concluded that Russia was not interested in such discussions.[60] Nevertheless, French President Emmanuel Macron rushed to Moscow for five hours of talks with Putin on February 9, insisting that some of Russia's demands left room for reasonable negotiation.

Another occasion came less than three weeks after the invasion, when Zelenskyy told British officials that "it is true, and it must be acknowledged" that Ukraine had no early hope of joining NATO.[61] At that late moment, too, Putin could have seized on Zelenskyy's comments. Profiting from Western alarm over the fighting, he could have pursued some kind of agreement to freeze or even reverse the invasion in return for solid commitments that Ukraine would never become part of the alliance. If he had gotten it, he would have been able to boast that just a few weeks of demonstrating Russian power had terrified NATO into abandoning Ukraine.

• **Putin did not believe the West would defend Ukraine.** Early in Putin's term, it was clear that the United States and its allies did not consider Ukraine a vital interest. The West was deep in "Ukraine fatigue," and NATO was in no hurry to add Ukraine to the alliance. What Putin missed was that, while the West was little concerned about Ukraine, it was increasingly concerned about Russia. Russian aggressiveness in Syria, the expansion of its influence and mercenary armies in Africa, its money-laundering and interference in Western elections, its assassinations abroad,

---

[60] Harris, Shane, et al., "Road to War: US Struggled to convince allies, and Zelensky, of risk of invasion," *The Washington Post*, August 16, 2022, https://www.washingtonpost.com/national-security/interactive/2022/ukraine-road-to-war

[61] Carey, Andrew, et al., "Zelensky signals he doesn't expect Ukraine to join NATO anytime soon," *CNN*, March 16, 2022, https://www.cnn.com/2022/03/15/europe/ukraine-nato-zelensky-shift/index.html

60 | HOW RUSSIA LOSES

and growing repression at home left the West looking for ways to demonstrate its strength. Just as Russia had dispatched bombers and warships to Latin America to antagonize the United States, Ukraine was an obvious vector to challenge Putin on his own border. It was an easy matter for the West to support the young, photogenic Maidan demonstrators fighting a Putin-backed strongman. And it seized the opportunity.

After Maidan and Russia's 2014 invasion, Europe and the United States showed surprising unity in imposing and tightening economic sanctions on Moscow. NATO countries also began pouring weapons and military trainers into Ukraine. Still, Putin could calculate that the West had no stomach for becoming involved in military actions against Russia. Although German Chancellor Angela Merkel led the imposition of the sanctions, she continued to support the Nord Stream 2 pipeline, which would make Western Europe even more dependent on Russian energy. Less than a year after the death of 200 Dutch passengers when pro-Russian separatists shot down a jet over Ukraine, Holland-based Royal Dutch Shell signed up as a shareholder in Nord Stream 2.

Such obvious contradictions in Western policy were carefully noted in the Kremlin. During the Trump administration, Putin never challenged the US directly; the American president was serving Russian interests well enough by sowing chaos in the US and NATO, and Putin may have considered Trump too vain and unstable to risk a test of will. With Trump's departure, however, the Russian leader apparently saw an irresistible opportunity for a new adventure, and Ukraine was the obvious place.

Joe Biden was 77 years old and consumed by an urgent domestic agenda. He had been vice president to President Barack Obama, who told an interviewer in 2016 that Ukraine will "be vulnerable to military domination by Russia no matter what" and "we have to be very clear about what our core interests are and what we

Ukraine: From Obsession to Catastrophe | 61

are willing to go to war for."[62] The EU was struggling with the aftermath of Brexit, and the Western security community was focused on China. Adds former CIA official Peter Clement:

> Putin may have assessed that geopolitical circumstances offered a narrow opportunity to decisively break the seven-year stalemate in eastern Ukraine. As Moscow saw it, the United States was politically polarized; the American public was largely indifferent to Ukraine and wary of new foreign wars, especially after the messy U.S. departure from Afghanistan; longtime German Chancellor Angela Merkel was leaving office; the world was still preoccupied with the pandemic; and Europe had a heavy dependence on Russian oil and gas.[63]

If Putin had been able to capture all of Ukraine in a *blitzkrieg*, all these factors might well have blocked any Western response. Instead, the Russian leader massed his armies along the Ukrainian border for an entire year before invading.

This slow striptease, with Kremlin video highlighting to the world the daily arrival of Russian troops and armor, was another fundamental miscalculation. The full year of saber-rattling gave time for a large international coalition against Russia to form, aided by skilled lobbying by Ukraine and its East European allies.

In the United States, Trump and his clique of isolationists, Russia sympathizers, and Ukraine skeptics had been replaced by an administration with a far more clear-eyed view of the overall

---

[62] Goldberg, Jeffrey, "The Obama Doctrine," *The Atlantic*, April 2016, https://www.theatlantic.com/magazine/archive/2016/04/the-obama-doctrine/471525
[63] Clement, Peter, "Putin's Risk Spiral," *Foreign Affairs*, October 6, 2022, https://www.foreignaffairs.com/ukraine/putin-risk-spiral-logic-of-escalation-in-war. For other indications of Western weakness that Putin might have taken into consideration, see "Why Russia Went to War," op. cit.

62 | HOW RUSSIA LOSES

threat from Moscow. West European political leaders who had long been convinced that talk and trade could manage Russia's ambitions had time to convince themselves that those strategies were not blunting Putin's Ukraine obsession. Putin's rhetoric was becoming more insistent and intimidating by the week. At the same time, however, Russian officials vociferously denied that they intended to invade. Given the denials, even Western leaders who feared Russia felt they risked little by making ever-stronger public commitments to Ukraine's independence.[64]

Russia's last ploy was the December ultimatum. The Kremlin may have hoped this would force the West to impose some form of disarmed neutrality on Ukraine as a way of avoiding the more sweeping proposals made by Russia. If the ultimatum had worked and Ukraine were militarily neutered, Putin would never have had to invade. He could have withdrawn his troops, perhaps also gaining a relaxing of Western sanctions. He would then have been free to subvert Ukraine at his leisure, tormenting whatever defenseless government remained until the nation became a Russian vassal state.

However, the ultimatum turned out to be so outrageous that it was dead on arrival in almost all Western capitals. Putin ignored the few diplomatic feelers the West put out. Left with an enormous army freezing in the field, Putin apparently felt he had no choice but to invade. Even if the West had not realized it was doing so, it had called Putin's bluff. Western nations then acted on their promises to protect Ukraine—partly out of courage and principle, but also because they had painted themselves into a corner by making guarantees they thought they would never have to fulfill.

All that said, an entirely different narrative about Putin and Ukraine is also conceivable. In this interpretation, Putin

---

[64] For an account of Russian officials' many denials, see Taylor, Adam, "Russia's attack on Ukraine came after months of denials it would attack," *The Washington Post*, February 24, 2022, https://www.washingtonpost.com/world/2022/02/24/ukraine-russia-denials

concluded early in his presidency, and certainly after the Orange Revolution, that no matter how much diplomatic skill or goodwill he deployed, he could never overcome the military and political danger Ukraine represented.

In this view, Putin thought Kyiv was inevitably on the road to NATO membership, even if the process had halted. When full membership came to pass, the results for Russia would be catastrophic: western Russia would be vulnerable to a pincer attack from Ukraine, Poland, and the Baltics; NATO missiles in Ukraine would be in range of Russian strategic launch sites beyond the Urals; and Ukraine might even insist on the ouster of Russia's Black Sea Fleet from Crimea. People raised in Western countries easily understand that the prospect of an unprovoked Western attack on Russia is close to zero. But Russian leaders have had centuries of unhappy experiences with unlikely scenarios coming true. Land empires like Russia require large buffer zones for protection; as Catherine the Great put it, "I have no way to defend my borders but to extend them." Putin saw Belarus and Ukraine as indispensable protective territory between Russia and a hostile West.

Even putting the military threat aside, Putin may have genuinely believed that Ukraine's democratic development and swing to the West would inevitably create an unacceptable political danger to his regime. The boost in domestic popularity he enjoyed after the seizure of Crimea only lasted a few years, the end of the oil boom began to drag down the economy, and his decision to raise the retirement age in 2018 led to protests and petitions. Putin extended his right to remain in office only by means of a clumsy referendum in 2020. The COVID-19 pandemic only added to the stress in Russian society.

If one believed Putin's claim that Ukraine and Russia were one people, Ukraine offered an example of millions of those people living in a democratic, if chaotic, country with a range of human rights unheard of in Russia. Putin spoke of Ukraine as "a sort of anti-Russia," a parallel but democratic universe that Russia itself

64 | HOW RUSSIA LOSES

risked getting sucked into.[65] "Ukraine's domestic system was a threat to his remaining in power," said Lutsevych. "He needed Ukraine to fail. His real existential fear was not of the US, but of the collapse of Russia." In Belarus, the near-overthrow of Alyaksandr Lukashenka by pro-democracy demonstrators in 2020 added more reasons for Putin to be alarmed.

Assuming Putin saw all these dangers early on, his strategic approach to Ukraine may have stemmed not from any misunderstanding of his neighbor, but from a very calculated mix of fear and *realpolitik*. He may have understood perfectly that Russians and Ukrainians are different people. For precisely that reason, there was no common bedrock for Moscow and Kyiv to permanently share. Ukraine's historical experience and democratic expectations would inevitably pull it toward the West. Nothing was to be gained by trying to build a friendly relationship with Ukraine; the two countries would never be Germany and Austria.

The only solution was a combination of force and guile: to intimidate NATO from offering Ukraine membership for as long as possible, slash Ukraine's economic importance to the West by finding alternative routes for Russian gas, stoke the international image of Ukraine as a corrupt state unworthy of support, use Ukraine's democratic system to create constant internal chaos, and pick away at its territory whenever the West seemed timid or preoccupied elsewhere. Some believe the trigger for the actual invasion came in February or March 2021 after Zelenskyy shut down Medvedchuk's television channels—either out of fury at the insult to Putin's personal friend, or because the channels were Russia's last hope to maintain influence on the Ukrainian population.[66]

---

[65] "Putin thinks Ukraine is being transformed into an antipode of Russia," op. cit.

[66] Zheguyov, Ilya, "Как Путин возненавидел Украину [How Putin came to hate Ukraine]," *Vyorstka*, April 25, 2023, https://verstka.media/kak-putin-pridumal-voynu

Of course, Putin could have approached the whole Ukraine question quite differently. He might have allowed some level of democracy at home and not persistently bullied Ukraine and alienated its people. If Putin had offered Russians a system that afforded them some freedom and dignity, he might not have feared his state would disintegrate on contact with the "anti-Russia." Had Putin pursued a gentler policy toward Russia's neighbor, Ukraine's people might have been guided by their long history to continue carefully balancing their ties with both the West and the Russian behemoth to the north.

However, trust in the Russian people and respect for Ukraine were not in Putin's nature. Whether through true miscalculation, or a cynical, daring calculus that ran aground on execution, the Ukraine war was his doing—with all its catastrophic results.

Epilogue: After February 2022

As this book goes to press, the outcome of the Ukraine war remains unknown. However, the effect of miscalculations by Putin and his inner circle became evident within the first hours of the invasion. Russia was apparently convinced that most Ukrainians, awed by Russian power or refusing to view the Russian forces as enemies, would not mount significant resistance. Therefore, Russian strategists concentrated simply on preparations for a short invasion. As a British analysis concluded, "It appears that Russian planners succumbed to optimism bias as to the dislocating effect that speed itself could achieve in diffusing Ukraine's will to resist and therefore opted to undertake a shock and awe campaign with little preliminary shaping." According to the analysis, Russia expected Ukraine to be under its complete control by the summer of 2022.[67]

---

[67] Zabrodskyi, Mykhaylo, et al., "Preliminary Lessons in Conventional Warfighting from Russia's Invasion of Ukraine: February-July 2022," Royal United Services Institute, November 30, 2022, https://static.rusi.org/359-SR-Ukraine-Preliminary-Lessons-Feb-July-2022-web-final.pdf

The first days of the invasion saw Russian air assault troops seize an airport only 6 miles from Kyiv and infiltrate commandos to within 2 miles of Zelenskyy's office. But Ukrainians fought bravely, forcing back Russian tanks headed to Kyiv and dragging Russian forces into exhausting tank, artillery, and trench warfare. The Ukrainian troops were nothing like the poorly trained soldiers and volunteers whom Russia had routed in Donbas in 2014. These were professionals, equipped and trained by NATO and informed by detailed, real-time Western intelligence.

Putin declared on September 30, 2022, the annexation of more Ukrainian territory, including areas his forces did not even control. The battlefield became increasingly stalemated, with neither side able to gain significant new territory by the summer of 2023. Putin faced his own problems at home, including the June 2023 rebellion by Wagner Group head Yevgeny Prigozhin. Two months later, Prigozhin was dead, but his demise likely presaged more turbulence in Russia's centers of power and money. The outcome of the war seemed to depend on continued Western arms supplies, Ukrainian endurance, and Putin's ability to maintain political stability and an effective fighting machine.

2.

South Africa: The Deal Too Big to Succeed

For any outside power seeking to spread its influence in Africa, South Africa is perhaps the greatest prize. Its per capita GDP is one of the largest of any African nation; its government one of the best-organized; and its science, technology, and cultural life highly advanced. South Africans have won 11 Nobel Prizes. The nation boasts a rich economy based on mining, manufacturing, and agriculture, is strategically located on the Atlantic and Indian oceans, and has a long history of peaceful transfers of power.

At the same time, the nation of 60 million has the world's highest level of income inequality.[1] South Africa's 47 million Blacks, subjugated by apartheid until the 1990s, earn one-third the average wages of the five million Whites. (Colored and Indian-Asian people earn wages between those of Blacks and Whites.[2]) Crime levels are high, with many prosperous South Africans living behind walls topped with barbed wire and broken glass. South Africa has the world's highest level of HIV/AIDS and was badly struck by COVID-19. Protests are common over poverty, inequality, working conditions, and politics and have often spiraled into violence.

For the Soviet Union, South Africa presented an enormous opportunity. For three decades during the apartheid regime, the

---

[1] See https://hdr.undp.org/system/files/documents/global-report-document/hdr2021-22pdf_1.pdf, Gini coefficient scores on pp. 281-284.

[2] http://www.statssa.gov.za/?p=12930

68 | HOW RUSSIA LOSES

Soviet Union and its allies poured advice, training, weapons, and logistical support into the South African Black liberation struggle. It educated and cared for thousands of South Africans in exile. Moscow clearly had a geopolitical goal of replacing Western influence in Africa with its own, but it also occupied a moral high ground in the fight against apartheid.

Ironically, when South Africa finally became a multiracial republic in 1994, Russia reaped little immediate benefit. Its support for the anti-apartheid cause declined precipitously under Mikhail Gorbachev and Boris Yeltsin. Under Vladimir Putin, however, Russia made building influence in Africa a priority again. The Kremlin leaned heavily on the reserve of goodwill still present in South Africa from the fight against apartheid and styled itself as a battle-tested ally deeply committed to the nation's success.

The zenith of Russian influence in South Africa came during the presidency of Jacob Zuma, an anti-apartheid fighter with a long association with the Soviet Union. Under Zuma's presidency from 2009 to 2018, South Africa's "anti-colonialist" foreign policy aligned it closely with Russia and China, and against the United States and the European Union. Zuma and Putin met regularly and often talked on the telephone. Russia's influence in South Africa rose so high that it was almost able to clinch a huge nuclear deal with South Africa that could have made the nation's entire economy beholden to Moscow.

Yet the nuclear project was a classic example of Russian overreach. Russia (with Zuma's help) felt it could trample South Africa's government institutions, judiciary, civil society, and free press to force the deal through. However, its size was so extravagant, and its potential for Russian control of the entire country so great, that it played a major role in destroying Zuma's presidency. With Zuma gone and the nuclear deal in ruins, Russia lost a financial lever that could have solidified its dominance in South Africa for decades.

All was not lost for the Kremlin, however. In an outcome unusual for the case studies in this book, Moscow's political influence endured. South Africa even served as something of an ally to Russia during the Ukraine war, refusing to condemn the invasion and continuing

South Africa: The Deal Too Big to Succeed | 69

trade. Still, South Africa's relationship with Moscow seemed rooted in nostalgia and ideology more than ongoing benefit, and the counties lacked the deep personal ties Putin had enjoyed with Zuma.

The Soviet Union and the Struggle Against Apartheid

Russian involvement in the affairs of southern Africa dates as far back as 1899. Tsarist Russia sent weapons and volunteers to help the Boers, South Africans of Dutch origin, in their unsuccessful war against the British Empire. Since Russia and Britain were rivals, even Russia's first intervention in Africa had a geopolitical motive.

After the 1917 Bolshevik Revolution, the Communist Party of South Africa (CPSA) eagerly joined the Comintern, the international organization for communist parties. By then, White domination of the Black majority had been firmly established in South Africa. The CPSA, which opposed White dominance, saw in the Soviet Union a model egalitarian society. Many of the CPSA's first members were White, but by the end of the 1920s most were Black.

South Africa had close ties with Russia during World War II, when they were allies against Nazi Germany. Relations deteriorated, however, after South Africa began passing formal apartheid laws in 1949 and banned the African Nationalist Congress (ANC), which promoted anti-capitalist and anti-racist ideology. The Suppression of Communism Act in 1950 allowed almost anyone agitating for social change to be branded a communist. South Africa broke off diplomatic relations with Moscow in 1956.

The breakdown of official relations presented an opportunity for Nikita Khrushchev, who ruled the Soviet Union from 1953 to 1964. Khrushchev had sought to reassert Russian power wherever possible in the postwar world, and Africa was a particular opportunity. Decolonization in the 1950s and 1960s allowed Moscow to win substantial influence in Egypt, Ghana, Guinea, Tanzania, Zambia, and elsewhere.

70 | HOW RUSSIA LOSES

Apartheid was already making South Africa an international pariah; in 1962, the UN General Assembly called on all nations to impose a trade embargo on the country. Moscow saw in South Africa a chance to pursue two opportunities at once. It could become a leader in the campaign for the liberation of the country's Black population—a morally virtuous cause with overwhelming international support—while laying the groundwork to expand its geopolitical influence all the way to Africa's strategic tip.

Economic advantage was also not far from Moscow's mind; Soviet enterprises continued to deal with South Africa's De Beers diamond interests, jointly controlling much of the world's diamond market.

Under pressure from the government, the CPSA dissolved itself and became the underground South African Communist Party (SACP) in 1953. In 1955, the ANC, the SACP, and others adopted the Freedom Charter, a call for radical transformation of the country through nationalization of the economy and redistribution of its wealth. In 1960, after police killed 69 Black protesters in the Sharpeville Massacre, the ANC was banned. In 1961, SACP and ANC members, meeting secretly inside the country, decided their only option was to turn their campaign into an armed struggle. They secured an agreement with Moscow for help with armed operations and created Umkhonto we Sizwe ("Spear of the Nation") to carry out the plan.

Nelson Mandela was a co-founder of the group, commonly known as "MK," which carried out sabotage against electrical substations and other targets. In 1963, South African security forces captured MK's leadership. Mandela and seven colleagues were sentenced to life in prison. MK subsequently engaged in several failed operations, including efforts backed by the Soviet military to infiltrate guerrillas into the country. Not until the 1980s did the cell reassert itself.

The Soviets continued to work intensively with the ANC as well as the SACP. The two organizations' leadership largely overlapped, which facilitated their cooperation. After a visit to Russia by ANC

Deputy President Oliver Tambo, military training for ANC and SACP personnel began in Moscow, Odesa, Tashkent, and elsewhere. Thousands of anti-apartheid cadres also trained with Soviet support in Tanzania, Angola, Algeria, Egypt, and Morocco. Soviet operatives had the opportunity to observe the South African trainees and identify those who might best help Soviet objectives in the future. In some cases, close personal friendships developed. Ronnie Kasrils, a trainee who became South Africa's minister of intelligence services in 2004, said, "To us, the Soviet Union was like a dream, and it was held with much love and respect."[3]

Soviet support remained robust under Khrushchev's successor, Leonid Brezhnev, who came to power in 1964. Aid included not only military assistance but diplomatic support, international solidarity campaigns, supplies to build and equip camps, and training of medical workers. In 1966, the Soviet Union began supporting Namibian and Angolan fighters in their war with the South African Defense Force.

All this activity put heavy pressure on South Africa's White regime. However, with the Soviet Union, Cuba, and East Germany so obviously involved in the conflict, South Africa's government managed to portray itself to many in the West as a bulwark against communism. The ANC, Prime Minister P. W. Botha said in 1983, was "a small clique of Blacks and Whites, controlled by the Kremlin."[4] In the United States, Ronald Reagan condemned apartheid but said it should be ended gradually in cooperation with the South African authorities. He said the United States would not turn against a country "that has stood by us in every war we've ever fought, a country that, strategically, is essential to

---

[3] Barnett, Marcus, "Sabotaging Apartheid," *Jacobin*, March 11, 2017, https://www.jacobinmag.com/2017/11/south-africa-apartheid-sacp-london-recruits

[4] Lelyveld, Joseph, "Black Challenge to Pretoria: Rebellion, still puny, is showing more muscle," *The New York Times*, October 12, 1983, https://www.nytimes.com/1983/10/12/world/black-challenge-to-pretoria-rebellionstill-puny-is-showing-more-muscle.html

the free world in its production of minerals."[5] In the United Kingdom, Prime Minister Margaret Thatcher also opposed sweeping sanctions, though she pushed the South African regime to release Mandela from prison and make reforms.

Despite the caution of major Western governments, strong anti-apartheid movements grew in the US and Europe. Congress began in the 1960s to impose restrictions on US relations with the White government. In 1984, over Reagan's veto, Washington promulgated far-reaching sanctions through the Comprehensive Anti-Apartheid Act. An outpouring of films, books, and activism in Europe and the United States documented the repressiveness of apartheid. Still, although humanitarian organizations and some Western governments, especially Sweden, helped the ANC, the Soviet Union remained the movement's main outside material supporter.

Inside South Africa, the anti-apartheid movement struggled, suffering the arrest of many activists in the early 1970s. The 1976 Soweto Uprising changed the picture dramatically. Protests by Black children in Soweto, an impoverished township on the edge of Johannesburg, turned into violent confrontations with police that left 176 people dead and 1,000 injured. Not only did the violence bring major global condemnation of the apartheid regime and new sanctions, but thousands of young people left South Africa. Many wound up at military camps in Angola run by Soviet, Cuban, and Angolan trainers and soon joined the ANC and MK.

SACP delegates were invited in 1984 to a meeting of the Communist Party Central Committee, the top Soviet ruling body. The SACP profited from the occasion to hold its own sixth

---

[5] Interview with Walter Cronkite, CBS News. Transcript at https://www.reaganlibrary.gov/archives/speech/excerpts-interview-walter-cronkite-cbs-news. Joe Biden, as a senator in 1986, blasted the Reagan administration for tolerating the "ugly," "repulsive," and "repugnant" apartheid system. See video at https://www.independent.co.uk/news/world/americas/us-election-2020/joe-biden-anti-apartheid-senate-reagan-south-africa-video-a9547471.html

congress in Moscow, bringing together a wide array of South Africans studying and training in the country. Beyond military training, tens of thousands of South Africans were being educated by the Soviet Union in non-military subjects, preparing them for careers and government posts in a post-apartheid nation.

Meanwhile, South Africa's government faced spiraling strikes and protests after Soweto. A revived MK moved beyond its previous attacks on property and began launching bloody operations that targeted military command centers, energy resources, a shopping center, restaurants, and a bank.

By the early 1980s, influential figures in the South African government had reached the conclusion that White domination could not endure endlessly. Under pressure from domestic protests, world opinion, economic sanctions, and MK's continuing attacks, officials of the ruling National Party opened secret negotiations with Mandela.

When Mikhail Gorbachev came to power in Moscow in 1985, a negotiated end to apartheid in South Africa seemed possible. Soviet diplomats helped engineer a settlement to South Africa's border war with Angola and Namibia. Some in South Africa's power structure began to look at Moscow less as a *rooi gevaar* ("red threat" in Afrikaans) and more as an ally in creating conditions for domestic peace.[6] Envoys from the South African government proposed further cooperation with the Soviets in gold and diamond marketing and suggested at times that they could replace their knee-jerk anti-communism by neutrality in the competition between East and West.[7]

The biggest accommodation between South Africa's government and anti-apartheid forces came under President F. W. de Klerk, who took office in 1989. He freed Mandela in 1990 and allowed

---

[6] Filatova, Irina, "South Africa's Soviet Connection," *History Compass*, February 27, 2008, https://doi.org/10.1111/j.14780542.2007.00508.x
[7] Shubin, Vladimir, "The Soviet Union/Russian Federation's Relations with South Africa, with Special Reference to the Period since 1980," *African Affairs*, January 1996, https://www.jstor.org/stable/723723

74 | HOW RUSSIA LOSES

the ANC and SACP to resume activity. Soon the government agreed to free 1,300 political prisoners and allow as many as 22,000 exiles to return home. On August 7, 1990, the ANC announced the end of its violent activity, though Mandela said strikes and demonstrations would continue against White domination.

Once Mandela was freed and the armed struggle ended, the contacts that had been quietly forged between the Kremlin and the de Klerk government became much more visible. The ANC was alarmed because the rights of Blacks in the country had still not been established. A top South African diplomat visited Moscow a month before Mandela was freed, ostensibly because Moscow was such a convenient place to change planes on the way to Tokyo; the ANC was informed of his arrival at the last moment. The two nations' governments agreed to open diplomatic interest sections in each other's capitals, a step just short of embassies. Stanley Mabizela, the deputy ANC international affairs director, worried that the Soviets had offered the apartheid government "an important break from isolation" and that the interest section agreement was "a big victory for them, a big victory particularly over the ANC, because the ANC and the Soviets have always claimed such closeness."[8]

The Soviets frustrated the ANC and SACP further in 1990 with a five-year diamond deal with De Beers. There were other irritants as well. Gorbachev's transfer of foreign affairs responsibilities from the Communist Party Central Committee to the Foreign Ministry shifted relations with South Africa away from officials who had dealt with the ANC for decades. In November 1991, South African Foreign Minister R. F. "Pik" Botha arrived in Moscow. "I don't see any reason why we should be apart anymore," Botha told a Moscow news conference. "I am convinced

---

[8] Davidson, Joe, "Pretoria and Moscow Forge Links That May Turn Gold," *The Wall Street Journal*, March 28, 1991.

South Africa: The Deal Too Big to Succeed | 75

from what I've learned that there is a vast scope for close cooperation."[9]

Gorbachev increasingly put a premium on relations with the West instead of the Kremlin's traditional allies. Mandela, who was traveling the world after his release, was eager to meet Gorbachev. This was never arranged. There were some genuine scheduling problems, but many felt Gorbachev believed receiving Mandela would feed the idea that the Kremlin was still intent on spreading communism. What is more, people close to Gorbachev were making their own contacts with South African authorities behind the backs of both the Soviet Communist Party and the ANC, wrote Vladimir Shubin, a senior Soviet official who oversaw much of the aid to the Black struggle.[10]

In December 1991, the Soviet Union collapsed. Gorbachev's successor in the Kremlin, Boris Yeltsin, only intensified the reverse course on South Africa that his predecessor had begun. Russia re-established diplomatic relations with South Africa in 1992, and Yeltsin met de Klerk in Moscow—seven years before he found time to meet Mandela. "While major Western powers were doing their best to build or to broaden the bridges to the ANC (which had been ignored or even opposed by them previously) the new rulers in Moscow were in a hurry to develop ties with the outgoing South African government," said Shubin.

Moscow's embrace of South Africa's White leadership was not based only on the Kremlin's overall pro-Western course. Moscow also hoped for large mineral deals with South Africa and, perhaps, new South African investments in Russia's struggling economy. Irina Filatova of the University of KwaZulu-Natal, a specialist on Russian–South African relations, said some senior Russian

---

[9] "Botha Bullish on Relations with Soviet Union and Russia," *The Associated Press*, November 8, 1991, https://apnews.com/article/47037445eac6448844c0b047536a2f2b
[10] "The Soviet Union/Russian Federation's Relations with South Africa, with Special Reference to the Period since 1980," op. cit.

officials believed the White government would never actually give up power.[11]

Shubin also cited "the rise of xenophobia and even of outright racism largely fuelled by the gross deterioration of living standards in Russia. The obverse side of this was a sympathy for the whites in South Africa, who were portrayed by the dominant mass-media as potential victims of 'black majority rule.' " Further, Yeltsin and other Russian politicians were questioning how much of a return Moscow had received from its aid to Africa and to developing regions in general. Some Russian aid projects in Africa were stopped on the spot, and embassies and cultural centers were cut back.

All these developments meant Moscow's relationship with South Africa's anti-apartheid struggle ended in a far different place than where it started. The more that justice for South Africa's Blacks looked likely, the more the Soviet Union and Russia engaged with the country's White authorities. Ironically, however, the Kremlin's renunciation of communism, and its diminished support for its traditional allies, may have also helped speed up negotiations on South Africa's future. In Filatova's words:

> The collapse of the Soviet Union destroyed the validity of the *rooi gevaar* idea even in the eyes of those who had firmly believed in it. This, in the system of notions and values of apartheid supporters, meant that there was no need to be worried about the ANC: it was no longer going to install either Soviet troops or a communist order. On the other hand, from then on the ANC leadership knew that despite a powerful international lobby, there would be no one to bail the party out, had it failed to accept compromises and negotiate. In effect even the very collapse of

---

[11] Filatova, Irina, "Third time lucky? Establishing diplomatic relations between Russia and South Africa," *South African Journal of International Affairs* 22:4, 2018, https://doi.org/10.1080/10220461.2015.1115369

South Africa: The Deal Too Big to Succeed | 77

the Soviet Union and the withdrawal of Soviet support played a role in bringing the ANC to power sooner than might otherwise have happened.[12]

In 1993, negotiators finally agreed on an interim constitution for a multiracial South Africa and a transitional executive council to prepare the way for a democratic election. The ANC won the election in April 1994, and Mandela became president on May 10. His two deputies were de Klerk and Thabo Mbeki, an ANC international relations official who, during a long exile from South Africa, had received Soviet military training. Several other members of Mandela's cabinet, and dozens of parliament members, also were deeply familiar with and respected the Soviet Union.

Russia and the New South Africa

Despite the Soviet connections of so many officials, Moscow's relationship with Mandela's South Africa was initially limited. Gorbachev and Yeltsin had significantly damaged relations between the ANC and Moscow. Each country was also distracted by other problems. Mandela was trying to reverse a century of Black poverty and convince Whites that they had a future in the country. His international attention was focused largely on resolving African conflicts. Yeltsin, trying to mend decades of Soviet economic failures, had pulled back from foreign adventures. South Africa's new foreign and defense ministers visited Moscow in 1994 and 1995, signing a handful of agreements with few concrete results. South Africa joined the Non-Aligned Movement in 1994, effectively declaring that it did not want to be part of any great power bloc.

The 21st century dawned with new leadership in both countries. Vladimir Putin took over from Yeltsin on New Year's Eve. Mbeki had become South African president in June 1999 after Mandela, who was about to turn 81, declined to seek a second term. The

---

[12] "South Africa's Soviet Connection," op. cit.

Putin administration announced it would expand relations with Africa. It began reopening diplomatic missions and inviting African leaders to Moscow. Relations between Moscow and South Africa began to flower, led by Russian economic investments. In 2005, Viktor Vekselberg, one of Russia's richest men, became a member of Mbeki's international investment advisory forum. Putin met Mbeki during a G8 summit in St. Petersburg in 2006. He visited Mbeki in Cape Town later that year, signing a Treaty of Friendship and Cooperation that had languished in its preliminary form since Mandela's much-delayed Moscow visit in 1999.

Along with bilateral trade relations, the countries began to consult on political issues, too, especially after South Africa became a rotating member of the UN Security Council in 2007. Yet Mbeki emphasized South Africa's move from a strong reliance on Russia toward nonalignment, believing that the end of the Cold War would ultimately reduce Moscow's support for the ANC.[13] Mbeki's rhetoric on issues such as neo-colonialism and non-intervention coincided with positions inherited from the Soviet Union, but they were just as much tenets of nonaligned ideology in general. Mbeki also tended to ties with the United States, receiving President George W. Bush in Cape Town in 2003 and visiting him at the White House in 2005. Some proposals for expansive economic projects with Russia failed to gain any traction. When Dmitry Medvedev, sitting in for Putin as president, traveled to Africa in June 2009, he did not include South Africa as a stop—though his itinerary included Namibia and Angola.

South Africa's ties with Russia changed significantly again with the election of Jacob Zuma as president. Zuma, a Zulu, was born in 1942 in KwaZulu-Natal province on South Africa's east coast. He had no formal education. He joined the ANC as a teenager and soon became a member of MK. He was arrested almost immediately and sent to the same prison as Mandela and other ANC leaders. He also became a member of the SACP. Once freed from prison, he led ANC operations in Mozambique and Zambia

---

[13] Gevisser, Mark, *Thabo Mbeki: The Dream Deferred* (Johannesburg, Jonathan Ball Publishers, 2007), 483–484.

South Africa: The Deal Too Big to Succeed | 79

and became head of the organization's intelligence service—responsible, among other matters, for a secret police unit that rooted out spies. For three months he received military and leadership training in the Soviet Union. He became deputy president of South Africa under Mbeki in 1999, president of the ANC in 2007 and president of South Africa in May 2009 at the age of 67.

Zuma, who described himself as a socialist, oriented South Africa strongly toward Russia and China. His rhetoric was sharply anti-Western, and he visited Russia at least seven times during his presidency. His first visit as president was in 2010, accompanied by 11 government ministers and more than 100 business representatives. Happily for Moscow, his realignment of South African policy came just as Putin, who invaded Georgia in 2008, was looking for new allies to counteract his plunging relations with the West. South Africa, along with the Organization of African Unity, became the first focus of a broad new Russian outreach to the African continent.

In 2010, Zuma accepted an invitation for South Africa to join the BRICS economic bloc, formed a year earlier by Russia, China, India, and Brazil as a counterweight to Western economic institutions. Zuma was an enthusiastic supporter of BRICS and its New Development Bank, which he said would aid developing countries in a more equal way than Western institutions. He told Russia's *RT* television in 2015 that Africa's relationship with Western powers had not changed since decolonization: "They still regard us as the Third World as a kind of people who must be related to as the former subject, etc. That talks also to the economics. ... Their intention has never been to make the former colonial countries develop."[14] (In the West's view, what Zuma was looking for was funding without the monitoring and accountability that Western aid usually entails.)

---

[14] "West still treats Africa as former vassals – South Africa's Zuma to RT," May 10, 2015, *RT*, https://www.rt.com/news/257353-zuma-africa-russia-china-brics

80 | HOW RUSSIA LOSES

A discussion document prepared for the ANC's 2015 National General Council typified Zuma's and the ANC's view of Russia, China, and the West. The ANC, it declared, was a "revolutionary national liberation movement which is an integral part of the international revolutionary movement to liberate humanity from the bondage of imperialism and neo colonialism."

Russia's leaders, the document said, are constantly being attacked by Western media as "monsters abusing human rights"—and "whatever genuine concerns may exist," these were being exploited to contain Russia's global rise. (The document was issued a year after the first Russian invasion of Ukraine.) The discussion paper said China's "economic development trajectory remains a leading example of the triumph of humanity over adversity. The exemplary role of the collective leadership of the Communist Party of China in this regard should be a guiding lodestar of our own struggle." By contrast, the document said the United States was trying to destabilize progressive governments in Latin America, the Middle East, and Africa, and expressed concern about the growing footprint of the US Africa Command.[15]

When Mandela came to power, South Africa publicly espoused democracy, respect for national borders, and non-interference in other countries' affairs. Under Zuma, these principles were interpreted with an ideological overlay. South Africa condemned the US interventions that overthrew regimes in Libya and Iraq, supported Cuba's government, and backed the Palestinians against Israel. It abstained in the 2015 UN vote defending the territorial integrity of Ukraine after the Russian invasion. (No BRICS country voted to support Ukraine.) In fact, South Africa stepped up its food exports to Russia in response to Western sanctions over the invasion.[16] In May 2015, Zuma and nearly 80 officials traveled to Moscow for celebrations of the Soviet World

---

[15] Document at https://new.anc1912.org.za/wp-content/uploads/2021/03/NGC-2015-Discussion-Document-International-Relations.pdf
[16] World Food Moscow, "South African Food in Russia," October 3, 2016, https://web.archive.org/web/20191129144527/https://world-food.ru/Articles/south-african-food-in-russia

War II victory over Nazi Germany, an event boycotted by most Western countries.

Zuma tended not to publicly disparage dictatorial African regimes, though he eventually became critical of Zimbabwe's Robert Mugabe. In 2015, the government allowed Sudanese President Omar al-Bashir to come and go from South Africa despite a warrant from the International Criminal Court for his arrest. Zuma's government was also wary of Western democracy-promotion efforts, adopting the Russian view that they were regime-change plots in disguise. In that spirit, Nikolai Patrushev, director of the Russian Federal Security Service (FSB), and David Mahlobo, the South African minister of state security, were reported to have discussed at a November 2015 meeting "countering 'coloured revolutions' and preventing external interference in internal affairs" of African states."[17]

Zuma also opened the way for potential Russian involvement in Africa's own peacekeeping operations. South Africa has been an active contributor to negotiating and enforcing peace in the Democratic Republic of the Congo, Burundi, Sudan, and Uganda. During a Moscow visit in 2014, Zuma asked for support for the African Capacity for Immediate Response to Crises (ACIRC), which he had helped create. Speculation at the time hinted that Zuma was looking for airlift capacity.[18] This would have brought Russian embassies and military officers deeply into the details of African peacekeeping operations while raising the image of Russian power and benevolence in the eyes of local populations.

Meanwhile, intelligence ties grew between the two countries. South Africa reportedly sent 90 intelligence agents to Russia for training in 2012. The intelligence relationship with Russia, a South African spokesman said, was "cordial and warm." (On the negative side, one South African source said, "The sad part is that

---

[17] Russian Embassy in South Africa, Twitter, November 26, 2015, https://twitter.com/EmbassyofRussia/status/669956807528460293

[18] "Jacob Zuma's mysterious mission to Russia," *News24*, August 31, 2014, https://www.news24.com/News24/Jacob-Zumas-mysterious-mission-to-Russia-20140831

82 | HOW RUSSIA LOSES

the Russians have recruited at least four of our people, which means we are sitting with double agents."[19]) In 2015, Patrushev and Mahlobo met at least four times.

South Africa's military intelligence service began a program with Russia to develop a spy satellite, launched in 2014 and known as "Project Condor." The arrangements were so secret that South Africa's civilian intelligence agency reportedly had to turn to an agent in Russia to learn what its military counterpart at home was up to. The opposition Democratic Alliance said the project, which involved 30 Russian specialists based in South Africa, was set up "outside all government procurement legislation and regulations." The government denied it had failed to follow proper procedures.[20]

Zuma's frequent visits to Russia were reciprocated by three trips by Putin to South Africa. In one 10-month period in 2014–2015, the heads of state held four in-person meetings in Moscow and at international conferences. Little was publicly reported about the sessions, or the frequent phone conversations they also reportedly had. Zuma explained one trip to Moscow in 2014 by saying he was receiving medical treatment after being poisoned. The president and his entourage frequently implied he was the victim of poisoning plots organized by the US, the UK, local enemies, or a former wife.[21] Irrespective of whether he was indeed poisoned and by whom, Zuma seemed convinced he was a poisoning victim and that he owed his life to Russian doctors.[22]

---

[19] Shoba, Sibongakonke, "Double-agent fear as local spies sent to train in Russia," *The Sunday Times* (Johannesburg), August 31, 2014.

[20] Jordan, Will, "S Africa spied on Russia for satellite project details," *Al Jazeera*, February 25, 2015, https://www.aljazeera.com/news/2015/2/25/s-africa-spied-on-russia-for-satellite-project-details

[21] "Poison," *BBC*, December 17, 2021, https://www.bbc.co.uk/sounds/play/m0012fxl

[22] Maughan, Karyn, et al., *Nuclear: Inside South Africa's Nuclear Deal* (Cape Town: Tafelberg, 2022).

South Africa: The Deal Too Big to Succeed | 83

'A Scarcely Believable Picture of Rampant Corruption'

Accusations of corruption predated Zuma's time as president. In 2005, Mbeki removed him as deputy president after a Zuma associate was convicted of making illicit payments to Zuma in connection with an enormous arms deal—the 1999 purchase of $4.8 billion in ships, submarines, and aircraft for the South African military. Prosecutors began efforts in 2002 to indict Zuma for corruption, fraud, racketeering, and money laundering related to the deal; they stopped when he became president in 2009. In 2005, Zuma was charged with rape. To many at that time, the corruption and rape allegations together meant Zuma's political career was already over. The *Mail & Guardian* newspaper wrote confidently during the rape trial that "even Zuma's most diehard supporters privately acknowledge that he cannot now be president, regardless of the trial outcome."[23]

Those who dismissed Zuma's future political chances did not fully comprehend his power within the ANC. South Africa's president is elected by parliament, which has been controlled by the ANC since the end of apartheid. Becoming president, therefore, depends on the dominance of the ANC parliamentary majority, rather than a national vote. As former ANC intelligence chief, he had detailed knowledge of key ANC figures. Zuma, who was acquitted of the rape charge, also enjoyed staunch support from Zulu activists and trade unions.

A gulf soon opened within the party between Zuma and Mbeki, who was facing a population increasingly frustrated with the economy, his minimizing of growing crime, and his claims that AIDS could be cured with herbal remedies. Mbeki also found himself on the ideological defensive against ANC cadres who still wanted to radically restructure society in line with the Freedom Charter.[24] Further, Zuma knew how to get his supporters into the

---

[23] Robinson, Vicki et al., "23 Days that Shook Our World," *Mail & Guardian*, April 28, 2006, https://mg.co.za/article/2006-04-28-23-days-that-shook-our-world

[24] For a discussion of the ideological conflict, see Filatova, Irina, "The Lasting Legacy: The Soviet Theory of the National-Democratic

streets. When Mbeki dismissed Zuma as vice president, hundreds of Zuma supporters staged rallies, some burning T-shirts with Mbeki's face on them. (During his rape trial, 2,000 Zuma-backers surrounded the courthouse.) Zuma won the ANC leadership in 2007, and Mbeki was forced to resign as president the following year. After an interim presidency under Kgalema Motlanthe, Zuma became the nation's leader.

Zuma became president at the start of the global financial crisis in 2008, accompanied by a recession at home. Despite the financial pressure, he increased social welfare benefits, expanded access to water and electricity, and made higher education free. He invested heavily in a national infrastructure plan and took resolute action against AIDS. Zuma was a gifted orator in Zulu, charismatic at rallies with a mix of populist rhetoric, humorous asides, and mockery of his opponents.

However, South Africa's average growth during Zuma's time in power barely topped 1.5 percent per year. Public debt rose, and stock prices fell. Unemployment reached nearly 28 percent in 2017. By 2018, South Africa was the only OECD country still in recession. Political instability—Zuma reshuffled his cabinet 12 times—and uncertainty over economic policies led to a fall in foreign investment and an increase in capital flight. Zuma roiled markets with proposals to ban exports of strategic minerals and allow government seizure of land without compensation.

The most significant financial aspect of his reign, however, was a spectacular level of corruption and mismanagement. By one widely quoted estimate, the country lost 470 billion rand in GDP ($40 billion at 2018 rates) due to "corruption, maladministration and misguided policies" just from the start of his second term in 2014 to his resignation in 2018.[25] By other calculations, "state

---

Revolution and South Africa," *South African Historical Journal*, April 23, 2012, https://doi.org/10.1080/02582473.2012.665077
[25] The estimate was by the chief economist of Nedbank, one of the nation's largest banks. See Dykes, Dennis, "Trimming state fat and cutting red tape for investors can save country," *Business Day* (Johannesburg), February 19, 2019, https://www.businesslive.

capture" by corrupt interests cost South Africa as much as a third of its GDP.[26]

How could corruption have reached such a spectacular level?

As soon as he became president, Zuma moved to establish a grip on South Africa's most powerful institutions. These included the ANC's internal structures, the security establishment, the judiciary, and government entities with big budgets. Other targets were the South African Revenue Service, a tax agency respected internationally for its professionalism, and the Scorpions, an FBI-like organization that had investigated corruption charges against Zuma.

As Zuma settled into power, he faced mounting allegations that he was creating a web of corrupt interests that intervened in ministerial appointments and seized control of contracts from state-controlled entities, including South African Airways, the Eskom electric utility company, and Transnet, a transportation and pipeline entity. The first installment of the report of the Zondo Commission, established after Zuma's fall to probe state capture by corrupt interests, said events at major state corporations presented "a scarcely believable picture of rampant corruption."[27]

Many allegations focused on the Guptas—three brothers of Indian origin who built close connections to Zuma as they steadily expanded their wealth in mining, media, and other industries. By

---

co.za/bd/opinion/2019-02-19-trimming-state-fat-and-cutting-investor-red-tape-two-ways-to-rescue-sa Conversion to dollars at the rate the day Zuma resigned.

[26] Merten, Marianne, "State Capture wipes out third of SA's R4.9-trillion GDP – never mind lost trust, confidence, opportunity," *Daily Maverick*, March 1, 2019, https://www.dailymaverick.co.za/article/2019-03-01-state-capture-wipes-out-third-of-sas-r4-9-trillion-gdp-never-mind-lost-trust-confidence-opportunity

[27] Report at https://www.gov.za/sites/default/files/gcis_speech/Judicial%20Commission%20of%20Inquiry%20into%20State%20Capture%20Report_Part%201.pdf

one NGO's estimate, some $3.5 billion flowed to the Gupta family directly from state-controlled entities.[28]

Zuma built a powerful security and intelligence apparatus that abetted his political and economic dominance. He kept personal control over key security appointments, sometimes selecting leaders with little security background but who were certain to be loyal. According to testimony before the Zondo Commission, he established a national domestic espionage network, including some operatives who worked separately from the state security agencies and were accountable only to him. A former agent said Mahlobo oversaw some of this separate work and cooperated with a man named Markhov, who spoke with a Russian or East European accent and often carried transcripts of wiretaps between agents and Mahlobo.[29] The operatives had access to large amounts of cash, a great deal of which reportedly disappeared without a trace.

Agents penetrated media, civil society, and student groups, monitored phone calls and emails of political opponents, and tried to influence judiciary officials in cases involving Zuma. Opponents of Zuma were investigated for supposedly being CIA agents. Zuma mistrusted even his colleagues in the ANC; by some accounts, he required party members voting on internal

---

[28] Davis, Rebecca, "The total(ish) cost of the Guptas' State Capture: R49,157,323,233.68," *Daily Maverick*, May 24, 2021, https://www.dailymaverick.co.za/article/2021-05-24-the-totalish-cost-of-the-guptas-state-capture-r49157323233-68

[29] The former agent, a whistleblower, made his allegations in a sworn affidavit to Paul O'Sullivan, a private investigator and founder of the anti-corruption organization, Forensics for Justice. The former agent also quoted Mahlobo as saying Russia would provide money to bribe senior ANC officials to advance their and Mahlobo's interests. Hogg, Alec, "SSA insider spills beans, names those tapped, exposes Mahlobo," *BizNews*, March 11, 2019, https://www.biznews.com/undictated/2019/03/11/ssa-insider-spills-beans-names-those-tapped-exposes-mahlobo

South Africa: The Deal Too Big to Succeed | 87

appointments to provide photos showing how they had marked their ballots.[30]

What was remarkable was that, while the espionage was secret, the financial manipulations by Zuma's circle largely were not. Rarely have government officials in a democratic country engaged in so much questionable activity under such a glare of publicity.

In 2016, the government's own "public protector," a monitor of government integrity, published a 355-page report, "State of Capture," on "improper and possibly corrupt" relationships between the government and the Guptas.[31] Yet little happened once the report was published. Not until a month before his resignation did Zuma agree to appoint an official inquiry into its findings.

The most potent challenges to Zuma came from South Africa's vibrant civil society. Independent news media and civil society groups had been fixtures in South Africa even under apartheid. Newspapers exposed the injustices of the apartheid system, using elaborate strategies to evade censorship laws and interview people who were banned from being quoted. In the new multicultural South Africa, civil society groups remained prominent, providing health and welfare services the government failed to deliver and campaigning for affordable housing, workers' rights, and more generous welfare payments.

---

[30] See Brock, Joe, et al., "How Zuma, the smiling spy, controls South Africa," *Reuters*, May 4, 2016, https://www.reuters.com/article/us-safrica-zuma-insight-idUSKCN0XV1RB; Thamm, Marianne, "Zuma's spy state: A decade of unfettered surveillance, secrets, lies and lootings, propped up by a private army of spies," *Daily Maverick*, January 30, 2021, https://www.dailymaverick.co.za/article/2021-01-30-zumas-spy-state-a-decade-of-unfettered-surveillance-secrets-lies-and-lootings-propped-up-by-a-private-army-of-spies; and Torchia, Christopher, "South Africa to investigate spy allegations," *The Associated Press*, March 5, 2015, https://apnews.com/article/da2005cbf98c4b008546553a63359698
[31] Report at https://www.sahistory.org.za/sites/default/files/2019-05/329756252-state-of-capture-14-october-2016.pdf

Independent media and civil society had helped topple Mbeki over his AIDS denialism and disregard for opposition voices. Public campaigns by civil society groups created a safe space for senior ANC members to set aside "party unity" and push Mbeki out of office.

Under Zuma, media and civil society worked nonstop to expose corruption and defend those whom he attacked. In 2017, five news and investigative outlets jointly analyzed 200,000 leaked emails between the Gupta family and its government and business associates. The same year, investigators from four universities published a detailed report that accused Zuma of a "silent coup"—with the stunning goal of controlling the entire national treasury. Books by investigative reporters exposed not only corruption but also the structures and people that made it possible. Among them were Jane Duncan's *The Rise of the Securocrats* in 2015, Jacques Pauw's *The President's Keepers* in 2017, and Robin Renwick's *How to Steal a Country* in 2018.

Activists went to court to block public contracts awarded illegally. They rallied to defend government officials such as Thuli Madonsela, whom a government official accused of being a CIA agent after she questioned government-paid improvements to Zuma's private residence. They collaborated with the South African Council of Churches, which issued its own reports on corruption and offered protection to whistleblowers. Groups such as Corruption Watch and United Against Corruption organized protests that attracted thousands of participants.

Civil society groups were even powerful enough to affect foreign policy. Under pressure from NGOs, South Africa in 2016 reversed its position at the UN and voted to establish an independent expert on sexual orientation and gender identity.

Sometimes the NGOs needed to normalize the very idea of political protest in a country where the concept did not always make cultural sense. In the words of one veteran activist, traditional norms of deference to authority led people to support corrupt leaders "simply on the basis of their blackness or whiteness."[32]

Many politically active NGOs received funding from foreign governments and foundations. Civil society organizations working in health and education could raise money from large South African corporations; however, the companies feared being cut off from government contracts if they became involved in political causes. For instance, Right2Know, a freedom of expression organization, has received funds from the US Luminate Foundation, Germany's Heinrich Böll Foundation, Norwegian People's Aid, and George Soros' Open Society Foundations.[33] "Foreign funding became increasingly important for advocacy NGOs because local businesses were afraid to contribute to them for fear of Zuma's reaction," said Barbara Groeblinghoff of Germany's Friedrich Naumann Foundation, who worked in South Africa under Zuma.[34]

Zuma was aware of the challenge these NGOs represented. His circle, like heavy-handed regimes everywhere, had been put on its guard by the Arab Spring in the early 2010s and popular movements elsewhere in the world. Government and ANC spokespeople began to see any unrest, even a student protest over school fees, as subversive activity that could lead to "regime change." In 2014, South Africa led a group of nations, including Russia, China, Cuba, and Saudi Arabia, in trying to weaken a UN Human Rights Council resolution protecting the rights of peaceful protesters.[35]

---

[32] Gumede, William, "Policy Brief 28: How civil society has strengthened democracy in South Africa," Democracy Works Foundation, May 8, 2018, https://democracyworks.org.za/policy-brief-28-how-civil-society-has-strengthened-democracy-in-south-africa
[33] Donor list at https://www.r2k.org.za/about/donors/
[34] Barbara Groeblinghoff, interview with author, May 5, 2022.
[35] "Shaky road to important peaceful protest resolution," UN Watch, April 1, 2014, https://unwatch.org/shaky-road-to-important-peaceful-protest-resolution

African governments, Mahlobo said in 2017, were under threat from "color revolutions" resulting from "nefarious activities of rogue NGOs threatening national security." The danger of such official attitudes, wrote journalism professor Jane Duncan, was that "local NGO's and protest movements engaging in lawful advocacy can now be accused of engaging in subversion, and investigated on these grounds."[36] Zuma and his officials denounced opposition NGOs as remnants of apartheid-era interest groups, or as fronts for foreign enemies. Black civil society activists were accused of being puppets of "White monopoly capital." Those NGOs that received government support found that support withdrawn if they did not endorse the government's political agenda.

ANC Secretary General Gwede Mantashe told party supporters in 2016:

> As we mobilize our people, we must say be vigilant. You must see through anarchy and people who are out there in a program of regime change. We are aware of the meetings taking place regularly in the American Embassy. These meetings in the embassy are about nothing else other than mobilization for regime change. We are aware of a program that takes young people to the United States for six weeks, brings them back and plants them everywhere in the campuses and everywhere.[37]

Zuma claimed that critical media, too, were out to destroy him. He sued major newspapers for defamation, and his bodyguards were

---

[36] Duncan, Jane, "Why South Africans should be worried by ANC talk of a 'colour revolution,'" *The Conversation*, November 14, 2017, https://theconversation.com/why-south-africans-should-be-worried-by-anc-talk-of-a-colour-revolution-87019

[37] Munusamy, Ranjeni, "Chasing butterflies and bogeymen: Mantashe beats 'regime change' drum," *Daily Maverick*, May 13, 2016, https://www.dailymaverick.co.za/article/2016-05-13-chasing-butterflies-and-bogeymen-mantashe-beats-regime-change-drum

South Africa: The Deal Too Big to Succeed | 91

accused of arresting and manhandling reporters. Zuma said South Africa's news media should be "patriotic," downplaying bad news to better promote the country.[38] The ANC discussed creating a Media Appeals Tribunal, a government body that would be authorized to judge news coverage and punish journalists for unfair reporting. The idea faded after international protests and a plan by the ANC to open its own newspaper fizzled out. Ultimately, Zuma tried other tactics to change the nation's news agenda. An ally of Zuma and the Guptas was appointed president of the state-owned South African Broadcasting Corporation. Journalists there soon reported he was manipulating news coverage in Zuma's interests. The Gupta family also set up its own newspaper and TV station, which ran pro-Zuma content. Later, Zuma said he had suggested the idea to the Guptas because South Africa needed "alternative" media.[39]

Still, the government was never able to stifle independent media in a country where freewheeling newspapers and magazines had become thoroughly embedded in the culture. Zuma and his enablers were never able to stop the flow of revelations about corruption, block civil society groups from operating, or control the country's legal system. Democracy advocates had learned much about survival. They adroitly used legal procedures and constitutional guarantees to pursue their work. There was no legal framework in place to shut down the media or politically active NGOs, Groeblinghoff said. "South Africa isn't North Korea. They couldn't just go out and destroy them."

That said, had Zuma's officials been more organized and assertive, they could have created more difficulties for troublesome media and NGOs. They could have picked up some tips from their

---

[38] Van Onselen, Gareth, "A brief history of Jacob Zuma's hatred for the media," *Rand Daily Mail*, February 26, 2016, https://www.businesslive.co.za/amp/rdm/politics/2016-02-26-a-brief-history-of-jacob-zumas-hatred-for-the-media
[39] Dlamini, Penwell, "Zuma says Gupta newspaper and TV station was his idea," *Sowetan Live*, July 15, 2019, https://www.sowetanlive.co.za/news/south-africa/2019-07-15-zuma-says-gupta-newspaper-and-tv-station-was-his-idea

92 | HOW RUSSIA LOSES

Russian colleagues. In 2012, Russia passed the first of a series of "foreign agent" laws directed against protest-minded NGOs— many of which, like those in South Africa, received foreign funding. The Russian laws allowed authorities to impose burdensome reporting requirements on the organizations and created a pretext for raids on their offices to check on compliance. Some Russian activists and reporters were followed, beaten, or killed. Zuma's regime may not have felt it could get away with killings, but there were ample opportunities for other forms of harassment if they had been more vigorous and committed.

The thoroughly documented exposés of Zuma's conduct would have brought down the leader of almost any democratic country. Yet with a solid ANC majority in parliament, and government prosecutors unlikely to charge a sitting president, Zuma survived for years. Ever since its struggle in exile, the ANC had placed a premium on party unity, which made it difficult for members to publicly oppose the president they elected, whatever his transgressions. When the public protector found in 2014 that Zuma had benefited personally from $22 million in improvements the government made to his home, Zuma settled the matter with a payment of $538,000.

Forcing Zuma from power would take a clear public perception that the president's malfeasance was imperiling the country's whole future. It would also require a concerted effort by media, civil society, and a significant part of the ANC. That point was reached at the end of 2017. Ironically, much of the responsibility for this turn of events stemmed from miscalculations and overreach by Putin, his close ally.

The Nuclear Deal

Russian investments in South Africa grew substantially under Putin. The Russian president saw opportunities to enrich Russian companies, guarantee strategic minerals that Russia needed, and gain political advantage, all at the same time. Vekselberg's Renova Group acquired a near-majority stake in a large manganese mining venture, and Norilsk Nickel bought a 20-percent stake in

South Africa: The Deal Too Big to Succeed | 93

the major South Africa mining company Gold Fields.[40] Numerous personal interactions occurred between top Russian business figures and South African officials. Norilsk General Director Vladimir Strzhalkovsky met with Zuma in 2011 and presented a mobile medical laboratory for the people of Nkandla, the town where Zuma's home was located.[41]

Given the nature of both the Putin and Zuma regimes, it was not surprising that some of these deals sparked questions about influence and transparency. The other partner in Vekselberg's manganese deal was a company owned by the ANC. When the government granted broad prospecting rights to the venture, a corruption watchdog group said that "diplomatic expediency and the party's funding needs may well, in our view, have trumped the public interest."[42] An investigative journalist reported that the mobile laboratory Strzhalkovsky brought to Nkandla was accompanied by a substantial shipment of cash.[43] Questions were also raised about a 2017 mining deal between the Russian gas company Rosgeo and the South African state oil company PetroSA. Two PetroSA directors told a court that the company

---

[40] Pham, J. Peter, "Back to Africa: Russia's New African Engagement," in Mangala, Jack, ed., *Africa and the New World Era: From Humanitarianism to a Strategic View* (New York: Palgrave Macmillan, 2010).

[41] Campbell, Keith, "Russian mining group head in discussions with South African President," *Mining Weekly*, April 8, 2011, https://www.miningweekly.com/print-version/russian-mining-group-head-in-discussions-with-south-african-president-2011-04-08

[42] Robinson, Vicki, et al., "SA Democracy Incorporated: Corporate fronts and political party funding," Institute for Security Studies, November 2006, https://www.africaportal.org/documents/3601/PAPER129_2.pdf

[43] According to investigative journalist Jacques Pauw, the laboratory and cash were initially impounded by South African revenue agents. Soon, however, a close friend of Zuma called the airport to ask that the cargo be released. The minister of state security took possession of it, saying it was a security matter. The ultimate recipient of the cash, Pauw said, was never determined. Pauw, Jacques, *The President's Keepers* (Cape Town: Tafelberg, 2017). Norilsk denied it brought any cash with the medical equipment.

was pressured to do the deal despite a lack of management compliance and competitive bidding.[44]

All these projects paled in size, however, to a massive nuclear venture that Zuma and Putin worked to pull off during the entire course of their relationship. Starting with his first visit to South Africa in 2006, Putin made clear that nuclear contracts were a top priority. Nuclear power is one of Russia's most valuable industrial sectors; foreign contracts help fund Moscow's own sprawling activities in nuclear research, power generation, and warheads. Atomic power is also Russia's answer to the declining popularity of fossil fuels, a major Russian export. For developing countries, nuclear power can be a matter of prestige. "Nuclear plants are a symbol that you've made it into the big leagues now," said Hartmut Winkler, a physicist at the University of Johannesburg who writes on the intersection of energy and politics. "Never mind that most developed nations have now moved beyond nuclear."[45]

At the 2006 summit, the two countries signed a contract to supply Russian fuel to South Africa's only nuclear power station, at Koeberg near Cape Town. (The plant was a legacy of the apartheid state's nuclear weapons program, which produced six nuclear devices that were dismantled under de Klerk.) "We propose expanding this joint effort and to make our cooperation in developing atomic energy for peaceful purposes long-term and large-scale," announced Putin during a news conference.[46]

There was no doubt South Africa needed more electricity. State-owned Eskom began struggling in the mid-2000s as demand grew, coal-fired generating plants approached the end of their useful lives, and coal supplies became unreliable. Two new coal

---

[44] Helmer, John, "Dodgy Russia gas deal is riddled with intrigue," *BusinessDay*, October 11, 2017, https://www.businesslive.co.za/bd/opinion/2017-10-11-dodgy-russia-gas-deal-is-riddled-with-intrigue

[45] Hartmut Winkler, interview with author, April 22, 2022.

[46] Text at http://www.kremlin.ru/events/president/transcripts/copy/23778

plants were constructed but quickly encountered operational problems. Blackouts began hitting some areas in 2007. Millions of poor people were still awaiting electric service, and the cost of electricity to consumers rose rapidly.

About 75 percent of South Africa's energy came from coal, 5 percent from nuclear, and a smaller slice from hydroelectric sources. The cheapest large new sources of power would have been the new coal plants if they could be gotten into operation, natural gas, or renewable sources such as wind or solar (which at the time were viewed as expensive and experimental). Nuclear power was reliable and much cleaner than coal, but it was the most expensive option for electricity consumers. It would also lock South Africa into energy dependence on foreign partners.

The ANC had taken a strong anti-nuclear stance during the struggle against apartheid, associating nuclear energy with the apartheid regime's nuclear weapons. The 1986 Chornobyl disaster and the 2011 accident at Fukushima hardened anti-nuclear feelings. Still, under Mandela and Mbeki, South African politicians began to say nuclear power should at least be considered as an option. The Mbeki government proposed purchasing nuclear reactors from France and the United States. However, the worldwide recession was closing in and officials decided that a deal would be too expensive.

The year 2010 was a turning point for nuclear energy in South Africa. In August, during Zuma's first visit to Moscow, he and then-President Medvedev discussed again the possibility of building Russian nuclear power plants. In October, Zuma's government presented an Integrated Resources Plan on the country's energy future, calling for 9.6 gigawatts (GW) of nuclear power. The 9.6 GW figure was significant. "This is the exact total one would obtain from eight plants with the 1.2 GW specifications of Russian reactors," said Winkler. Plants from other countries, he said, had different standard capacities that would not add up precisely to 9.6 GW.

Although the plan to use nuclear power was still officially preliminary, the smart money seemed to have made the

96 | HOW RUSSIA LOSES

appropriate conclusions: the Gupta family acquired a uranium mine that could provide raw material for the reactors. Among the loans that financed the purchase was $35 million from a state investment corporation. The Guptas' partners in the acquisition were Zuma's son and other businesspeople connected to the ANC.[47]

Finance Minister Pravin Gordhan told the Zondo Commission it was clear to him that Zuma wanted to buy the nuclear plants from Russia. He warned the president that proper contracting procedures must be followed and that bypassing them could be as dangerous to the president politically as the arms deal charges had been.[48]

The cost of renewable energy plummeted, but the government remained focused on nuclear power and Russia. Zuma and Putin reportedly worked personally on the provisions of a deal at meetings in Durban, South Africa, in March 2013 and in Sochi, Russia, in May.[49]

At the end of 2013, the South African Department of Energy presented a detailed draft feasibility study for the project. Nhlanhla Nene, who had replaced Gordhan as finance minister, told the Zondo Commission that "it became apparent to me that regardless of the underlying policy rationale to develop nuclear energy capacity, the costs associated with it are astronomical." Relative to the size of the national economy, he said, the deal would have been one of the largest public investment projects in the world. He added:

---

[47] Sparks, Allister, "At Home and Abroad: A cautionary tale about the Guptas' dud uranium mine," *BusinessLive*, May 11, 2016, https://www.businesslive.co.za/archive/2016-05-11-at-home-and-abroad-a-cautionary-tale-about-the-guptas-dud-uranium-mine

[48] Testimony at https://www.corruptionwatch.org.za/wp-content/uploads/2018/11/Pravin-Gordhan-Zondo-statement.pdf

[49] Kachur, Dzvinka, "How State Capture went Nuclear," in Callaghan, Nina, et al., eds., *Anatomy of State Capture* (Stellenbosch: African Sun Media, 2021), p. 335.

> The total investment required would have had material consequences for Eskom's and the country's foreign and domestic debt, fiscal and financial position, the balance of payment and sovereign balance sheet for decades to come, as well as investment grading, which would have had implications for all South Africans.[50]

The exact cost of the deal was almost impossible to understand because many details were kept secret and the final cost of such an undertaking could be defined in so many different ways. The costs were also vulnerable to overruns (common in the nuclear industry, as Nene noted) and to shifts in the value of the South African rand, a volatile currency whose value has bounced between 9 and 18 rand to the US dollar in the past ten years. (The deal was to be denominated in dollars.)

A government estimate in 2011 set the initial cost of the project at between $43 billion and $58 billion at the then-current exchange rate. An official estimate in 2015 put the cost at $41 billion but did not reveal how much of the project was included in that figure. An academic study estimated the cost at $71 billion, and estimates by civil society and businesses put the total figure as high as $125 billion.[51] To give a sense of the scale of these costs, South Africa's entire government budget was $125 billion in 2015, its GNP $335 billion and its national debt $156 billion.

Importantly, details also were not released about how payment to Russia for the plants would be structured. In some cases, Russia has sold nuclear plants with little initial payment required. Interest on the loan accrues at 3 percent a year, but payments do not start for 10 to 13 years. By then, the interest due will have

---

[50] Testimony at https://www.statecapture.org.za/site/files/documents/16/Nene_1.pdf

[51] Figures converted from South African rand amounts cited in Martin, Brenda, et al., "Final Report: Findings of Africa Nuclear Study," Heinrich Böll Stiftung, 2015, https://www.academia.edu/14922005/Martin_B_and_D_Fig_2015_Final_Report_Findings_of_Africa_Nuclear_Study_Cape_Town_Heinrich_Boell_Stiftung?auto=download

raised the cost of the project by up to 40 percent—and the officials who made the agreement are almost certain to have left office.[52] South African treasury analysts estimated that deal could, depending on its details, raise the country's debt-to-GDP ratio to between 75 and 95 percent by 2030.[53] (It is currently around 71 percent.)

Some officials expressed concern that the cost of the project could further raise electricity prices. But Zuma remained intent on the idea. In 2011 he moved government discussions on the deal to special cabinet committees, which he began in 2013 to chair personally. This structure kept discussions of the matter away from the public and parliament.

If the deal were to go through without full public scrutiny, the potential for corrupt dealings would be unlimited. The project would involve the expenditure of enormous sums by state companies, allocated through processes that had already proven highly remunerative to the Guptas and other Zuma associates. The deal could also benefit Putin's close associates. If the level of corruption under Zuma had been substantial, the nuclear deal could make it stratospheric.

Zuma asserted that the deal, despite the sum involved, was the only way to solve South Africa's power problems. "All what people could say was, 'the thing is expensive, will we afford it?' That's the only query we could have had. But the fact of the matter is nuclear could solve our problems, once and for all," Zuma told a journalist after leaving power. As for the Russians pressuring South Africa if it could not pay the debt, he added:

> They would not come for us. They would understand, we would have an agreement to work out another arrangement. Others will come

---

[52] Winkler, Hartmut, "Why nuclear power for African countries doesn't make sense," *The Conversation*, May 15, 2018, https://theconversation. com/why-nuclear-power-for-african-countries-doesnt-make-sense-96031

[53] *Nuclear: Inside South Africa's Nuclear Deal*, op. cit.

South Africa: The Deal Too Big to Succeed | 99

for us, will force us to go to some financial thing so that they suck our funds forever. We know [the Russians] are trusted people. We know they will never sink us, they will lift us.

Zuma also said the deal was a way of "rewarding" Russia for its support of the ANC during the anti-apartheid struggle.[54] That a country with millions of impoverished residents should financially reward a resource-rich superpower is not intuitive, but the comment reflected the depth of Zuma's commitment to Russia.

The expense of the nuclear deal and the secrecy around it led to constant protests and inquiries by the Democratic Alliance, civil society, and the media. As early as 2011, investigative reporters from the *Mail & Guardian*, the *amaBhungane* investigative journalism center, *City Press*, *Business Day*, and the *Daily Maverick* raised concerns. Their reporting included information from whistleblowers inside the government.[55] Weekly public protests brought together anti-nuclear activists and organizations close to the ANC, including the mineworkers' union and the Congress of South African Trade Unions.

On August 28, 2014, Zuma met with Putin during a six-day visit to Moscow, accompanied only by Mahlobo and a deputy foreign minister.[56] Less than a month later, South Africa's energy minister and the head of Rosatom signed an agreement in Vienna that, according to a press statement, "lays the foundation for the large-scale nuclear power plant (NPP) procurement and development programme of South Africa." The statement quoted Rosatom's director as saying the deal would also allow Russia and South

---

[54] *Nuclear: Inside South Africa's Nuclear Deal*, ibid.

[55] "How State Capture went Nuclear," op. cit., p. 347.

[56] The main reason for Zuma's trip was reportedly to receive medical treatment for a poisoning he suffered in South Africa. See *Sunday Times*, "Zuma 'poison plot,' " February 22, 2015, https://www.pressreader.com/south-africa/sunday-times-1107/20150222/281479274859744

Africa to operate joint projects in Africa and elsewhere.[57] The document the officials signed was kept secret.

The event led to immediate protests from the deal's opponents, who organized demonstrations at Eskom headquarters and parliament. South African officials rushed to insist that the document was nothing more than a "potential framework of cooperation" and that similar agreements existed or would be signed with the United States, France, China, and South Korea.[58] Yet given Zuma's support for the deal, the secrecy of the document, and the celebratory tone of the Vienna press release, many in South Africa believed Russia was on the verge of walking away with the project. A top South African nuclear power official did not help matters by telling a news briefing that the official tender for the project, which was still to be issued, "might not be an open tender," but a non-public or government-to-government agreement.[59]

New revelations about the project soon followed. In February 2015, the environmental group Earthlife Africa obtained a copy of the unreleased Vienna agreement. The Russian ecology group Ecodefense had received it from a source in the Russian Foreign Ministry and relayed it to Makoma Lekalakala, the Johannesburg director of Earthlife. The document was published by the *Mail & Guardian*, which said the "shocking details of the deal" held "many dangers for South Africa." Prominent among them was the language regarding any possible nuclear "incident." In such an event, all responsibility would fall on South Africa. Russia would be fully indemnified for any consequences, inside or outside South Africa.

---

[57] Press statement at https://rosatom-centralasia.com/en/press-centre/highlights/russia-and-south-africa-signed-the-agreement-on-strategic-partnership-in-nuclear-energy-11
[58] Paton, Carol, "SA resolute on nuclear build," *BusinessLive*, October 2, 2014, https://www.businesslive.co.za/archive/2014-10-02-sa-resolute-on-nuclear-build
[59] Ibid.

South Africa: The Deal Too Big to Succeed | 101

The agreement would be binding on South Africa for 20 years. Russia would benefit from "special favorable treatment" in tax and other financial matters. The document lacked any reference to legal procedures in the event of a disagreement about its implementation. It said simply that disputes would be resolved "by consultations or negotiations through diplomatic channels." This suggested that any issues that might arise, even commercial ones, would be resolved at a political level.[60]

The Russian Ecodefense group opposed the project not only on environmental grounds. It also feared it would create a huge liability for Russia if South Africa did not pay—as well as make South Africa geopolitically dependent on Moscow. "This is what Russia does," said Ecodefense co-founder Vladimir Slivyak. "They make you dependent on an energy source that they supply and then they control you. If you make a wrong decision, then they find a way to teach you a lesson about it." (His comments were prophetic for how Russia worked to make Europe dependent on its natural gas in advance of its 2022 invasion of Ukraine.)

Zuma continued to press his officials for a fast deal with Russia. Zuma's last trip to Russia as president was for the July 2015 BRICS summit in Ufa. Finance Minister Nene told the Zondo Commission of a meeting he had there with Zuma, who attacked him for not moving quickly enough on the project. Nene refused to sign a letter, which Zuma wanted to hand to Putin, guaranteeing that South Africa would agree to the deal if Russia would provide financing. Nene told the commission that "my signature would have resulted in a binding financial commitment by the South African government." Nene became even more concerned about the deal when the Russian deputy finance minister told him at the summit that he had not been involved in the negotiations.[61] On

---

[60] See Faull, Lionel, "Exposed: Scary details of SA's secret Russian nuke deal," *Mail & Guardian*, February 12, 2015, https://mg.co.za/article/2015-02-12-exposed-scary-details-of-secret-russian-nuke-deal. An apparent Russian version of the agreement is at https://docs.cntd.ru/document/420234777

[61] Statement of Nhlanhla Nene to the Zondo Commission.

102 | HOW RUSSIA LOSES

December 9, Zuma's cabinet gave its approval to acquiring 9.6 GW in nuclear power. He fired Nene the same day.

Opponents of the project were already in court. Lekalakala and Liz McDaid, another long-time anti-apartheid and environmental activist, had taken the agreement with Russia to South Africa's High Court in October. Although the government claimed the document was not a contract, but simply a statement of intent, the activists asked the court to stop the "rush by government in decision-making on the deal" and force the authorities to observe normal contracting processes.

Rosatom tried to back the government up. "No deal was struck," Viktor Polikarpov, the head of the company's Sub-Saharan operations, told a news conference in 2016. "It has been much exaggerated by the press, who says it is a done deal. It's not a done deal." As for the ebullient Rosatom press statement in 2014, he said, "Frankly, that was a mistake."[62]

On April 26, 2017, the High Court ruled. It found that the agreement with Russia amounted to "a firm legal agreement" that set the parties "well on their way to a binding, exclusive agreement in relation to the procurement of new reactor plants" without the observance of required vetting procedures.[63] The agreement was invalidated.

Still, Zuma and Russia worked frantically to keep the project alive. In October 2017, Zuma made Mahlobo, who had extensive Russian connections through his security portfolio, head of the Department of Energy. A report by the *Sunday Times* said the

---

https://www.reuters.com/article/us-safrica-politics-finmin/south-africas-zuma-fired-me-for-blocking-russian-nuclear-power-deal-nene-idUSKCN1MD0TJ

[62] "Russia's Rosatom: SA nuclear contract not a done deal," February 17, 2016, *News24*, https://www.news24.com/Fin24/russias-rosatom-sa-nuclear-contract-not-a-done-deal-20160217

[63] Roelf, Wendell, "South African court declares nuclear plan with Russia unlawful," *Reuters*, April 26, 2017, https://www.reuters.com/article/us-safrica-nuclear-court/south-african-court-declares-nuclear-plan-with-russia-unlawful-idUSKBN17S25R

South Africa: The Deal Too Big to Succeed | 103

elevation of Mahlobo came after a set of sudden events: a trip to Moscow in June by Energy Secretary Nkhensani Kubayi, who told the Russians she needed more time to study the deal; the dispatch of a Russian delegation to Zuma to complain about Kubayi; a trip to Moscow by Mahlobo in August to reassure the Russians that the deal was still on; and a visit by four Russians to Zuma just hours before he replaced Kubayi with Mahlobo.[64] Zuma's office denied there had been any contacts with Russians on the eve of the cabinet shuffle. The Russian Embassy said the *Sunday Times* report was Russophobic sensationalism that could not be true because Russia never interferes in other countries' affairs.[65]

The reported Russian pressure raised the question of whether Moscow believed that Zuma was still a full ally on the deal, or needed to be leaned on more heavily. As South African commentator Max du Preez wrote, Putin "must find Zuma's explanations of court orders and parliamentary processes as reasons for the delays simply annoying, or amusing at best—such democratic niceties don't exist in Moscow."[66]

The turbulence over the nuclear deal, combined with other pressures on Zuma, put him on the political defensive throughout 2016 and 2017. In the 2016 municipal elections, the ANC's vote share tumbled to 54 percent compared to 62 percent in 2011; the party lost control of Tshwane (formerly Pretoria) and Johannesburg. Financial markets were shaken when Zuma fired Nene, who was widely seen as an opponent both of the Russian nuclear project and dubious aircraft acquisitions for South African Airways. Eventually Zuma brought back Gordhan as

---

[64] Afrika, Mzilikazi Wa, et al., "From Russia with love: How Putin had a hand in Cabinet reshuffle," *Sunday Times*, October 22, 2017, https://www.timeslive.co.za/sunday-times/news/2017-10-21-from-russia-with-love-how-putin-had-a-hand-in-cabinet-reshuffle/

[65] Embassy statement at https://web.archive.org/web/20171028130058/https://russianembassyza.mid.ru/-/embassy-s-comment-on-the-article-how-putin-had-a-hand-in-cabinet-reshuffle-sunday-times-

[66] Du Preez, Max, "Did Zuma cross Putin?" *news24*, October 24, 2017, https://www.news24.com/news24/Columnists/MaxduPreez/did-zuma-cross-putin-20171024

104 | HOW RUSSIA LOSES

finance minister but fired him anew in a massive cabinet reshuffle in March 2017.

Again, markets and the rand's value plunged. International rating agencies downgraded South Africa's debt. Deputy President Cyril Ramaphosa criticized the cabinet bloodletting, and senior ANC officials called for Zuma's resignation. Tens of thousands of people marched against Zuma in April. By December, Ramaphosa was able to seize the presidency of the ANC on an anti-corruption platform. (Ramaphosa, an activist in South Africa during the anti-apartheid struggle who later became one of the country's richest businessmen, called himself a "capitalist with a socialist instinct."[67]) Without control of the ANC, Zuma's national presidency and projects were increasingly untenable. In January 2018 Ramaphosa told the Davos economic conference that the nuclear program would be assessed on the basis of South Africa's needs and ability to pay.[68]

On February 8, Sergey Donskoy, Russia's acting minister of natural resources and the environment, flew to South Africa to meet with Mahlobo, but the Zuma administration was finished. Zuma resigned as president on February 14, and parliament elected Ramaphosa to take his place. In April, the Gupta brothers left South Africa.

One month after Zuma resigned, the national prosecutor's office renewed its attempts to prosecute Zuma over the 1999 arms deal. Despite periodic rumors he might flee to Russia,[69] Zuma remained in the country and pleaded not guilty. The trial dragged on into 2023.

---

[67] Harvey, Ebrahim, "Is Ramaphosa still a shoo-in?" *Mail & Guardian*, September 10, 2015, https://mg.co.za/article/2015-09-10-is-ramaphosa-still-a-shoo-in

[68] "South Africa has no money for major nuclear expansion, Ramaphosa says," *Reuters*, January 26, 2018, https://www.reuters.com/article/ozatp-uk-davos-meeting-safrica-nuclear-idAFKBN1FF1JT-OZATP

[69] Hogg, Alec, "Gatvol SAs speak: Let Zuma flee SA, then he'll be Russia's problem," *BizNews*, February 2, 2021, https://www.biznews.com/global-citizen/2021/02/02/gatvol-sas-zuma-flee

South Africa: The Deal Too Big to Succeed | 105

The final chapter in the nuclear deal—at least on the scale Putin and Zuma had envisaged—took place in July 2018. Putin was in Johannesburg for a BRICS summit; humiliatingly for Zuma, he was in court at the time over the arms deal prosecution. Ramaphosa told Putin the deal was off. "The issue of nuclear expansion was discussed, as it relates to our broader energy mix," Ramaphosa's spokesperson said. "The president reiterated that South Africa can only afford it at an appropriate time, and at a pace and scale it could afford."[70]

Three months earlier, Ramaphosa's energy minister, Jeff Radebe, signed 27 deals for renewable energy that had been blocked under Zuma. Nuclear power advocates, including some close to Zuma, continued to press for a nuclear program, describing renewable energy as serving private Western interests. Ultimately the government issued a new Integrated Resources Plan in 2019. Its modest reference to nuclear power called for "preparations for a nuclear build programme to the extent of 2.5 GW at a pace and scale that the country can afford."[71]

The failure of the nuclear deal and the fall of Zuma were major setbacks for Russia. Russian influence in South Africa appeared to plunge. In an analysis for Russia's Institute of African Studies just a week after Zuma resigned, Shubin wrote that "today the majority of the South African population has no real idea about our country and accepts as true many charges against Moscow, and South African media forge an extremely distorted image of Russia." He added:

> A situation has been created in which the friendly relations established between Russia's leadership and Zuma turned into a brake on bilateral cooperation since the overall negative feelings about Zuma carried over onto our country and its president. ... Unfortunately, the

---

[70] Friedman, Daniel, "Zuma faces charges while his friend Putin visits SA," *The Citizen*, July 27, 2018, https://www.citizen.co.za/news/south-africa/1987715/zuma-faces-charges-while-his-friend-putin-visits-sa
[71] "How State Capture went Nuclear," op. cit.

106 | HOW RUSSIA LOSES

aftermath of the malignant and dirty anti-Russian campaign that focused on the [nuclear] "deal" and even "the collusion between Zuma and Putin" ... is still being felt after Zuma's resignation. There is a basis to believe that this anti-Russian campaign is being fed by the US and EU, trying to block the deepening of mutual activity between Russia and South Africa."[72]

The Cost of Overreach

Zuma's regime had been the ideal partner for Putin in advancing Russian influence on the African continent. Russia's role in the fight against apartheid was widely recognized and appreciated by South Africa's most influential people. The ANC's worldview fit well with the Kremlin's anti-Western stance. More concretely, Russia stood to gain from South Africa's extensive financial interests and connections throughout the continent, as well as its occasional role in mediating conflicts in strategic countries. South Africa, in turn, benefited from membership in the BRICS alliance and from Russia's deep experience in mining, energy, and other sectors essential to its economy.

Zuma himself had much in common with Putin. Both were former intelligence agents who had leveraged their skill and connections to reach the pinnacle of power. Both had little regard for public accountability. The nuclear deal would be their crowning achievement—binding the two countries together for decades, modeling for the whole world how Russia could solve the energy problems of developing nations, and vastly enriching well-connected figures at every stage of the process.

Russia, however, made a series of miscalculations:

---

[72] Shubin, V.G., "О смене высшего руководства в ЮАР [The leadership change in the Republic of South Africa]," Africa Institute of the Russian Academy of Sciences, February 21, 2018, https://www.inafran.ru/node/1563

South Africa: The Deal Too Big to Succeed | 107

- **The nuclear deal was a huge overreach by Russia.** Its size raised fundamental questions about South Africa's ability to pay the bill and whether Zuma was sacrificing his country's economic future for the benefit of a few. If the plan had gone through, future governments might have ultimately decided they needed to try to cancel it. Assuming Russia stood firm, the deal could have become a cautionary tale, in Africa and elsewhere, about making massive economic commitments to Russia.

- **Putin (and Zuma) underestimated the resistance the deal would provoke in South Africa.** If Zuma, or Putin's advisors, told Putin that the deal would slide through, the Russian leader was badly served. Despite all of Zuma's attempts to undermine institutions of accountability, enough checks and balances remained in the nation's government, media, civil society, and courts to make the deal impossible. In the words of a study by the Carnegie Endowment for International Peace:

> The Kremlin overplayed its hand. Its pursuit of a massive, nontransparent nuclear deal mobilized South African civil society and Zuma's political opponents. Instead of anchoring Moscow's relationship with Pretoria, the nuclear deal demonstrated Russia's limited reach and lack of appeal as a partner to a country resilient in terms of democratic governance, strong civil society organizations, press freedoms, and political competition. Another unintended consequence was the impression that the failed nuclear deal was all there was to the South Africa-Russia relationship.[73]

- **Popular affection for Russia was not enough to save the deal.** Moscow might have expected that a reservoir of public

---

[73] Weiss, Andrew, et al., "Nuclear Enrichment: Russia's Ill-Fated Influence Campaign in South Africa," Carnegie Endowment for International Peace, December 16, 2019, https://carnegieendowment. org/2019/12/16/nuclear-enrichment-russia-s-ill-fated-influence-campaign-in-south-africa-pub-80597

gratitude for the Soviet Union's solidarity against apartheid would ultimately have rescued the nuclear project.

However, historic affections must be constantly tended to remain potent. South Africans who worked closely with Russians had been retiring from posts of importance. Zuma was 75 when he resigned. About two-thirds of South Africa's current population was younger than 10 at the time apartheid ended.[74] They had no personal experience of the struggle or the Soviet part in it. All South Africans are taught in school about the Soviet Union's vital role but were not likely to sacrifice their future as a "reward" to another country. South Africa's free press had also reported on the increasingly autocratic nature of Putin's regime.

Rosatom attempted to build a positive profile for itself through women's health and wildlife initiatives and by trying to ease fears around nuclear power. Polikarpov of Rosatom told reporters:

> We have a good PR team in South Africa. We are working hard to change the perception and eradicate the myths, which are circulating around nuclear and around Rosatom. The South African public is frankly very emotional. We cannot deal with nuclear on emotions only. We all have to be very knowledgeable and very pragmatic.[75]

Most of Russia's efforts, however, were devoted to nourishing tight relations with a narrow group of powerful people who were influenced mainly by money.

"This has always been the Russian complaint: 'We have very good political relations, but no people-to-people relations.' It was mostly just about big business and politics," Filatova said.[76] Indeed, across Africa few Russia-connected foundations or civil society organizations are in operation. Africans who receive Russian aid through multilateral organizations are often unaware

---

[74] Derived from https://www.statista.com/statistics/1116077/total-population-of-south-africa-by-age-group/
[75] "Russia's Rosatom: SA nuclear contract not a done deal," op. cit.
[76] Irina Filatova, interview with author, April 30, 2022.

of its origin. Only 4 percent of African students studying abroad go to Russia.[77] In a comment particularly relevant to South Africa, one Russian specialist noted that, although Russia has a positive "historical heritage" in Africa, "it is necessary to go further and propose new initiatives and formats for dialogue."[78]

Russia might have strengthened its image through actions that showed it was committed to the South African people, rather than just to deals with its elite, said Joseph Siegle of the Africa Center for Strategic Studies in Washington. "They could have done real capital investment instead of everything being about patronage and projects that would have to be paid for by the South African public," he said. "They could have built infrastructure that would be a vote of confidence in the stability of the country, acted with respect for the rule of law, so they'd have a long-term partnership."[79]

Many ordinary South Africans, it turned out, felt negatively or ambivalently toward Russia. In a poll during Zuma's last year in office, 44 percent of South Africans had an unfavorable view of Russia, 34 percent felt positively, and 22 percent expressed no opinion. By contrast, 50 percent had a positive view of the United States and 46 percent a favorable view of China.[80]

---

[77] "Африка: перспективы развития и рекомендации для политики России [Africa: prospects for development and recommendations for Russian policy]," Higher School of Economics, 2021, https://global affairs.ru/wp-content/uploads/2021/11/doklad_afrika_perspektivy-razvitiya.pdf

[78] Kulkova, Olga, "Мягкая сила России в Африке: новые перспективы и вызовы [Russian soft power in Africa: new prospects and challenges]," Russian Council on International Affairs, October 9, 2019, https://russiancouncil.ru/analytics-and-comments/analytics/myagkaya-sila-rossii-v-afrike-novye-perspektivy-i-vyzovy/

[79] Joseph Siegle, interview with author, September 27, 2022.

[80] Figures from https://www.pewresearch.org/global/2018/12/06/image-of-putin-russia-suffers-internationally and derived from https://www.pewresearch.org/global/database/indicator/27/country/ZA

110 | HOW RUSSIA LOSES

Despite the deterioration of political relations, the West retained its own strong influence in South Africa under Zuma. As in many other nations, Western economic power was a factor no South African government could ignore. For all the business deals Russian companies and oligarchs made and promised, Russia's economic profile was minimal under Zuma. In his last year in power, South Africa's top trading partners were China, Germany, the United States, India, and the United Kingdom. Russia ranked 38th, accounting for about half of 1 percent of South African imports and exports.[81]

Cultural ties between South Africa and the West were also powerful. South Africans are far more familiar with Western societies than with Russia's or China's. They are well aware of racism in Western countries but still attracted by their wealth and opportunity. "The average South African looked and looks to the West culturally and economically," said Patrick Gaspard, US ambassador to South Africa from 2013 to 2016.

Aware of Western economic and cultural strengths, US officials avoided giving in to pique over anti-American statements by Zuma and his lieutenants.

"Because of their ideology, we really felt no surprise over these statements," Gaspard said of that period. He also said the US took in stride the possibility that Russia was giving Zuma funds to assure the loyalty of ANC members. "We felt this will pass, that it wasn't influencing the overall direction of culture, or the economy." Gaspard said that whenever South African journalists asked him about some anti-Western remark by Zuma, he tried to move the conversation back to the positive elements of US–South African relations.[82]

---

[81] Trade with the US totaled about $18 billion a year at the end of the Zuma administration in 2018, with Russia about $1 billion. Figures derived from https://comtrade.un.org/data. In 2018, US investments in South Africa were worth $9 billion, while South Africa had $3 billion worth of investments in the US. See https://apps.bea.gov/international/factsheet/factsheet.html#436

[82] Patrick Gaspard, interview with author, September 30, 2022.

South Africa: The Deal Too Big to Succeed | 111

The US also did not let political differences with Zuma stop its aid to South Africa, which averaged around $460 million a year.[83] Most was devoted to health projects. The United States won broad appreciation in South Africa for assistance with its programs to combat HIV/AIDS.

"By and large, the US and UK don't want to provoke instability or fight with South Africa," said John Matisonn, a South African journalist and author. "Their attitude toward Zuma was one of concerned tolerance."[84]

Thus, the Zuma era ended with Russian influence at a low point and Western economic and cultural interests strong. Western nations bided their time under Zuma, promoting whatever was positive in their relationships with South Africa, continuing the flow of aid and avoiding quarrels with the government that could alienate the public. After years of being on the political defensive in South Africa, the US and its allies could hope for a more balanced policy under Ramaphosa.

Epilogue: South Africa After Zuma

Ramaphosa's administration began with a public commitment to a "new dawn" in domestic affairs and to regaining the moral authority abroad that South Africa had enjoyed under Mandela. Ramaphosa seemed at first to be trying to keep South African relations with Russia and the West carefully balanced. At the UN, South Africa voted against a US resolution of support for opposition leader Juan Guaidó in Venezuela and opposed US calls for targeted sanctions against Zimbabwean leaders. At the same time, it supported the US by voting against China and Russia on resolutions regarding Syria and Somalia.

Ramaphosa met Putin on the sidelines of the first Russia-Africa Summit in October 2019, held in Sochi. Ramaphosa said that Putin raised the nuclear deal again and that he responded that South

---

[83] See https://foreignassistance.gov/cd/south%20africa
[84] John Matisonn, interview with author, April 21, 2022.

112 | HOW RUSSIA LOSES

Africa could not afford it. In their public speeches, Putin reeled off a list of areas where he said the two countries were cooperating, including natural resources and energy. Ramaphosa responded with generalities, not mentioning any specific areas.[85] Russia reportedly signed deals with other countries at the summit worth $12.5 billion; however, nothing was signed with South Africa. Ramaphosa suggested no large new deals were in sight.

Ramaphosa and his lieutenants, however, had limited time for foreign affairs. They were bedeviled by constant crises at home, including a massive economic downturn, frequent power cuts, water system failures, the COVID-19 pandemic, and deadly riots against foreign workers. Ramaphosa's position within the ANC was also tenuous. When Zuma was imprisoned in July 2021 for refusing to testify to the Zondo Commission, rioting swept two provinces, leaving 354 people dead and costing the economy $3 billion, according to official figures.[86] Many attributed the riots to other factors as well, including poverty, corruption, and COVID restrictions, but it was clear that Zuma and his supporters—many with pro-Russian sympathies—remained a force to reckon with. In addition, joint projects by the ANC's investment arm and Russian business interests were feeding money to the cash-strapped organization.[87]

As Western relations with Russia plunged over Ukraine, Syria, Russian cyberattacks, and Putin's crackdown on Russian dissenters, public statements by Ramaphosa's administration defaulted increasingly to Moscow's side. Officials regularly engaged in sniping at Western countries, either directly or through general rhetoric about "colonialism" and "imperialism." Few knew what Ramaphosa personally thought about the issues,

---

[85] Texts at http://www.kremlin.ru/events/president/news/61881

[86] Official inquiry at https://www.thepresidency.gov.za/download/file/fid/2442

[87] See, for example, Van Rensburg, Dewald, "ANC's manganese 'gold' mine joint venture with sanctioned Russian oligarch," *amaBhungane*, May 9, 2022, https://www.dailymaverick.co.za/article/2022-05-09-ancs-manganese-gold-mine-joint-venture-with-sanctioned-russian-oligarch

South Africa: The Deal Too Big to Succeed | 113

but it seemed clear that taking pro-Western positions would entail political risk for the president.

Russia reportedly prepared to intervene in the 2019 parliamentary elections in the ANC's favor. According to the Dossier Center, a project of exiled Russian oligarch Mikhail Khodorkovsky, Russian operatives developed a plan to buttress the ANC against the liberal Democratic Alliance and the extreme-left Economic Freedom Fighters. The Dossier Center said it obtained the text of the plan, drawn up by associates of Yevgeny Prigozhin, who had long been active in disinformation, as well as business and mercenary operations in Africa.[88] (The ANC lost seats in the election but held on to its parliamentary majority.) Ramaphosa declined an invitation to Biden's Summit for Democracy at the end of 2021. Foreign Minister Naledi Pandor said she was taken aback by the invitation letter: "The letter says things like, 'America, a country that has always supported human rights.' Really?"[89]

Russia's invasion of Ukraine in February 2022 came as Ramaphosa was facing claims that he was involved in corruption and fears that the continuing economic crisis would cost the ANC its parliamentary majority in 2024, forcing it into a coalition. The second-biggest party in parliament was the pro-Western Democratic Alliance, but many observers felt the most natural coalition partner ideologically would be the Economic Freedom Fighters. In either case, Ramaphosa would benefit from further burnishing his anti-West credentials—to forestall claims he had sold out ideologically in a coalition with the DA, or to prevent

---

[88] Popkov, Roman, "Южная Африка: как политтехнологи Пригожина помогают на выборах правящей партии [South Africa: how Prigozhin's political technicians are helping the ruling party in the elections]," *MBK Media*, May 7, 2019. Documents at https://mbk-news.appspot.com/files/2019/05/Краткая-справка.pdf and https://mbk-news.appspot.com/files/2019/05/Обобщённые_рекомендации.pdf

[89] Fabricius, Peter, "Ramaphosa gives US president's democracy summit the cold shoulder," *Daily Maverick*, December 10, 2021, https://www.dailymaverick.co.za/article/2021-12-10-ramaphosa-gives-us-presidents-democracy-summit-the-cold-shoulder

114 | HOW RUSSIA LOSES

being outflanked as an "anti-imperialist" by coalition partners from the EFF.

Immediately after Russia invaded Ukraine, South Africa initially condemned Moscow's actions.[90] But soon it joined many other African nations in abstaining on a series of UN resolutions condemning Russia. Ramaphosa seemed to dismiss the invasion as simply part of the "historical tensions" between Russia and Ukraine and argued that "a sustainable and lasting peace" could come only through negotiations.[91] While opposing violence, South Africa did not call for a Russian withdrawal. Ramaphosa also suggested the war could have been avoided if NATO had not expanded to the east.[92]

It was not clear that South Africans as a whole supported Ramaphosa's view. Major news outlets in South Africa were favorable to Ukraine. A November 2022 survey found that 75 percent of South Africans believed Russia's invasion was "an act of aggression that must be condemned."[93] Another poll, conducted largely among urban and educated citizens, found 57 percent favored taking in Ukrainian refugees. Two-thirds said that doing nothing in Ukraine would encourage Russia to take further military action elsewhere and that sanctions against Russia were an effective tactic.[94] However, the Ukraine war was far away for most South Africans, who were consumed with much more local issues. "Polling of ordinary people doesn't reflect the

---

[90] Statement at https://www.facebook.com/DIRCOza/posts/the-republic-of-south-africa-is-dismayed-at-the-escalation-of-the-conflict-in-uk/317854733700968

[91] Statement at https://www.thepresidency.gov.za/newsletters/desk-president%2C-7-march-2022

[92] Cocks, Tim, "South Africa's Ramaphosa blames NATO for Russia's war in Ukraine," *Reuters*, March 18, 2022, https://www.reuters.com/world/africa/safricas-ramaphosa-blames-nato-russias-war-ukraine-2022-03-17

[93] Brenthurst Foundation survey at https://www.thebrenthurstfoundation.org/news/brenthurst-survey-shows-vast-majority-of-south-africans-condemn-russia

[94] Ipsos survey at https://www.ipsos.com/en-us/news-polls/war-in-ukraine-april-2022

South Africa: The Deal Too Big to Succeed | 115

government's own ideologically driven logic," said Matisonn, whose book *Cyril's Choices* described many of the issues facing Ramaphosa. "Foreign policy in South Africa is not driven by overall public sentiment. It is driven very much by ideology and alliances of the ruling party."

Russian trade with South Africa remained miniscule. It totaled less than $1 billion in 2022, compared to $34 billion with China, $19 billion with the United States, and $17 billion with Germany.[95] The countries with the largest investments in South Africa were the UK, the Netherlands, Belgium, the United States, and Germany.[96] China and Western countries became South Africa's biggest allies in solving its energy problems.[97]

Ramaphosa declared that South Africa would scour the world for $100 billion in foreign investments, a task that would be greatly eased by maintaining a modicum of good relations with the West. In 2022, more than 600 US companies had investments in South Africa, employing more than 220,000 people.[98]

Cultural ties with the West also remained strong. Asked in a 2022 poll what country they would go to if they left South Africa, half of South Africans cited Western countries, 16 percent other African countries, and 8 percent said Russia or China.[99]

---

[95] Statistics from https://tradingeconomics.com/south-africa/exports-by-country and https://tradingeconomics.com/south-africa/imports-by-country

[96] See https://www.state.gov/reports/2022-investment-climate-statements/south-africa

[97] The US, UK, EU, Germany, and France agreed in 2021 to provide $8.5 billion in financing to help the nation transition to green energy sources. China agreed at the 2023 BRICS summit to provide new aid in operating coal-fired generating plants and with power distribution.

[98] Fabricius, Peter, "South Africa's relations with US 'not under duress' over Ukraine, says American ambassador," *Daily Maverick*, October 21, 2022, https://www.dailymaverick.co.za/article/2022-10-21-sa-us-relations-not-under-duress-over-ukraine-american-ambassador

[99] Brenthurst Foundation survey, op. cit.

116 | HOW RUSSIA LOSES

The US continued its attempts to avoid public clashes with the South African government, possibly believing Ramaphosa had little room for maneuver on foreign policy. "South Africa has always been a tough nut for the West to engage, very independent-minded," Siegle said. "There was recognition of Russia's interest, but the West's economic and cultural and political ties were quite extensive. Moreover, prospects for a robust, mutually beneficial partnership with South Africa are stronger than many other African countries. These are not things you throw away lightly."

Washington was also a major contributor to the South Africa Just Energy Transition Partnership, in which the US, UK, EU, Germany, and France agreed in 2021 to provide $8.5 billion in financing to help the nation transition to green energy sources.

By early 2023, Ramaphosa was continuing to pursue a foreign policy line that served Russian interests. South Africa conducted naval exercises with Russia and China in February 2023, just as the world was marking the first anniversary of the Russian invasion. The ongoing war, however, did not stop Ramaphosa from visiting Biden in Washington, or keep Secretary of State Antony Blinken and Treasury Secretary Janet Yellen from holding talks in South Africa. On each occasion the two sides took pains to avoid public clashes about Ukraine.

It was clear, however, that the war troubled South Africa. Ramaphosa took part in a mission of African leaders to Kyiv and Moscow in June 2023 to try to help negotiate a peace agreement, but nothing came of it. The war frayed US–South African relations when Ambassador Reuben Brigety set off a storm in May 2023 by claiming South Africa had loaded arms onto a freighter bound for Russia.[100] Russia and South Africa also had to agree that Putin

---

[100] Imray, Gerald, "South Africa summons US ambassador over weapons for Russia allegations," *The Associated Press*, May 12, 2023, https://apnews.com/article/united-states-south-africa-russia-weapons-sanctions-f54587d43db7bb5d13d043fa87d2e87a. South African officials said a subsequent inquiry found no arms were loaded onto the ship.

South Africa: The Deal Too Big to Succeed | 117

would not come to Johannesburg for the BRICS summit in August; Ramaphosa's government was unable to overcome political and judicial realities that would have forced it to arrest Putin on war crimes charges filed by the International Criminal Court (ICC).

South Africa's tolerance of the Russian invasion carried risks for its own foreign policy. It was obvious that South Africa had chosen fealty to Russia over Mandela's clear principle of respect for national borders. Many ethnic groups in Africa live on different sides of national borders. African nations might also conclude that, while Mandela and Mbeki put themselves forward as honest brokers in mediating African conflicts, any South African mediation now might have an additional goal of advancing Russian interests.

Meanwhile, the ANC's entire position in South Africa remained unstable because of poverty, inequality, inflation, and power. Russia's visibility faded as South Africa became increasingly dependent on Chinese and Western aid and investment.

Perhaps most important to the nation's future was whether a majority of South Africans believed that continued leftist approaches were the surest way to reduce poverty. Critically important as well would be how much confidence foreign investors had in South Africa's commitment to democracy and rule of law.

3.

The Sputnik Vaccine: From Breakthrough to Footnote

On August 11, 2020, Russian President Vladimir Putin made a stunning announcement to a world ravaged by the coronavirus. Russia, he said, had granted official approval for the world's first vaccine against COVID-19.[1] Putin said the vaccine, known as Sputnik V and created by Moscow's Gamaleya Research Institute of Epidemiology and Microbiology, was close to mass production inside Russia and would soon be made available worldwide.

The vaccine's name was chosen to recall the Sputnik I spacecraft in 1957, which made the Soviet Union the world leader in space. Sputnik's rollout website contained an animation of a beeping satellite, labeled Sputnik V in Russian colors, destroying a COVID-19 virus that had locked itself around the earth.[2] Russia expected the new vaccine to have all the impact of the satellite, both scientifically and geopolitically. With Sputnik V, Russia would once again beat every country, including the United States, this time in the race to

---

[1] As will be described later in this case study, it is highly questionable whether Sputnik can properly be called the world's first COVID-19 vaccine—even though Russia granted it official approval before other countries formally approved the vaccines they had developed.

[2] Russian Direct Investment Fund, "Sputnik Vaccine," https://web.archive.org/web/20200812125506im_/https://sputnikvaccine.com/upload/satelite.mp4?v2

stop a pandemic that had already infected 20 million people worldwide and killed 800,000.[3]

From the start, Russia presented Sputnik as "a vaccine for all mankind," including people in developing countries who cannot afford drugs from Western companies. Sputnik would be produced in multiple countries and would cost less than $10 a shot. Within days of Putin's announcement, Sputnik's marketers proclaimed that countries around the world had already asked for a billion doses. With Sputnik, Russia might become a lifesaver on every continent.

Yet by 2023, the Sputnik vaccine was almost a footnote in the vaccine competition, its use minimal compared to vaccines from Western companies and China. Key international regulators refused to approve the Russian vaccine. As a result, the drug was excluded from international vaccination programs, and people inoculated only with Sputnik were barred from many countries that required vaccination certificates for entry. Some nations officially rejected Sputnik, citing questions about its safety and formulation. Others complained of production flaws and slow deliveries and opted for other vaccines.

The stakes involved in producing the world's first COVID-19 vaccine were enormous. The project had top-level support from Putin, whose daughter was vaccinated with one of the first batches. Sputnik's production and foreign marketing were organized by the Russian Direct Investment Fund (RDIF), a $10 billion state entity. Given the political strength behind the project, the resources of the RDIF, and Russia's ability to focus resources on top state goals, how did Russia fail to capitalize on this enormous medical and geopolitical opportunity?

---

[3] Figures for August 11, 2020, derived from World Health Organization, "WHO Coronavirus (COVID-19) Dashboard," https://covid19.who.int

The Sputnik Vaccine: From Breakthrough to Footnote | 121

'The World's First Vaccine'

Putin announced Sputnik's registration amid a frantic worldwide effort to find a COVID vaccine. Scientists had cooperated well in sharing information about the virus' genetic makeup, but vaccine development became a highly competitive undertaking. US President Donald Trump's "Operation Warp Speed" funneled more than $11 billion to US companies for this purpose. The world's largest pharmaceutical corporations built alliances with universities and each other to jointly develop a drug. Chinese laboratories were equally active, already injecting soldiers with a trial version of the vaccine at the time of Putin's announcement.

Russia had a modest vaccine industry but much history and experience in the field. In the 18th century, Catherine the Great had been an early advocate of vaccines and had herself inoculated against smallpox by a British doctor.[4] Odesa-born Nikolai Gamaleya studied in Paris with Louis Pasteur in 1886, returning to oversee Russian vaccination programs against rabies, anthrax, and smallpox.

Despite Cold War tensions, the Soviet Union worked with American researchers and others to develop polio vaccines in the late 1950s. In the 1960s, the US supplied financing that enabled Moscow to provide a half-billion doses of smallpox vaccines for use worldwide. The Gamaleya Research Institute, run by the Russian Ministry of Health, had also worked on vaccines against Ebola, Middle East Respiratory Syndrome (MERS), and influenza. In 2012, Russia published a strategic document calling for the country to become a global leader in biotechnology, including vaccine development, within the decade.[5]

As COVID-19 ravaged the world in mid-2020, top Western scientists were predicting that a vaccine would not be available for a year to 18 months. More optimistic predictions flooded out

---

[4] She underwent variolation, an early form of vaccination, receiving the contents of a smallpox pustule from an infected person.
[5] Document at http://static.government.ru/media/files/
41d4e85f0b854eb1b02d.pdf

122 | HOW RUSSIA LOSES

of Moscow. On April 7, 2020, the head of a Siberian research center announced that three COVID vaccines had been tested on animals for safety and efficiency and that tests on humans would begin in June.[6] By July, some members of the Russian business elite were reportedly already receiving experimental vaccines.[7]

At the end of July 2020, Russian officials could barely contain themselves about an imminent victory in the vaccine race. Officials told *CNN* on July 30 that a Russian vaccine would likely be approved within two weeks. "It's a Sputnik moment," gloated Kirill Dmitriev, CEO of the RDIF, whose pedigrees included Harvard Business School, Goldman Sachs, and McKinsey & Company. "Americans were surprised when they heard Sputnik's beeping. It is the same with this vaccine. Russia will have got there first."[8]

Putin's announcement, to a meeting of cabinet ministers on August 11, was treated by the Russian media as an event with vast political and scientific significance. The nightly newscast "Vremya" ("Time") called it "the story of the day, and maybe of the year." It showed clips of American networks saying Russia had shocked the world with its breakthrough. Dmitriev appeared on the program to say that five countries would be producing the vaccine along with Russia. Sputnik, he added, was already experiencing "a great number of information attacks, because many big Western companies and many Western politicians do

---

[6] "Russia Ready to Start Testing Coronavirus Vaccines on Humans in June," *Agence France-Presse*, April 7, 2020, https://www.themoscow times.com/2020/04/07/russia-ready-to-start-testing-coronavirus-vaccines-on-humans-in-june-a69906

[7] Kravchenko, Stepan, et al., "Russian Elite Given Experimental COVID-19 Vaccine Since April," *Bloomberg*, July 19, 2020, https://www.bloomberg.com/news/articles/2020-07-20/russian-elite-got-experimental-covid-19-vaccine-from-april?sref=Y2tgfPTW

[8] Chance, Matthew, "Exclusive: Russia says foreign inquiries about its potential fast-track COVID-19 vaccines are pouring in. But questions abound," *CNN*, July 30, 2020, https://www.cnn.com/2020/07/28/europe/russia-coronavirus-vaccine-approval-intl/index.html

The Sputnik Vaccine: From Breakthrough to Footnote | 123

not want Russia to become one of the standards for anti-coronavirus vaccines."[9]

Vremya said the "V" in Sputnik's name stood for "vaccine." However, a website for the vaccine explained the designation in terms of competition with America:

> The vaccine was named in honor of the space achievements of the USSR, of which Russia is the heir, which launched the first satellite, which signified victory over the Americans of that time. The symbol "V" is the generally accepted abbreviation for victory, from the English "victory."[10]

In his televised comments to the ministers, Putin duly sounded a note of caution about the rollout: "The main thing, of course, is that in the nearest future we can assure the unconditional safety and effectiveness of this vaccine. I hope this will be the case." Yet, he added, "I hope that in the very near future we can start mass production—and that is what is important—mass production." His clear implication was that he anticipated that any safety issues would be resolved immediately, and mass production started forthwith.

Russian officials wasted no time. Before Putin's announcement, scientists had completed only phase I and phase II trials of Sputnik, involving 76 people. Normally, vaccines are released only after successful phase III trials with thousands of participants—the only way to assess their effectiveness and side effects in a statistically significant way. After Putin's announcement, Russian scientists launched their phase III trials but did not await the outcomes to start administering Sputnik to

---

[9] Program recording at Channel One Russia, "Выпуск программы 'Время'" [Broadcast of the Program 'Time'], August 11, 2021, https://www.1tv.ru/news/issue/2020-08-11/21:00#1

[10] https://spytnik-v.ru/kak-pravilno-sputnik-v-ili-5. The spytnik-v.ru website was registered in 2021 alongside the main sputnikvaccine.com site; the function of the spytnik-v website is unclear.

124 | HOW RUSSIA LOSES

healthcare workers, teachers, soldiers, and high-risk individuals. No official information was released about side effects; Russians had to turn to social networks to discuss any reactions they experienced.[11]

By December 2, 2020, when Putin announced the start of large-scale vaccinations across the country, 100,000 Russians had already been immunized with Sputnik.[12] (His announcement came just hours after the United Kingdom approved, for immediate use, a shot made by US-based Pfizer and Germany's BioNTech.[13]) Russia also moved quickly to get its vaccine to foreign countries. Just ten days after Putin's announcement, Mexico reported that it would receive 2,000 doses of Sputnik for testing.

The day before Putin's announcement, a coalition of Russian clinical trial companies had warned about the dangers of haste. In an open letter to the Ministry of Health, the Association of Clinical Trials Organizations (ACTO) said six vaccines worldwide were already in large-scale trials and that the Russian vaccine should not be registered until it had gone through the same process. The organization further stressed that there was no substitute for the gold standard of randomized, double-blind, and placebo-controlled testing. The statement added:

> None of these recommendations has yet been observed in the development of [Sputnik]. Unfortunately, one must state that the Russian regulator is ready to introduce into civilian

---

[11] Yasny, Ilya, " 'Спутник' и ложь во спасение. Почему у работоспособной вакцины плохая репутация ['Sputnik' and white lies. Why a workable vaccine has a bad reputation]," *The Insider*, May 28, 2021, https://theins.ru/opinions/ilya-yasnyi/242196?ysclid=kz99f58tm3

[12] "В России от COVID-19 вакцинировали уже более 100 тыс. Человек [More than 100,000 people vaccinated against COVID-19 in Russia]," *Interfax*, December 2, 2020, https://www.interfax.ru/russia/739638

[13] The Pfizer-BioNTech vaccine is formally known as Comirnaty; it will be referred to subsequently in this case study as the Pfizer vaccine.

The Sputnik Vaccine: From Breakthrough to Footnote | 125

circulation a vaccine that meets much lower requirements and, accordingly, is less safe and effective.

The coalition was especially concerned that the drug's developers intended to use it quickly on elderly citizens, though it had not been tested on them, and that steps had not been taken to ensure all batches of the vaccine would be of uniform quality.[14] ACTO Executive Director Svetlana Zavidova told *Bloomberg*: "This is Pandora's box, and we do not know what will happen to people injected with an unproven vaccine."[15]

The World Health Organization (WHO) expressed its own caution the day after Putin's announcement. It said it was looking forward to learning more about the Russian trials but added diplomatically, "Accelerating vaccine research should be done following established processes through every step of development, to ensure that any vaccines that eventually go into production are both safe and effective."[16]

Many foreign scientists expressed deep skepticism about the Russian product. "I hope that the Russians have actually, definitively proven that the vaccine is safe and effective. I seriously doubt that they've done that," said Anthony Fauci, head

---

[14] Association of Clinical Trials Organizations, "Открытое обращение Ассоциации организаций по клиническим исследованиям в связи с анонсированной государственной регистрацией вакцины [Open Letter of the Association of Clinical Research Organizations in Connection With the Announced State Registration of a Vaccine]," August 10, 2020, https://web.archive.org/web/20200813202757/http://acto-russia.org/index.php?option=com_content&task=view&id=411

[15] Arkhipov, Ilya, et al., "Industry Body Calls Russian Covid-19 Vaccine a Pandora's Box," *Bloomberg*, August 10, 2020, https://www.bloomberg.com/news/articles/2020-08-10/russian-covid-19-vaccine-is-pandora-s-box-industry-body-warns?sref=Y2tgfPTW

[16] *Agence France-Presse*, "WHO keen to review Russian vaccine trials," December 8, 2020, *Agence France-Presse*, https://www.france24.com/en/20200812-who-keen-to-review-russian-vaccine-trials

126 | HOW RUSSIA LOSES

of the US National Institute of Allergy and Infectious Diseases.[17] Many news outlets quoted Francois Balloux, a geneticist at University College London, who said:

> This is a reckless and foolish decision. Mass vaccination with an improperly tested vaccine is unethical. Any problem with the Russian vaccination campaign would be disastrous both through its negative effects on health, but also because it would further set back the acceptance of vaccines in the population.[18]

Christa Wirthumer-Hoche, board chair of the European Medicines Agency (EMA), the European Union's drug regulator, said using Sputnik in the EU would be "somewhat comparable to Russian roulette."[19]

Sputnik's developers were unapologetic. Sputnik's Twitter account demanded a public apology from Wirthumer-Hoche, saying her comments "raise serious questions about possible political interference in the ongoing EMA review."[20] Denis Logunov, the head of the team that developed Sputnik, declared, "If we have something that is proven to be safe and that has the chance to save a person, it is unethical not to try and do so."[21] Russian officials and commentators argued that the West was

---

[17] Andreano, Caterina, "Fauci says he has serious doubts Russia's COVID-19 vaccine is safe, effective," *ABC News*, August 11, 2020, https://abcnews.go.com/US/fauci-doubts-russias-covid-19-vaccine-safe-effective/story?id=72309297

[18] "Expert reaction to Russia's approval of a COVID-19 vaccine," Science Media Centre, August 11, 2020, https://www.sciencemediacentre.org/expert-reaction-to-russias-approval-of-a-covid-19-vaccine

[19] Video at https://www.youtube.com/watch?v=Wgroz4CnrPI

[20] Sputnik V, Twitter, March 8, 2021, https://twitter.com/sputnikvaccine/status/1369042868216692745?lang=en

[21] Yaffa, Joshua, "The Sputnik V vaccine and Russia's race to immunity," *The New Yorker*, February 1, 2021, https://www.newyorker.com/magazine/2021/02/08/the-sputnik-v-vaccine-and-russias-race-to-immunity

The Sputnik Vaccine: From Breakthrough to Footnote | 127

disparaging Sputnik out of "Russophobia" and jealousy that Russia's vaccine was certified first.

Sputnik works differently from many vaccines. Traditionally, vaccines have been made from weakened or dead versions of the virus that causes a disease. The body recognizes them as foreign, potentially dangerous substances and manufactures antibodies to protect against the virus should it appear in a live form. China's Sinovac and Sinopharm COVID-19 vaccines, as well as India's Covaxin, are based on this inactivated virus technology.

Sputnik, by contrast, delivers the gene of the COVID-19 virus to the body's cells. The cells then transcribe this into messenger RNA, or mRNA, an acid that triggers the cell to create the protein of the virus' "spikes" and display it on its surface. The body sees this foreign substance and creates antibodies that will fight real COVID if it appears.

Sputnik delivers the genetic material to the cells by inserting it into vehicles, or vectors, consisting of two viruses. The viruses used are adenoviruses, which cause the common cold, sore throat, and other conditions. (The viruses in Sputnik do not cause disease as they are modified not to replicate.) Sputnik uses two different adenoviruses, known as rAd26 and rAd5, which are used in separate shots 21 days apart.

The AstraZeneca–Oxford University and Johnson & Johnson (J&J) vaccines also use adenoviruses—chimpanzee and rAd26, respectively. Gamaleya claims Sputnik is more reliable because it uses two adenoviruses in case the person inoculated has or builds resistance to one of them.

("Messenger RNA" vaccines, such as Moderna and Pfizer-BioNTech, work differently. Instead of delivering genetic material that cells transcribe into mRNA, they provide the mRNA molecules themselves that trigger the construction and display of the spike protein.)

Gamaleya claimed its experience working on adenovirus vaccines against MERS and Ebola made it logical that it would be able to

128 | HOW RUSSIA LOSES

develop Sputnik quickly. Not everyone, however, was impressed with its previous work. ACTO's letter to the Ministry of Health raised questions about the Ebola vaccine, saying it also was not adequately tested before it received Russian registration. (The vaccine was used to inoculate 2,000 people in Guinea, but the WHO licensed only Ebola vaccines produced by Merck and J&J.) The MERS vaccine, ACTO said, had not even received Russian registration, and "there is no way that another unregistered vaccine, for which data is still being collected, can be considered as the basis for accelerated registration of a new vaccine."[22]

More troublesome still for skeptical scientists was the way in which Russian authorities tested Sputnik, and the information they released about the trials.

Russia revealed the first official information about trials of COVID only in September 2020, a month after Putin's announcement. In an article published in the British medical journal *The Lancet*, Russian scientists reported they had conducted a combined phase I-II trial with 76 participants, who all developed antibodies to COVID with no serious side effects.[23]

Several aspects of the test were questioned within Russia and internationally. Rather than dividing the participants into one group that received Sputnik and another that received a placebo, the two groups instead used two formulations of Sputnik. No control group was used that received only a placebo.

The trial was not randomized, using only participants who were healthy and younger than age 60. (COVID-19 is particularly dangerous for the elderly and people with obesity, diabetes, and

---

[22]"Open Letter of the Association of Clinical Research Organizations in Connection With the Announced State Registration of a Vaccine," op. cit.

[23] Logunov, Denis Y. et al., "Safety and immunogenicity of an rAd26 and rAd5 vector-based heterologous prime-boost COVID-19 vaccine in two formulations: two open, non-randomised phase 1/2 studies from Russia," *The Lancet*, September 4, 2020), https://www.thelancet.com/article/S0140-67362031866-3/fulltext

other pre-existing conditions.) Further, the statistics presented from the trial were challenged in an open letter to *The Lancet* by three dozen international scientists, who questioned very similar results for several participants in the study.[24] The Sputnik researchers responded that the similarities were coincidental or caused by rounding errors.

In February 2021, Russian researchers again tried to prove the effectiveness of Sputnik with the publication of interim data from a phase III study in *The Lancet*. This was a randomized, double-blind and placebo-controlled study based on nearly 22,000 adults in Moscow from September 7 to November 24, 2020. The researchers claimed the vaccine was 91.6-percent effective in preventing a COVID infection, again with minimal side effects.[25]

Accompanying the study in *The Lancet* were two editorials praising Sputnik. One, by two British researchers, enthused that the results of the phase III trial wiped away all previous doubts about Sputnik:

> The development of the Sputnik V vaccine has been criticised for unseemly haste, corner-cutting, and an absence of transparency. But the outcome reported here is clear, and the scientific principle of vaccination is demonstrated, which means another vaccine can now join the fight to reduce the incidence of COVID-19.[26]

Other scientists, again, were less impressed. Russian and foreign researchers questioned discrepancies between the number of

---

[24] Bucci, Enrico, "Note of Concern," *Cattivi Scienziati*, September 7, 2020, https://cattiviscienziati.com/2020/09/07/note-of-concern
[25] Logunov, Denis Y. et al., "Safety and efficacy of an rAd26 and rAd5 vector-based heterologous prime-boost COVID-19 vaccine: an interim analysis of a randomised controlled phase 3 trial in Russia," *The Lancet*, 397, no. 10275 (February 2, 2021), https://pubmed.ncbi.nlm.nih.gov/33545094
[26] Jones, Ian, et al., "Sputnik V COVID-19 vaccine candidate appears safe and effective," *The Lancet*, 397, no. 10275 (February 2, 2021), https://www.thelancet.com/article/S0140-67362100191-4/fulltext

130 | HOW RUSSIA LOSES

people who were vaccinated for the study and the number for whom results were reported, whether bad reactions to the shot were properly recorded, the procedure for determining whether subjects had developed COVID, and the exclusion of some trial participants from an analysis of Sputnik's safety.[27] Only 2 percent of those whose results were reported were not White. (Russia has few Black citizens but many of Asian descent.) Only 10 percent were older than age 60.

"There are figures of 92 percent [efficacy], 90 percent, and 91 percent whether they are for people older than 60 or for people between 18 and 30," said Jean-Daniel Lelièvre, a French vaccine expert. "In general, effectiveness declines with age. So this is fairly unusual."[28] Critics also faulted the Russian researchers for not releasing more raw data from the trial. The researchers listed in their article several conditions that would have to be satisfied by anyone wanting the data, including approval by an unnamed "security department."

The concerns of these critics, however, received little public attention. Instead, Sputnik's promoters seized on *The Lancet*'s coverage, treating it as if it amounted to approval by a major

---

[27] See Collis, Helen, et al., "Russia's 'geopolitical' vaccine: Is Sputnik too good to be true?" *Politico*, February 17, 2021; and Bucci, Enrico, "More Concerns on the 'Sputnik' Vaccine," *Cattivi Scienziati*, February 9, 2021, https://cattiviscienziati.com/2021/02/09/more-concerns-on-the-sputnik-vaccine

[28] Reltien, Philippe et al., "Vaccin Spoutnik V: les raisons d'un retard qui nourrit les complotismes [Sputnik V vaccine: the reasons for delay that nourish conspiracy theories]," *Radio France Inter*, June 25, 2021, https://www.franceinter.fr/vaccin-spoutnik-v-les-raisons-d-un-retard-qui-nourrit-les-complotismes. Questions about the age distribution in the Sputnik trial's statistics continued into 2022 with a study that concluded the statistics reported by Gamaleya were "very unlikely to occur in genuine experimental data." See Sheldrick, Kyle A., "Plausibility of Claimed Covid-19 Vaccine Efficacies by Age: A Simulation Study," *American Journal of Therapeutics* 29, no. 5 (September/October 2022), https://journals.lww.com/americantherapeutics/Fulltext/2022/10000/Plausibility_of_Claimed_Covid_19_Vaccine.1.aspx

The Sputnik Vaccine: From Breakthrough to Footnote | 131

regulator. The RDIF followed up with press releases reporting more good news. It announced in April 2021 that Sputnik had proven 97.6-percent effective for 3.8 million Russians vaccinated in a four-month period.[29] In June, the RDIF said the vaccine had proven 97.8-percent effective among 81,000 people in the United Arab Emirates.[30] Russia also announced that a single dose of Sputnik had been found to be 79.4-percent effective against COVID-19.

At the same time as the February *Lancet* article, Russia applied to the WHO and EMA for approval of Sputnik. EMA approval would mean that Sputnik could be immediately distributed within the EU, where vaccines were in short supply through the first half of 2021. WHO endorsement would allow Sputnik to be included in the COVAX program, an international alliance to distribute vaccines to lower-income countries. The EMA announced on April 3 that it had begun a "rolling review" of Sputnik, which allows the agency to start assessing a new drug even before all relevant data is received.

Given the *Lancet* coverage and the torrent of positive news that the RDIF was generating about Sputnik, many countries began pressuring the two agencies to approve it quickly. Some began using Sputnik immediately, without WHO or EMA approval. Christoffer Van Tulleken, a British infectious disease specialist, wrote in May 2021:

> The *Lancet* paper seems to have given other countries confidence. Before publication of the phase III trial, 16 countries had authorised

---

[29] "Sputnik V Demonstrates 97.6% Efficacy According to Analysis of Data From 3.8 Million Vaccinated Persons in Russia Making It the Most Efficient COVID-19 Vaccine in the World" Russian Direct Investment Fund, April 19, 2021), https://sputnikvaccine.com/newsroom/pressreleases/sputnik-v-demonstrates-97-6-efficacy-according-to-the-analysis-of-data-of-3-8-million-vaccinated-per

[30] "Эффективность "Спутника V" в ОАЭ составила 97,8% [Effectiveness of Sputnik V vaccine reaches 97.8% in UAE]," *TASS*, June 29, 2021, https://tass.ru/obschestvo/11775049

> Sputnik V for use—now, over 40 have authorised it. ... Understandably, because of the desperate global shortage of vaccines approved by a major regulator, they may have had no choice but to rely on the *Lancet*'s vetting of the science. But despite its international reputation, is the *Lancet*'s peer review process adequate for this?[31]

The EMA and WHO reviews soon ran into trouble. Western pharmaceutical companies know the exacting requirements of these regulators, who demand precise documentation of all stages of vaccine development and testing. For instance, every batch of vaccines must be tested at multiple stages, and the origin of batches used in trials must be precisely identified. The regulators did not find the documentation they sought for Sputnik; thus, they set about trying to revalidate each stage of the original trials.

Meanwhile, the WHO and EMA began inspecting the Russian plants producing Sputnik for export. In July 2021, an inspection of a plant in the city of Ufa discovered a number of problems, including insufficient safeguards against contamination. The WHO suspended its approval process in September over concerns that "best practices in manufacturing" were not being observed.[32]

In October, an anonymous source told Reuters that the EMA was unlikely to reach a decision on Sputnik until at least the first quarter of 2022 because data was still missing on how it would be produced and how the finished product would be bottled. The source also reported that Russia kept changing which plants would provide Sputnik for the EU, complicating the EMA's inspection job. The EU ambassador in Moscow, Markus Ederer,

---

[31] Van Tullekin, Christoffer, "Covid-19: Sputnik vaccine rockets, thanks to Lancet boost," *BMJ*, 2021, no. 373 (May 6, 2021), https://www.bmj.com/content/373/bmj.n1108

[32] "Sputnik V: WHO suspends approval process for COVID vaccine due to 'manufacturing' concerns, September 16, 2021, *Euronews*, https://uk.news.yahoo.com/sputnik-v-suspends-approval-process-123324733.html

The Sputnik Vaccine: From Breakthrough to Footnote | 133

argued that Russia, while accusing the West of political bias against Sputnik, had itself been delaying EMA inspection visits. "When Russian officials talk about delays and politicization from the European side, it sometimes seems to me that they are mainly talking about themselves, since it is really they who are politicizing this issue," he said.[33]

In March 2021, Thierry Breton, head of the EU's vaccine task force, declared that "we have absolutely no need of Sputnik V" because the EU could supply 300 to 350 million doses of Western vaccines by the end of June. In response, Putin posed a rhetorical question during a meeting with Russian health officials: "Whose interests are such people protecting—those of pharmaceutical companies or of European citizens?"[34] Sputnik's promoters fired back at Breton on the Sputnik Twitter account:

> Europeans want a choice of safe and efficient vaccines, which you so far failed to provide. Sputnik V is already registered in 54 countries. If this is an official position of the EU, please inform us that there is no reason to pursue EMA approval because of your political biases.[35]

The WHO and EMA reiterated that their approval delays were based simply on scientific and manufacturing issues. "This is a technical, not a political process," Ederer said.[36] Russian spokespeople occasionally seemed to agree that the issues were indeed technical and could be ironed out. "We have not yet provided some of the information [to regulators] that should be provided because we had a different understanding" of what was

---

[33] "Посол ЕС - РБК: 'Озеленение' наших отношений - шаг к их стабилизации [EU ambassador: The "greening" of our relations is a step toward their stabilization]," *RBC*, October 8, 2021, https://rbc.ru/interview/politics/08/10/2021/615ec6999a79473db7670633?from=column_1

[34] Text at http://kremlin.ru/catalog/keywords/50/events/65181/print

[35] Sputnik V, Twitter, March 21, 2021, https://twitter.com/sputnikvaccine/status/1373748199823933441l

[36] "Putin Comments on EU Rejection of 'Sputnik' ," op. cit.

134 | HOW RUSSIA LOSES

needed, said Kremlin spokesman Dmitry Peskov at the end of 2021.[37] For his part, Putin said that he hoped for early approval and that 200 million people worldwide had already received the vaccine.[38]

Vaccines Roll Out

Neither EMA nor WHO approval was necessary for Russia to strike bilateral agreements with individual countries to manufacture and distribute Sputnik. Russia's readiness to distribute Sputnik globally in late 2020 and early 2021 came at a perfect moment for Putin. By February 2021, according to UN Secretary-General António Gutierrez, 75 percent of all vaccine doses had been administered in only ten countries, and more than 130 countries had not received a single dose.[39] As a result, Russia could capitalize on the slowness, selfishness, and inefficiency of Western countries:

- Trump had exuded a general arrogance toward most of the world, especially developing countries. His administration took the United States out of the WHO and refused to participate in COVAX. The "Warp Speed" initiative prioritized vaccines for the US, though the plan was for eventual international distribution. Even before vaccines were produced, the US, the UK, and Canada bought up enough doses to vaccinate their populations several times over. This covered their bets if some

---

[37] "Russia misunderstood WHO demands for Sputnik V vaccine approval, says Kremlin," *Euronews*, December 14, 2021, https://www.euronews.com/2021/12/14/russia-misunderstood-who-demands-for-sputnik-v-vaccine-approval-says-kremlin

[38] "Russia Renews Push For WHO Approval Of Sputnik V COVID-19 Vaccine, *Radio Free Europe/Radio Liberty*, December 5, 2021, https://www.rferl.org/a/russia-who-approval-sputnik/31594929.html

[39] United Nations, "Secretary-General Calls Vaccine Equity Biggest Moral Test for Global Community, as Security Council Considers Equitable Availability of Doses" (press release, February 17, 2021), https://press.un.org/en/2021/sc14438.doc.htm

The Sputnik Vaccine: From Breakthrough to Footnote | 135

vaccines proved not to work but left little supply for other countries.

- The Joseph Biden administration, which took office in January 2021, had far more gracious rhetoric toward the outside world but no comprehensive strategy to rush vaccine deliveries. In February, Biden promised $4 billion to finance vaccines for the developing world. In June, the Group of Seven (G7) leaders meeting in Cornwall promised 870 million doses of vaccine to poor nations, with half to be delivered by the end of the year. (This included 500 million doses of the Pfizer vaccine to be donated by the United States.) However, the Cornwall promises seemed to largely aggregate previous pledges. The promises were also not accompanied by a delivery mechanism and lacked a full timetable for fulfillment. They fell far short of the WHO's call for the G7 leaders to provide for vaccinating 70 percent of the world's population within a year. Former British Prime Minister Gordon Brown, an activist for vaccine distribution, called the Cornwall summit "an unforgiveable moral failure."[40]

Western leaders seemed to give short shrift not only to humanitarian concerns for developing nations but also to the scientific argument that COVID-19 could not be conquered decisively until it was conquered everywhere. Populist sentiments in major Western countries had already cut into public support for foreign aid. Given the political climate, only a remarkably brave politician would have proposed distributing vaccines worldwide on a truly equitable basis—which would mean, for example, prioritizing shots for doctors and the elderly in Africa over middle-aged people in prosperous countries.

---

[40] Philip, Catherine, "G7 leaders denounced by Gordon Brown for moral failure over 1bn Covid vaccine donations," *The Times,* June 14, 2021, https://www.thetimes.co.uk/article/g7-leaders-denounced-by-gordon-brown-for-moral-failure-over-1bn-vaccine-donations-rzqpl6nld

136 | HOW RUSSIA LOSES

- In October 2021, at a special vaccine summit, Biden boosted US commitments to 1.1 billion doses for needy nations. However, he wavered on whether to release a large stock of the AstraZeneca vaccine—which had not even been approved yet for use in the US—to the EU and developing countries that were willing and frantic to use it. White House spokeswoman Jen Psaki had declared earlier in the year that the administration wanted to be sure "we have maximal flexibility, that we are oversupplied and over-prepared, and that we have the ability to provide vaccines—whatever the most effective ones are—to the American public. There are still 1,400 people who are dying in our country every single day, and we need to focus on addressing that."[41] The new administration also took time to allow vaccine components to be exported from the United States.

- The first US vaccine donation to COVAX was not until June 2021, and COVAX did not begin distributing vaccines in quantity until the last quarter of 2021.

- The West's rollout of its vaccines was hardly a pretty process, even for its own citizens. Some pharmaceutical giants, such as France's Sanofi, US-British GlaxoSmithKline, and America's Merck, did not come up with vaccines at all. Reports of blood clot side effects slowed the acceptance of the AstraZeneca and J&J vaccines. (The Astra-Zeneca shot was never accepted for routine use in the US, and officials limited the situations in which the J&J vaccine could be used.) The US and UK got the fastest start in distributing vaccines to their own citizens, with 30 percent of the American population fully vaccinated by the end of April 2021, despite initial delays.[42] In Europe, the EU's vaccine rollout was slower.

---

[41] Transcript at https://www.whitehouse.gov/briefing-room/press-briefings/2021/03/12/press-briefing-by-press-secretary-jen-psaki-march-12-2021
[42] Centers for Disease Control and Prevention, "COVID-19 Vaccine Breakthrough Infections Reported to CDC – United States, January 1-

The Sputnik Vaccine: From Breakthrough to Footnote | 137

Governments ordered vaccines too late, and distribution varied widely from country to country. Sniping over vaccines broke out among Paris, London, and Brussels—exacerbated by tensions over Britain's exit from the EU. By April's end, only 17 percent of EU citizens had received at least one dose.[43] (The EU, from early on, did export some vaccines to needy nations.)

It was clear to all that, given the hostility between the West and Russia, and the West's preoccupation with taking care of its own citizens, no combined effort could take place with Moscow to deliver vaccines around the world. No arrangement would be made in the spirit of the US-Russian collaboration to distribute the smallpox vaccine during the Cold War.

The moment was right, therefore, for Russia's go-it-alone strategy. Over the previous decade and half, the Kremlin had re-established itself as a world power mainly through military action, support for authoritarian governments, and business deals with elites in the Global South. Sputnik gave it an opportunity to be famous through benevolence. Russia would showcase its scientific skills and compassion, while Western countries would be perceived as bumbling and selfish. Sputnik also promised to burnish Russia's reputation vis-à-vis China in the developing world. Beijing had far outstripped Moscow's ability to help developing countries economically; Sputnik gave the Kremlin a chance to win back attention and gratitude by saving lives.

Between December 2020 and February 2021, Argentina, Bolivia, Venezuela, Paraguay, and Nicaragua all began national vaccination campaigns using Sputnik. By March 2021, Russia had announced deals to distribute 1.2 billion doses to more than 50 countries, including Turkey, Brazil, Peru, Ghana, Guinea, Nigeria, and the Philippines. Serbia became a vaccine superpower in the

---

April 30, 2021," May 28, 2021, https://www.cdc.gov/mmwr/volumes/70/wr/mm7021e3.htm

[43] Derived from Our World in Data, "Coronavirus (COVID-19) Vaccinations," https://ourworldindata.org/covid-vaccinations

138 | HOW RUSSIA LOSES

Western Balkans, distributing Sputnik and Chinese vaccines—and Western ones when they later became available—to Bosnia-Herzegovina, Montenegro, and North Macedonia.

International production of Sputnik was a key part of Moscow's strategy, both to increase supply and to position Russia as a licenser of high technology. Putin told Russian businessmen in April 2021 that international turnover on Russian vaccines could be worth $100 billion.[44] Serbia and Argentina began producing Sputnik in their own factories, with Putin watching by video as production started simultaneously in both.[45] Companies in Vietnam, India, China, and South Korea joined the production effort, even though Beijing and Seoul did not authorize Sputnik for their own populations. With international production, Russia claimed, Sputnik could be provided to 700 million people outside Russia by the end of 2021.[46]

There was even talk of the European Union buying Sputnik, at least while it sorted out its own vaccine woes. Russia said it could provide enough vaccine to inoculate 50 million EU citizens. Excitement over the Russian drug reached the point at which travel agencies in Norway, Turkey, Moldova, and Germany organized "vaccine tours" to Russia for Sputnik injections.[47] Slovakia and Hungary, the friendliest nations to Russia within NATO, bought Russia's shot in bilateral deals. Several other EU members began to agitate for buying the vaccine. They included Italy, which had long cultivated good relations with Moscow and

---

[44] Text at http://special.kremlin.ru/events/president/news/642535

[45] "Serbia and Argentina start producing Russia's Sputnik V vaccine," *Reuters*, June 4, 2021, https://www.reuters.com/business/healthcare-pharmaceuticals/serbia-argentina-start-producing-russias-sputnik-v-vaccine-2021-06-04

[46] Meyer, Henry, "Russia Wants to Vaccinate Nearly 1 in 10 Globally This Year," *Bloomberg*, March 11, 2021, https://www.bloomberg.com/news/articles/2021-03-12/russia-wants-to-vaccinate-nearly-1-in-10-on-the-planet-this-year?sref=Y2tgfPTW

[47] Antelava, Natalia, "Sputnik V vacations and peak vaccine diplomacy on Mount Everest," *Coda Story*, April 2, 2021, https://www.codastory.com/newsletters/infodemic-april-2

The Sputnik Vaccine: From Breakthrough to Footnote | 139

felt particularly underserved by the EU at the start of the pandemic. In France, Russia-friendly populist politicians called for Sputnik's import. The RDIF reached production deals with factories in Italy and Bavaria, contingent on EMA approval of Sputnik.

"In a war—which this situation is, though we fight against an invisible enemy—you need to do whatever you can to make it stop," said Czech President Miloš Zeman, a long-time ally of Moscow. "I frankly don't think that receiving vaccines means losing independence, or any similar repercussions. It's a business deal, for God's sake."[48] Zeman fired Foreign Minister Tomáš Petříček and Health Minister Jan Blatný after they opposed using Sputnik. Still, Czech authorities did not approve the use of the Russian vaccine—a decision Peskov called a Czech "provocation" linked to revelations that Russian agents blew up a Czech warehouse housing arms to be sent to Ukraine.[49] Among EU citizens in Central and Eastern Europe, eagerness for Sputnik was minimal. Those who preferred the Russian vaccine over others ranged from 1 percent of the population in Romania to 15 percent in Slovakia.[50]

In the EU, more than just the Sputnik deal was at stake for Russia. Moscow had been campaigning aggressively for an end to EU economic sanctions over its 2014 invasion of Ukraine. Some EU members already believed the sanctions were having little effect on Russia while hurting their own business interests. The Kremlin

---

[48] Serhan, Yasmeen, "Here's How Russia and China Are Helping the U.S.," *The Atlantic*, March 30, 2021, https://www.theatlantic. com/international/archive/2021/03/heres-how-russia-and-china-are-helping-us/618443

[49] "Czechs says they lack info needed to assess Sputnik vaccine for use," *Reuters*, April 29, 2021, https://www.reuters.com/world/europe/czechs-says-they-lack-info-needed-assess-sputnik-vaccine-use-2021-04-29

[50] The preference for Sputnik was 4 percent in Hungary and 3 percent in the Czech Republic. See Hajdu, Dominika, "GLOBSEC Vaccination Trends: Perceptions from Central & Eastern Europe," GLOBSEC, April 27, 2021, https://www.globsec.org/wp-content/uploads/2021/04/GLOBSEC-Vaccination-Trends.pdf

140 | HOW RUSSIA LOSES

had reaped favorable publicity by sending masks and other equipment to European nations at the start of the pandemic; if it could now deliver a life-saving vaccine at a moment of critical need, support for sanctions could crumble even further. Russia and 17 other nations, including several others targeted by sanctions regimes, called on the UN General Assembly in March 2020 to cancel all economic sanctions in the interest of fighting COVID-19.[51]

China, too, was busy distributing its own vaccines, powered by its enormous industrial capacity. It leapt into vaccine distribution in early 2021. By late in the year, according to the consulting group Airfinity, its Sinovac and Sinopharm vaccines had been used for half of all COVID injections worldwide.[52] The Chinese vaccines were expensive due to the complexities of working with inactivated viruses. Even so, Beijing gave many doses free of charge to needy nations. Like Russia, China did not wait for authorization of its vaccines by the WHO, which approved Sinopharm and Sinovac in May and June, respectively. By late 2021, however, experts began warning that the immunity created by the Chinese vaccines tapered off quickly and was not as effective for older people.[53]

From the start of 2021, Russia and China were both active in providing COVID vaccines to developing nations. Russia provided far fewer doses than China, but from a geopolitical viewpoint, many saw the two countries together as saviors for those nations least able to obtain vaccines from the wealthy West. By March 2021, the Economist Intelligence Unit suggested the West was on the ropes in "vaccine diplomacy":

> G7 states are increasingly concerned about being perceived as unreliable partners by developing

---

[51] Text of the proposal at https://digitallibrary.un.org/record/3856500/files/A_74_768--S_2020_238-EN.pdf

[52] Airfinity data cited in Mallapaty, Smriti, "China's COVID vaccines have been crucial – now immunity is waning," *Nature*, October 14, 2021, https://www.nature.com/articles/d41586-021-02796-w

[53] Mallapaty, "China's COVID Vaccines Have Been Crucial," op. cit.

The Sputnik Vaccine: From Breakthrough to Footnote | 141

countries, but we expect Western countries to engage in vaccine diplomacy only later this year, once the bulk of their population is vaccinated. This will probably be too late to catch up with Russia and China, which are winning the public relations battle. By then, the damage to Western countries' reputations will be hard to repair.[54]

Trouble for Sputnik

Signing deals to sell Sputnik to eager buyers was an easy task for the RDIF. However, by the middle of 2021, word began to spread of manufacturing and shipping delays. Some customers also began questioning Sputnik's safety and effectiveness.

By May, Sputnik's makers had produced a cumulative total of just over 33 million doses of Sputnik and exported fewer than 15 million two-dose combinations, according to a tally by *Reuters*.[55] (By comparison, China had produced 600 million doses of its vaccines, the US and the EU together had manufactured about 630 million, and India 250 million.[56]) Contractors manufacturing the vaccine in Russia claimed they needed to build new plants to handle the production demands. They also had trouble finding equipment and skilled workers. The head of one contractor reported that the work was complicated by the need to create a first dose with the rAd26 vector and a second with rAd5: "The

---

[54] Economist Intelligence Unit, "EIU Global Outlook: Some thoughts on vaccine diplomacy," March 16, 2021.

[55] Ivanova, Polina, et al., "Big promises, few doses: why Russia's struggling to make Sputnik V doses," *Reuters*, May 14, 2021, https://www.reuters.com/business/healthcare-pharmaceuticals/big-promises-few-doses-why-russias-struggling-make-sputnik-v-doses-2021-05-14

[56] Airfinity data cited in Guetta-Jeanrenaud, L. et al., "A world divided: global vaccine trade and production," *Bruegel Blog*, July 20, 2021, https://www.bruegel.org/2021/07/a-world-divided-global-vaccine-trade-and-production

142 | HOW RUSSIA LOSES

product is difficult enough, and you actually have to make two different drugs."[57]

This was a key difference from other two-dose vaccines, which used the same formula for each injection. Whatever the scientific merits of the two-vector approach, it required tight coordination of production, delivery, and inventory all the way from manufacturing plants to the individual clinics that administered Sputnik.

Production of Sputnik was also delayed in India and Serbia; some producers abroad depended on vaccine components sent from Russia.[58] When the one-shot Sputnik Light vaccine was registered in May 2021, some believed it was a way to distract attention from shortages of the second vaccine. A survey in July 2021 found Sputnik had shipped 99 million doses, compared to two billion for Sinovac and Sinopharm together, 951 million for Pfizer, and 239 million for Moderna.[59]

The production issues meant severe delays in Sputnik deliveries to RDIF clients. At least 16 African countries had authorized Sputnik for use, but shipments were delayed to Algeria, Tunisia, Guinea, Ghana, and others. Some African countries reportedly received only enough doses to vaccinate a few thousand members of their elites.[60] An Indian distributor put its rollout of imported Sputnik doses on hold because Russia could not provide equal

---

[57] Ivanova et al., "Big Promises, Few Doses."

[58] "COVID: Stalled Russian vaccines cause global anger," *BBC*, July 29, 2021, https://www.bbc.com/news/world-europe-58003893

[59] Statistics from Airfinity reported in Rudnitsky, Jake, "Russia's Global Supply Ambitions Stumble During Supply Shortage," *Bloomberg*, July 30, 2021, https://www.bloomberg.com/news/articles/2021-07-30/russia-s-global-vaccine-ambitions-stumble-amid-supply-shortage?sref=Y2tgfPTW

[60] Keir, Grace, et al., "Russia's Vaccine Diplomacy Is Mostly Smoke and Mirrors," Carnegie Endowment for International Peace, August 3, 2021, https://carnegieendowment.org/2021/08/03/russia-s-vaccine-diplomacy-is-mostly-smoke-and-mirrors-pub-85074

The Sputnik Vaccine: From Breakthrough to Footnote | 143

numbers of the first and second shots.[61] Iran received only two million of the 60 million doses it ordered.[62]

In the Philippines, where President Rodrigo Duterte had volunteered to be a personal "guinea pig" for Sputnik, the vaccine's arrival also lagged. By September, 46 million doses of Sinovac and US vaccines had arrived in the Philippines, compared to 380,000 Sputnik doses.[63] Duterte, who had become increasingly disenchanted with Russia, ultimately had himself vaccinated with Sinopharm. He said his gratitude for the US vaccine deliveries led him not to cancel the agreement allowing the American military to operate in the Philippines.[64]

In Latin America, Sputnik had started off strong, with Bolivia, Venezuela, Paraguay, and Nicaragua making it the first COVID-19 vaccine they used. However, all those countries suffered subsequent delivery delays, as did Mexico, Peru, Honduras, and Guatemala.

Sputnik was particularly proud of its relationship with Argentina, the foreign country that received the largest number of Sputnik doses. President Alberto Fernández, who had pursued a range of policies friendly to Russia, rejected an early vaccine deal with Pfizer on the grounds that its terms violated Argentina's sovereignty.[65] He then signed a contract for Sputnik, reportedly

---

[61] Das, Krishna N., "Exclusive: Sputnik V second dose shortage to delay India's full rollout – Dr. Reddy's," *Reuters*, July 12, 2021, https://www.reuters.com/world/india/exclusive-sputnik-v-second-dose-shortage-delay-indias-full-rollout-dr-reddys-2021-07-12

[62] "COVID: Stalled Russian vaccines cause global anger," op. cit.

[63] Sanglee, Tita, "The Forgotten Vaccine: Russia's Sputnik V in Thailand and Southeast Asia," *The Diplomat*, September 17, 2021, https://thediplomat.com/2021/09/the-forgotten-vaccine-russias-sputnik-v-in-thailand-and-southeast-asia

[64] Ranada, Pia, "Duterte says US vaccine donations led him to keep VFA," *Rappler*, Aug. 3, 2021, https://www.rappler.com/nation/duterte-says-united-states-vaccine-donations-decision-keep-vfa

[65] An investigative journalism group said Pfizer bullied Argentina and other governments, sometimes demanding that the company be indemnified even for its own negligence. See Davies, Madlen, et al., "

144 | HOW RUSSIA LOSES

ignoring concerns of Argentina's own medical regulators over its possible effects on older people.[66]

Fernández also worked to smooth the way for Sputnik elsewhere in Latin America, even though he contracted COVID himself only two months after his Sputnik shots. Yet, supply problems bedeviled Sputnik's Argentine success story. By mid-2020, several million Argentines were forced to wait more than three months for their second dose. Public anger reached the point at which officials feared political consequences. A top aide to Fernández, Cecilia Nicolini, wrote a tough letter to the RDIF on July 7, calling urgently for new shipments. According to a leaked version, she warned:

> At this point the entire contract risks being publicly canceled. We understand the shortages and production difficulties a few months ago. But now, seven months later, we are still very much behind, while we are starting to receive doses from other suppliers on a regular basis, and on time. ... We have always done everything possible for Sputnik V to be a major success, but you are leaving us with very few options to keep fighting for you and this project! And as I also mentioned once, we are facing legal prosecution as public servants due to these delays, putting our government at risk.

In a comment likely to be particularly frustrating for Moscow, Nicolini added, "We recently issued a presidential decree that

---

'Held to Ransom': Pfizer demands governments gamble with state assets to secure vaccine deal," *The Bureau of Investigative Journalism*, February 23, 2021.

[66] "Argentina rolls out a Russian Vaccine," *The Economist*, January 2, 2021, https://www.economist.com/the-americas/2021/01/02/argentina-rolls-out-a-russian-vaccine

The Sputnik Vaccine: From Breakthrough to Footnote | 145

allows us to sign contracts with American companies and receive donations from the United States."[67]

Fernández's coalition, beset by a series of failings related to the pandemic and the economy, lost control of the Argentine Senate in the November 2021 elections. The political opposition claimed Fernández had "prioritized ideology and geopolitics when it was time to save lives."[68] Argentina gave emergency authorization to Sinopharm and announced that it would offer AstraZeneca or Moderna shots to those who had received only one dose of Sputnik.

Sputnik's response to its delayed deliveries was to attribute them to Sputnik's virtues and the dangers of other vaccines. It declared on Twitter:

> Given unprecedented worldwide demand, all vaccine producers are experiencing some short-term supply issues. Sputnik V is in enormous demand as it has demonstrated outstanding efficacy and safety while not having any rare side effects that have been linked to other vaccines.[69]

The RDIF also attributed the shortage to an EU "smear campaign" against the vaccine and efforts by Brussels to slow down production abroad.[70]

---

[67] Pagni, Carlos, "La carta a Rusia que revela la encrucijada del Gobierno por la falta de vacunas [The letter to Russia that reveals the government's conundrum over the lack of vaccines]," *La Nación*, July 22, 2021, https://www.lanacion.com.ar/politica/la-revelacion-de-la-encrucijada-mas-desesperante-del-gobierno-nid22072021
[68] Centenera, Mar, "Argentina reclama a Rusia por la demora de la entrega de la vacuna Sputnik V [Argentina complains to Russia over the delay in deliveries of Sputnik V]," *El País*, July 22, 2021, https://elpais.com/internacional/2021-07-22/argentina-reclama-a-rusia-por-la-demora-en-la-entrega-de-la-vacuna-sputnik-v.html
[69] Sputnik Vaccine, Twitter, July 28, 2021, https://twitter.com/sputnikvaccine/status/1420343276725485575?s=20
[70] European External Action Service, "EEAS special report update: Short Assessment of Narratives and Disinformation Around the COVID-

146 | HOW RUSSIA LOSES

However, production delays were not the only issue for Sputnik. Brazil's health regulator, Anvisa, rejected several states' requests to import Sputnik in April 2021, citing a lack of safety and manufacturing data about the drug. Brazil said its inspectors found fault with Russian production sites and that the adenovirus in Sputnik seemed capable of replicating, potentially with disease-causing effects.[71] In the summer, Brazil finalized a large deal with Pfizer. Sputnik went on the attack, publicly accusing Brazil of bowing to US pressure and threatening to sue Anvisa for libel.[72] Anvisa subsequently allowed some states to import Sputnik under stringent conditions but again recommended against its import in October.

Initially, Thailand announced it would purchase Sputnik, but its medical regulator did not approve the transaction.[73] Indonesia approved Sputnik only in August 2021, after five other vaccines had received emergency-use authorizations and China had become its biggest vaccine supplier.[74]

---

19 Pandemic," April 28, 2021, https://euvsdisinfo.eu/uploads/2021/04/EEAS-Special-Report-Covid-19-vaccine-related-disinformation-6.pdf

[71]Brito, Ricardo, et al., "Brazil health regulator rejects Russia's Sputnik vaccine," *Reuters*, April 26, 2021, https://www.reuters.com/world/americas/brazil-health-regulator-anvisas-technical-staff-recommend-against-importing-2021-04-2

[72] In its 2020 annual report, the US Department of Health and Human Services announced in a section titled "Combating malign influences in the Americas" that the US had convinced Brazil not to buy Sputnik. See Biller, David, et. al., "Sputnik vaccine helping Russia regain LatAm foothold," *The Associated Press*, April 12, 2021, https://apnews.com/article/technology-world-news-brazil-rio-de-janeiro-south-america-c979506337e838680bdaa87f382082ae

[73] Sanglee "The Forgotten Vaccine, op. cit."

[74] Majumdar, Anwesha, "COVID: Indonesia Approves Russia's Sputnik V Vaccine For Emergency Use," *Republic World*, August 25, 2021, https://www.republicworld.com/world-news/rest-of-the-world-news/covid-indonesia-approves-russias-sputnik-v-vaccine-for-emergency-use.html

The Sputnik Vaccine: From Breakthrough to Footnote | 147

A scandal erupted in Slovakia, where Prime Minister Igor Matovič was forced to resign over a deal to buy Sputnik, which other members of his coalition said was done behind their backs. Worse, the State Institute for Drug Control said batches that had arrived in the country were not the same as those used in the *Lancet* trial. "It is only its name that links it to the Sputnik V vaccines used in about 40 countries around the world," the regulator proclaimed.[75] Sputnik demanded the vaccine back and accused the regulator of "disinformation," "fake news," and "an act of sabotage."[76] In the end, only a few thousand Slovaks were vaccinated with Sputnik.

In Africa, multiple foreign companies sought out facilities to produce their vaccines in South Africa, perhaps the continent's most scientifically advanced country, for distribution throughout the continent. However, South Africa, despite its BRICS membership and friendly relations with Russia, withheld approval of Sputnik. South Africa has the world's highest level of HIV/AIDS, and its authorities feared Sputnik's rAd5 vector could increase susceptibility to HIV among men.[77]

Pricing was an issue for Sputnik as well. At $10 a shot, the vaccine's price was quite high for African nations. In February 2021, the *Financial Times* reported that the African Union would pay $9.75 per dose for 300 million shots, compared to $3 for AstraZeneca and the US Novavax vaccine (both manufactured by the Serum Institute of India), $6.75 a dose for the Pfizer vaccine, and $10 for the one-dose J&J shot.[78]

---

[75] "Slovak regulator voices misgivings about Sputnik vaccine," *Medical Xpress*, April 8, 2021, https://medicalxpress.com/news/2021-04-slovak-voices-misgivings-sputnik-vaccine.html

[76] Sputnik Vaccine, Twitter, April 8, 2021, https://twitter.com/sputnikvaccine/status/1380158709985329155?lang=en

[77] South African Health Products Regulatory Authority, "Update on the Sahpra Review of the Sputnik V Vaccine," press release, October 18, 2021, https://www.sahpra.org.za/wp-content/uploads/2021/10/MEDIA-RELEASE-Sputnik-Vaccine_18Oct-2021.pdf. Sputnik said the concerns were baseless.

[78] Pilling, David, et. al., "Africa will pay more for Russian Covid vaccine than 'western' jabs," *Financial Times*, February 25, 2021,

148 | HOW RUSSIA LOSES

Questions also abounded about Sputnik being sold in Africa by intermediaries based in the United Arab Emirates at well over the $10-per-dose maximum Russia had publicly announced. Ghana canceled a $65 million contract with a UAE company to buy Sputnik at $19 per dose. Kenyan officials reportedly blocked a deal for the UAE supplier to deliver the vaccine to a private Kenyan company, which would have paid $18.50 a dose and resold them for $42 each.[79] A UNICEF table of vaccine prices in early 2022 showed Sputnik being sold at $19 a dose in Ghana's and Lebanon's private markets, as well as $27.15 in the Pakistani market.[80]

As 2021 went on, vaccines from wealthy nations finally began to arrive in large quantities to countries of all economic levels. By March 2022, the United States had become the biggest contributor to COVAX in both funding and vaccine supplies.[81] Many of the doses contributed were mRNA vaccines. Not only did these have the cachet of being widely used in the world's most developed nations, but the mRNA technology in the Pfizer and Moderna vaccines had been the subject of much scientific excitement.

"Adenovirus-based vaccines in general didn't get the attention mRNA vaccines did," said David Heymann, an infectious disease specialist who has held senior posts at the WHO and other government health bodies. The mRNA vaccines, he said, had

---

https://www.ft.com/content/ffe40c7d-c418-4a93-a202-5ee996434de7

[79] Cordell, Jake, et al., "Kenya's Failed Sputnik V Deal Used Emirati Resale Scheme," *The Moscow Times*, July 19, 2021, https://www.themoscowtimes.com/2021/07/19/kenyas-failed-sputnik-v-deal-used-emirati-resale-scheme-a74554

[80] "COVID-19 Market Dashboard," UNICEF, https://www.unicef.org/supply/covid-19-vaccine-market-dashboard.

[81] Rouw, Anna et al., "Vaccinating the World: How Does the U.S. Stack Up Against Other Donors?" KFF, March 3, 2022, https://www.kff.org/coronavirus-covid-19/issue-brief/vaccinating-the-world-how-does-the-u-s-stack-up-against-other-donors

The Sputnik Vaccine: From Breakthrough to Footnote | 149

already captured the imagination of scientists who had been following the technology for its use in anti-cancer therapy.[82]

The manufacture of mRNA vaccines also involves no outside biological components, eliminating quality control issues with vaccines that use genetic or dead-virus material. They can be manufactured faster than other vaccines. The Pfizer and Moderna vaccines use fat cells to convey the molecules to body cells, avoiding the problem of people developing immunity to adenoviruses.

As mRNA vaccines increasingly dominated the market, Sputnik fell by the wayside. Hungary announced in late 2021 that it would buy no more Russian or Chinese vaccines because they were not needed. About 80 percent of the vaccines already in Hungary were of Western origin, according to a Hungarian television report.[83]

By mid-2022, fewer than 2 percent of COVID vaccine doses produced in the world had come from Russia, according to the World Trade Organization.[84] (The figure would not include Sputnik produced elsewhere.) In developing nations, where Russia had hoped Sputnik would be particularly successful, it became a statistical footnote. By May 2023, according to WHO Africa, less than 0.3 percent of COVID vaccine doses administered on the continent were Sputnik. J&J accounted for 33 percent, Sinovac and Sinopharm together 20 percent, Pfizer 19 percent, AstraZeneca and Covishield (its India-produced version) 15 percent, and Moderna 4 percent.[85] While in May 2021 Sputnik

---

[82] Heymann, David, interview with author, August 1, 2022.
[83] Makszimov, Vlad, "Budapest skips Eastern vaccines, EU joint procurement in new jab haul," *Euractiv*, November 24, 2021, https://www.euractiv.com/section/politics/short_news/budapest-skips-eastern-vaccines-eu-joint-procurement-in-new-jab-haul
[84] World Trade Organization, "WTO-IMF COVID-19 Vaccine Trade Tracker," https://www.wto.org/english/tratop_e/covid19_e/vaccine_trade_tracker_e.htm
[85] WHO Africa, "COVID-19 Vaccination Dashboard," https://app.powerbi.com/view?r=eyJrIjoiOTI0ZDlhZWEtMjUxMC00ZDhhLWFjOTY

150 | HOW RUSSIA LOSES

accounted for more than half of all COVID-19 inoculations in Argentina, by the end of 2022, the Russian vaccine had been overtaken by Sinopharm, AstraZeneca, and Pfizer.[86] In Mexico at the end of 2022, 36 percent of inoculations had been with AstraZeneca, 35 percent with Pfizer, 12 percent with Sinovac, and 7 percent with Sputnik.[87]

The Information Struggle

Russia's announcement that it had registered the world's first COVID-19 vaccine came at a moment of high tensions between the Kremlin and the West. Russia was in its sixth year of Western sanctions over its invasion of Ukraine in 2014. Putin's government was cracking down on independent voices inside Russia, accusing them of being "foreign agents." The Kremlin was disrupting Western societies with cyberattacks and election interference. And Russian troops, mercenaries, and information outlets were advancing Moscow's influence in Latin America, Africa, and the Middle East.

In such circumstances, the appearance of Sputnik could not be isolated from its geopolitical context. Scientists were properly suspicious of a vaccine announced with no rigorous data on its safety and effectiveness. But suppose, ultimately, Sputnik worked? Western politicians could hardly oppose saving the lives of millions. Yet, they recognized that Sputnik could hand the Kremlin an enormous propaganda victory. Western media emphasized the political significance of Sputnik. *The New York*

---

tYjZlMGYzOWI4NGIwIiwidCI6ImY2MTBjMGI3LWJkMjQtNGIzOS04MT BiLTNkYzI4MGFmYjU5MCIsImMiOjh9

[86] Ruiz, Iván, "Dos años después de las primeras dosis, cuáles fueron las vacunas contra el COVID-19 más aplicadas en Argentina [Two years after the first doses, what COVID-19 vaccines were most used in Argentina]," *Infobaé*, December 12, 2022, https://www.infobae.com/politica/2022/12/12/dos-anos-despues-de-las-primeras-dosis-cuales-fueron-las-vacunas-contra-el-covid-19-mas-aplicadas-en-argentina

[87] Escobar, Cristian, "¿Cuál es la vacuna contra COVID-19 más aplicada en México?" *Serendipia*, December 23, 2022, https://serendipia.digital/covid-19/vacuna-covid-mas-aplicada-en-mexico

The Sputnik Vaccine: From Breakthrough to Footnote | 151

Times story on Putin's announcement said the leaders of the United States, Russia, and China were treating the vaccine race as "a proxy war for their personal leadership and competing national systems."[88] In London, *The Independent* said the speed and lack of transparency in Sputnik's rollout "has fuelled concerns that geopolitics may have been prioritised at the expense of science."[89]

After an EU summit in March 2021, French President Emmanuel Macron spoke of a "new type of world war" over vaccines. He accused Russia and China of using vaccines in "attacks" and "attempts at destabilization."[90] A month earlier, he had warned that, if Europe were slow to deliver vaccines to countries in Africa, they would turn to Russia and China and "the strength of the West will no longer be a reality."[91] Lithuanian Prime Minister Ingrida Šimonytė lamented, "Regretfully, Sputnik comes packed with many layers of propaganda and not even hidden ambition to divide the EU."[92] European Council President Charles Michel

---

[88] Andrew E. Kramer, "Russia Approves Coronavirus Vaccine Before Completing Tests," *The New York Times*, August 11, 2020, https://www.nytimes.com/2020/08/11/world/europe/russia-coronavirus-vaccine-approval.html

[89] Oliver Carroll, "Coronavirus Russia: Putin says world's first vaccine has been approved for use," *Independent*, August 11, 2020, https://www.independent.co.uk/news/world/europe/coronavirus-russia-world-first-vaccine-approval-putin-latest-a9664376.html

[90] "Virus: le ton monte sur les vaccins, Moscou se défend de 'mener une guerre,' [Tones Sharpen Over Vaccines, Moscow Denies 'Waging a War']," *Agence France-Presse*, March 26, 2021, https://www.lalibre.be/dernieres-depeches/afp/2021/03/26/virus-le-ton-monte-sur-les-vaccins-moscou-se-defend-de-mener-une-guerre-ZSWJAPNGR5CNXIJ2TVKS2USSWU

[91] "Covid-19: le G7 s'engage à renforcer l'aide à la vaccination des pays pauvres [Covid-19: the G7 promises more help for vaccinations in poor countries]," *France-24*, February 19, 2021, https://www.nytimes.com/2021/02/19/world/europe/russia-coronavirus-vaccine-soft-power.html

[92] Von der Burchard, Hans, "POLITICO Brussels Playbook: From Russia, no love – Sputnik row – Lux still leaky," *POLITICO*, February 8, 2021, https://www.politico.eu/newsletter/brussels-playbook/politico-brussels-playbook-from-russia-no-love-sputnik-row-lux-still-leaky.

152 | HOW RUSSIA LOSES

declared, "We should not let ourselves be misled by China and Russia, both regimes with less desirable values than ours, as they organize highly limited but widely publicized operations to supply vaccines to others."[93]

At a White House briefing, Psaki seemed to imply that Russian and Chinese vaccine deliveries were a way to encourage nondemocratic countries:

> Of course, we're concerned by Russia and China using vaccines to engage with countries in a way where they're not holding them, at times, to the same standard the United States and a number of other countries would hold them to—on human rights, on freedom of speech, freedom of religion, freedom of media, even.[94]

Psaki's implication seemed to be that it was wrong to deliver vaccines to countries without asking them to improve their human rights records.

Along with warnings about prospective geopolitical threats, Western intelligence agencies alleged that Russian hackers were trying to access research by Western companies. One report said they had stolen key information about the AstraZeneca vaccine.[95] Russian officials ridiculed the claims, saying they had no need of Western data to create their own products.

---

[93] Chalmers, John, et. al., "EU rejects accusations of 'vaccine nationalism,' " *Reuters*, March 9, 2021, https://www.reuters.com/world/china/eu-rejects-accusations-vaccine-nationalism-2021-03-09

[94] Transcript at https://www.whitehouse.gov/briefing-room/press-briefings/2021/03/02/press-briefing-by-press-secretary-jen-psaki-march-2-2021

[95] Walker, Amy, "UK '95% sure' Russian hackers tried to steal coronavirus vaccine research," *The Guardian*, July 17, 2020, https://www.theguardian.com/world/2020/jul/17/russian-hackers-steal-coronavirus-vaccine-uk-minister-cyber-attack

The Sputnik Vaccine: From Breakthrough to Footnote | 153

Putin added to the combative atmosphere by comparing Sputnik and Sputnik Light to weapons of war. With a slight smile, he proclaimed at a government meeting in May 2021:

> As one European specialist said, they are as reliable as a Kalashnikov rifle. That is not us talking; this was said by a European specialist. And I think that he undoubtedly was right: simple and reliable, like a Kalashnikov rifle.[96]

In the first months after Sputnik was announced, Western media were as skeptical about the vaccine's effectiveness as about Russia's political motives. However, the publication of the Russian study in *The Lancet* in February substantially changed the narrative. The media covered the study heavily. Just as Sputnik's developers would have hoped, many outlets conflated the Russian scientists' claim of 91.6-percent effectiveness, the two accompanying editorials, and the prestige of *The Lancet* to give the impression that Sputnik had been rousingly endorsed by the global medical community.

By the time scientific experts started questioning the data behind the study and the competence of *The Lancet*'s peer-review process, the media had moved on. It became common to see phrasing in media articles to the effect that, "according to the prestigious medical journal The Lancet, Sputnik is 91.6-percent effective against COVID-19." Western think tanks also largely dropped any questions about Sputnik's quality, though they continued to write regularly about Sputnik's propaganda value to Russia.

Russia was aware from the start that Sputnik would become a major issue in the information war between Moscow and the West. Since the beginning of the pandemic, Russian information assets had been suggesting that COVID was intentionally created by secret US laboratories as a biological weapon. (This was essentially a reprisal of "Operation Infektion," a 1980s campaign by the KGB that claimed secret Pentagon labs had created AIDS.)

---

[96] Video at https://www.youtube.com/watch?v=dGZz0-4gH1I

154 | HOW RUSSIA LOSES

When Sputnik appeared, the Russian narrative expanded to allege that the West had its knives out for Russia's product. The day Putin announced the vaccine, Sputnik's website published what it called a "forbidden op-ed"—an opinion column by Dmitriev that supposedly had been "rejected by all leading Western media." In it, the RDIF CEO accused "some international politicians and media" of trying to undermine Sputnik's credibility out of political motivations: "We believe that such an approach is counterproductive and call for a political 'ceasefire' on vaccines in the face of the COVID-19 pandemic."[97]

Russian assets then proceeded to double down on their propaganda campaign surrounding the pandemic and Sputnik. There was no ceasefire from the official Russian media, Russian proxies worldwide, or Sputnik's own Twitter feed; all launched vicious assaults against those who criticized Sputnik. (Sputnik was the only vaccine that had its own Twitter account.)

In Russia's view, Sputnik became another litmus test by which countries could be judged: Ukrainian authorities were committing "genocide" by not using Sputnik, Belarus deserved praise for rapidly adopting it, and Georgia was refusing it under orders from the West. Pro-Russian media accused the EMA, "Big Pharma," and the European Union of conspiracies against Sputnik. Russia's *RT* ran headlines such as, "Are Western Attacks on the Russian COVID-19 Vaccine a Corporate Cold War Against Humanity?"[98] The Russian news agency *TASS* quoted a "high-level Kremlin source" as saying the West was preparing an elaborate plot to fake large numbers of people dying following vaccination with Sputnik.[99]

---

[97] RDIF, https://sputnikvaccine.com/newsroom/forbidden-op-ed-the-sputnik-vaccine-as-a-lifesaving-global-partnership-eng

[98] Text at https://www.rt.com/op-ed/500981-sputnik-v-cold-war-covid

[99] The plot supposedly involved USAID, George Soros' Open Society Foundations, the Thomson Reuters Foundation, the *BBC*, and the international journalism NGO Internews. See "West readies information attack on Sputnik V by faking deaths – Kremlin source," TASS, March 12, 2021, https://tass.com/politics/1265511

The Sputnik Vaccine: From Breakthrough to Footnote | 155

The Russian campaign amplified legitimate concerns about some Western vaccines, such as indications that, in rare cases, the AstraZeneca and J&J vaccines could induce blood clots and that Pfizer's product could cause anaphylaxis, a life-threatening allergic reaction. But Russia went much further, questioning the science behind mRNA vaccines, claiming that the Pfizer vaccine had been linked to disorders including ALS and Alzheimer's. Kremlin propaganda suggested that the AstraZeneca shot could turn people into chimpanzees because it uses a chimpanzee adenovirus.[100] (Peskov opined that the AstraZeneca shot was a "monkey vaccine," while Sputnik was a "human vaccine."[101])

A chart published on Sputnik's Twitter feed claimed that people were most likely to die as a result of taking the Pfizer vaccine. Sputnik was listed as the safest option.[102]

In October 2021, at the annual Valdai political conference, Putin asserted that Europeans were traveling to Russia to gain access to its "more reliable, safer vaccine" and then faking papers at home to show they had received Pfizer. The only source he gave

---

[100] See Woollacott, Emma, "Facebook Shuts Down Russian Campaign That Claimed Vaccine Turns People Into Chimpanzees," *Forbes*, August 11, 2021, https://www.forbes.com/sites/emmawoollacott/2021/08/11/facebook-shuts-down-russian-campaign-that-claimed-vaccine-turned-people-into-chimpanzees/?sh=78db68b767a0; and EUvsDisinfo, "Disinfo: the Pfizer vaccine could be a biological weapon," July 1, 2021, https://euvsdisinfo.eu/report/the-pfizer-vaccine-could-be-abiological-weapon

[101] Pfanner, Eric, et al., "Scientists Cast Doubt On Results From Russian Covid Vaccine," September 8, 2021, *Bloomberg*, September 8, 2020, https://www.bloomberg.com/news/articles/2020-09-08/scientists-cast-doubt-on-results-from-russian-covid-vaccine?sref=Y2tgfPTWe

[102] For the chart, See Sputnik V, Twitter, April. 23, 2021, https://twitter.com/sputnikvaccine/status/1385580036162560002?lang=en. Its validity is questioned in "Why a workable vaccine has a bad reputation," op. cit.

156 | HOW RUSSIA LOSES

for this information: "Doctors are saying this."[103] Earlier in the year, social media influencers in Western Europe reported that they had been approached by a Russia-based company to post videos disparaging Pfizer.[104]

If they had been so inclined, Western actors could have found grounds to disparage Sputnik in return. For instance, Sputnik's logo included the phrase "proven human adenoviral technology." This claim was something of a stretch. Adenoviruses have long been used in biological research and are being considered for gene therapy. However, until some companies began using the technology for COVID-19 vaccines, only a single adenovirus vaccine—the Merck and J&J Ebola product—was in widespread use. An opposition campaign might also have argued that an adenovirus vaccine against one disease risks making future vaccines useless if the body creates antibodies against those vectors used.

However, no such campaigns ever materialized—and rightly so. Western companies and governments would have rejected any such tactics not only for moral reasons but also on the grounds that they could fan anti-vaccine sentiment in general. In the same spirit, Boeing and Airbus rarely publish anything questioning the safety of each other's products; although they are fierce commercial competitors, both fear undermining confidence in air travel as a whole. Sputnik's promoters, in contrast, apparently had no trouble frightening people about other vaccines.

Rarely mentioned by Sputnik promoters was Russia's internal vaccination situation. For a country promising to save the world with its vaccine, the Russian authorities had great difficulty

---

[103] Gutterman, Steve, "The Week In Russia: 'Values' And The Virus," *Radio Free Europe/Radio Liberty*, October 29, 2021, https://www.rferl.org/a/putin-covid-values-virus-russia/31535207.html

[104] Krutov, Mark, et al., "Exclusive: Meet The Murky Russian Network Behind An Anti-Pfizer Disinformation Drive In Europe," *Radio Free Europe/Radio Liberty*, May 27, 2021, https://www.rferl.org/a/russia-pfizer-covid-disinformation-serebryanskaya-murky-vaccine-influencers/31277170.html

The Sputnik Vaccine: From Breakthrough to Footnote | 157

convincing their own people to trust Sputnik. They tried cash payments, raffles, discounts on merchandise, and shutting down workplaces until people were vaccinated. Officials eventually began requiring vaccination certificates for people who worked in service industries and schools, as well as for anyone wanting to enter a restaurant. (Underground operators soon started to offer fake certificates.)

By the end of March 2021, 3 percent of Russians were fully vaccinated; by June, 9 percent; by September, 26 percent; and by December, 40 percent. The December figure for Germany was 69 percent, for the United States 61 percent, and for Mexico 50 percent.[105] Kremlin spokesman Peskov blamed "total nihilism" for Russians' failure to get vaccinated.[106] A wave of Delta-variant COVID-19 in the summer of 2021 spurred some Russians to suddenly seek out vaccinations. Supply shortages inside Russia were the result; authorities had become used to low domestic demand and had been focused on satisfying angry foreign customers whose shipments had not arrived. Some supplies of the Russian drug had to be imported into Russia from factories in South Korea.[107]

In a *CNN* interview in March 2021, Dmitriev blamed resistance to Sputnik within Russia on a Western "disinformation campaign."[108] A Russian senator insisted that anti-vax content on social networks was "all coming from the West."[109] Other factors,

---

[105] Derived from https://ourworldindata.org/coronavirus

[106] "Kremlin blames nihilism and low vaccine uptake for COVID-19 surge," *Reuters*, June 18, 2021, https://www.reuters.com/world/kremlin-says-nihilism-low-vaccination-rate-behind-fresh-covid-19-surge-2021-06-18

[107] Nikolskaya, Polina, "Push to get wary Russians vaccinated leaves some COVID clinics short," *Reuters*, July 21, 2021, https://www.reuters.com/world/europe/push-get-wary-russians-vaccinated-leaves-some-covid-clinics-short-2021-07-21

[108] Video at https://edition.cnn.com/videos/world/2021/03/04/kirill-dmitriev-sputnik-v-coronavirus-vaccine-ctw-vpx.cnn

[109] "Джабаров: Антипрививочная кампания в соцсетях идет с Запада [Dzhabarov: Anti-injection campaign on social networks is being carried out by the West]," *TASS*, June 28, 2021, https://rg.ru/

however, were more likely to have affected Russian attitudes. At least initially, the country's own doctors mistrusted Sputnik. A poll of 3,000 doctors immediately after Putin's announcement on August 11, 2020, found that 52 percent were not ready to receive the injection themselves, compared to 24.5 percent who were. The doctors worried about a lack of data and the speed at which Sputnik was developed.[110]

Many ordinary Russians distrusted anything the government said about COVID-19, given widespread dissatisfaction with the state health system and rumors that COVID deaths were being disguised as deaths from pneumonia. Lurid accounts in Russian state media of side effects from Western vaccines (infertility, neurological symptoms, blood clots, and death) may have made people worry if Sputnik injections could have the same consequences. Russians saw little leadership from Putin: he was largely silent about the pandemic, asserting that the situation was "under full control" and offloading responsibility for caring for citizens on regional governors.

Some skeptical Western news reports about Sputnik undoubtedly penetrated Russia's information space. However, it was Moscow, in its propaganda products aimed abroad, that elevated anti-vax conspiracy theories to the level of state policy. Russian information organs actively encouraged citizens in Western countries to oppose vaccinations and lockdowns and promoted narratives that COVID-19 was created by shadowy forces to dominate the world. Posts by Western anti-vaxxers likely reached some Russians, but Russian anti-vax posts were shared on a wide variety of anti-vax platforms and may well have come back to the Russian Federation.[111]

2021/06/28/dzhabarov-antiprivivochnaia-kampaniia-v-socsetiah-idet-s-zapada.html

[110] "Опрос продемонстрировал недоверие врачей к вакцине от коронавируса [Survey shows doctors' mistrust of coronavirus vaccine]," *RBK*, August 14, 2020, https://www.rbc.ru/society/14/08/2020/5f35d9579a79471d249e8374

[111] "How pro-Kremlin outlets and blogs undermine trust in foreign-made COVID vaccines," DFRLab, January 27, 2021,

The Sputnik Vaccine: From Breakthrough to Footnote | 159

Russian authorities had an ambiguous relationship with their own anti-vaxxers. In his first announcement about Sputnik, Putin emphasized that vaccination would be voluntary. Although the authorities were violently breaking up any political protest against the regime, an anti-vax demonstration at a Moscow office of the ruling United Russia party in June 2021 was allowed to proceed unhindered.[112] The government attitude suggested that officials may have seen the anti-vaxxers as the vanguard of a much larger number of Russians who considered the government incompetent or untrustworthy.[113] In that case, actively repressing anti-vaccine forces could be politically dangerous—especially ahead of the September 2021 parliamentary elections. When Putin was vaccinated in March 2021, no photo coverage was provided and, initially, Russians were not even told what vaccine he had received. (Putin later said it was Sputnik.)

'A Flawed and Irredeemable Venture'

Sputnik triumphed initially in two areas: in the information space and in its initial rollout to nations desperate for vaccines. Russia failed at winning endorsements from international scientific bodies and in producing enough vaccines for Sputnik to become a global go-to product. If Russia had won approval from international regulators and been able to deliver Sputnik in the promised quantities when Western vaccines were still lacking, its success would have been far greater.

---

https://medium.com/dfrlab/how-pro-kremlin-outlets-and-blogs-undermine-trust-in-foreign-made-covid-vaccines-4fa9f9f19df1

[112] "Противники принудительной вакцинации пришли к приемным 'Единой России.' В Кремле сказали, что они 'неверно видят ситуацию' [Opponents of forced vaccination come to the reception office of 'United Russia.' The Kremlin says that 'they view the situation incorrectly']," *Rain TV*, June 25, 2021, https://tvrain.ru/teleshow/notes/protivniki_prinuditelnoj_vaktsinatsii_prishli_k_priemn ym_edinoj_rossii_v_kremle_skazali_chto_oni_neverno_vidjat_situatsiju-532651

[113] Such sentiments among Russians became quite visible later regarding Russia's conduct of its war against Ukraine.

160 | HOW RUSSIA LOSES

In the information arena, Russia's announcement that it had registered Sputnik was a *coup de théâtre* heard round the world. Sputnik put Russia on the consumer map; before Sputnik, almost no one sought any consumer product from Putin's Russia. Many ordinary news consumers took at face value that Russia had beaten the rest of the world in vaccine development. In fact, the Russian authorities had simply chosen to inoculate substantial numbers of citizens after small and rushed phase I-II trials. By the time of Putin's announcement, the Pfizer and Moderna vaccines were already in their phase III trials. That point was lost on the global public, however. "The Russian PR campaign worked," said Niclas Poitiers, who studies vaccine economics at the Bruegel Institute in Brussels. "We [Western nations] were at the same stage they were at, but that was lost in the discussion."[114] As Fauci put it on the day of Putin's announcement:

> If we wanted to take the chance of hurting a lot of people, or giving them something that doesn't work, we could start doing this, you know, next week if we wanted to. But that's not the way it works.[115]

Western pharmaceutical companies strongly backed Fauci's position. Their eyes, ironically, had not been set on Russia but on Trump. They feared Trump would force them to cut corners on testing to roll out vaccines before the November 2020 presidential election. Trump clearly was frantic to declare vaccine success; on the day of Putin's announcement, Trump told a radio interviewer that "we're getting to an end. We're getting to, and the vaccines are ready to rock. We're going to be very close to a vaccine. We're ready to distribute."[116] Nine pharmaceutical companies signed a pledge in September to "stand with science"

---

[114] Niclas Poitiers, interview with author, March 23, 2022.

[115] "Fauci says he has serious doubts Russia's COVID-19 vaccine is safe, effective," op. cit.

[116] Transcript at https://hughhewitt.com/president-trump-on-a-scotus-vacancy-china-college-football-joe-bidens-vp-and-more

The Sputnik Vaccine: From Breakthrough to Footnote | 161

and not release vaccines until their safety and effectiveness were certain.[117]

Another major information success for Russia was the phase III study in *The Lancet*, which largely ended public debate about Sputnik's quality. In an analysis for the Institute of Modern Russia, Vera Michlin-Shapir and Olga Khvostunova speculated that the Kremlin may have planned the information campaign around Sputnik from the very start as a *dvukhkhodovka*—a Russian chess term for a pair of moves conceived in advance. In this case, it would have been Moscow's plan to awe the world by announcing the first vaccine, let critics have their day complaining that scientific processes had not been followed, and then shut down the critics decisively with the positive phase III study in *The Lancet*.[118]

Russia also lost no opportunity in publicizing Sputnik's international rollout. Every vaccine delivery was chronicled in news releases and videos. Russian media presented a parade of doctors and scientists extolling the vaccine. Whatever "soft power" could do for Sputnik, Russia's information specialists did. The Kremlin also attempted to leverage maximum geopolitical advantage in Sputnik's international trials. Countries selected for the trials included India, Brazil, Saudi Arabia, and Turkey— middle-level powers whose political sympathies oscillate between Russia and the West and which Moscow wanted to bring closer to its orbit.

Despite all the efforts and accomplishments, however, Sputnik was ultimately a shadow of what it might have been. The reasons for this included production issues, failure to collaborate with regulators and foreign drug companies, prioritizing propaganda

---

[117] Thomas, Katie, "9 Drug Companies Pledge to 'Stand With Science' on Coronavirus Vaccines," *The New York Times*, September 8, 2020, https://www.nytimes.com/2020/09/08/health/9-drug-companies-pledge-coronavirus-vaccine.html

[118] Michlin-Shapir, Vera, et al., "The Rise and Fall of Sputnik V," Institute of Modern Russia, October 2021, https://imrussia.org/images/stories/Reports/Sputnik-V/IMR_Sputnik_eng_final_web_v2.pdf

162 | HOW RUSSIA LOSES

over reality, and Russia's failure to position itself as a magnanimous international donor:

• **Russia's production capabilities were inadequate to support its promises.** "Russia didn't have the manufacturing capacity, and they overpromised. Even after the *Lancet* piece, they never really got out of the box," according to J. Stephen Morrison, director of the Global Health Policy Center at the Center for Strategic and International Studies. Russia was in a sweet spot from late 2020, when the world was desperate for vaccines and China was the only other main supplier, until mid-2021, when Western vaccines became widely available outside the wealthiest countries. During that period, Russia and its foreign producers were unable to deliver enough quantity to make a difference. As Morrison concluded:

> China was so much better organized than Sputnik. They had vast production capacity and vast marketing capacity. AstraZeneca and J&J both had their stumbles, but Russia really lost their opportunity. No one trusted them. They had serious reputational problems. They got outhustled by the Chinese.[119]

Did Russian officials know their extravagant estimates—such as the immunization of 700 million people outside Russia by the end of 2021—would be impossible to fulfill? Perhaps. In authoritarian systems, it is common for promises of success offered by (or wrung from) working-level officials to be quickly relayed to top policymakers, who cast them in stone. All those involved in the chain benefit from sending good news to the top, and the working level can always be blamed if something goes wrong. Without an aggressive press or truly independent regulators, those at the top have no reason to question what they are told.

There was also ambiguity about who was responsible for what. Gamaleya developed a product whose two-drug formula made for complicated production. Contractors hired to make the two drugs

---

[119] J. Stephen Morrison, interview with author, April 6, 2022.

The Sputnik Vaccine: From Breakthrough to Footnote | 163

stumbled due to a lack of equipment and personnel. The RDIF, which issued nonstop good news about Sputnik, had little experience with the complexities of drug production and marketing.

Astute Russian analysts know well their country's tendency to overpromise. A 2021 report from the National Research University Higher School of Economics argued that, in Russian relations with Africa, "intentions are often put forward as results, projects not yet agreed to are described as underway, and there is an overrating of our capabilities." The report said:

> An example is the delivery of Russian vaccines to Africa, when Russian exporters that had concluded contracts to supply Sputnik V to a series of African countries were unable to fulfill their obligations on time—and contracts were not concluded with the majority of countries where the vaccine was approved, again because of shortages.[120]

• **Russia failed to get sufficient outside help with production.** Moscow had tried for years to build up the utility of the BRICS economic bloc, made up of itself, Brazil, India, China, and South Africa, as a counterweight to Western economies. All BRICS members, except South Africa, had significant vaccine industries. At an online BRICS summit in November 2020, Putin pushed for the bloc to coalesce around Sputnik:

> There are Russian vaccines. They work. They work effectively and safely. The question is about carrying out mass production. This is not a problem, but this is the issue we face and, of

---

[120] Higher School of Economics, "Африка: перспективы развития и рекомендации для политики России [Africa: prospects for development and recommendations for Russian policy]," 2021, https://globalaffairs.ru/wp-content/uploads/2021/11/doklad_afrika_perspektivy-razvitiya.pdf

164 | HOW RUSSIA LOSES

course, it is very important here to produce this
product on a large scale for the general public.[121]

As it turned out, Brazilian and South African regulators were wary of Sputnik. Most of China's effort went into its own vaccines. India approved Sputnik for domestic use and manufactured it, but most of its own citizens were vaccinated with Covishield, the locally produced version of AstraZeneca.

Russia might have partnered with a major international vaccine-maker skilled in large-scale production and distribution, rather than basing its full production chain on plants inside Russia and individual contractors in a few countries. Most vaccine production is a coordinated international effort. "It's hard to brand a lot of vaccines as actually being 'from' one country or another," said Poitiers. "They may be conceived in one country, manufactured in another, and bottled and shipped from another." To truly compete with other vaccines, he continued, Russia needed to build a high-level relationship with international partners, share information, and "forget about autarky." Sputnik's marketers might at least have contracted with respected foreign consultants to manage their safety and effectiveness trials. This would have ended concerns about the data around Sputnik—though it would have required broad foreign access to Russia's laboratories and testing process.

If Russia had taken this road, Sputnik's development timeline might have allowed routine approval from the WHO by the first quarter of 2021—the same period in which Pfizer, AstraZeneca, and J&J received emergency authorization. Another adenovirus-based COVID vaccine was not an "earth-shattering development," Morrison said, and would not have raised concern in and of itself. Sputnik might also have been promoted without attacking products by other companies. Sputnik could then have entered the world market as a fully approved vaccine, officially recognized

---

[121] *RIA Novosti*, "Путин рассказал о планах по производству вакцины 'Спутник V' за рубежом [Putin talks about plans to produce 'Sputnik V' abroad]," November 17, 2020, https://ria.ru/20201117/vaktsiny-1585000663.html?ysclid=kzoorxi8l2

The Sputnik Vaccine: From Breakthrough to Footnote | 165

as the technical equal of major Western products had been marketed in an internationally acceptable way. "Everything would have been fine if there had not been all this hype and lack of transparency," asserted Ilya Yasny, a scientist at a Russian pharmaceutical investment fund.[122]

Russia would also have made more money. While Putin had talked to businesspeople about a $100 billion turnover, Sputnik's revenue was $2.74 billion in 2021 and was expected to reach $3.97 billion in 2022, according to Airfinity.[123] (Pfizer was the revenue leader, with $36.7 billion in 2021 and $37.8 billion in 2022.)[124]

• **Russia prioritized propaganda over producing a successful vaccine.** Co-production with a Western country would have saved more lives but ultimately undermined the propaganda value of a fully Russian vaccine. Russian scientists must have been aware that the world's scientific community would be put off by Moscow's registration of the vaccine after minimal trials, not to mention the belligerent tone of Russia's information assets. Flags would be raised that would lead to intense scrutiny of Sputnik when Gamaleya sought WHO and EMA approval.

However, the propaganda advantages to be gained by announcing the world's first vaccine were apparently too great for the Kremlin to pass up. What would lodge in the world's consciousness, top officials might have reasoned, was that Russia was a scientific superpower that had been first with a vaccine. Russia would be quick to deliver Sputnik to countries in need—in at least enough volume for some airport ceremonies. Perceptions of Russia's scientific power and concern for developing nations might be created even if Russia did not deliver significant

---

[122] "The Sputnik V vaccine and Russia's race to immunity," op. cit.

[123] Airfinity, "COVID-19 Vaccine Revenue Forecasts: 2022 revenue forecasts," January 21, 2022, https://assets.ctfassets. net/poihmvxzgivq/7rLG80qQCuV6C1EEFAqSRR/728370efe9eb6484d ef512e7cf3b7621/2022_Vaccine_Revenue_Forecast.pdf

[124] Pfizer revenue report at https://s28.q4cdn.com/781576035/ files/doc_financials/2022/q4/Q4-2022-PFE-Earnings-Release.pdf

166 | HOW RUSSIA LOSES

amounts of Sputnik never materialized. The vaccine could also be conscripted into Moscow's broader information operations. The bellicose tone of Russian propaganda around Sputnik perfectly matched that of Russian operators in other domains, attacking the West and trying to justify Moscow's actions internationally.

- **The Kremlin largely blew off international regulators.** Moscow might have decided that delays in WHO and EMA certification were an acceptable risk; Russia had little prospect of selling Sputnik to the EU or other advanced countries, at least in the long term, and no international approval was needed for bilateral deals with developing nations. In terms of propaganda, Russian information operators have long been drawn to narratives that paint Russia as a virtuous, compassionate nation, incessantly blocked and libeled by Western forces as acting out of geopolitical scheming and greed. Western-controlled vaccine regulators refusing to endorse lifesaving Sputnik fit that propaganda line deliciously.

Russia's ineligibility to join the COVAX distribution system was actually a plus. The principle of COVAX—though exceptions were eventually allowed—was that its administrators, not donors, would decide where the vaccines went. If Moscow stayed out of COVAX, it would have a completely free hand to target those countries it considered most important to its interests.

One significant cost of non-approval by regulators was that people around the world who were vaccinated only with Sputnik found it difficult to travel to major Western countries. Throughout the pandemic, many required arriving travelers to provide proof of immunization with an internationally approved vaccine. Such Western rules, Russian Foreign Ministry spokeswoman Maria Zakharova wrote on Facebook, amounted to "racism, imperial hegemony and neo-Nazism."[125]

---

[125] *Reuters*, "Moscow mayor says COVID-19 situation stabilising, but cases still high," July 8, 2021, https://www.reuters.com/world/europe/moscow-mayor-says-covid-19-situation-stabilising-cases-still-high-2021-07-08

The Sputnik Vaccine: From Breakthrough to Footnote | 167

Putin proposed in November 2021 that all nations allow "mutual recognition of vaccines and vaccine certificates"—a step that would have neutered the WHO and EMA and forced countries to accept travelers inoculated with vaccines approved anywhere.[126] The proposal went nowhere. Russians began to go to countries such as Croatia, Serbia, and Armenia, which they could enter easily, to receive Western vaccines—especially the single-shot J&J—that would let them travel more widely.[127]

• **Russia never established a profile as a major donor of free vaccines.** The doses of Sputnik that Russia did manage to distribute internationally were almost all sold, rather than donated to show Russian magnanimity. According to UNICEF, the biggest vaccine donor as of the end of 2022 was the United States, with 191 million doses donated directly and 502 million co-financed with COVAX. China donated 256 million doses. Russia donated 2.2 million doses of Sputnik to 23 countries, with the largest recipients being Mongolia, Sri Lanka, Belarus, and Syria.[128]

An alternative view of the whole Sputnik affair is that, despite all the excitement Russia tried to generate around the vaccine, it was actually not that important to the Kremlin. There was little indication that Putin made Sputnik a top national priority on the level of Trump's "Warp Speed." The Russian president may have seen Sputnik as a harmless, opportunistic venture that, if it did not save the world, might at least be helpful somewhere on the propaganda front. As Morrison said:

> I did not ever really feel that Putin had his whole heart in this enterprise. Like his disastrous

---

[126] "Путин выступил за создание процедуры признания вакцинации от COVID-19 [Putin calls for creating a procedure to recognize COVID-19 vaccination]," *RBC*, October 27, 2021, https://www.rbc.ru/rbcfreenews/61796d0c9a794720840c6d76
[127] "Le 'tourisme vaccinal' en plein essor chez les Russes, [Russians flock to 'vaccine tourism']," *Radio France Culture*, January 13, 2022, https://www.franceculture.fr/emissions/le-reportage-de-la-redaction/le-reportage-de-la-redaction-du-jeudi-13-janvier-2022
[128] https://www.unicef.org/supply/covid-19-market-dashboard

168 | HOW RUSSIA LOSES

> [2022] invasion of Ukraine, he had a grossly inflated notion of his capacities and discovered far too late what a flawed and irredeemable venture he had launched.

Putin might have calculated that if Sputnik worked at all reliably, it would at least spare Russia the embarrassment of having to import vaccines from the West or China. In that respect, it succeeded. Sputnik did pay some propaganda benefits, mainly when the West appeared to have abandoned the developing world and before Sputnik's manufacturing failures became obvious. Sputnik came on the scene as the Kremlin was punching back at Western claims that it had poisoned Alexei Navalny, that it was brutalizing Syrians, and that it had practically stamped out freedom of speech at home. If Sputnik had become a recognized vaccine widely used around the globe, it would have improved Russia's image. But a real boost to Sputnik required cooperation with international regulators, which Moscow seemed to have little interest in.

In fact, Moscow's approach to regulators was so careless as to suggest that a lack of international approval could have been part of Sputnik's strategy. With its global activities in many industrial and financial fields, Russia knows how to find lawyers and consultants who exquisitely understand how to get things done. Yet, Moscow made what appeared to be rookie mistakes in trying to push Sputnik through the regulatory process. In Europe, it uploaded documents to the wrong website and failed to create a required EU-based entity to formally submit its application. A former French official said that researchers from her country and others tried to coach Gamaleya on the regulatory approval process, but staff there did not engage.

Ultimately, Sputnik was little more than a footnote in the fight against COVID-19. Russian propaganda, aggressive as it was, could not make up for Moscow's inability to efficiently produce a scientifically credible product. It was Putin's good fortune that Sputnik injections did not prove ineffective or cause major side effects—though given its small and fragmented distribution, it was difficult to create a full picture of Sputnik's patient outcomes.

The Sputnik Vaccine: From Breakthrough to Footnote | 169

The overall story of Sputnik V was much like the story of Sputnik I, the first spacecraft to orbit the earth. The immediate effect of the launch was electric, capturing world headlines and raising fears that the West was hopelessly behind in conquering space. Twelve years later, when American astronauts landed on the moon, there was no question that Russia had lost the space race. In the case of the vaccines against COVID-19, there were many more players, and the timeframe was much more compressed. However, the story was similar: after a strong start, Russia's lead quickly faded. Russia's scientific prowess, its appetite for risk, and its skill in propaganda had been upended by bluster, overreach, and economic weakness.

Epilogue: Variants, Sanctions, and War

As new variants of COVID appeared in 2022 and health authorities began recommending booster shots, Sputnik's backers tried to breathe new life into their vaccine. They announced a nasally administered version and promoted "heterogeneous" vaccination—that is, strengthening a person's immunity to COVID by switching vaccines for a booster shot. Sputnik seized on reports that people who had received Chinese vaccines needed boosters and said the one-shot Sputnik Light "can become a solution." RDIF said Sputnik could be used as a booster for people who received an mRNA vaccine and that a new version of Sputnik to combat the Delta and Omicron variants had been developed.[129]

Some scientists, however, said Sputnik was weaker than mRNA vaccines against Omicron.[130] In June, *The New England Journal of Medicine* published a warning by Argentine and British

---

[129] RDIF press release, February 21, 2022, https://sputnikvaccine.com/newsroom/pressreleases/sputnik-light-can-become-a-major-booster-for-those-vaccinated-with-inactivated-chinese-covid-vaccine

[130] For example, see "Sinopharm, J&J, Sputnik Vaccines Are Weaker Against Omicron in New Study," *Bloomberg*, December 17, 2021, https://www.bloomberg.com/news/articles/2021-12-17/sinopharm-j-j-sputnik-shots-weaken-against-omicron-study-sees?sref=Y2tgfPTW

170 | HOW RUSSIA LOSES

researchers that Sputnik could cause the same kind of dangerous blood clots in rare cases as the AstraZeneca and J&J vaccines.[131]

Sputnik's publicity machine kept pumping out good news about the vaccine even after its use had declined sharply. When Argentina won the World Cup soccer tournament in December 2022, Sputnik's Telegram channel said:

> The largest number of all doses of the Russian vaccine 'Sputnik V' was exported to Argentina. Even the nation's president was vaccinated with 'Sputnik V.' Today the national team defeated France by penalty kicks and became world champion. Coincidence? We think not.[132]

(The post ignored the issue of whether Argentina's players were vaccinated with Sputnik; many play for teams in Western Europe, where Sputnik was generally unavailable.)

Russia's invasion of Ukraine in February 2022 administered a new blow to Sputnik. The United States and the European Union sanctioned the RDIF, and, although sanctions supposedly exempted humanitarian activity, anyone abroad still interested in the drug would have to wonder about its continued availability and how to pay for it. The US Treasury said the RDIF is "widely considered a slush fund for President Vladimir Putin and is emblematic of Russia's broader kleptocracy." The US also personally sanctioned Dmitriev, whom it called "a close associate of Putin."[133]

---

[131] Herrera-Comoglio, Raquel, "Vaccine-Induced Immune Thrombocytopenia and Thrombosis after the Sputnik V Vaccine," *The New England Journal of Medicine*, Oct. 13, *2022,* https://www.nejm.org/doi/full/10.1056/NEJMc2210813

[132] Sputnik V, Telegram, December 18, 2022.

[133] US Treasury, press release, February 28, 2022, https://home.treasury.gov/news/press-releases/jy0612. Russia denied the US claims. See RDIF, press release, February 28, 2022, https://sputnikvaccine.com/newsroom/pressreleases/rdif-statement-28

The Sputnik Vaccine: From Breakthrough to Footnote | 171

International regulators ceased their inspection trips to Russia, further delaying any possibility of WHO or EMA approval of the Russian vaccine.

172

4.

Nord Stream 2: So Near and Yet So Far

Few projects promised Russia as much geopolitical advantage as the Nord Stream 2 gas pipeline. The pipeline would run directly from Russia to Germany under the Baltic Sea, doubling the amount of natural gas Europe was receiving from the parallel Nord Stream 1 pipeline that opened in 2011. From the first discussions of Nord Stream 2 until the last of its 200,000 pipes were welded together in 2021, there was never a doubt that Nord Stream 2 would further cement Europe's energy dependence on the Kremlin.

Some in the West argued the pipeline was essential for Europe's growing gas needs. They pointed to decades of reliable gas supplies from Moscow to Europe, even at times of high political tension. Others said European gas use would decline, and the pipeline was not needed at all. They said the project's main value was to Russia, to further marginalize Ukraine in the short run and to blackmail Europe in the long. The more Europe depended on gas from Russia by any route, they believed, the easier it would be for Moscow to dominate Europe in a crisis by threatening to turn off the taps.

Russia always proclaimed the same public position on Nord Stream 2: that whatever happened in the world, Moscow would be a rock-solid energy supplier. Any assertions to the contrary, it claimed, amounted to "Russophobia" and a betrayal of Europe's own interests. For a decade, the argument worked. Backed by the German government of Angela Merkel, a host of well-placed

174 | HOW RUSSIA LOSES

lobbyists, and some of the most powerful energy companies in Europe, Russia largely succeeded in insulating the Nord Stream 2 project from other East-West tensions.

Yet Russia failed to appreciate the power of public opinion, the meticulousness of European institutions and regulators, the worries of some Western governments, and the potential for sudden political change inside Germany. Russia's aggressive behavior at home and abroad, including its nonstop threats against Ukraine and the imprisonment of Alexei Navalny, eventually chipped away at the pipeline's political invulnerability. Another blow came from the European Green Deal, adopted in 2020, which committed the European Union to significantly reduce the use of hydrocarbons.

Delays by Denmark over the pipeline's route, along with sanctions by the United States, put Nord Stream 2 behind schedule by two years. By the time it was completed, Germany's government coalition had changed, with a powerful role for the anti-pipeline Greens. German and European regulators tied a legal web around the pipeline, drawing Gazprom into a bureaucratic nightmare. Further legal trouble, fueled by environmentalists as well as Central and East European nations, waited in the wings. Ultimately, the pipeline lost its political invulnerability entirely. On the eve of Russia's invasion of Ukraine, Germany's new government withdrew an essential permit for Nord Stream 2, all but sealing the fate of the mega-project.

In September 2022, explosions destroyed at least part of Nord Stream 2, along with sections of Nord Stream 1. Even before the blasts, however, many expected that Nord Stream 2 would remain, literally, dead in the water so long as Putin remained in power. Even after Putin, there may never be a need to repair and open the €9.5 billion Nord Stream 2, as Europe steadily becomes independent of Russian hydrocarbons.

Russia's Blue Gold

Natural gas is one of the world's most versatile fuels. It can be found by itself in underground rock formations, or along with coal or oil deposits. Homes use gas for cooking, heating, and cooling. Gas generates electricity more cleanly than oil, at a price similar to coal. The chemical components of gas can be separated out to produce fertilizers, pharmaceuticals, plastics, and fabrics. Gas powers motor vehicles with less pollution than gasoline or diesel. Gas can be reliably transported over long distances by pipeline or liquefied for shipment by sea. Despite its advantages, however, gas is a non-renewable hydrocarbon that contributes to global warming. It is a greenhouse gas itself, discharging carbon dioxide into the atmosphere when burned.

The Soviet Union was rich in natural gas, as Russia is today. The Soviets began exporting gas in the mid-1960s, delivering supplies to Poland, Czechoslovakia, and Austria from fields in Ukraine. The Soviets, however, lacked the technology to build large-diameter pipes to expand their export network. In 1959, after the United States and its allies removed pipeline tubes from their CoCom export restrictions, West Germany began rapidly exporting pipes to the Soviet Union.

The US forced a halt to the shipments in 1962 after the Cuban Missile Crisis and the construction of the Berlin Wall. By 1970, however, Washington had relaxed its position, and West Germany signed a major deal with Moscow known as "gas for pipes." In return for pipes to expand Russia's export network, Germany obtained a 20-year contract for 3 billion cubic meters (bcm) of gas per year. Thousands of East Germans worked on installing the pipes in Ukraine, and gas began flowing in 1973. Deliveries to Finland began in 1974. And in 1975, Germany and other West European countries contracted with the Soviet Union to pipe them gas from Iran.

The 1973 OPEC oil embargo, followed by Iran's Islamic Revolution in 1979, increased European interest in gas and oil from the Soviet Union. Moscow proposed a new pipeline from the Urengoy field in Siberia, also running through Ukraine and known as the Urengoy–Pomary–Uzhhorod project. Not only did the Kremlin seem to be a more reliable supplier to Europeans than the Middle East or North Africa, but the Soviets were looking to Western companies to produce many of the pipeline's

176 | HOW RUSSIA LOSES

components. Europe was in recession in the early 1980s, with unemployment around 8 percent in major economies. The pipeline promised big orders for steel, pipes, compressor stations, and turbines. Companies in West Germany and Britain said the project could generate more than 5,000 jobs. A French engineering group said it could occupy up to half the employees in many of its factories. European banks offered Moscow generous financing for the $10 billion enterprise, much of it to be repaid with gas.[1]

Negotiations for the project began in 1980 but once again ran into resistance from Washington. Tensions between the West and the Soviet Union had been soaring over intermediate nuclear missiles in Europe and the 1979 Soviet invasion of Afghanistan, which led to US sanctions and a boycott of the 1980 Moscow Olympics. In 1981, Poland's Soviet-backed government imposed martial law in an attempt to stop the Solidarity movement. Ronald Reagan, who became president that year, argued that the new pipeline would provide money for Moscow to spend on its military and subject Western Europe to energy blackmail if Moscow ever turned off the gas. Western experts estimated that with the new pipeline, Russia would supply 30 percent of Germany's gas, 32 percent of France's, 35 percent of Italy's needs, and 24 percent of Spain's.[2]

Reagan ordered sanctions against the use of American equipment or technology for the project. Under pressure from US companies that also stood to profit, as well as from European leaders including Margaret Thatcher, he lifted the sanctions in November 1982, four days after the death of Soviet leader Leonid Brezhnev. The pipeline was completed two years later.

The easy availability of Russian gas induced Europe to reduce its own energy extraction. EU nations began to shut down their coal industries to reduce greenhouse emissions. Several nations decided to phase out nuclear power as well. After the Fukushima

---

[1] Lewis, Paul, "A Soviet Project Tempts Europe," *The New York Times*, May 30, 1982, https://www.nytimes.com/1982/05/30/business/a-soviet-project-tempts-europe.html
[2] Ibid.

nuclear disaster in Japan in 2011, Chancellor Angela Merkel decided to speed up the end of nuclear power in Germany, setting full shutdown for 2022.[3] Europe's own gas production was in decline with the depletion of Britain's North Sea and Dutch gas fields. By 2021, Russia was supplying 40 percent of Europe's gas, including 55 percent of Germany's supply.

Meanwhile, Western energy companies became increasingly involved in profitable deals with Russia's energy industry. BP, Shell, and others set up joint production and technology ventures to extract oil and gas in and outside of Russia. Russian state gas company Gazprom, in turn, gained interests in West European gas production, marketing, and storage. By the time Russia invaded Ukraine in 2022, Russian interests owned Germany's biggest gas storage facility, a majority stake in the nation's most important gas transportation company, and an oil refinery that served Berlin.[4]

Russia's poor relations with Ukraine, however, complicated the gas picture for Moscow. Most Russian gas arrived in Europe through pipelines in Ukraine. After Ukraine's independence in 1991, Moscow's relations with Kyiv went through a series of political crises. Russia, alarmed by Ukraine's 2004–2005 Orange Revolution and its talk of joining the EU and NATO, steadily increased political and economic pressure on Kyiv. These tensions aggravated the two nations' quarrels over the price of Russian gas for Ukrainian customers and the fees Ukraine charged to feed its gas to Europe. "For Russia, relying on Ukraine [to transmit gas] was as dangerous as Germany relying on Russia," said Karel Svoboda, an energy expert at Charles University in Prague.[5] The disputes between Moscow and Kyiv led Russia to shut off the flow of gas to Ukraine for several days in

---

[3] After Russia's invasion of Ukraine, the shutdown was delayed. All generation of electricity from nuclear power ceased in April 2023..
[4] Morris, Loveday, et al, "Flow of Russian gas and cash entangled German state in dependent web," *The Washington Post*, November 23, 2022, https://www.washingtonpost.com/world/2022/11/23/germany-gas-russia-dependence
[5] Karel Svoboda, interview with author, May 40, 2022.

178 | HOW RUSSIA LOSES

2006 and two weeks in 2009, thereby stopping supplies to European customers. (Ukraine prefers the wording, "Russia shut off the flow of gas to Europe.") The cutoffs forced gas rationing and factory shutdowns in Slovakia and the Balkans, as well as a heating crisis in Poland.

Nord Stream 1: 'A Secure, Resilient Partnership'

It soon became a priority for Russia to find ways to route gas to Europe other than through Ukraine. To that end, Moscow engaged in a massive project to rewire its entire system of gas transmission to the West. In 1999, the Yamal-Europe pipeline had opened, bringing gas from fields in Russia's northern Yamal Peninsula to Poland and Germany via Belarus. The Blue Stream pipeline, opened in 2005, routed gas to Turkey. Turk Stream, inaugurated in 2020, ran through Turkey and served customers in Greece, Bulgaria, Serbia, and Hungary. In a rare setback, Russia's South Stream pipeline project, which was to bring gas to southern Europe under the Black Sea, failed in 2014 due to European regulations. Nevertheless, Russia remained intent on finding any opportunity to route gas around Ukraine.

On September 8, 2005, Russian President Vladimir Putin and German Chancellor Gerhard Schröder presided over the signing of a letter of intent for a huge project that had been under discussion since the late 1990s: a direct pipeline from Russia to Germany that would run for 760 miles under the Baltic Sea. The €7.4 billion project, which opened in 2011 and became known as Nord Stream 1, was in fact a pair of pipes with a combined capacity of 55 bcm per year that run from Vyborg near Russia's Finnish border to the northern German town of Lubmin.

The project saved fees for shipping gas across other countries' territories and provided a gas route free from potential interference from any other country. Gazprom owns 51 percent of the Nord Stream 1 project, with the remainder belonging to energy companies E.ON and Wintershall Dea of Germany, Gasunie of the Netherlands, and France's ENGIE.

Nord Stream 2: So Near and Yet So Far | 179

When it was proposed, Nord Stream 1 revived all the past fears about the political dangers of depending on Russian gas. "I wonder as a US official how much diversification anybody can develop by having more pipelines into the same supplier," State Department official Matthew Bryza said at the time.[6] Ukraine protested Nord Stream 1, and Poland's defense minister compared the deal to the 1939 Molotov-Ribbentrop pact.[7] Some feared that a platform to be built in Swedish waters for pipeline maintenance could be used for Russian espionage.

EU Energy Commissioner Andris Piebalgs chided Germany for not consulting its neighbors on the project. "We should never have the situation we will with this pipeline, where one partner country decided a project that is not acceptable to others, not even discussing it," he said.[8] The EU announced new intentions to increase the diversity of gas supplies, but little came of them.

Through it all, Germany took the position that the pipeline was purely a commercial proposition (though Gazprom had been totally controlled by the Russian state since 2005). Any risk involved, Berlin felt, was primarily a financial one for European companies that invested in the project.

Schröder was succeeded as chancellor in November 2005 by Angela Merkel. Many considered Merkel and her Christian Democratic Union party clear-eyed about the possibility of Russian energy blackmail. The first years of Merkel's chancellorship saw Putin's landmark denunciation of the West at the 2007 Munich Security Conference and his 2008 invasion of Georgia. Still, she allowed the project to proceed. German industry

---

[6] Daniel Dombey et al., "US criticizes Russia-Germany gas deal," *Financial Times*, October 29, 2006, https://www.ft.com/content/50e6faec-6779-11db-8ea5-0000779e2340

[7] Castle, Stephen, "Poles angry at pipeline pact," *Independent*, May 1, 2006, https://www.independent.co.uk/news/world/europe/poles-angry-at-pipeline-pact-6102171.html

[8] Beunderman, Mark, "Poland compares German-Russian pipeline to Nazi-Soviet pact," *EUobserver*, May 2, 2006, https://euobserver.com/world/21486

180 | HOW RUSSIA LOSES

strongly favored the pipeline, as did Schröder's Social Democratic Party, an essential part of Merkel's "grand coalition" in the Bundestag.

The pipeline was also a job-creator for the state of Mecklenburg-Western Pomerania, formerly part of East Germany and home to Merkel's own electoral district. Many people there still held affection for Russia and the orderly, if authoritarian, days of the German Democratic Republic. Officially speaking, the EU was still in favor of cooperation with Russia; an EU paper designed to guide the bloc's relations with Russia for 2007–2013 spoke of building a "strategic partnership" with Moscow.[9]

"Merkel never had any love for Putin. She knew who he was," said Jeffrey Rathke, president of the American Institute for Contemporary German Studies at Johns Hopkins University. "She was aware Russia wanted to peel back as much of the European security order as it could. She was trying to make the best of a situation that was not ideal for Germany: that there was a strong belief, and perception in the public eye, that a good relationship with Russia had been a force for stability, and had been in Germany's interest, for decades."[10]

Merkel's position was indeed consistent with long-standing German policy. During and after the Cold War, successive German governments insisted that mutual respect and commerce were the best ways to inspire constructive behavior by Russia at home and abroad. A series of chancellors, starting with Willy Brandt and his *Ostpolitik* in 1969, sought to forge "special relationships" with the Soviet Union. This official attitude played well with Germany's substantial pacifist community, whose slogan was *Waffen bringen kein Frieden,* or "weapons don't bring peace." Brandt oversaw the pipes-for-gas deal, Helmut Kohl had warm ties with Mikhail Gorbachev and Boris Yeltsin, and Schröder went so far as to call Putin a "flawless democrat." After the Soviet collapse, Germany's

---

[9] "Country Strategy Paper 2007-2013: Russian Federation," European Union, https://eeas.europa.eu/archives/docs/russia/docs/2007-2013_en.pdf
[10] Jeffrey Rathke, interview with author, September 15, 2022.

philosophy toward Russia, often summarized during the Cold War as *Wandel durch Annäherung* ("change through rapprochement"), evolved to a much closer *Annäherung durch Verflechtung* ("rapprochement through interdependence").

Such attitudes in Germany had long rankled US officials, who thought the nation with Western Europe's strongest economy should be one of the wariest toward Moscow. They worried that the constant contacts and exchanges involved in *Ostpolitik* allowed Russia to build a web of connections, institutions, and agents across Germany that could jeopardize its faithfulness to NATO. German politicians responded that their country's relationship with Moscow was not a liability to the Western alliance but a plus—a tool to guarantee peace.

Helmut Schmidt, chancellor from 1974 to 1982, referred to Germany as an "interpreter" between Washington and Moscow, implying that Germany occupied some kind of space between the two superpowers and could prevent misunderstandings and worse between them.[11] Americans worried that such language telegraphed an attitude, on the part of both Germans and Russians, that they needed to jointly strive to keep America's obstreperous instincts under control.

Indeed, for decades, many in Germany had seen Washington as overly aggressive toward Moscow—during the Cold War, when hundreds of thousands of Germans demonstrated against new US missiles in Europe, and after the Soviet collapse, when the United States emerged as the world's sole superpower. Some Germans saw parallels between the humiliation of Germany by the Allies at the end of World War I and American triumphalism over Russia after the disintegration of the Soviet Union. The diplomatic history of German states and Russia began long before the United States even existed. Washington, many Germans feared, was provoking Russia from across the Atlantic with little understanding of the realities of Russia's immutable importance on the European continent.

---

[11] At the same time, Schmidt supported the deployment of US medium-range nuclear missiles in Europe.

182 | HOW RUSSIA LOSES

Pipe-laying under the Baltic for Nord Stream 1 started in 2010. The first conduit began operation on November 8, 2011, following a ceremony in Germany with Merkel and then–Russian President Dmitry Medvedev. Merkel declared that the project promised "a secure, resilient partnership with Russia in the future."[12] When gas began to flow through Nord Stream's second conduit in late 2012, Russia began reducing gas transmission through Ukraine and Poland. In 2009-2011, 60 to 70 percent of Russian gas sent to Europe transited Ukraine; by 2013-2014, this had fallen to 40 percent.[13]

Nord Stream 2: Security or Vulnerability?

In 2011, active discussions began about adding a second pair of pipelines to Nord Stream, a project to be known as Nord Stream 2. This line would start from Ust-Luga, located between St. Petersburg and the Estonian border, then run parallel to the first Nord Stream pipelines along the Baltic seabed and terminate alongside Nord Stream 1 at Lubmin. Like Nord Stream 1, the two channels of Nord Stream 2 would have an annual total capacity of 55 bcm.

However, by the time construction of Nord Stream 2 began in 2018, many things had changed since the time of Nord Stream 1. The legal landscape was one such area. EU institutions had begun to take a much stronger role in regulating European energy, meaning the new project would not simply be based on agreements between Russia and Germany. Berlin and Brussels had already sparred over regulatory issues involving Nord Stream 1. That pipeline fed into the newly constructed Opal pipeline, which routed gas from Lubmin to the Czech border.

---

[12] Text at https://www.bundesregierung.de/breg-de/service/bulletin/rede-von-bundeskanzlerin-dr-angela-merkel-802270

[13] Aurélie Bros, "There Will be Gas: Gazprom's Transport Strategy in Europe," Institut français des relations internationales, October 2015, https://www.ifri.org/sites/default/files/atoms/files/ifri_rnr_21_eng_aurelie_bros_october_2015.pdf.

Nord Stream 2: So Near and Yet So Far | 183

Germany wanted to give Gazprom full use of the pipeline; the European Union, concerned about monopoly control of Opal by just one company, authorized Gazprom to use only half of the pipeline's capacity. Such disputes could affect Nord Stream 2 even more due to the EU's growing authority.

The economic picture had also changed. The need for Nord Stream 2 depended greatly on forecasts of Europe's future demand for gas. Proponents of the project argued that the EU's gas consumption, which ranged between 380 and 450 bcm in the 2010s, was certain to rise.[14] Gazprom estimated in 2013 that European countries would consume 700 bcm in 2020.[15] Russia's capacity for gas transmission to Europe at the time totaled about 245 bcm.[16] Given Europe's falling gas production, it seemed obvious that, if Gazprom's estimates were right, Europe could use all 55 bcm of Russian gas that the new Nord Stream 2 could provide—and much more.

Gazprom's bullish forecasts, however, ignored the fact that Europe was moving to conserve its use of energy and develop power sources with less environmental impact than hydrocarbons. By 2021, Europe's gas consumption was about 490 bcm.[17] Nord Stream 2 backers tried to leverage Europe's

---

[14] EU consumption statistics from Eurostat: https://ec.europa.eu/eurostat/databrowser/view/NRG_CB_GAS_custom_3280796/default/table?lang=en.

[15] " 'Южный Поток' - гарантия будущей энергетической безопасности Европы ['South Stream' - Guarantee of the future of Europe's energy security]," Gazprom, archived March 7, 2013, https://web.archive.org/web/20210410175343/https://www.gazprom.ru/f/posts/88/600522/south_stream_spb.pdf

[16] This included pipelines running through Ukraine. See Kardaś, Szymon, "Gas business as usual? The new agreements between Gazprom and EU energy companies," Centre for Eastern Studies, https://www.osw.waw.pl/en/publikacje/analyses/2015-09-09/gas-business-usual-new-agreements-between-gazprom-and-eu-energy

[17] Figure based on Eurostat calculation of EU consumption of 413 bcm at https://ec.europa.eu/eurostat/databrowser/view/NRG_CB_GASM_custom_5672433/default/table?lang=en, and consumption of 78.5 BCM reported by UK government at https://assets.publishing.

184 | HOW RUSSIA LOSES

environmental consciousness by arguing that natural gas was cleaner than oil or coal and would support an orderly transition to fully green energy. They noted as well that natural gas could be converted in Europe or Russia to hydrogen gas, a clean fuel favored by Brussels. However, hydrogen gas can also be made from renewable sources instead of natural gas, with less damage to the environment.

As for political risk, Nord Stream 2 supporters continued to deride claims that dependence on Russian gas was politically dangerous. Russia depended on gas revenues as much as Europe depended on gas supplies, they said, and the Kremlin would do nothing to jeopardize its income. (Half of Russia's gas exports went to Europe.) Russian gas would be even more dependable, they added, if delivery depended less on Ukraine—whose pipeline system, they claimed, was a leaky mess that might, at any moment, break down or explode in flames.[18]

Another guarantor of Europe's energy security, pipeline backers said, was that Europe's huge gas consumption would always guarantee market alternatives. The whole world would compete to serve Europe if Russian supplies disappeared. Pipelines had already been constructed to bring gas to Europe from Azerbaijan. The Baltic Pipe project, to begin operation in 2022, would supply Norwegian gas to Denmark, Poland, and their neighbors. Liquefied national gas (LNG) was always available from the US and the Middle East. It was just that, from an economic standpoint, Nord Stream 2 was the bargain option—a brand new pipeline, as reliable as its twin, that offered immediate cost

---

service.gov.uk/government/uploads/system/uploads/attachment_dat a/file/1147110/ET_4.1_MAR_23.xlsx#:~:text=Gas%20consumption%2 0decreased%20by%2013,well%20as%20higher%20gas%20prices

[18] Putin himself made a point of the Ukrainian networks' supposed decrepitude. In October 2021 he said, "They haven't repaired the gas transmission there for decades and if the pressure is increased there [to carry more gas], it could just burst, and Europe will be totally deprived of this route." Text at http://www.kremlin.ru/events/ president/news/page/77

savings because no fees had to be paid to transit countries or shipping vessels.

Opponents of Nord Stream 2 bought none of these arguments. First, they said Russia did have a history of using energy pressure for political ends, including against the EU.[19] Second, the existing 245 bcm pipeline capacity from Russia was sufficient for Europe's needs, given its success in conserving energy and transition to green sources. Third, as Europe's demand for gas fell, alternative suppliers would have less motivation to compete with Gazprom. Europe could not instantly modify its sources of supply, meaning Gazprom could raise prices or indeed engage in energy blackmail whenever it wished. Fourth, the pipeline would stall, rather than ease, Europe's green energy transition: if cheap gas flowed reliably from Russia, there would be less incentive for Europe to move to more sustainable energy sources.

As for the cost savings that Nord Stream 2 would supposedly provide, any such calculation would have to take into account the costs of Nord Stream 2's construction and how much money would actually be saved on transit fees over several decades. Nord Stream 2 might lead to profitable future deals with Russia for the energy companies involved, but that was apart from any public value from Nord Stream 2 itself. "There was no economic necessity for Nord Stream 2, not at any point," said Claudia Müller, a pipeline opponent in the Bundestag from the Greens. "It was economical only if Ukraine was not to be used any more. We needed gas to replace coal, but that didn't mean we needed more

---

[19] For examples, see Larsson, Robert L., "Nord Stream Sweden and Baltic Sea Security," Swedish Defence Research Agency, March 2007, https://inis.iaea.org/collection/NCLCollectionStore/_Public/39/015/3 9015071.pdf. The report was issued before the 2009 interruptions to Ukraine and Gazprom's reduction of supplies to the EU between October 2014 and March 2015—possibly to show displeasure over reverse flows of gas from the EU to Ukraine. See also Bros, Aurélie, "German-Russian Gas Relations," German Institute for International and Security Affairs, December 2017, https://www.swp-berlin.org/publications/products/research_papers/2017RP13_wep_EtAl.pdf

186 | HOW RUSSIA LOSES

gas overall."[20] The German Institute for Economic Research published a searing paper in 2018 calling Nord Stream 2 "superfluous":

> Nord Stream 2 is not a profitable investment project. From a business perspective, it therefore appears highly questionable. The project operator's profitability calculations are probably based on implausibly high assumptions for natural gas consumption and market prices. However, the facts are unclear due to the lack of transparency of the calculations. ... The planned second Baltic Sea pipeline is not necessary to secure the natural gas supply in Germany and Europe. Rather, it is to be feared that its construction will hinder the energy transition towards a complete decarbonization of the economic system in Germany and Europe.[21]

The pipeline's critics argued that Nord Stream 2 would bring Europe exactly the same molecules of Russian gas it was already getting through existing pipelines, but through an expensive new route whose sole purpose was to help Russian bully Ukraine.[22] The trouble with gas transmission through Ukraine, they said, was not really about transmission issues or transit fees, but rather Russia's vendetta against the government in Kyiv. The timing of Russia's pipeline deals seemed suspiciously related to its frustrations with Ukraine: Moscow signed the Nord Stream 1

---

[20] Claudia Müller, interview with author, June 10, 2022.

[21] "Erdgasversorgung: Weitere Ostsee-Pipeline ist überflüssig [Natural gas supply: Additional Baltic Sea pipeline is superfluous]," German Institute for Economic Research, 2018, https://www.diw.de/%20documents/publikationen/73/diw_01.c.593445.de/18-27-1.pdf

[22] Gazprom's intent was no secret. Its CEO said in 2016 that, once Nord Stream 2 began operation, Russian gas transit through Ukraine would fall steeply. Zhdannikov, Dmitry, "Gazprom warns of steep gas transit cuts via Ukraine after 2020," *Reuters*, June 16, 2016, https://www.reuters.com/article/us-gazprom-exports-ukraine/gazprom-warns-of-steep-gas-transit-cuts-via-ukraine-after-2020-idUSKCN0Z20YR

contract with Germany eight months after Russian authorities were alarmed by Ukraine's people-power Orange Revolution; the Turk Stream deal came ten months after the Maidan uprising; and the Nord Stream 2 contract was signed as pro-Russian and Ukrainian forces dueled in Donbas. "It was crystal clear that Nord Stream 2 meant throwing Ukraine under the bus," said Polish energy analyst Bartosz Bieliszczuk.[23]

Nord Stream 2 opponents said Ukraine's pipelines were old but replete with backup routes and excess capacity.[24] The Ukrainian system also had storage capacity that the point-to-point Nord Stream pipelines lacked. Fixing whatever Ukrainian facilities needed repair would be far cheaper than a whole new pipeline, and the EU and Western financial institutions were already at work updating Ukraine's pipeline infrastructure.

It was not even clear that the pipeline would make money for Gazprom. Alex Fak, an analyst for Russian state-controlled Sberbank, was reportedly fired in 2018 after he co-authored a report that called Nord Stream 2 and two other pipeline projects "deeply value-destructive" to Gazprom. He estimated Nord Stream 2's internal rate of return to the company, a measure of profitability, at only 3 percent. Gazprom, he calculated, would not recoup its investment in the pipeline for 20 years.[25] Many critics also found Gazprom itself a thoroughly unsavory business partner for Europe, less of a commercial enterprise than a machine to advance Russian foreign policy interests and shuffle money to Russian elites. (As a sign of its fealty to the state,

---

[23] Bartosz Bieliszczuk, interview with author, May 17, 2022.

[24] In 2017, Ukraine transported about 93 bcm of Russian gas through its system, compared to a system capacity of more than 140 bcm.

[25] Fak assumed Nord Stream 2 would run at 60 percent of capacity, and that gas would also continue to flow through Ukraine. For Fak's firing, see *Bne IntelliNews*, "Sberbank oil analyst Alex Fak fired for being openly critical of state-owned gas giant Gazprom," May 23, 2018, https://www.intellinews.com/sberbank-oil-analyst-alex-fak-fired-for-being-openly-critical-of-state-owned-gas-giant-gazprom-142134. For his report, see "Russian Oil and Gas: Tickling Giants," Sberbank CIB, May 2018, https://globalstocks.ru/wp-content/uploads/2018/05/Sberbank-CIB-OG_Tickling-Giants.pdf

188 | HOW RUSSIA LOSES

Gazprom bolstered Russia's 2022 invasion of Ukraine by financing front-line units formed from its own security guards.[26])

Finally, critics said, Nord Stream 2 would deal a new blow to Ukraine, just after Crimea and much of the Donbas region had been seized by Russia and its allies. Ukraine needed the $2 billion a year Russia paid it in transit fees, which came close to 2 percent of Ukrainian GDP. Kyiv feared that, if Russia had no more need for its pipelines, Moscow would find it easier to intimidate Ukraine and attack it again.

Still, Nord Stream 2 moved forward. A shareholders' agreement on the project was signed at an energy conference in Vladivostok on September 4, 2015. Nord Stream 2 was to be 51-percent owned by Gazprom and the rest by E.ON, Wintershall Dea, ENGIE, and Royal Dutch Shell.[27] Nearly 30 financial institutions agreed to provide credit for the project's costs, which were initially estimated at €9.5 billion. Construction began in May 2018 from the German end, with the partners expecting completion by 2019.

Given the huge gulf between opposing views of the project's technical and economic merits, the debate over Nord Stream 2 increasingly defaulted to the political. Putin's invasion of Ukraine in 2014 had led the EU to enact sanctions on Moscow and pledge once again to diversify its energy sources. Nord Stream 2 was the opposite of energy diversification. It also meant partnering on a new mega-project with a regime that was growing increasingly authoritarian at home and had seized territory from both Ukraine and Georgia. Nord Stream 1 and 2 would lock Europe and Russia together for an "infrastructure generation," a period of 30 or 40

---

[26] Ivanova, Polina et al., " 'Stream' and 'Torch': the Gazprom-backed militias fighting in Ukraine," *Financial Times,* June 2, 2022, https://www.ft.com/content/4dd0aa0a-4b37-4082-8db0-0b969c539677

[27] Regulators in Poland forced a restructuring of the project in 2017 by threatening action against those European energy companies involved that also had operations in Poland. Gazprom became the sole owner-operator of Nord Stream 2, and the European companies became investors. (Austria's OMV energy company joined the European companies involved in 2015.)

Nord Stream 2: So Near and Yet So Far | 189

years in which Moscow's policy could make many unpredictable turns.

The political argument in favor of Nord Stream 2 was based on the idea that, however distasteful Putin's policies might be, Europe's greatest interest was to live harmoniously with Russia. The risks of living in Russia's shadow could not be mitigated; the risk of depending on the transmission of gas through Ukraine could. If Russia was intent on bullying Ukraine, perhaps it was wiser to do deals with the bully than line up with the victim. Great swaths of Eastern Europe, including most of Ukraine, had changed hands almost routinely throughout history with minimal impact outside the region; in contrast, Germany and Russia were enduring centers of power that had to remain in balance to avoid disaster. Some German officials, Rathke said, seemed to proceed from the concept that Ukraine was. at root, an unreliable and corrupt country. Russia—in Germany's postwar experience—had been a reliable partner.

At an Atlantic Council seminar in April 2016, Friedbert Pflüger, an energy lobbyist and former Bundestag member, cast the question in terms of accepting the reality of Russia while maximizing the benefits the relationship offered. Germany's major political parties, he said, had always been strong Atlanticists. He added, however:

> But we have also understood that Russia is there and will remain to be there. And most probably Mr. Putin, too. So we can of course have hundreds of arguments about why we don't like Gazprom, or why we don't like Russia and its human rights record and so on. But it is there. It's a reality. And it has nuclear weapons, and it is ambitious. So we have to find some sort of accommodation with the Russians. ... And if it is smart in the present situation—I'm just talking geopolitics right now—in the present situation with all these tensions, to tell the Russians that—especially in the field that has worked, at least from the Western European perspective, very reliable

> through the Cold War, a reliable flow of energy—
> that especially here we want to jump in and have
> a new source of tensions, is another question. I
> think this would be a grave mistake.[28]

If Europe turned down Nord Stream 2 for political reasons, pipeline supporters said, then both sides would be equally guilty of basing energy decisions on politics. Supporters also argued that US objections to the pipeline went far beyond solicitude for European security: the US, flush with oil and gas from fracking, would benefit commercially if Europe started freezing out Russian gas. Some even asked whether opposition to Nord Stream 2 was a too-little-too-late attempt by Washington to regain respect after having failed to help Ukraine when Russia was seizing its territory in 2014.

Some pipeline supporters went so far as to argue that stopping the transmission of gas through Ukraine would actually benefit Kyiv. The transport of Russian gas to Europe kept Ukraine's economy entangled with Russia's, and the huge sums of money involved fed corruption in both countries. Kyiv, the argument went, would do well to rid itself of this whole relationship with a hostile state and focus on developing energy sources of its own. (Ukraine had promising gas drilling operations in the Black Sea near Crimea until Russia seized them as part of its annexation of the peninsula.)

If Russia sought to convince Europeans that it was a benign, friendly country, its behavior during the key years of the Nord Stream 2 debate seemed aimed in the opposite direction. Russia threw planes, troops, and mercenaries into Syria's civil war, drawing condemnation from the EU, which said Russian forces might have committed war crimes through their involvement in poison gas attacks. Artillery duels continued daily between Russia's allies in Donbas and Ukrainian forces. The 2014 and 2015 Minsk I and II Agreements and the Normandy Format, painstaking diplomatic efforts pursued by the US, France, and

---

[28] For video, see https://www.atlanticcouncil.org/unused/webcasts/ nord-stream-2-is-it-a-threat-to-european-energy-security

Nord Stream 2: So Near and Yet So Far | 191

Germany to involve Russia in resolving the Ukrainian crisis, failed. The Kremlin was widely accused of interfering in the 2017 French and German elections, much as it had in the 2016 US election. In 2018, Russian agents poisoned former spy Sergei Skripal and his daughter in the UK with the nerve agent Novichok, sparking outrage across Europe.

Moscow also seemed to go out of its way to provoke Merkel's government, despite Germany's long history of friendship with Russia and the importance of Nord Stream 2. In 2015, operatives believed to be from the Russian APT28 group hacked their way into the Bundestag's internal computer network. The following year, Russian media played on German domestic tensions over migrants with a fake story about Lisa, a 13-year-old Russian-German girl who allegedly was raped by foreigners seeking asylum in Germany. In 2017, Siemens sharply reduced its operations in Russia after two gas turbines, manufactured by the company for a plant in southern Russia, were diverted by Russia to Crimea in violation of EU sanctions. In 2018, a dissident Chechen separatist, Zelimkhan Khangoshvili, was shot to death in broad daylight less than two miles from Merkel's office; German prosecutors said it was a hit ordered by Moscow.

As Germany's September 2021 elections approached, *RT*'s German-language service, which had become one of the most prominent media outlets in the country, promoted anti-vax conspiracies and the right-wing Alternative für Deutschland party. Right before the election, Russian cyber operators sent a wave of phishing emails to German lawmakers in a new hacking attempt, leading to a German demand to Russia "in all urgency to end this unacceptable cyber activity immediately."[29]

As Moscow likely had anticipated, the official German reaction to Russia's provocations rarely went beyond public statements and an occasional diplomatic expulsion. "The broad dependency on

---

[29] Donahue, Patrick, "Germans See Russian Meddling in Tight Election Intensifying," *Bloomberg*, September 17, 2021, https://www.bloomberg.com/news/articles/2021-09-17/germans-see-russian-meddling-in-tight-election-intensifying?sref=Y2tgfPTW

Russia in Germany made it more difficult to react to these things," said Sascha Müller-Kraenner, CEO of Environmental Action Germany, which fought the pipeline. "The government was thinking, 'Next week we have this meeting with them on Iran. We need them for Syria. We need them for stability in Donbas.' " Russian propaganda in Germany, he said, had worked hard to sow "seeds of doubt" over whether Moscow was truly responsible for malign acts it allegedly committed. "A significant part of the public debate has always been whether or not Russia was really behind these things or not," Müller-Kraenner said.

Another reason Germany did not respond more forcefully to Russia's actions may have been its mistrust of Donald Trump. With Trump's electoral win in 2016, many European leaders wondered if the United States would be there if they wound up in a crisis with the Kremlin. Trump questioned the whole basis of NATO and took an abrasive attitude toward Europe in general. He sparred with leaders there about steel and auto imports, the Paris climate agreement, the Iran nuclear deal, and COVID lockdowns.

He bullied Merkel at a 2018 NATO conference for not contributing enough to Europe's defense, and later announced the United States would withdraw a quarter of its forces in Germany—reportedly without even consulting Berlin. As Europe debated the best way to help Ukraine, Trump declared that Ukraine was a "very corrupt" country and pressured President Volodymyr Zelenskyy to produce evidence against Joe Biden's son. Not only were Europeans repelled by Trump personally and his policies toward Europe, but they also worried that US racial and political unrest could threaten America's overall stability.

Against this background, many in Europe felt the time was hardly ripe to risk Moscow's wrath. This included any wavering on the pipeline, which Trump opposed vociferously. For all his friendliness toward Putin, Trump said European gas purchases from Russia were strategically dangerous, and he opposed them absolutely. Merkel had already made clear that she would protect

Ukraine from the pipeline's effects[30]; however, Ukraine was the least of Trump's concerns. He thought the money Europe sent to Russia for gas should be used to buy LNG from the United States, increase European contributions to NATO, or remedy Trump's many grievances about US-EU trade.

"You know, we're protecting Germany, we're protecting France. We're protecting everybody," Trump told reporters after the 2018 NATO conference. "And then numerous of the countries go out and make a pipeline deal with Russia where they're paying billions of dollars into the coffers of Russia." Germany "is a captive of Russia," Trump said. "They got rid of their coal plants. They got rid of their nuclear. They're getting so much of the oil and gas from Russia. I think it is something NATO has to look at. It is very inappropriate."[31]

Soon the conflict over Nord Stream 2 moved from debate to confrontation, between the United States and Germany and within Europe itself.

In 2016, then–Vice President Joe Biden had denounced the project during a European trip, calling it "a fundamentally bad

---

[30] As early as 2018, Merkel's government had recognized that Nord Stream 2 was more than simply a commercial project. Upending years of German claims that the project was just business, she said after a meeting with Ukrainian President Petro Poroshenko, "I made very clear that a Nord Stream 2 project is not possible without clarity on the future transit role of Ukraine. So you can see that it is not just an economic issue but there are also political considerations." Yet her government allowed construction of the pipeline to go ahead without insisting that such "clarity" be established. See "Merkel says Nord Stream 2 not possible without clarity for Ukraine," *Reuters*, April 10, 2018, https://www.reuters.com/article/germany-ukraine/merkel-says-nord-stream-2-not-possible-without-clarity-for-ukraine-idUSB4N1PH00K

[31] Text at https://trumpwhitehouse.archives.gov/briefings-statements/remarks-president-trump-nato-secretary-general-jens-stoltenberg-bilateral-breakfast

194 | HOW RUSSIA LOSES

deal for Europe." He added, "To lock in great reliance on Russia will fundamentally destabilize Ukraine."[32]

With Trump taking the same position, US opposition to the project grew further. US officials shuttled across Europe to argue against the pipeline. Some of them resurrected speculation from the Nord Stream 1 debate that Russian equipment monitoring the pipeline could collect intelligence about NATO military movements in the Baltic.[33]

In January 2019, just 11 months before the project was due to be completed, Richard Grenell, the US ambassador to Germany, began to threaten US sanctions against German companies taking part. Public opinion in Germany reacted sharply. A poll found 91 percent of Germans opposed Grenell's threats and 77 percent took them as blackmail. Nearly 70 percent said Trump was wrong to believe the pipeline threatened Germany's security, and 90 percent said Trump was denouncing Russia only because the US wanted to sell LNG to Europe.[34]

---

[32] "Biden warns EU against Russian gas dependency," *Deutsche Welle*, August 25, 2016, https://www.dw.com/en/biden-warns-europe-against-dependency-on-russia-for-heating-oil-and-natural-gas/a-19503334

[33] Shalal, Andrea, "Russia-Germany gas pipeline raises intelligence concerns – U.S. official," *Reuters*, May 17, 2018, https://www.reuters.com/article/uk-usa-germany-russia-pipeline/russia-germany-gas-pipeline-raises-intelligence-concerns-u-s-official-idUKKCN1II0V7. Some European officials worried about the possible intelligence functions of a compressor station that might be built off Sweden, or the installation of ship monitoring devices along the sides of the pipeline. See also Honczar, Mychajło et al., "Wojskowe zastosowania Nord Stream 2. Eksperci: może być użyty do szpiegowania [Military applications of Nord Stream 2. Experts: It can be used for espionage]," *Energetyka 24*, May 18, 2021, https://energetyka24.com/gaz/wojskowe-zastosowania-nord-stream-2-eksperci-moze-byc-uzyty-do-szpiegowania-analiza

[34] "Deutsche werfen Trump Erpressung vor [Germans accuse Trump of blackmail]," *Ntv*, January 21, 2019, https://www.n-tv.de/politik/Deutsche-werfen-Trump-Erpressung-vor-article20820218.html

Not all Europeans supported Germany, however. Many saw the same strategic dangers in Nord Stream 2 that the Americans saw, and resented Germany trying to impose its desires on the rest of the continent. Soon after the Nord Stream 2 deal was signed in 2015, ten Central and East European countries demanded an EU summit to discuss the deal. "Preserving the transport route through Ukraine," they said, "is the strategic interest of the EU as a whole, not only from an energy security perspective, but also in terms of reinforcing the stability of the eastern European region."[35]

As pipe-laying work went on, opposition only increased. In an open letter to Merkel in November 2018, nearly 200 members of the European Parliament and national parliaments across the continent said of Germany's eagerness for the pipeline:

> It antagonizes many of Germany's partners because it leaves their interests unaddressed, and it gives Russia additional strategic leverage over the EU because it increases the EU's energy dependency on Russia. Your government, Madam Chancellor, is allowing a major rift between EU member countries to fester at a time when the EU needs cohesion more than ever before. Europe cannot afford this. Nor can Germany. ... Choose the European way, not the "Germany first" way.[36]

American opposition to the project was welcomed by like-minded Central and East European nations, who often felt marginalized in the EU.

In 2017, construction of Nord Stream 2 was suddenly blocked in an unexpected place. Denmark, a NATO member, had approved the passage of Nord Stream 1 through its territorial waters.

---

[35] Lewis, Barbara, "Ten EU nations say Nord Stream gas extension not in EU interests," *Reuters*, November 27, 2015, https://www.reuters.com/article/us-ukraine-crisis-nordstream-idUSKBN0TG0JX20151127
[36] Text at https://rebecca-harms.de/post/joint-open-letter-regarding-nord-stream-2-to-german-chancellor-angela-merkel-57995

196 | HOW RUSSIA LOSES

Denmark's own gas supplies had come from the North Sea for more than a decade, and Copenhagen saw no reason to interfere with a Russian-German project. Denmark also had reasonably good relations with Russia for a NATO country; Premier Lars Løkke Rasmussen visited St. Petersburg in 2009 and Putin, as prime minister, traveled to Denmark in 2011.

The situation with Nord Stream 2 was different. In April 2017, Russia applied to build the new pipeline through Danish territorial waters alongside Nord Stream 1. By then, however, views of Russia had darkened across the EU due to the invasion of Ukraine. The application put Denmark in a difficult position. On one hand, Denmark highly valued its security relationship with the United States. It knew the pipeline was opposed by the volatile Trump (who in 2019 would propose that the US acquire Denmark's territory of Greenland). At the same time, Germany was Denmark's largest export market. Copenhagen had no desire to anger Berlin by blocking so serious a project as Nord Stream 2. Denmark was also not keen to directly provoke Russia.

Denmark found it easiest to stall, hoping that, *deus ex machina*, something might come along to spare it a painful decision. In November 2017, parliament gave the government the power to stop the pipeline if it chose to do so, voting overwhelmingly to make security considerations a legal basis for blocking projects in its territorial waters. Major political parties and civil society groups called on the government to block the project.

The government deliberated, and then deliberated some more. The stalling went on for two and a half years. Schröder blamed the delay on US pressure,[37] but Denmark said it was acting on its own. In March 2019, Foreign Minister Anders Samuelson said that, when the time came for a decision, Copenhagen would evaluate "what is going on in Russia and the way they treat Ukraine."

---

[37] "Schroeder says U.S. pressure on Denmark the main reason for Nord Stream 2 delay," *Reuters*, June 7, 2019, https://www.reuters.com/article/us-russia-forum-nordstream2-schroeder-idUKKCN1T80H4

Russia, he added, is "definitely not working in the interest of Denmark in general."[38]

Denmark stretched out the process by repeatedly asking Gazprom to propose new possible routings for Nord Stream 2. Finally, Gazprom offered a plan to run it outside Danish territorial waters, in Denmark's exclusive economic zone (EEZ). The new route would be 70 miles longer but under international law activities in economic zones cannot be restricted for political reasons. Copenhagen finally approved the project at the end of October 2019. The new routing enabled Denmark to satisfy the needs of Russia and Germany, while demonstrating to Washington that it had delayed the pipeline as long as reasonably possible.

By the time Denmark gave its go-ahead, all of Nord Stream 2 had been built except for the segment now planned for its EEZ. With luck, backers felt, the pipeline might be completed by its original 2019 target. But America's attitude had hardened, not only in the White House but in Congress as well. Thanks to the Danish delay, there was still time to act—and the United States did. Congress passed legislation imposing sanctions on any company laying pipe for Nord Stream 2, and Trump signed it on December 20, 2019. The law's effect was immediate: Allseas Group, the Swiss-based company that had been laying the pipe, announced on December 21 that it had stopped work because of the legislation.

With Nord Stream 2 now radioactive legally for Western companies, Russia had to lay the remaining pipe itself. As time slipped by, Gazprom was forced into a lengthy reconfiguration of Russian vessels to do the work. Denmark then had to approve those ships and their equipment. Further delays ensued due to a fish spawning season in the area. Ultimately, no pipe was laid in all of 2020, with Russian vessels starting work only in January 2021.

---

[38] "Denmark: No decision yet on Russian-German pipeline," *The Associated Press*, March 6, 2019, https://apnews.com/article/ed9c6594979f43079d1ad0bb13d08fed

198 | HOW RUSSIA LOSES

For more than a decade, Gazprom had vowed it would stop transiting gas through Ukraine by the end of 2019.[39] With Nord Stream 2 on ice because of Denmark's delay and US sanctions, Russia was forced to conclude a new deal with Kyiv. On December 30, 2019, Russia agreed to ship 65 bcm of gas through Ukraine in 2020 and 40 bcm annually from 2021 to 2024.[40] It also paid Ukraine a $2.56 billion settlement in a case Ukrainian energy company Naftogaz had won against Gazprom in a Stockholm arbitration court. Germany let it be known that it had pressed Russia to give Ukraine the best terms possible for the transit deal. Merkel then asserted after a meeting with Putin that the Ukrainian question had been solved so far as Nord Stream 2 was concerned, and the pipeline was once again "essentially an economic project."[41]

However, trouble for Nord Stream 2 kept piling up. The United States was not done with its opposition to the project. Repression inside Russia sparked new opposition to the pipeline in Europe. Germany ran into new legal issues with other EU nations and European courts. Finally, the EU committed itself to new environmental goals that took direct aim at the increased use of hydrocarbons that Nord Stream 2 would bring.

First was the issue of the United States. Many believed that even if Merkel's enthusiasm for the project was dimming because of Russian behavior, she could not oppose the project for fear of seeming to buckle under Trump's demands. Not only was he repeatedly obnoxious to her personally, but his brash demands

---

[39] See, for example, "Russia to stop gas delivery via Ukraine by 2019, push ahead with Turkish Stream – Miller," *RT*, April 13, 2015, https://www.rt.com/business/249273-gazprom-ukraine-gas-transit/..
[40] Soldatkin, Vladimir, "Russia, Ukraine clinch final gas deal on gas transit to Europe," *Reuters*, December 30, 2019, https://www.reuters.com/article/us-ukraine-russia-gas-deal/russia-ukraine-clinch-final-gas-deal-on-gas-transit-to-europe-idUSKBN1YY1FY
[41] Dornblüth, Gesine, "Die geopolitische Gasröhre [The geopolitical gas pipeline]," *Deutschlandfunk*, January 21, 2020, https://www.deutschlandfunk.de/zukunft-der-pipeline-nordstream-2-die-geopolitische-100.html

on the pipeline and other issues had antagonized people across Europe. Not only Berlin was wary of giving Trump a victory.

One point Europeans missed, however, was that opposition to the pipeline was not just one of Trump's personal grudges. Particularly in Germany, politicians thought some transactional deal, perhaps involving purchases of American LNG, would satisfy Trump's venality and thus end all opposition in Washington. They were unprepared for the bipartisan anti–Nord Stream coalition in Congress, led by such powerful figures in the Senate as Republican Ted Cruz and Democrat Bob Menendez.

For decades, many US lawmakers had been unimpressed with German politicians who viewed themselves as *Russlandversteher*, or "understanders" of Russia, who would tutor America in Moscow's needs and sensitivities. To Congress, Nord Stream 2 was less about a confidence-building partnership with Russia and more about Berlin risking European energy security in its eagerness to control the continent's gas market. (Most of Nord Stream 2's gas would go to customers outside Germany through German companies.)

In June 2020, US lawmakers began preparing various bills that would sanction insurers, technical certification companies, and others working on Nord Stream 2. By one estimate, the measures threatened 120 companies from 12 European states.[42] In July, the State Department issued a new interpretation of a 2017 sanctions law that made it potentially usable against both Nord Stream 2 and Turk Stream.[43] "This action puts investments or other activities that are related to these Russian energy export pipelines at risk of US sanctions," Secretary of State Mike Pompeo said on July 15. "It's a clear warning to companies [that] aiding and

---

[42] Solomon, Erika, "Germany warns new US sanctions endanger Nord Stream 2 pipeline," *Financial Times*, July 1, 2020, https://www.ft.com/content/81a1d823-730f-4412-a698-670e4fc4f6f1

[43] The 2017 legislation was the Countering American Adversaries Through Sanctions Act (CAATSA).

abetting Russia's malign influence projects will not be tolerated. Get out now, or risk the consequences."[44]

Europe girded for battle. On July 1, Merkel denounced any "extraterritorial sanctions" as illegal, declaring "we still believe it's right to get the project done."[45] Josep Borrell, the EU's foreign policy chief, said in a statement two days after Pompeo's warning:

> As a matter of principle the European Union opposes the use of sanctions by third countries on European companies carrying out legitimate business. Moreover, it considers the extraterritorial application of sanctions to be contrary to international law. European policies should be determined here in Europe not by third countries.[46]

The EU talked of imposing counter-sanctions against the United States or protecting European companies through the EU Blocking Statute.[47] The state of Mecklenburg-Western Pomerania established a public foundation that was ostensibly an environmental organization but in fact was prepared to continue pipeline-related construction. (Although the foundation was funded by Gazprom, officials felt that as a German state entity, it would be more difficult for the US to sanction.)[48]

By year's end, the US had imposed no sweeping sanctions; however, it did sanction companies providing insurance,

---

[44] Transcript at https://2017-2021.state.gov/secretary-michael-r-pompeo-at-a-press-availability-9/index.html
[45] "Germany warns new US sanctions endanger Nord Stream 2 pipeline," op. cit.
[46] Statement at https://www.eeas.europa.eu/eeas/statement-high-representativevice-president-josep-borrell-us-sanctions_en
[47] The Blocking Statute protects EU companies and individuals from the extraterritorial application of third-country laws. It has been used to nullify the effect of US sanctions over trade with Cuba, Iran, and Libya.
[48] "Flow of Russian gas and cash entangled German state in dependent web," op. cit.

certification, and other services for the pipeline. On January 4, 2021, Norwegian company DNV GL said that, because of the new legislation, it would no longer work on certifying the technical integrity of the Nord Stream 2 infrastructure.

While Washington was busy creating difficulties for the pipeline, Russia created new perils of its own. On August 20, 2020, Russian agents poisoned Alexei Navalny, the leader of Russia's anti-corruption movement. Navalny was transported to a Berlin hospital for treatment and spent two weeks in a medically induced coma, deeply affecting the German public. Senior members of the Greens called for Nord Stream 2 to be canceled. Even Merkel and her ministers seemed to waver on their commitment to the pipeline.

"It is certain that Alexei Navalny is the victim of a crime," Merkel said. "He was meant to be silenced and I condemn this in the strongest possible terms, on behalf of the German government."[49] A government spokesman said that, if the poisoning were not investigated to Germany's satisfaction, sanctions involving Nord Stream 2 could result.[50] Foreign Minister Heiko Maas told the newspaper *Bild*, "I hope the Russians don't force us to change our position on Nord Stream 2."[51] The European Parliament overwhelmingly passed a resolution demanding that the pipeline be halted because of the poisoning.

---

[49] Statement at https://www.bundesregierung.de/breg-de/aktuelles/pressestatement-von-bundeskanzlerin-merkel-zum-fall-nawalny-am-2-september-2020-1781830

[50] "Merkel schließt sie nicht aus: So denken Bürger über neue Putin-Sanktionen [Merkel does not rule them out: What citizens think of new Putin sanctions]," *Focus Online*, September 9, 2020, https://m.focus.de/politik/deutschland/civey-umfrage-fuer-focus-online-merkel-schliesst-sie-nicht-aus-so-denken-buerger-ueber-neue-putin-sanktionen_id_12406147.html

[51] Röpcke, Julian, et al., "Nord stream 2 wegen Nawalny stoppen? [Stop Nord Stream 2 because of Navalny?]," *Bild*, September 6, 2020, https://www.bild.de/politik/inland/politik-inland/nord-stream-2-wegen-nawalny-stoppen-so-viel-putin-steckt-in-der-union-72772532.bild.html

202 | HOW RUSSIA LOSES

Navalny returned to Russia in January 2021 and was sentenced to prison the next month. The sentencing brought another call by the European Parliament to stop Nord Stream 2 and a tweet about the poisoning from teenage environmentalist icon Greta Thunberg: "So in the year 2021 Europe chooses to meet its energy demand by building a pipeline to transport more fossil fuels from the ones responsible for this. Shameful on so many levels. #FreeNavalny."[52]

Yet as Navalny's name receded from the headlines, Merkel's administration swung back to favoring Nord Stream 2. In February, Merkel said her government reserved its right to impose other sanctions over the poisoning but added, "The position on Nord Stream 2 is not affected by this for the time being; this is a project on which you know the position of the federal government."[53] German President Frank-Walter Steinmeier again raised the argument that Germany could hope to influence the situation in Russia only if it maintained ties to Moscow, stressing that "energy relations are almost the last bridge between Russia and Europe." He also invoked Germany's war guilt:

> We can look back on a very checkered history with Russia. There were phases of fruitful partnership, but even more times of terrible bloodshed. June 22nd marks the 80th anniversary of the start of the German invasion of the Soviet Union. More than 20 million people in what was then the Soviet Union fell victim to the war. That doesn't justify any wrongdoing in Russian politics today, but we mustn't lose sight of the bigger picture. Yes, we live in the presence of a difficult

---

[52] Greta Thunberg, Twitter, February 2, 2021, https://twitter.com/GretaThunberg/status/1356669038664032257

[53] Text at https://www.bundesregierung.de/breg-de/suche/pressekonferenz-von-bundeskanzlerin-merkel-und-praesident-macron-anlaesslich-des-deutsch-franzoesischen-verteidigungs-und-sicherheitsrates-am-5-februar-2021-1851512

relationship, but there is a past before and a future after.[54]

Steinmeier's comments outraged officials in Kyiv. They noted that Ukraine, too, was part of the Soviet Union that Germany had invaded and that Germany had just as much of a moral obligation to Kyiv as to Moscow.[55] Müller of the Greens agreed with the Ukrainian view. "The Germans were thinking of Russia as equivalent to the Soviet Union," she said, "disregarding all the parts of the Soviet Union besides Russia that suffered in the war."

Russia took advantage of the fading of the Navalny story to continue its threats against Ukraine. In the spring of 2021, it massed 300,000 troops on Ukraine's border. While most units pulled back, many troops remained, along with a large store of heavy equipment.

Meanwhile, legal developments were complicating the future of Nord Stream 2. Germany had worked hard to keep the pipeline away from the jurisdiction of EU officials, who had long been far more skeptical than Berlin about Russia's intentions. German Economics and Energy Minister Sigmar Gabriel told Putin at a 2018 meeting, "The most important thing is that regarding legal issues, we are trying to make certain that everything possible remains within the scope of German bodies. So that, if we manage

---

[54] Text at https://www.bundespraesident.de/SharedDocs/
Reden/DE/Frank-Walter-Steinmeier/Interviews/2021/210206-
Interview-Rheinische-Post.html. After Russia's invasion of Ukraine,
Steinmeier said Germany had misjudged how far Putin would go in "his
imperial madness." He also said Germany's support for the pipeline
was a mistake because it "not only destroyed a billion-dollar project,
but also because it cost us a lot of credit and credibility with our
Eastern European partners." See "Putin ein 'eingebunkerter
Kriegstreiber' [Putin is a 'warmonger in a bunker']," *ZDF*, May 4, 2022,
https://www.zdf.de/nachrichten/politik/steinmeier-putin-ukraine-
krieg-russland-100.html
[55] "Kyiv angry at Steinmeier over Nord Stream, WW II comments,"
February 9, 2021, *Deutsche Welle*, https://www.dw.com/en/germanys-
steinmeier-angers-kyiv-with-his-comments-on-nord-stream-wwii/a-
56515956

204 | HOW RUSSIA LOSES

to do that, the possibilities of interference from outside will be limited."[56] (It was telling that, to Gabriel, the EU was an "outside" force.)

In 2019, however, Germany agreed to a compromise with France that would later cause deep trouble for Nord Stream 2. The deal allowed the EU to approve an amendment to its Third Gas Directive that would subject pipelines from abroad to an anti-monopoly principle that had applied previously to pipelines within the EU. Under that principle, the producer of gas and the operator of the pipeline must be separate entities. Gazprom was to be both owner and operator of Nord Stream 2. Under the compromise, it was Germany that would apply the EU law; nevertheless, this gave little comfort to pipeline advocates. Since the amendment came only shortly before Nord Stream 2 was originally due to be completed, "one must indeed speak of a certain discrimination against Russia here," said Andreas Metz, spokesperson for the German Eastern Business Association, which had promoted German-Russian trade.[57]

More seriously, in 2020, the EU adopted the European Green Deal, a set of policies aimed at making the EU climate neutral by 2050. Measures to reach this target included decreasing gas imports by 13 to 19 percent by 2030 and 58 to 67 percent by 2050, as compared to 2015 levels. Hydrocarbons would be replaced by fuels such as hydrogen gas produced from green sources. The Green Deal threw into question whether there would ever be a need for new major sources of gas—from Russia or anywhere else.

The replacement of Trump by Joe Biden at the start of 2021 sharply improved relations between the United States and Europe, but Washington was still worried about the pipeline. Construction was almost complete and the Biden administration was not eager for a new transatlantic confrontation, especially with Germany. "We inherited a pipeline that was over 90%

---

[56] Text at http://kremlin.ru/events/president/news/50582
[57] Andreas Metz, interview with author, June 9, 2022.

complete and so stopping it has always been a long shot," said an anonymous State Department official quoted by *Reuters*.[58]

The two nations' interests were nimbly addressed in a two-step move. In May 2021, despite frantic efforts by Ukraine, Biden decided to waive sanctions on Nord Stream 2 AG and CEO Matthias Warnig, even though Congress had authorized them. (The US did issue sanctions against several Russian vessels trying to complete the pipeline.) Then in July, Germany and the US signed an agreement under which Germany promised to provide seed money for a billion-dollar project to develop clean energy in Ukraine, to use "all available leverage" to encourage Russia to prolong its gas transit agreement with Ukraine, and, most importantly, to "take action" in response to any Russian effort to use energy as a weapon against Kyiv.

The agreement did not define what specific Russian actions would trigger a German response, or that the response would necessarily target Nord Stream 2. The agreement said only that, in the event of a Russian effort to weaponize energy or other aggressive acts against Ukraine, Berlin would act "at the national level and press for effective measures at the European level, including sanctions, to limit Russian export capabilities to Europe in the energy sector, including gas, and/or in other economically relevant sectors." Still, the agreement could be read as a threat of retaliation for a wide range of potential aggressive acts by Russia. It committed Germany to take some action, and it specifically targeted gas exports as one of several possible areas for retaliation. The agreement also said Germany would abide by "the letter and the spirit" of EU energy regulations.[59]

---

[58] Shalal, Andrea, "U.S. waives sanctions on Nord Stream 2 as Biden seeks to mend Europe ties," *Reuters*, May 19, 2021, https://www.reuters.com/business/energy/us-waive-sanctions-firm-ceo-behind-russias-nord-stream-2-pipeline-source-2021-05-19
[59] Text at https://www.state.gov/joint-statement-of-the-united-states-and-germany-on-support-for-ukraine-european-energy-security-and-our-climate-goals

206 | HOW RUSSIA LOSES

Biden did not want Nord Stream 2 to be the defining issue in US relations with Germany, Rathke said, "so US diplomacy used the potential [US] sanctions as leverage to obtain a stronger and more explicit German commitment to counter attempted Russian weaponization of energy supplies."

The pipeline was finally completed on September 10, 2021, Gazprom announced. Yet German and European regulators still needed to give Nord Stream 2 their sign-off, and such agencies work at their own pace. The German regulator, the Bundesnetzagentur, said in September that it had received all necessary paperwork from Nord Stream. In November, however, it suspended its review because the company lacked a legal entity in Germany. The request, which surprised some energy experts, required Gazprom to create such an entity and transfer assets and personnel to it. Only after that would Germany complete the approval process, after which the matter would move to European regulators. Both sets of regulators were expected to look closely at a raft of anti-monopoly issues, including whether Gazprom could develop a way to split the supply and transmission of gas between two credibly different legal entities.

Meanwhile, Ukraine's Naftogaz and Polish gas company PGNiG exercised their right to consult with the Bundesnetzagentur regarding Nord Stream 2's impact on their business. Environmental activists also kept raising new legal challenges to the project. A German court indicated that methane released into the atmosphere in Russia when gas was extracted for Nord Stream 2 could be considered by German authorities as part of the pipeline's environmental impact. Poland, which feared the pipeline's strategic significance and the loss of transit revenues from Russia, looked likely to challenge the project in EU courts. In late 2021, the most optimistic forecast for the pipeline going into operation was March 2022; some believed it would take far longer.

Russia was losing patience. Gazprom had been a reliable "swing supplier" of gas, always ready to provide supplies above contract levels when needed. But as early as April 2021, Gazprom began reducing these supplemental deliveries. Gas prices on European

Nord Stream 2: So Near and Yet So Far | 207

markets began to rise in May because of low inventories, increased demand with the end of COVID lockdowns, and falling domestic production. "The time has come to agree on reasonable, mutually beneficial parameters for the operation of the gas pipeline," Russian Foreign Ministry spokeswoman Maria Zakharova declared on September 9.[60] By October, as Putin resumed massing troops on Ukraine's border, European gas prices reached €116 per megawatt hour (MWh), compared to €35 four months earlier. With a frigid winter expected, Russia essentially held the additional gas hostage to Nord Stream 2 going into operation. Putin said in October that gas flows could increase "the day after tomorrow" if regulators approved the pipeline "tomorrow."[61]

The showdown over gas coincided with the German federal elections on September 21. Merkel had decided not to run again after nearly 16 years in power, leading to an enormous range of speculation over what kind of coalition might take over running the country. Ahead of the election, the leaders of the largest parties—Merkel's center-right Christian Democratic Union (CDU) and the center-left Social Democrats—continued to officially support Nord Stream 2. The Greens opposed it over environmental and Russian human rights concerns.

The election failed to yield a decisive result, leading to two months of negotiations over a new coalition. The result was a government led by the Social Democrats and bolstered by the Greens and Free Democrats, with Merkel's CDU and its Bavarian

---

[60] Zakharova added: "For many years we explained, answering questions, responding to criticism, and combatting fake narratives, that Nord Stream 2 is a purely economic project, and Russia has no plans to use it for any other purpose. We sincerely hope that Nord Stream 2 will cease to be the subject of all sorts of political speculations, bogus stories, information campaigns, a pretext for illegal restrictive measures and will vanish from such a confrontational agenda altogether." "Захарова: начало поставок газа по 'Северному потоку – 2' зависит от немецкого регулятора [Zakharova: Start of gas via Nord Stream 2 depends on German regulator]," *TASS*, September 9, 2021, https://tass.ru/ekonomika/12343777

[61] Text at http://kremlin.ru/events/president/news/66975 6

208 | HOW RUSSIA LOSES

sister party, the Christian Social Union, in opposition. The Greens received the Foreign Ministry and the newly created Ministry of the Economy, Energy and Climate. The new coalition remained, on the record, in favor of the pipeline, but its enthusiasm dimmed with new Russian provocations against Ukraine. By the time Olaf Scholz took over as chancellor on December 8, Russian troops on Ukraine's border were reported to number at least 70,000. The US predicted an invasion in early 2022 with 175,000 troops. Officials in Washington pressured Berlin anew to cancel the pipeline.

On December 21, Russia cut off gas supplies via the Yamal pipeline, and gas prices spiked to €178 per MWh. The new Green foreign minister, Annalena Baerbock, said Germany could suspend the pipeline "in the event of further escalation."[62] Still, it was unclear what kind of "escalation" would trigger German action. Biden dangerously muddied the waters on January 19, suggesting that, if Russia committed only a "minor incursion" into Ukraine, the allies might have to "fight about what to do and not to do, etc."[63]

Putin helped the West out of any ambiguity. He delivered an angry speech on February 21 making clear that Russia would not tolerate the existence of the current Ukrainian state. The same day he recognized the independence of the separatist-held Luhansk and Donetsk "people's republics," making clear he was unilaterally redrawing Ukraine's borders. On February 24, he launched a full-scale invasion of Ukraine, taking any worries about the Western response to a "minor incursion" off the table.

There was no way that business or political circles in Germany could protect Nord Stream 2 in such circumstances. On February 22, the day after Putin recognized Donetsk and Luhansk, Scholz

---

[62] Video at https://web.archive.org/web/20220704065347/
https://www.zdf.de/nachrichten/heute-journal/heute-journal-vom-12-12-2021-100.html
[63] Text at https://www.whitehouse.gov/briefing-room/speeches-remarks/2022/01/19/remarks-by-president-biden-in-press-conference-6

ordered the withdrawal of an official government opinion stating that the pipeline did not pose a threat to the security of Germany's gas supplies. Without that document, the regulatory review was suspended indefinitely. Medvedev, who had become deputy head of the Russian Security Council, snapped back on Twitter, "Well. Welcome to the brave new world where Europeans are very soon going to pay €2.000 for 1.000 cubic meters of natural gas!"[64]

The US sanctioned Nord Stream 2 AG on February 23. With the invasion, Germany admitted the failure of its whole strategy of *Ostpolitik*. In a stunning speech on Sunday, February 27, to an emergency session of the Bundestag, Scholz said Germany had reached a *Zeitenwende*, or turning point, in its relationship with Moscow. Berlin would sharply increase its defense spending and send weapons to the Ukrainian military. Germany had pivoted dramatically away from Moscow. And Nord Stream 2 was one of the biggest victims of that change.

Money and Influence

Nord Stream 1 and 2 were both described by their promoters as purely commercial projects, beneficial to Europe as much as to Russia. Yet the history of the two pipelines was replete with allegations of corruption, greed, and political arm-twisting.

Few industries involve so much money and potential profit as energy. Putin's rise to president in 2000 happened to come shortly before a jump in world energy prices—a dazzling opportunity to restore the Russian economy after the financial disaster of the Yeltsin years. At a small dinner with journalists that this author attended in 2006, it was obvious that Putin had deeply studied the European gas market; he spoke fluently about

---

[64] Dmitry Medvedev, Twitter, February 22, 2022, https://twitter.com/ MedvedevRussiaE/status/1496112456858574849. At the time, the European benchmark price of gas was €0.58 per cubic meter, so Medvedev was speculating about a price increase of about 250 percent. By the end of 2022, gas prices were even lower than when Medvedev made his threat.

210 | HOW RUSSIA LOSES

pipeline routes and pricing. Not only did energy offer a way for Russia to make huge profits, but the nature of the industry lent itself to a small group of officials and business interests controlling finance, production, transport, and distribution..

In 2006, Gazprom received the exclusive right to export gas from Russia. Gazprom's leadership had tight connections to Putin and other senior government officials; through various deals and schemes, it steadily took over other Russian gas companies from their private owners.[65] Gazprom's first focus for exports was Eastern Europe, where pipelines already existed from the Soviet era. The company signed long-term gas supply deals, with rates pegged to the price of oil. (Oil prices can be more easily manipulated by producers, including Russia, than gas prices.) The Gazprom contracts also contained "destination clauses" that prohibited buyers from reselling excess gas to other countries. The effect was to keep gas sales on a bilateral basis between Russia and each customer, blocking them from exchanging supplies or benefiting from the movement of global spot prices.[66] The big money for Russia, however, would come not from its former satellites, but from Western Europe. Germany was the ideal main partner because of its decades of *Ostpolitik*, its voracious need for gas, and its central position in Europe's gas

---

[65] For an account of this process, including allegations of intimidation tactics, see Zaslavskiy, Ilya, "Corruption pipeline: the threat of Nord Stream 2 to EU Security and Democracy," Free Russia Foundation, October 16, 2017, https://www.4freerussia.org/wp-content/uploads/2017/10/Corruption-Pipeline-web.pdf

[66] The EU filed antitrust charges against Gazprom in 2015, accusing it of violating EU rules by illegal partitioning European customers, opportunistic pricing, and refusal to let other companies use its pipelines. Alexei Miller, chairman of Gazprom's Management Committee, fired back against the EU's price claims, saying that if Brussels wanted the same prices everywhere, then all customers might wind up paying the highest. See "Выступление Алексея Миллера на конференции 'Европа и Евразия: на пути к новой модели энергобезопасности' [Speech by Alexei Miller at the 'Europe and Eurasia: on the road to a new model of energy security' conference]," April 13, 2015, https://web.archive.org/web/20180509104452/https://www.gazprom.ru/press/news/miller-journal/2015/223594

distribution network. Putin had personal experience with Germany from his Cold War KGB work there, spoke German, and could feel comfortable interacting with German officials. Germany's business elites controlled huge investments across Europe; if they were dealing with Moscow, it would be hard for other countries and companies not to follow suit.

The first big project under Putin to cement the gas relationship with Germany was Nord Stream 1. Russia reactivated ties dating to Soviet times, with officials who had dealt with Western executives on behalf of the Soviet government re-emerging as Gazprom officials. Russia was pushing on an open door; Western companies were only too pleased to join a project that promised large revenues and a chance for future deals. At home, Russian tycoons stood to make their own profits through construction and other contracts. Outside analysts had long suspected that enriching well-connected oligarchs was at least as important for Gazprom as the company's own profits. In the report that reportedly led to his firing, Sberbank researcher Alex Fak wrote, "Gazprom's decisions make perfect sense if the company is assumed to be run for the benefit of its contractors, not for commercial profit."[67]

To further ensure the success of the Nord Stream pipelines, Russia offered lucrative jobs and consulting contracts to a host of former European politicians. These figures brought prestige and credibility to the projects and—Russia might have assumed—all the necessary connections to keep legal and political problems at bay.

The best-known German promoter of the Nord Stream projects was Schröder, the former chancellor and a close friend of Putin. He was sworn in as head of Nord Stream 1's shareholder advisory board in 2006, just four months after losing his re-election bid to Merkel. His salary in that post was €250,000 per year.[68] Later, he

---

[67] "Russian Oil and Gas: Tickling Giants," op. cit.
[68] "Former Chancellor Schröder Sworn in at Russia's Gazprom," *Deutsche Welle*, March 30, 2006, https://www.dw.com/en/former-chancellor-schr%C3%B6der-sworn-in-at-russias-gazprom/a-1949349

became chairman of Nord Stream AG. Putin insisted that Schröder was hardly Moscow's pawn; at a 2022 news conference, the Russian president called him "an honest man whom we respect and who, of course, looks first of all to protect the interests of his own country."[69]

Some Germans were discomfited by what they saw as Schröder's *Männerfreundschaft*, or bromance, with Putin and his revolving-door transformation from chancellor to Nord Stream executive. Many in Europe, however, have traditionally seen a sharp distinction between a person's public and private lives, considering the retirement activities even of senior government officials to be their own affair.

Many other top figures benefited in retirement from Russian jobs. Former French Prime Minister François Fillon served on the boards of two Russian companies; former Austrian Chancellor Wolfgang Schüssel was on the board of Russia's Lukoil; former Austrian Foreign Minister Karin Kneissl, whose wedding Putin attended in 2018, joined the board of the Rosneft oil conglomerate; former Finnish Prime Minister Paavo Lipponen was a consultant on the application for Nord Stream 1 to run through Finnish waters; Ulrica Schenström, a former senior official in the Swedish prime minister's office, worked for Nord Stream 1 in Sweden; and the former mayor of Hamburg, Henning Voscherau, became chairman of the failed South Stream. Matthias Warnig, a major in East Germany's Stasi secret police at the time Putin was working for the KGB in Germany, was named CEO of Nord Stream AG in 2012.

There was no secret about these top former officials working for Russian concerns. "This is all transparent. For instance, everybody knows what Schröder does. Yes, he supports Nord Stream. Yes, he's paid money. That's his job," said Metz of the German Eastern Business Association.

---

[69] Text at http://www.special.kremlin.ru/events/president/news/67774

Nord Stream 2: So Near and Yet So Far | 213

The West, too, has no shortage of former politicians who have become lobbyists, including in energy. Former German Foreign Minister Joscha Fischer was hired as a strategic advisor to the Nabucco pipeline project, which was to bring gas to Europe from Iraq but was abandoned in 2013. Richard Burt, a former US ambassador to Germany, lobbied for Nord Stream 2 on behalf of participating Western companies. Rasmussen Global, a consulting firm founded by former NATO Secretary-General Anders Fogh Rasmussen, served as an advisor to Ukraine, with Rasmussen himself speaking out strongly against Nord Stream 2.

Russia sought not only to influence governments and regulators, but Germany's people. Germans widely supported good relations with Russia. Many were tired of the US crying wolf about supposed dangers from the Kremlin. But for good measure, Gazprom was active in promoting its own public image and building support for the continued use of gas. A cover story in its house magazine showed an ice-coated windmill with the caption, "Alternative reality: 'green' energy is expensive and inefficient."[70] Gazprom funded German schools and sports clubs, as well as art and classical music events. For thrill-seekers, it paid for the heart-stopping Blue Fire roller coaster at Germany's largest theme park. (The attraction's name evoked a gas flame.) For yachtsmen, Gazprom organized races along the pipeline's route.

Companies worldwide engage in such publicity activities, but Gazprom's were different, said Müller-Kraenner of Environment Germany. "Here we're talking about state companies, like Gazprom, whose job is to implement a Kremlin agenda," Müller of the Green Party said. "Gazprom's sponsorships were open, but you're not doing sponsorships unless you want to get something out of them."

---

[70] Magazine from 2020 at https://web.archive.org/web/ 20200414205647/https://www.gazprom.ru/f/posts/32/005727/jour nal-gazprom-2010-12.pdf.pdf

214 | HOW RUSSIA LOSES

Dead in the Water

For Russia, everything about the Nord Stream 2 project was a plus. Gas from Russia would cement Europe's reliance on the Kremlin for the very survival of its economies. By keeping gas cheap, Russia could discourage Europe from looking for other suppliers, and perhaps slow the development of green alternatives. Nord Stream 2 would starve Ukraine of gas transit revenues and diminish the country's importance to Western Europe. Any conflict over the pipeline between the US and Europe would create strains inside NATO and particularly antagonize Germany, whose support for the alliance was already weak. The opening of the pipeline would be a signal achievement for Russia and Germany, a trouncing for the US, and a humiliation for EU and East European officials who had opposed it. Nord Stream 2 might not make much money for Gazprom, especially if European gas demand fell, but Gazprom contractors with Kremlin connections would still make out nicely.

Russia also had the advantage of having reliably supplied gas to Western Europe for years. European energy companies found their cooperation with Russia highly profitable. Gazprom and the European companies could make credible-looking public arguments that the continent's demand for gas would grow, even if more rigorous analysis showed the contrary. Russia could also play on Germany's passion for doing business with Moscow— born of decades of *Ostpolitik*, war guilt, and a sense that trade was the surest way to guarantee peace.

Further, US opposition to Nord Stream 2 could be painted as simply the latest edition of a paranoid America blocking something good for Europe. Washington fought the shipment of pipes to the Soviet Union in 1962, the Urengoy–Pomary–Uzhhorod project in the early 1980s, and Nord Stream 1. In each case, the projects went ahead with no catastrophic effects. For much of its postwar history, Germany had resented US economic and political dominance over Europe. With Nord Stream 2, Berlin could demonstrate anew that it would make its own decisions.

Nord Stream 2: So Near and Yet So Far | 215

Russia's brace of arguments for Nord Stream 2, its lineup of prestigious Western advocates, and its skill at publicity made any battle over Nord Stream 2 seem highly winnable for Russia. Yet for years, Russia struggled. Even if Putin had not invaded Ukraine, it was unclear if the pipeline would ever have opened, or been needed. Russia's efforts were bedeviled by its own miscalculations, smart tactics by pipeline opponents, and a few chance events that had enormous impacts.

• **Russia misunderstood the legal obstacle course that Nord Stream 2 would have to navigate.** Russia is used to dealing with political and business powerbrokers who can make anything happen, including in political and judicial institutions. Moscow gives short shrift to international organizations, such as the EU, believing that, if it can pull the right strings in the countries that control them, the institutions will fall into line. As Polish energy analyst Bieliszczuk put it, "The Russians don't get Europe. They think they can get anything they want through bilateral deals with Germany or whoever, that everything can be agreed with national leaders, and the EU will have to follow."

Yet Germany's power was not unlimited. Trade with Germany is important to Denmark, but that had little effect on the snail's pace review of the pipeline in Copenhagen. Germany is the largest contributor to the EU, but it failed to cut out Brussels politicians and regulators from the Nord Stream 2 process. Especially after the compromise with France in 2019, it was clear that EU rules would prevail. The German government could not even keep its own regulatory agency from delaying the pipeline's approval in the critical last months of 2021, when it suddenly forced Nord Stream AG to create a German entity.

Poland remained a huge threat to the project throughout and might well have continued its opposition even if German and EU regulators had finally approved the project. In the view of some, this could even have led to a top-level fight and threat of a Polish veto in the EU's highest councils. "Poland would have made life miserable for the EU if the pipeline had looked like it was opening," said Thierry Bros, an energy specialist at Sciences Po

216 | HOW RUSSIA LOSES

university in Paris. "The probability of Nord Stream 2 going online was always very low for me."[71]

• **Moscow believed the project would be embraced by Europe as a whole.** Supporters of the pipeline "always tried to advance the narrative that Nord Stream 2 was somehow a European project," said Benjamin L. Schmitt, a research associate at Harvard University who worked as an energy security advisor in the State Department from 2015 to 2019. He added:

> The truth is that there was not only never a broad coalition in favor of Nord Stream 2, but in fact, there was a broad coalition opposing the project. This included not only nearly every nation across NATO's eastern flank, but countries like Sweden, Denmark, the United Kingdom, and Canada. The Kremlin-advanced pipeline was never defined as an EU Project of Common Interest[72] by the European Union, and the European Parliament voted by broad majorities on at least three different occasions, passing resolutions calling for the project to be ended. If we are being honest, the only countries that vigorously promoted the project were Germany and Austria—and the Russian Federation of course.[73]

The opposition that sprung up to Nord Stream 2 was just the kind of situation that Russia's high-powered lobbyists were hired for. People like Schröder were supposed to be able to make problems evaporate with a quiet word to the right people. But Moscow's well-pedigreed operatives failed to deliver. The very appointment of Schröder even backfired on Moscow because of the controversy over a former chancellor becoming an employee of Russia. "Schröder's job was to get all the politicians onside, to fix

---

[71] Thierry Bros, interview with author, February 16, 2023.
[72] The EU uses this term for cross-border energy projects of particularly high priority.
[73] Benjamin L. Schmitt, interview with author, October 21, 2022.

Nord Stream 2: So Near and Yet So Far | 217

everything with Denmark, the EU and so forth. At that he didn't succeed," said Svoboda of Charles University. Metz of the German Eastern Business Association added, "To Putin, hiring Schröder might have seemed the right thing to do, but all the German media were constantly doing investigations about Schröder and Putin. In the end, Schröder was not effective. He caused problems."

- **Russia underestimated the US and other pipeline opponents.** Putin may have felt that, given his strong relationship with Trump, the US president could be talked out of his opposition to the project—especially since Nord Stream 2 had little to do with Trump's domestic political agenda. If that was Putin's thought, he erred in thinking that a single powerbroker—even the president—can dictate US policy. Republican and Democratic administrations had consistently opposed the pipeline. Trump's denunciations of the project encouraged both parties to continue their opposition through the grueling Obama-Trump transition. Key members of Congress were furious about Nord Stream 2 and dead set on sanctions. Congress gave the Trump administration no choice but to act.

As Putin might have expected, US pressure tactics over the pipeline antagonized many Europeans. But the US also gathered support from East European nations fearful of Russia, and from other EU constituencies that resented German *diktat*. Conservative Russia hawks and leftist environmentalists found a common cause. Pipeline opponents in wealthy Western Europe joined with like-minded allies in the EU's poorest nations, who had direct experience with Kremlin domination and vigorously opposed its restoration.

Beyond that, US power could not be ignored, as when Washington's sanctions instantly halted Allseas' work at the end of 2019. Those sanctions were a perfect surgical strike: they targeted a critical link in Nord Stream 2's construction, paralyzing the project but avoiding the blowback that would have come if Washington had gone after large numbers of European companies.

218 | HOW RUSSIA LOSES

The US-German agreement on energy security in July 2021 was widely criticized in the US as a retreat by the Biden administration and a gift to Russia. There was particular criticism of the seemingly vague promise Washington extracted from Berlin to "take action" if Russia used energy as a weapon against Ukraine. However, the deal had three virtues, little recognized at the time in the United States.

First, it contained unusually strong language, by German standards, about potential Russian "aggression" and the responses Germany would make. Second, Germany's agreement to respect "the letter and the spirit" of EU energy regulations cemented the application of EU law to the project, abandoning Berlin's long efforts to keep it exclusively under German control. Third, the deal gave Biden an excuse not to sanction European companies. Although pipeline hawks in the US had desperately hoped he would, such an action would have immediately brought on a crisis with Europe as a whole. The EU would have backed Germany, as it had threatened to do. Brussels might even have found some reason to sanction American companies. The row would likely have affected Germany's September elections, which the US hoped would yield a government more supportive of American policy. As it turned out, the elections brought an excellent result for Washington.

Denmark's role in Nord Stream 2 was critical. Russia had designed the pipeline to stay clear of waters controlled by Poland and the Baltic nations, all members of NATO. But an efficient route to Germany could not avoid the territorial waters of Denmark. Given its economic dependence on Germany and desire not to unnecessarily offend the Kremlin, Denmark might have been excused for signing off quickly on the arrangements. But Copenhagen insisted on a full review and was willing to take the heat for the time it took. In the end, Denmark dragged its feet on authorizing the pipeline for two and a half years, making time for European opposition to the project to grow and for the United States to enact sanctions. Had Denmark speedily approved the project, the pipeline could have been finished before the US snapped its sanctions into place.

- **Russia may well have misread Germany's political scene.** Much as German officials fancied themselves *Russlandversteher* with a deep understanding of Russia, Putin may have imagined himself a master of German politics. During the key final years of the Nord Stream 2 project, Moscow treated Germany with open contempt—hacking the Bundestag, assassinating a political opponent in the heart of Berlin, and boosting a right-wing political party. Putin may have felt such provocations were justified given Merkel's marshaling of EU countries to maintain sanctions against Moscow. Alternatively, Russian power centers that deal with destabilizing democracies and killing people may simply been carrying out their own agenda, with little regard to Nord Stream 2.

However they came about, such actions, along with the poisoning of Navalny, reinforced a Darth Vader–type image of Putin that cost Russia public support in Germany and throughout Europe. Supporters of the pipeline found it increasingly hard to claim Russia was a benign power. Advocates' arguments for the pipeline began to center increasingly on the need to make a quick deal with Russia lest Moscow become even more violent, and on the eternally unrequited hope that a successful gas relationship could somehow help restore Russian civil freedoms.

Germany's 2021 elections brought Moscow a rude shock. Voters demonstrated that they were no longer happy with business-as-usual leadership by the CDU, which had stood up for Nord Stream 2 despite all of Moscow's provocations. The pipeline, and foreign policy in general, received little direct mention in the election campaign. But a third of voters said the top issue on their minds was the environment; no other subject was mentioned as frequently.[74] When the coalition's cabinet was announced, with the Greens winning the ministries responsible for foreign affairs, the economy, energy, and climate, the implications for Russia on many levels were worrisome. The Greens had long ago abandoned pacifism for a pro-Western, values-driven foreign

---

[74] "ARD-DeutschlandTREND September 2021," https://www.infratest-dimap.de/umfragen-analysen/bundesweit/ard-deutschlandtrend/2021/september

220 | HOW RUSSIA LOSES

policy, and they were implacable opponents of Nord Stream 2. Russia's invasion of Ukraine was the last straw, though the Greens had many incentives to slow-walk Nord Stream 2 even if Russia had not acted so blatantly.

• **Putin miscalculated by launching his invasion of Ukraine before the opening of Nord Stream 2.** If the new pipeline had been in operation when the invasion began, the Kremlin could have freely attacked Ukraine's gas pipelines, confident that it could satisfy Europe's gas needs via its undersea routes to Germany. "It's just so crazy he didn't wait. He would have been in a much better position," said Meghan O'Sullivan of Harvard's Kennedy School. O'Sullivan added that Putin likely believed Russia's energy business with Europe would continue despite the invasion, which he expected to succeed in a matter of days. "But I think that just speaks to his idea that there is nothing that would lead Europe to shut down these energy flows. I think he really had confidence that dependency really brought him immunity," she said.[75]

That confidence was another miscalculation. Unless, of course, the Kremlin had finally recognized the seriousness of the legal problems besetting Nord Stream 2 and had lost faith in a quick resolution—especially with the Greens in key government positions. If Putin had finally decided that the pipeline was lost, there was no point in delaying his invasion.

There are counterintuitive views on the Nord Stream 2 saga. Some believe Trump never cared that much about the pipeline. He had bigger matters to settle with Russia, including issues involving Syria and Iran. The pipeline was good for flaying the Europeans about their supposed spinelessness toward Russia, but Trump could only go so far: Merkel held the key to the renewal every six months of the EU's sanctions against Moscow. Trump railed against Nord Stream 2 at the July 2018 NATO conference in Brussels, but a week later, at a news conference

---

[75] "How Putin Has Played His Energy Cards," *The New York Times*, May 31, 2022, https://www.nytimes.com/2022/05/31/opinion/ukraine-energy-war-europe-gas.html

Nord Stream 2: So Near and Yet So Far | 221

with Putin in Helsinki, he spoke about it quite mildly: "I'm not sure necessarily that it's in the best interest of Germany or not, but that was the decision that they made. ... I discussed with Angela Merkel in pretty strong tones. But, I also know where they're all coming from."[76]

Asked by reporters in September 2018 about sanctions against German companies over the pipeline, Trump said, "We're not looking to do that. We just think it's very unfortunate for the people of Germany that Germany is paying billions and billions of dollars a year for their energy to Russia. And I can tell you the German people don't like it."[77]

Another theory is that Putin himself did not consider Nord Stream 2 essential, despite the Kremlin's full-court press to bring it to fruition. In this view, Russia understood perfectly well that gas demand was declining in Europe and that existing delivery channels were enough. Still, the project served the purpose of dividing the West, enriching Gazprom contractors, and deepening Russian influence in European political and financial circles—all useful accomplishments in and of themselves. Putin may have decided years earlier to invade Ukraine, whatever the cost to his relations with West European countries. This would explain his willingness to antagonize Germany, even with Nord Stream 2 hanging in the balance.

Some believe Nord Stream 2 should be viewed as a Russian influence success, halted only at the last minute by Putin's decision to invade Ukraine. In this view, the project was just too big to fail. If there had been no war, some way would have been found through the regulatory thicket to let the pipeline open, even if new companies had to be added to the project to satisfy EU rules. This theory assumes that the pipeline's backers would have

---

[76] Text at https://trumpwhitehouse.archives.gov/briefings-statements/remarks-president-trump-president-putin-russian-federation-joint-press-conference

[77] Text at https://www.presidency.ucsb.edu/documents/remarks-prior-meeting-with-president-andrzej-duda-poland-and-exchange-with-reporters

overwhelmed concerns from the Greens in government; that Germany's environmentally conscious public would accept the opening of another source of hydrocarbons; that lawsuits filed by climate activists and East European nations would have all failed; that Washington, Brussels, and Warsaw would not have found new ways to block the project; and that Scholz would have felt a continuing obligation to a project he inherited.

By most accounts, however, Russia desperately wanted Nord Stream 2 and failed to bring it to life. Russia's failure stemmed from its belief that its powerful German allies could bulldoze European nations and EU institutions into backing the pipeline; that the European public's environmental concerns, and revulsion over Russians actions at home and abroad, could be disregarded; that US sanctions on pipeline laying could be avoided; that Germany's government would always support the project; and that, even if Russia invaded Ukraine, Europe had no choice but to keep importing Russian energy. Putin wound up so near and yet so far from success in one of his biggest gambles in Europe.

Epilogue: Nord Stream 2 After the Invasion of Ukraine

The invasion of Ukraine was a watershed moment in Europe's attitude toward Russian energy. The EU, which received 40 percent of its gas from Russia in 2021, announced its intention to cut its reliance on Russian gas by two-thirds by the end of 2022 and to end all imports of Russian fossil fuels by 2027. Scholz announced that Germany would replace all Russian energy imports, including gas, as early as mid-2024.

EU imports of Russian gas began to tumble, from about 2,500 million cubic meters (mcm) per week in March 2022 to 500 mcm per week in December.[78] Overall European gas consumption in

---

[78] See https://www.bruegel.org/dataset/european-natural-gas-imports

2022 totaled 430 bcm compared to 490 bcm the year before.[79] Households and businesses conserved gas, the 2022–2023 winter proved mild (Christmas temperatures in Paris were above 50 degrees Fahrenheit); factories reduced production or switched to other fuels; and Norway, Azerbaijan, and Algeria sent additional supplies. Going into the winter of 2022–2023 the EU's gas storage tanks were full beyond the 80-percent target level.[80]

Far from Medvedev's apocalyptic predictions, gas prices declined, from a record €339 per MWh in August 2022 to €67 in January 2023. The price was around €40 in the fall of 2023.

Any prospect that Europe might resume its previous levels of energy dependence on Russia in a postwar world seemed unlikely, especially with Europe's commitment to reducing fossil fuel use overall. In 2022, for the first time, the EU generated more electricity from wind and solar sources than from natural gas.[81] The delay in Nord Stream 2 had given Europe more energy options: had the pipeline gone into operation when originally planned, Europe would have had fewer LNG import terminals, and the US and Azerbaijan might have done less to increase their export capabilities. After the invasion, Europe also began to look

---

[79] 2022 figure based on Eurostat calculation of EU consumption of 357 bcm at https://ec.europa.eu/eurostat/databrowser/ view/NRG_CB_GASM_custom_5672433/default/table?lang=en, and consumption of 73 BCM reported by UK government at https://assets.publishing.service.gov.uk/government/uploads/system /uploads/attachment_data/file/1147110/ET_4.1_MAR_23.xlsx#:~:text =Gas%20consumption%20decreased%20by%2013,well%20as%20hig her%20gas%20prices

[80] Buli, Nora, "European gas storage levels survive winter but summer refilling looms," *Reuters*, February 18, 2022, https://www.reuters. com/business/energy/european-gas-storage-levels-survive-winter-summer-refilling-looms-2022-02-18. Putin could have made Europe's energy situation much worse if he had cut off gas in April 2022, when storage tanks were only 20-percent full; by August, the tanks were approaching 70 percent.

[81] Jones, Dave, "European Electricity Review 2023," *Ember*, January 31, 2023, https://ember-climate.org/insights/research/european-electricity-review-2023

at its energy goals through a different lens; its motivation was no longer just to decarbonize for the environment's sake but to diversify energy sources for geopolitical security as well. The Bundestag passed an "Easter package" of laws vastly simplifying licensing procedures for large-scale energy projects.

Still, Europe needed some Russian gas for its immediate needs. As such, supplies ebbed and flowed after the invasion. Europe initially continued to buy Russian gas from Nord Stream 1, despite protests from Ukraine. But in June 2022, Gazprom cut deliveries through the pipeline from 170 mcm per day to 40 mcm, claiming it needed the gas to refill its domestic storage tanks. In July, Gazprom stopped the gas flow completely for ten days, blaming pipeline maintenance. It restored the flow afterward at 20 mcm, but then stopped transmission at the start of September, blaming equipment problems.

In May 2022, Russia stopped gas supplies to Poland through the Yamal-Europe pipeline and to Bulgaria after those countries refused Moscow's demand to pay in rubles. This left Russian pipeline gas reaching Europe only through Ukraine and Turkey. In all, Europe imported about 32 bcm of pipeline gas from Russia in all of 2022, compared to 146 bcm in 2021.[82] However, several nations, including Belgium, France, Spain, and the Netherlands, continued to import large amounts of Russian LNG, resulting in an increase in EU LNG imports from Russia to 19 bcm in 2022 from 14 bcm in 2021.[83] High rates of Russian LNG imports continued in 2023.[84]

On September 26, explosions rocked the Nord Stream pipelines, severely damaging both conduits of Nord Stream 1 and at least

---

[82] Figures from https://www-statista-com.ezproxy.cul.columbia.edu/statistics/1331770/eu-gas-imports-from-russia-by-route

[83] Figures from https://www.bruegel.org/dataset/european-natural-gas-imports

[84] O'Carroll, Lisa, et al., "EU imports of Russian liquified gas leap by 40% since Ukraine invasion," *The Guardian,* Aug. 30, 2023, https://www.theguardian.com/business/2023/aug/30/eu-imports-of-russian-liquified-gas-leap-by-40-since-ukraine-invasion

one strand of the still uncertified Nord Stream 2. The blasts in the Danish and Swedish economic zones appeared to be sabotage; seismologists in the two countries reported explosions equal in strength to 100 kilograms of TNT. The explosions sent some 500 mcm of gas bursting to the surface in bubbles as big as 1 kilometer in length, discharging the equivalent of 8 million tons of carbon dioxide into the atmosphere.[85]

NATO governments suspected Russia of the sabotage, though they released no evidence. The date of the attack was notable: it was the same day the Baltic Pipe opened, further diversifying Europe's energy sources by delivering Norwegian gas to Poland. But the rationale for a Russian attack was unclear. A Russian attack could have been simply an expression of anger, an effort to get out of delivery contracts based on *force majeure*, or a signal of Russia's ability to damage other critical energy and communications networks under the Baltic. Russia denied any responsibility. Some media reports claimed government or private actors from the US, Poland, or Ukraine could have been responsible.

The puzzle deepened in December 2022 with a report that Nord Stream AG had begun researching the restoration of the two pipelines. It was reportedly studying how long the pipes' internal polymer coating could withstand exposure to saltwater, as well as how much it would cost to get the pipelines back in operation.[86] Such repair work, however, could be stopped by US sanctions on Nord Stream 2 and would require review by Denmark and Sweden. The prospect of any near-term revival of gas transmission from Russia to Europe under the Baltic looked slim.

---

[85] Vakulenko, Sergey, "Shock and Awe: Who Attacked the Nord Stream Pipelines?" Carnegie Endowment for International Peace, September 30, 2022, https://carnegieendowment.org/politika/88062

[86] Ruiz, Rebecca, et al., "In Nord Stream Mystery, Baltic Seabed Provides a Nearly Ideal Crime Scene," *The New York Times*, December 26, 2022, https://www.nytimes.com/2022/12/26/world/europe/nordstream-pipeline-explosion-russia.html

5.

Macedonia: The Tank and the Lada

With the collapse of the Soviet Union, NATO moved swiftly to incorporate as many Central and East European nations as wanted to join. The first were Poland, Hungary, and the Czech Republic, former members of the Soviet Warsaw Pact alliance, which joined in 1999. NATO then extended membership to the Baltic states and more of the Warsaw Pact, and by 2009 to Balkan countries including Slovenia, Albania, and Croatia that had never been part of the Soviet sphere.

Increasingly alarmed at the alliance's growth, Putin appeared to draw a red line. As Montenegro moved close to NATO membership in 2016, Russia deployed political influence, economic pressure, and information operations in a bid to block that country's accession. By some accounts, Moscow was deeply involved in a coup attempt that nearly toppled the government. Yet the coup failed, and Montenegro joined the alliance.

Against this background, an increasingly testy Moscow faced yet another test in the Balkans in 2018–2019 when the nation of Macedonia prepared to take a critical step toward joining both NATO and the European Union. Moscow had cards to play in an effort to stop the process. But Western nations, along with their Macedonian allies, were intent on bringing Macedonia into both organizations.

228 | HOW RUSSIA LOSES

It was a great game in a tiny country, a contest where Russia and the West deployed an arsenal of influence tools—while each insisted that, unlike the other, it had no thought of "interfering" in Macedonian voters' freedom of choice. The winner was the West, thanks to miscalculations by Russia and its allies, as well as the West's economic strength and active campaigning. Western states also showed an unusual tolerance for machination and pressure tactics in the effort to obtain their desired goals.

Betrayal in Bucharest

Macedonia, a landlocked country with fewer than 2 million people, for centuries was the prey of its neighbors. It fell under Ottoman control in the 1300s, then spent time in the early 20th century under Serb and Bulgarian rule. After World War II, it became a people's republic within Josip Broz Tito's Yugoslavia. Macedonia largely avoided the horrors of the Yugoslav wars, seceding peacefully in 1991. However, its multiethnic make-up soon caused trouble internally. Much of this emanated from tensions between the majority Macedonians—Orthodox Christians with a Slavic language—and ethnic Albanians, who are largely Muslim and make up about a quarter of the population. An insurgency by ethnic Albanians in 2001 and retaliatory attacks by Macedonian troops and citizens left at least 200 people dead.

From the start of its independence, Macedonia's orientation was toward the West. Just two years after it became an independent state, the Macedonian Assembly, the nation's parliament, declared that it sought to join NATO. The US, NATO, and the EU brokered the agreement that ended the 2001 insurgency. Greece, however, complicated Macedonia's freedom of action, even imposing its will on the country's name. Athens insisted that only Greece's Macedonian region could legitimately be called "Macedonia," and that true Macedonians speak Greek. Macedonia, some Greeks claimed, even had designs on Greece's Macedonian territory. As a result of the Greek position, Macedonia was forced to enter the United Nations in 1993 under the ungainly name of the "Former Yugoslav Republic of Macedonia," or FYROM.

Macedonia: The Tank and the Lada | 229

From independence until 2006, Macedonia changed prime ministers eight times. The first premier to serve for a lasting period was Nikola Gruevski, who won the post in the 2006 election and held it for a decade. Hundreds of foreign observers descended on Macedonia to monitor the 2006 vote; with Albanian-Macedonian tensions still simmering, many had feared violence. The election was almost entirely peaceful, and incumbent Prime Minister Vlado Bučkovski conceded gracefully to Gruevski. Germany's *Deutsche Welle* broadcaster declared that Macedonia had passed "a crucial test of the Balkan country's bid for European Union and NATO membership."[1] Hopes were high that Gruevski, a 35-year-old with a Master of Arts in economics who had dabbled in boxing and acting, would attack Macedonia's 36-percent unemployment and lead the nation further on a pro-Western course.

Yet Macedonia was soon to be bitterly disappointed by the West. Its eyes set on full membership in both blocs, Macedonia had tried in every way to be a model participant in NATO and EU activities. Starting in 2003, it sent 250 soldiers to Afghanistan. It dispatched nearly 500 troops to support Operation Iraqi Freedom. It joined the EU's peacekeeping force in Bosnia and Herzegovina, losing 11 soldiers in a helicopter crash at the start of 2008. Gruevski's government made clear that its actions were just the start of even more political and military cooperation with Western institutions:

> The Republic of Macedonia has reaffirmed its strategic commitment for attaining membership to the EU by its resolute political commitment to support the Common Foreign and Security Policy (CSFP) and by declaring a concrete contribution to the civilian and military operations in the

---

[1] "Macedonian Opposition Leader Claims Victory," *Deutsche Welle*, July 6, 2026, https://www.dw.com/en/macedonian-opposition-leader-claims-victory/a-2080706

230 | HOW RUSSIA LOSES

framework of the Common Security and Defence Policy (CSDP).[2]

The reward for Macedonia's commitment was to be its formal admission to NATO at a summit in Bucharest in April 2008. The gathered leaders quickly granted membership to Croatia and Albania, and US President George W. Bush urged that Macedonia be accepted too. But the Greek government of Kostas Karamanlis insisted that Macedonia's name, even in the form of the clumsy FYROM, made an invitation to membership impossible. "We have said that no solution [regarding the name] means no invitation," Greek Foreign Minister Dora Bakoyannis told reporters.[3] The summit communiqué bent over backward to indulge Greece, not even making a reference to Athens as the party that had blocked Macedonia's accession. It blandly expressed the hope that "a mutually acceptable solution to the name issue" would be reached "as soon as possible."[4] (In 2009, Greece also used the name issue to block the EU from opening accession talks with Macedonia.)

The Macedonian delegation stormed out of the Bucharest summit. Gruevski was enraged. A cable from the US Embassy in Macedonia said "the psychological impact—for both the government and the public—of Bucharest should not be underestimated."[5] Gruevski claimed the Athens government was out to force Macedonia to change its national identity and was acting as a Trojan horse for Russia in an effort to undermine NATO. Gruevski sued Greece at the International Court of Justice for violating a previous agreement not to block Macedonia from membership in international organizations. (The court took its time, but

---

[2] "Contribution of the Republic of Macedonia to the EU Crisis Management Military Operation ALTHEA in Bosnia and Herzegovina," Army of the Republic of North Macedonia, http://www.arm.mil.mk/missions/althea/?lang=en

[3] Brunnstrom, David, et al., "Greece stands by NATO veto threat for Macedonia," *Reuters*, April 2, 2008, https://www.reuters.com/article/us-nato-macedonia/greece-stands-by-nato-veto-threat-for-macedonia-idUSL0238277320080402

[4] Text at https://www.nato.int/cps/en/natolive/official_texts_8443.htm

[5] Text at https://wikileaks.org/plusd/cables/09SKOPJE457_a.html

Macedonia: The Tank and the Lada | 231

ultimately ruled in Macedonia's favor in 2011.) Gruevski also bombarded world leaders with letters of complaint.

In a calculated affront to Greece, Gruevski began naming public places after Alexander the Great. It was a clear message to Athens that his country claimed as much right to Alexander's heritage— and to the term "Macedonia"—as did Greece. (Alexander was born in Greece's Macedonian region.) In 2011, a 78-foot bronze equestrian statue, complete with fountains, appeared in the main square of Skopje, Macedonia's capital. The monument's formal name was simply "Equestrian Warrior," but few doubted it was meant to represent Alexander.

NATO's snub of Macedonia was not the only source of tension between the West and Gruevski. The Macedonian leader's internal policies became a worry for Western governments. The prime minister and his VMRO-DPMNE party enjoyed a majority in parliament and controlled most local government organs. Opposition politicians, civil society, and foreign diplomats perceived a clear move by the government toward authoritarianism, corruption, and pressure on the media. "If Bucharest had said 'yes,' the pro-Western momentum would have continued," said Zvonko Naumoski, a Macedonian media development consultant. "There still would have been corruption, but the government would have been more careful."[6]

A cable from the US Embassy in 2009 said opposition and VMRO politicians who spoke out against the government had been arrested for abuse of office, charged with corruption, or invited to frightening "informal conversations" with the police.[7] In 2011, a public assessment by the State Department cited "the government's failure to fully respect the rule of law, which was reflected in its interference in the judiciary and the media, selective prosecution of political opponents of the country's leaders, and significant levels of government corruption and police impunity." It said Macedonia had also become a source, destination, and transit country for men, women, and children

---

[6] Zvonko Naumoski, interview with author, July 13, 2021.
[7] https://wikileaks.org/plusd/cables/09SKOPJE601_a.html

232 | HOW RUSSIA LOSES

involved in sex trafficking and forced labor.[8] The Council of Europe found in 2010 that, despite some improvements, there were still many reports of police beating suspects and threatening violence if they did not confess to crimes.[9]

Public discontent over the government's actions became increasingly evident. In 2010, tax officials backed by police raided a group of companies, including newspapers and a private television station, that critics claimed were targeted for their anti-government views. Some 10,000 people demonstrated against authoritarianism, government mismanagement, and Gruevski's failure to bring Macedonia closer to the EU and NATO.

Another major flashpoint was the beating death of a 21-year-old man, Martin Neskovski, by police on June 6, 2011. A plainclothes officer clubbed him to death, for no apparent reason, during celebrations of a VMRO victory in parliamentary elections. The officer was ultimately sentenced to 14 years in prison, but hundreds of youths protested for two weeks over the authorities' lack of transparency in the case.

Trying to bolster support from Macedonian nationalists, Gruevski became increasingly focused on national identity and cultural grandeur. His administration revived historical grievances with Bulgaria and Albania as well as Greece. In 2010, the government launched a massive "Skopje 2014" project, aimed at constructing more than 40 monuments, sculptures, and buildings that critics said had little to do with Skopje's actual needs. The plans included a version of Rome's Spanish Steps, but more ornate. Investigative reporters said the price tag, initially announced as €80 million, had risen to €560 million by 2015.[10]

---

[8] Text at https://2009-2017.state.gov/j/drl/rls/hrrpt/2011/eur/186377.htm

[9] Text at https://rm.coe.int/16806974db

[10] Jordanovska, Meri, "True Cost of 'Skopje 2014' Revealed," *BalkanInsight*, July 27, 2015, https://balkaninsight.com/2015/07/27/true-cost-of-skopje-2014-revealed

Many speculated that Gruevski, angry at domestic opponents and still smarting from NATO's rebuff, was starting to think that Russia would be a better ally than the West. The recession that began in 2007 had made EU leaders more wary of adding new countries to the bloc. The new US president, Barack Obama, seemed eager himself to improve relations with Russia. The Kremlin would give Gruevski none of the grief he was getting from Western countries about authoritarianism. Gruevski's nationalist agenda suited the Kremlin's purposes by provoking Greece and keeping Macedonia out of NATO. Some believed Gruevski had become increasingly drawn to the leadership styles of Putin, Hungary's Viktor Orbán, and Turkey's Recep Tayyip Erdoğan—all of whom based their leadership on strong government, nationalism, and conservative social and religious values.[11]

Gruevski may still have had an opportunity to move in the opposite direction. Aleksandar Nacev, a Skopje professor who served as a security official under Gruevski, said that, even after the Bucharest debacle, Gruevski still believed Macedonia should become a NATO country. Nacev believes Gruevski could have solved the name problem in 2010 or 2011 with a "double-formula" solution in which the country's name would remain Macedonia for internal purposes and something else that Greece could agree to internationally.

Such a deal could have flown with domestic voters, in Nacev's view. "Gruevski could have won a referendum to get into NATO," he said. "It would have been possible. VMRO-DPMNE then was dominant politically and all the Albanian parties would have given their support in that referendum. He just lacked the political courage to try it, for fear of being seen as a traitor, or he was afraid that he will not politically survive such a move."[12]

---

[11] See, for instance, Petsinis, Vassilis, "From pro-American to pro-Russian? Nikola Gruevski as a political chameleon," *openDemocracy*, May 22, 2015, https://www.opendemocracy.net/en/can-europe-make-it/from-proamerican-to-prorussian-nikola-gruevski-as-political-cha

[12] Aleksandar Nacev, interview with author, June 3, 2022.

234 | HOW RUSSIA LOSES

Whatever pro-NATO efforts he may have considered, Gruevski chose to visit Russia for three weeks in 2012, meeting with Putin and senior officials of energy giants Lukoil and Gazprom. The visit, a Macedonian statement said, "resulted in enhanced economic and political relations with the Russian Federation and with the largest and most powerful companies in Russia."[13] Gruevski's government declined to take part in Western sanctions against Moscow over its 2014 invasion of Ukraine, saying it would strain Macedonia's economy. Gruevski also favored connecting Macedonia to Russia's South Stream gas pipeline project. Once that project was abandoned, he backed a Russian plan to run its Turk Stream pipeline through Macedonia. Macedonian President Gjorge Ivanov attended the 2015 Victory Day parade in Moscow, which most Western leaders boycotted over Russia's invasion of Ukraine.

The Paint and Bubblebath Revolt

Macedonia held parliamentary elections in 2014, which Gruevski's VMRO party won. The opposition Social Democrats accused VMRO of electoral fraud and filed corruption charges against the prime minister for tax evasion and taking bribes.[14] Social Democratic leader Zoran Zaev, a former small-city mayor who became party head in 2013, accused Gruevski of "dictatorship," calling for a new government of national unity. Zaev declared his party had dramatic evidence of misdoings by top government officials. Gruevski, in turn, accused Zaev of trying to blackmail him. In January 2015, the government charged Zaev with plotting a coup.

The charges against Zaev were not enough to prevent the Social Democrats from releasing what they called their "bombs"—clips from thousands of wiretapped conversations. The recordings,

---

[13] Statement at https://vlada.mk/node/3612?ln=en-gb
[14] Marusic, Sinisa Jakov, "Macedonia Opposition Files Corruption Charges Against PM," *BalkanInsight*, April 23, 2014, https://balkaninsight.com/2014/04/23/criminal-charges-filed-against-macedonian-pm

Macedonia: The Tank and the Lada | 235

they said, showed the government had carried out illegal surveillance of more than 20,000 people, including judges, journalists, and government officials. Some recordings, which the party began releasing in February, captured Gruevski and other officials discussing ways to manipulate the judiciary and media. One of the most inflammatory recordings suggested that the government tried to cover up the police beating death of Martin Neskovski. Gruevski's interior minister claimed the tapes were manipulated by unnamed "foreign secret services" working with the opposition to destabilize the country.[15] The US, Germany, Britain, France, Italy, and the EU called on the government to carry out a credible investigation of what the wiretaps revealed.

In May 2015, violence broke out between Albanians and police in the northern town of Kumanovo, with 22 Albanians and police reported to have died. Gruevski said the police had foiled a terrorist group that had planned attacks on shopping malls, sports events, and government institutions. However, Gruevski's attempt to cast himself as a trooper in the international war on terror fell flat. His critics saw the violence as somehow inspired by the government to distract attention from its falling political fortunes. NATO and the EU demanded that his government conduct a "transparent investigation" of the events.[16]

Macedonia had many civil society organizations, dating from before Gruevski's reign and continuing today. They played an important role in opposing Gruevski, joining forces with other informal groups and movements opposed to his autocratic tendencies. About 20 to 30 organizations served as important vectors in opposing the regime, said Bardhyl Jashari of the civil society group Metamorphosis. Each had a core of five to ten people, plus 20 to 30 part-time associates. Most of the funding,

---

[15] "Macedonia Officials Attempted Murder Cover-up, Opposition Claims," *BalkanInsight*, May 5, 2015, https://balkaninsight.com/2015/05/05/macedonia-officials-attempted-murder-cover-up-opposition-claims

[16] "Violence between Macedonia police and 'terrorists' increases scrutiny of PM," *Reuters*, May 11, 2015, https://www.reuters.com/article/uk-macedonia-crisis-storm/a-perfect-storm-brews-in-macedonia-idUKKBN0NW19720150511

Jashari said, came from George Soros' Open Society Foundations (OSF), the EU, and USAID. (Jashari also said there was no tradition of local support for NGOs in Macedonia; companies that might have contributed funds were wary of getting involved in politics.)

The NGOs promoted the idea of honest government, and encouraged people to speak out. Many activists went beyond the normal mission of civil society, which is to foster democracy without becoming a direct political actor. "There is no independent civil society in Macedonia," said Ljupcho Petkovski, who headed the Eurothink NGO from 2017 to 2019. "Civil society did a lot of damage to Gruevski and probably crossed some red lines we shouldn't have. At the same time, the NGOs didn't create the situation in the country. People were genuinely angry over corruption, the wiretaps and so forth."

Gruevski and his VMRO allies reacted fiercely to civil society activities. Government inspectors entered the offices of a series of NGOs in 2015 and 2016; activists said the agents were intent on finding evidence that USAID funding had been mismanaged or used for illegal purposes. In December 2016, the government sent tax inspectors to 21 NGOs, all related in some way to Soros' foundations.[17] Some USAID workers reported harassment and surveillance, and personal information about them appeared on social media.

As the political crisis over Zaev's "bombs" grew, Macedonia's political parties asked the US and the EU to help reach a settlement. On June 2, 2015, the parties signed the Pržino Agreement, under which Gruevski agreed to step down pending new elections. He was replaced as prime minister on January 18 by VMRO politician Emil Dimitriev.

With Gruevski officially sidelined, President Ivanov became the focus of anger for pro-democracy forces. In April 2016, he issued

---

[17] Marusic, Sinisa Jakov, "Macedonia's NGOs Face Inspections After Political Threats," *BalkanInsight*, December 20, 2016, https://balkan insight.com/2016/12/20/macedonia-s-ngos-face-inspections-after-political-threaths-12-20-2016

Macedonia: The Tank and the Lada | 237

pardons to 56 officials involved in the wiretaps, setting off massive street protests. As many as 50,000 people joined the demonstrations, which became known as the "Colorful Revolution." The name stemmed from the participants' practice of splashing bright paint on buildings, walls, and monuments, including "Skopje 2014" creations that the protesters considered monstrosities and a waste of money. Protesters dumped red paint into the fountains around the "Equestrian Warrior" in sympathy with the victims of the regime; on another night, protesters used detergent to fill the water with bubbles.[18] Civil society activists made no secret of where their sympathies lay; paint for some of the Colorful Revolution protests was mixed in the office of a civil society group. Responding to the demonstrations and international protests, Ivanov revoked the pardons in June.

After two delays, the assembly elections required by the Pržino Agreement took place in December 2016. VMRO won 51 seats compared to 49 for the Social Democrats, both falling short of the 61 needed to form a governing coalition. The balance of power was held by ethnic Albanian parties, which said they would join a coalition with the Social Democrats in return for laws allowing broader use of the Albanian language. The sticking point was President Ivanov, whose formal permission was needed to form a new government. Zaev presented confirmation to Ivanov on February 27 that he had the seats to form a coalition; however, on March 1 the president refused to give Zaev a mandate to do so. Ivanov asserted that a Social Democratic government would implement the "platform of a foreign country" by allowing broader use in Macedonia of the Albanian language.

Major powers began to involve themselves in the Macedonian situation. On March 3, EU foreign affairs chief Federica Mogherini flew to Skopje. Significantly, she met first with civil society activists, whom she praised for "remarkable work." She then held a lengthy meeting with Ivanov. She told a news conference afterward, "I believe that it would be impossible for anyone to

---

[18] Ozimec, Kristina, " 'Colorful Revolution' paints raucous rainbow," *Deutsche Welle*, April 21, 2016, https://www.dw.com/en/macedonia-colorful-revolution-paints-raucous-rainbow/a-19203365

238 | HOW RUSSIA LOSES

convince anyone in the democratic world that the majority of members of Parliament, who represent the majority of citizens in a unitary state, cannot be allowed to form a government."[19]

Meanwhile, Gruevski accused foreign ambassadors, NGOs, and the opposition of plotting to steal what he called VMRO's election victory. Soros, he said, was financing "a modern army" of corrupt NGOs aimed at overthrowing him. "That is the reality and unfortunately that is how Soros works," he said. "They squash you and slam you. They will make you a criminal, a crook and a traitor, an idiot, incompetent and a monster—whatever they want."[20] Pro-government forces founded counter-NGOs of their own. One, called "Stop Operation Soros," said its mission was to "fight against one-mindedness in the civil sector, which is devised and led by George Soros."[21]

Gruevski also used PR consultants in Washington to reach out directly to conservatives in the US Congress. His strategy was to end-run the US Embassy and the State Department, which he viewed as complicit with his opponents. Six Republican senators, including Mike Lee of Utah and Ted Cruz of Texas, wrote to Secretary of State Rex Tillerson in March that they had received "credible reports" that the US mission had actively intervened in Macedonia's politics, "often favoring left-leaning political groups." The senators cited in particular US grants to Soros' foundations, which they asserted were "to push a progressive agenda."[22] The conservative US group Judicial Watch demanded that the State Department and USAID release records about the funding and activity of OSF in Macedonia. Conservative news outlets such as *Fox News*, *The New York Post*, and *Breitbart News* took up the

---

[19] Text at https://www.eeas.europa.eu/node/21847_en

[20] Marusic, Sinisa Jakov, "Race to Run Govt Heats up in Macedonia," *BalkanInsight*, January 5, 2017, https://balkaninsight.com/2017/01/05/race-for-new-government-resumes-in-macedonia-01-04-2017

[21] Marusic, Sinisa Jakov, "New 'Stop Soros' Movement Unveiled in Macedonia," *BalkanInsight*, January 18, 2017, https://balkaninsight.com/2017/01/18/macedonia-forms-anti-soros-movement-01-18-2017

[22] Text of letter at https://www.lee.senate.gov/2017/3/gop-senators-call-on-sec-tillerson-to-investigate-state-department-meddling

Macedonia: The Tank and the Lada | 239

story, probably marking the first time that Macedonia had roiled the US political scene. (The congressional pressure led to a two-year investigation by the US General Accountability Office, which found no wrongdoing by US officials.)

Throughout the winter and spring of 2017, nationalists demonstrated in the streets in favor of a VMRO government. On April 27, they stormed the parliament with guns, knives, and baseball bats after the new parliament elected Talat Xhaferi, an ethnic Albanian, as its president. (Xhaferi had deserted the Macedonian army to join the Albanian rebellion against the army in 2001; he was later amnestied and eventually rose to the position of defense minister.) About 100 people were injured in the melee; Zaev's face and body were splashed with blood from two head wounds. Zaev accused the attackers of a "premeditated murder attempt" and pointed an accusatory finger at Moscow. He told *The Sunday Times*, "After the loss of Montenegro, the Russian Federation is making a final push for influence in Macedonia."[23]

Ivanov's obstinacy and the invasion of the parliament rang alarms in Washington. Three days after the parliament attack, Deputy Assistant Secretary of State Hoyt Brian Yee arrived in Skopje to meet with Ivanov. He told reporters, "It is very important for the leaders to find a way to allow the majority in parliament, the coalition of MPs that have a majority, to propose a government and a government program."[24]

Finally, on May 17, after Zaev had vowed to create a government with or without Ivanov's approval, the president gave him the mandate. (Ivanov then headed to Moscow to meet with Putin.) Zaev became prime minister on May 31, 2017. He pledged to boost the economy, fight corruption, calm ethnic tensions, and bring Macedonia into NATO and the EU. With the attack on

---

[23] Pancevski, Bojan, "Macedonia 'at risk from Russian meddling,' " *The Sunday Times*, April 30, 2017, https://www.thetimes.co.uk/article/macedonia-at-risk-from-russian-meddling-q2k08f59t
[24] News conference text at https://mk.usembassy.gov/deputy-assistant-secretary-european-eurasian-affairs-hoyt-yee-press-availability

parliament and accusations of Russian involvement, Capitol Hill conservatives scaled back their complaints over US actions in Macedonia.

The dispute with Greece over Macedonia's name was the third rail of Macedonian domestic and international politics. It would be hard enough for Zaev to find some accommodation with Athens; getting such an agreement through Macedonia's turbulent politics would be equally excruciating. However, Zaev seemed convinced that Russia had designs on Macedonia, and that the country's future security and prosperity could be guaranteed only by the West.

Zaev's first move to make an impression on Athens was to sign a friendship agreement with Bulgaria on August 1, 2017. Although not directly related to the dispute with Greece, the agreement addressed long-standing linguistic and historical issues between Skopje and Sofia. It conveyed that Zaev was open to negotiation, even on the most sensitive matters of national identity. In January 2018, Zaev pledged to the World Economic Forum in Davos that he would find a speedy solution to the name dispute with Greece. Diplomats speculated that renaming the country "Northern Macedonia," "New Macedonia," or "Upper Macedonia" might be acceptable to Athens. In February, Zaev told reporters in Skopje that "we are ready for a geographical qualifier." Zaev signaled at the same news conference that he was looking to reduce tensions with Greece. In a turnabout from Gruevski's nationalist posturing, he said he was dropping Alexander the Great's name from Skopje airport and a major highway. The highway would be renamed "Friendship." He said the decision was aimed at "building friendship and confidence with Greece."[25]

For Greek Premier Alexis Tsipras, an agreement with Macedonia would hardly be popular at home. Yet he and his Syriza party were heading toward political defeat anyhow after five years of

---

[25] "Macedonia says ready to change its name and end row with Greece," *Reuters*, February 6, 2018, https://www.reuters.com/article/us-macedonia-greece/macedonia-says-ready-to-change-its-name-and-end-row-with-greece-idUSKBN1FQ2OY

Macedonia: The Tank and the Lada | 241

economic troubles and Western-dictated austerity. A deal with Zaev, much sought by NATO, the EU, and the UN, would give Tsipras, once a radical leftist, a more statesman-like image that could be politically useful in the future.[26] Strong ties between Athens and Skopje would also make sense given Greece's traditional rivalry with Turkey. A hostile Macedonia, with a large ethnic Albanian population friendly to Turkey, might become a center of Turkish influence on Greece's northern frontier.

On June 17, 2018, in a feat of diplomatic dexterity and political courage, Zaev and Tsipras reached agreement on the name dispute on the shores of Lake Prespa, which borders Macedonia, Greece, and Albania. Under the Prespa accord, which their foreign ministers signed before a brace of UN and EU representatives, Macedonia would change its name to North Macedonia. It was understood that Greece would then drop its objection to the country's NATO membership. Other provisions of the accord recognized that the term "Macedonia" means different things to each nation and called for a review of school materials in both countries to remove any claims on each other's territory.

The accord immediately ran into heavy opposition in both countries. In Athens, tens of thousands of protesters rallied against it. Tsipras barely survived a confidence vote in parliament. In Macedonia, President Ivanov threatened Zaev with imprisonment for betraying the country. With VMRO delegates boycotting the vote, the accord was ratified by Macedonia's parliament on June 20. Ivanov refused to sign it and in September denounced it in a speech to the United Nations General Assembly.

The June vote in Macedonia's parliament was not enough to formally change the country's name. This would require parliament to pass a set of four constitutional amendments, which VMRO could seek to block. Before these votes, Zaev called a national referendum on the issue to take place on September 30. A positive referendum result, the government felt, would force

---

[26] Armakolas, Ioannis et al., "Blueprint Prespa? Lessons learned from the Greece-North Macedonia agreement," Friedrich Ebert Stiftung, https://library.fes.de/pdf-files/bueros/skopje/15509.pdf

parliament to change the constitution to reflect the people's will. However, the referendum was officially described as "consultative," not binding. VMRO saw this as a sign that the government knew it was on shaky ground. "The referendum story was full of holes. Why didn't the government make the referendum binding? It was because they knew it wouldn't pass. They didn't have the public support," Nacev said.

The referendum question was: "Are you in favor of European Union and NATO membership by accepting the agreement between the Republic of Macedonia and the Republic of Greece?" Critics said the wording was intentionally deceptive, implying that NATO and EU membership were certain while not making clear that "the agreement" with Greece meant changing the country's name. The critics also claimed that by eliding acceptance of Prespa with the issues of EU and NATO membership, the wording violated Macedonia's law on referendums. Each issue in a referendum, the law states, should be presented separately, precisely and unambiguously.[27] The government argued that, in this case, the two issues were inextricably linked, since EU and NATO membership could not happen without acceptance of Prespa. The Constitutional Court ruled that the wording was acceptable.

Victory for Zaev in the referendum seemed possible. A July poll for the US International Republican Institute (IRI) found that 57 percent of Macedonians said they completely or somewhat supported Macedonia joining NATO and the EU under the new name. Only 28 percent somewhat or strongly opposed it. Half the respondents said they would go to polling stations to vote "yes," while 22 percent said they would vote against.[28]

---

[27] Pavlovska, Jacminka, "Референдумот распишан, дилемите останаа [Referendum announced, dilemmas continue]," *Nova Makedonja*, August 1, 2018, https://www.novamakedonija.com.mk/makedonija/ politika/референдумот-распишан-дилемите-оста. Text of the law at https://www.legislationline.org/documents/action/popup/id/5640
[28] Poll at https://www.iri.org/sites/default/files/iri_macedonia_july_ 2018_poll_public_final.pdf

Given numbers like that, opponents of the agreement decided their best strategy was to call for a boycott. With that approach, even if those who voted "yes" were in the majority, a low turnout would allow the legitimacy of the vote to be questioned. VMRO itself never officially urged a boycott, but its statements and actions clearly favored the boycott campaign.

With yet another Balkan country apparently on the verge of joining the West, the referendum took on high importance for Moscow, West Europe, and Washington. The vote would be decided by a public torn by years of political controversy and ethnic strife, and with the lowest media literacy rate in Europe.[29] The campaign to influence voters would be crucial. Macedonia was one of the world's smallest countries, but it suddenly became a laboratory for the influence tools of two rival superpower blocs.

Russia and Its Allies: Threats, Bots, and Motorcycles

Macedonia and Russia had almost no common history. As an Ottoman territory, Macedonia had little direct contact with Russia; as a people's republic within Yugoslavia, it was isolated from Moscow by Tito's wariness of the Soviet Union. No nostalgia for "Soviet times" could be evoked among Macedonians, since they were never part of the Soviet world. With the dissolution of the Soviet Union in 1991, Russian influence faded overall in Eastern Europe until Vladimir Putin moved to reassert his power in Russia's "near abroad." Even then, Moscow's influence efforts in the Balkans were directed mainly at Serbia, Bulgaria, and Greece. All three nations had quarrels with Macedonia, meaning close ties with Skopje were hardly a Russian priority.

Russian interest in Macedonia began to rise after 2008 when the nation's attempt to enter NATO failed. As Gruevski's government turned increasingly authoritarian and corrupt, Macedonia began to look like a country that might keep being snubbed by NATO and therefore could serve Russian interests. Gruevski's lengthy trip to

---

[29] 2018 media literacy index at https://osis.bg/wp-content/uploads/2018/04/MediaLiteracyIndex2018_publishENG.pdf

244 | HOW RUSSIA LOSES

Russia in 2012 opened a door to further cooperation. The Kremlin also felt increasingly embattled after its 2014 invasion of Ukraine and was grateful to countries, like Macedonia, that refused to join Western sanctions.

By May 2015, Russian Foreign Minister Sergei Lavrov was positioning himself as an outright backer of Gruevski. Apparently referring to Gruevski's claims that Zaev was trying to overthrow him, Lavrov warned that some in Macedonia might launch "anti-constitutional actions" because of "Macedonia's refusal to support sanctions against Russia, and construction of the Turk Stream pipeline."[30] In other remarks, likely to energize Gruevski's nationalist supporters, Lavrov painted an apocalyptic picture of how Macedonia might disappear if anti-regime plotters had their way. "The idea even has been expressed: why not divide it up, like an artificial state—to give part to Bulgaria, and part to Albania," he told the Russian parliament.[31]

The same month, the Russian Foreign Ministry took Gruevski's side in his battle against civil society organizations. A ministry statement charged that "the decision by a number of opposition movements and NGOs, including those inspired by the West, to follow the logic of the streets and the notorious 'color revolution' scenario, is fraught with grave consequences." Clearly disturbed by the idea that Macedonia's people might have something to say about their nation's future, it urged the resolution of contentious issues "strictly in an institutional and legal framework."[32]

Moscow's wide-ranging efforts to build influence in Macedonian society were catalogued by the Macedonian counterintelligence agency, then known as the UBK. Some UBK files on Russian operations were published in 2017 by the Organized Crime and

---

[30] "Лавров: обострение в Македонии может быть связано с отказом от санкций [Lavrov: Tension in Macedonia may be linked to refusing sanctions]," *RIA Novosti*, May 15, 2015, https://ria.ru/20150515/1064671852.html

[31] Speech at https://youtu.be/ta_TtCsvXJo

[32] Statement at https://www.mid.ru/ru/foreign_policy/news/1508181

Corruption Reporting Project (OCCRP), Macedonia's *NOVA TV* and Serbia's investigative Crime and Corruption Reporting Network. According to the UBK files, Russian agents attempted to recruit military and police officers to create "a critical mass of military-trained persons" who "at a certain political moment or situation are to be used for accomplishing Russian interests."

Russia also set out to fund and influence media outlets, including Albanian-language outlets, to spread "information and disinformation," the UBK said. Moscow created some 30 Russian-Macedonian "friendship associations" and constructed Orthodox crosses and churches across the country. According to the UBK files, Serbia aided Russia in trying to keep Macedonia out of NATO. The files said Serbian agents were involved in giving "instructions" to pro-Russian politicians and creating anti-Western narratives for friendly journalists to spread.[33]

The Russian Embassy denounced the news reports of the UBK's findings, saying they were characterized by "an incredible lack of professional competence, limitless fantasy, which fully correspond with the anti-Russian hysteria spread by the West."[34]

Russia also sought to spread economic influence in Macedonia, but the effect was limited. The Russia-connected Solway Investment Group began investing in 2005, and by 2015 was operating lead, zinc, and copper mines in Macedonia with a total revenue of €122 million. Russian companies increased gas deliveries to Macedonia but failed in several efforts to fully control the nation's gas and oil market. (Macedonia's main energy source is coal.) Russians did acquire substantial holdings in Macedonia through offshore companies with hard-to-trace owners. Sergei Samsonenko, a Russian businessman from Rostov-on-Don, was one of Macedonia's wealthiest men. He began

---

[33] Belford, Aubrey, et al., "Leaked Documents Show Russian, Serbian Attempts to Meddle in Macedonia," *OCCRP*, June 4, 2017, https://www.occrp.org/en/spooksandspin/leaked-documents-show-russian-serbian-attempts-to-meddle-in-macedonia

[34] Text of Russian statement at http://timemachine.truthmeter.mk/882049

activity in the country shortly after Gruevski became prime minister, profiting from construction, sports, and gambling businesses. Under Gruevski, he was named Russia's honorary consul in Bitola, a city close to the Greek border. After Gruevski fell from power, Samsonenko's fortunes declined.[35]

With operations in the intelligence, media, political, and economic realms, Russia had made itself something of a player in Macedonia and a visible supporter of the Gruevski regime. In March 2017, 52 percent of Macedonians felt their country should maintain strong relations with Russia. Strong ties with the EU were favored by 73 percent and with the US by 64 percent.[36]

Russia's greatest assets were Gruevski and VMRO. Since it had yoked itself so closely to their fortunes, Russia had little choice as the referendum approached but to double down on supporting their nationalist positions. In March 2018, Russia sent Alexander Dugin, a Slavophile philosopher close to Putin, to speak in Skopje under the banner of the pro-Russian United Macedonia party. "When they tell you that there is no alternative to EU and NATO, that represents blackmail, humiliation and colonization," he said. Audience members roared approval at each mention of Russia or Putin.[37]

In March, Macedonian media widely reported an unveiled threat by Russian Ambassador Oleg Shcherbak at a news conference. The ambassador said: "So how can we welcome the Republic of Macedonia's efforts to get into NATO? And for it to become a base for possible wars of this aggressive alliance? The Republic of

---

[35] For details of Russian mining and oil activity, see "Russian Negligent Influence on North Macedonian Politics," *The Kremlin's Influence Quarterly #2*," Free Russia Foundation, 2020,. https://www.4freerussia .org/wp-content/uploads/sites/3/2020/09/Malign_Influence_2_final-old.pdf

[36] Poll at https://www.iri.org/sites/default/files/iri_macedonia_ july_2018_poll_public_final.pdf

[37] Trpkovski, Goce, "Kremlin 'Guru' Rouses Anti-Western Feeling in Macedonia," *BalkanInsight*, March 5, 2018, https://balkaninsight.com/ 2018/03/05/kremlin-guru-rouses-anti-western-feeling-in-macedonia-03-05-2018/

Macedonia will become part of this military machine and part of the aggression against Russia with its inclusion. With that, you will become the target of retaliation from Russia. Is this something you and your children need?" Shcherbak added that, since Macedonia was surrounded by NATO on all sides, it could be attacked only "by NATO or aliens"[38]—a clever line, except that Macedonia has a border with Serbia, a non-NATO member that often makes common cause with Russia.

The following month, the ambassador told a university audience that Macedonia was safest as a neutral nation. "Throughout Europe there are many successful militarily neutral countries, and when regarding natural security, this is a rational approach," he said. "We know full well that when solidarity is put before common sense, it is fatal for national interests."[39] According to the UBK files, Shcherbak had been telling Macedonian officials that Moscow's political goal was for Montenegro, Bosnia and Herzegovina, Macedonia, and Serbia to form "a strip of militarily neutral countries" in the Balkans. Shcherbak reportedly also proposed that, instead of joining the EU, Macedonia join the Russia-led Eurasian Economic Union, a much weaker bloc whose other members included Belarus, Kyrgyzstan, Kazakhstan, and Armenia.[40]

When the nationalists stormed the parliament in response to Xhaferi's election, a Russian Foreign Ministry statement put all the blame on "the opposition, which lost the parliamentary election." Although Zaev and his ethnic Albanian allies had won the vote to elect the parliament president, the statement said Xhaferi was chosen "in gross violation of the established

---

[38] "Shcherbak: In case of an eventual war between Russia and NATO, Macedonia will be a legitimate target," *Meta.mk*, March 29, 2018, https://meta.mk/en/shcherbak-in-case-of-an-eventual-war-between-russia-and-nato-macedonia-will-be-a-legitimate-target

[39] "Shcherbak: Disaster for national interests when solidarity put before common sense," *Meta.mk*, April 24, 2018, https://meta.mk/en/shcherbak-disaster-for-national-interests-when-solidarity-put-before-common-sense/

[40] "Leaked Documents Show Russian, Serbian Attempts to Meddle in Macedonia," op. cit.

procedures" as part of "the unceremonious manipulation of the will of the citizens with the aim of removing the legitimate government from power." The statement added that the "lightning-fast coordinated reaction" with which the US and EU congratulated Xhaferi "is undoubtedly evidence that the incident was planned in advance, with the tacit knowledge of the 'external curators' of the Macedonian opposition."[41]

The Russian news agency *Sputnik* also tried to whitewash the attack on parliament, saying it "was truly not pretty to behold, but it cannot be said that it was not justified, to a point."[42] Xhaferi later said he could not exclude Russian involvement in the attack. He said a Serbian intelligence agent was present. He added, "Serbia has its own interests but things can't happen without coordination with Moscow."[43]

Even after Zaev became Macedonia's leader, Russia might still have believed that, given the passions on all sides, Skopje would never settle its conflict with Greece on the country's name. Any such confidence evaporated with Prespa. When the agreement was signed on June 17, 2018, Russia found itself suddenly dealing with an exceedingly tight timetable. Within two weeks, it was announced that the referendum on the name change would take place on September 30. Moscow had to consider that, if the referendum succeeded, the parliament could change the constitution and the country's name in short order—and membership in NATO and the EU could swiftly follow.

Initially, Russia could take heart from the wave of discontent over Prespa that welled up immediately in both Macedonia and Greece. The day after it was signed, 2,000 demonstrators shouting "Traitors!" and "To the gallows!" massed at the parliament building in Skopje to demand that Zaev resign. When they tried to breach a security cordon, police responded with tear gas and stun grenades; about 25 people were arrested. Members of the

---

[41] Statement at https://archive.mid.ru/ru/foreign_policy/news/-asset_publisher/cKNonkJE02Bw/content/id/2739769

[42] "Macedonia 'at risk from Russian meddling,'" op. cit.

[43] Talat Xhaferi, interview with author, July 15, 2021.

Macedonian branch of the Night Wolves, a Russian motorcycle club, took part in the protests. The leader of United Macedonia attended, carrying Macedonian and Russian flags.[44]

According to OCCRP, *BuzzFeed*, and Macedonia's Investigative Reporting Lab, Ivan Savvidis, a Georgian-born billionaire who moved to Greece after serving in the Russian parliament, paid Macedonian opponents of Prespa at least €300,000 to carry out public demonstrations. The outlets' reporting found that recipients of the funds included politicians, newly created nationalist organizations, and football hooligans associated with Komiti, a fan club of the Vardar football club owned by Samsonenko. Ten associates of Komiti were arrested in the protests in Skopje. Savvidis denied stoking protests in Macedonia, and the Russian Foreign Ministry said claims that pro-Russian businessmen were behind the protests were "unsubstantiated accusations against Moscow aimed at whipping up anti-Russian hysteria."[45] A dozen or so NGOs, mainly supported by nationalist diaspora groups, attracted thousands of people to their own rallies against the government's proposal.

Resistance to Prespa went beyond street protests. The powerful Macedonian Orthodox Church spoke out against the name change. Anti-NATO activists unrolled a massive online campaign to promote a boycott of the referendum. Macedonia was about to be blackmailed, the campaigners said, into a plot to destroy its

---

[44] Stojanovski, Filip, "Pro-Russia biker club admits participation in protests leading to violent attack of Macedonian Parliament," *Global Voices*, January 12, 2019, https://globalvoices.org/2019/01/12/pro-russian-biker-club-admits-participation-in-protests-leading-to-violent-attack-of-macedonian-parliament-trial-reveals; and Marusic, Sinisa Jakov, "In Pictures: Macedonia 'Name' Protest Turns Violent," *BalkanInsight*, June 18, 2018, https://balkaninsight.com/2018/06/18/in-pictures-macedonia-name-protest-turns-violent-06-18-2018
[45] See "Ιβάν Σαββίδης: Μήνυση κατά του BuzzFeed για τη συνέντευξη Ζάεφ [Ivan Savvidis: Lawsuit against BuzzFeed for the Zaev interview]," *KIPE*, July 17, 2018, http://www.kathimerini.com.cy/gr/ellada/iban-sabbidis-minysi-kata-toy-buzzfeed-gia-ti-synenteyxi-zaef; and Russian Foreign Ministry, Twitter, July 18, 2018, https://twitter.com/MID_RF/status/1019571707483508736

250 | HOW RUSSIA LOSES

identity and harm its people. Some messages claimed that NATO would poison citizens with depleted uranium munitions, that Google would no longer support the Macedonian language, and even that the language would be officially renamed "North Macedonian." Some posts raised the specter of the "Tirana Platform," a purported plan to create a "Greater Albania" with territory from Macedonia, Kosovo, Serbia, Montenegro, and Greece. (The supposed plan, which Albania says does not exist, has been a staple of anti-Albanian agitation in the Balkans.)

Posts with the hashtag #Бојкотирам ("I'm boycotting") garnered 20,000 retweets and 24,000 mentions. Rosana Aleksoska, head of the counter-disinformation program at the civil society group MOST, said harrowing accounts of what NATO membership could mean often started from anonymous websites. From there, they jumped to pro-VMRO sites and finally to mainstream media.[46] A few weeks before the referendum, 40 new pages agitating for a boycott were appearing every day on Facebook. The accounts, some managed from outside the country, posed questions such as, "Are you going to let Albanians change your name?" Bots bearing Macedonian names followed by a string of numbers reposted provocative messages at industrial speed. Accounts used by troll farms in the Macedonian town of Veles to interfere in the 2016 US presidential campaign turned to promoting a boycott, as did sensationalist Hungarian-owned media in Skopje. Sometimes identical narratives appeared from Russian and Serbian online sources and were then picked up by Macedonian outlets.[47] (The anti-NATO claims were no stretch for Serbian-controlled media, which had long been attacking the alliance and raising suspicions about Albanian intentions.)

Many automated tweets amounted simply to spam, drowning out any serious discussions of the issues involved. The intensity of the

---

[46] Aleksoska, Rosana, interview with author, July 15, 2021.
[47] See Metodieva, Asya, "Russian Narrative Proxies in the Western Balkans," German Marshall Fund, June 2019, https://www.gmfus.org/sites/default/files/Russian%2520Narrative%2520Proxies%2520in%2520Balkans.pdf; and "Russian Negligent Influence on North Macedonian Politics," op. cit.

Macedonia: The Tank and the Lada | 251

referendum battle split families, Aleksoska said. Overall, said Jashari of the Metamorphosis group, Russia activated a "campaign of small things, but well-synchronized." Voices ranging from football fans to motorcycle clubs, anti-NATO religious figures, social influencers, and outright Putin admirers—all encouraged people to vote "no" in the referendum or boycott it, he said.

Russia was also reportedly active inside Greece, where thousands protested the Prespa accord and sometimes clashed violently with police. Less than a month after Prespa, authorities expelled two Russian diplomats and blocked the entry of two more. A Greek newspaper said the diplomats had been trying to bribe Greek officials and that "various circles" tied to Russia had tried to intervene in domestic politics over Prespa.[48] One Greek official said the government had received evidence of "specific actions" by the expelled Russians to fund anti-Prespa protests.[49]

The official Greek support for Prespa stood out against Tsipras' generally friendly attitude toward Russia. When Sergei Skripal and his daughter were poisoned in England four months earlier, Greece had refused to join other NATO nations in retaliating by expelling Russian diplomats. (Macedonia, as a candidate NATO member, expelled a Russian diplomat from Skopje.)

Zaev maintained that, as a matter of policy, NATO membership for Macedonia was not aimed against Russia. He said in March 2018 that "Macedonia in its strategic goals intends to strengthen and promote cooperation with the Russian Federation."[50] But he was blunt about Russian involvement in domestic affairs. He told *BuzzFeed*, "The Russian representatives who were here, and also

---

[48] Nedos, Vassilis, "Greece decides to expel Russian diplomats," *Ekarthimerini.com*, July 11, 2018, https://www.ekathimerini. com/news/230551/greece-decides-to-expel-russian-diplomats
[49] Kantouris, Costas, et al., "Greece: Russians expelled over cash-for-protests allegation," *The Associated Press*, July 12, 2018, https://ap news.com/article/aaf032985e7341d3a7968f6ff6b95ce0
[50] "Zaev: Our integration into NATO is not directed against Russia," March 20, 2018, *Meta.mk*, https://meta.mk/en/zaev-our-integration-into-nato-is-not-directed-against-russia

others from Moscow, [do not hide] that they are against our integration in NATO. Part of them are connected with media, part of them ... encourage the young people to protest in front of the parliament, to attack policemen, that kind of things. It's very obvious."

Zaev said he had invited President Trump to visit Macedonia to campaign for a "yes" vote on the referendum, despite Trump's chilliness toward NATO. "The United States—still—is the huge example of democratic institutions, [rule] of law, free speech, and free media. That is the important thing," Zaev said. "It's a huge model for us and good example."[51]

Lavrov denied Russia was trying in any way to interfere in the referendum. Just nine days before the vote, the Russian foreign minister declared in Belgrade:

> The situation is dubious in Macedonia after the signing of the Prespa agreement, whose legitimacy is questioned by many Macedonian political forces. A referendum is coming. I invite you to watch in the media, social networks, on the Internet, what Russia says about this— we do not say anything that could be interpreted as campaigning for that or another option of voting.[52]

This came despite all of Moscow's efforts—including the Russian ambassador's speeches suggesting that, if Macedonians joined NATO, they would be signing their own death warrant in the event of a future conflict.

---

[51] Feder, J. Lester, "Macedonia Suspects A Greek-Russian Billionaire Paid For Violent Protests To Prevent It From Joining NATO," *BuzzFeed News*, July 18, 2018, https://www.buzzfeednews.com/article/lesterfeder/macedonia-russia-nato

[52] "Russian FM Lavrov, Republika Srpska President Dodik Hold Joint Press Conference," *Sputnik News*, September 21, 2018, https://sputnik news.com/20180921/conference-lavrov-dodik-1068232869.html

The West's Campaign: Star Power and the Team From DC

Even before the United States officially recognized Macedonia's independence, US aid was flowing into the country. USAID began operating there in 1993, a year before Washington's formal recognition. The US built a thick web of activity throughout Macedonian society. Its programs promoted democracy and civil society, wired schools to the internet, educated handicapped children, advanced women's rights, encouraged anti-corruption activists, and promoted agriculture, entrepreneurship, and the environment. Total US assistance to Macedonia reached a peak of $72 million in 2002. Much of the early help went to make Macedonia's government, which early on was firmly pro-Western, more efficient and better at communicating with its citizens. These US-taught lessons were inherited by the Gruevski government, which decided to build strong relations with Moscow. In 2018, the year of the referendum, Macedonia received $24 million from the US.

Aiding Macedonia alongside the United States was the European Union. Macedonia's application for EU membership in 2004 brought it €1.25 billion in "pre-accession" funds from 2007 to 2020. The European Investment Bank, an EU agency, also provided €940 million in loans starting in 1999. Other EU agencies and member governments offered support.

Along with aid came trade. Macedonia's trade in goods was heavily oriented toward the West. In the referendum year, its trade with the EU was €9.5 billion and with the US $400 million. Trade with Russia that year totaled $170 million.[53] Macedonia's diaspora, which sends substantial funds home, lives mainly in Western countries.

---

[53] See https://webgate.ec.europa.eu/isdb_results/factsheets/country/details_north-macedonia_en.pdf https://www.census.gov/foreign-trade/balance/c4794.html, and https://wits.worldbank.org/CountryProfile/en/Country/MKD/Year/2018/TradeFlow/EXPIMP/Partner/by-country.

254 | HOW RUSSIA LOSES

Both the US and the EU made democracy promotion central to their efforts. The EU contributed €24.3 million specifically to reinforce civil society between 2014 and 2020.[54] The UK ran its own programs, with such goals as strengthening civil society organizations and independent media, developing a "vision for democracy" among young Macedonians, and increasing the role of women in politics.[55]

The State Department, the US National Endowment for Democracy, and especially USAID provided more than $45 million in democracy assistance to Macedonia in 2012–2017.[56]

When the 2015 crisis broke out between Gruevski and the opposition, USAID opened a Skopje branch of its Office of Transition Initiatives (OTI), a specialized unit devoted to providing fast, short-term assistance to countries "with key political transition and stabilization needs." By 2016, OTI was working in two major areas: improvements in media quality and pluralism, and further development of civil society. In January 2017, Congress allocated $8 million specifically to fight Russian disinformation in Macedonia, though the money reportedly did not arrive for a year.[57]

US projects aimed to reach large audiences in Macedonia, especially those interested in news and politics. USAID sponsored short news videos on social networks titled "Vidi Vaka" ("Let me tell you"). The US agency deployed American and British consultants to help produce a political TV talk show, "Samo Vistina" ("Only the Truth"), which debuted in May 2017. Another

---

[54] 2018 US and EU aid figures from https://foreignassistance.gov. Other European figures from https://ec.europa.eu/neighbourhood-enlargement/system/files/2021-10/18102021_factograph_north_macedonia.pdf

[55] https://www.gov.uk/government/publications/programme-portfolio-of-the-british-embassy-skopje-2005-2014

[56] https://www.gao.gov/assets/gao-20-158.pdf

[57] Santora, Mark, et al., "In the Balkans, Russia and the West Fight a Disinformation-Age Battle," *The New York Times*, September 16, 2018, https://www.nytimes.com/2018/09/16/world/europe/macedonia-referendum-russia-nato.html

Macedonia: The Tank and the Lada | 255

television program aimed at reducing religious tensions. For Macedonians not deeply interested in politics, USAID ran a series of two- and three-day "civic festivals" around the country. These attracted crowds with music and art exhibitions and offered panels on democracy, citizen participation in society, and environmental issues.

There was discussion within the USAID team as to whether overt US branding would diminish the festivals' effectiveness. The decision was to be open about US involvement. If the funding were covert, the team reasoned, word of it would leak in any case—and damage the festivals' credibility.

The US also backed a satirical television show, "Vcherashni Novosti" ("Yesterday's News"). The show took shots at Gruevski and extreme nationalists, as well as opposition politicians including Zaev. Political satire is a risky business in any country, and USAID tried its best to keep the show from going over the top—especially since the USAID logo appeared in the credits. Mission staffers reviewed content to keep out vulgarity and maintained an Excel spreadsheet of jokes to enforce balance in terms of who was lampooned.

Another US-backed campaign was "Mrdni so prst." This could be translated as "Make an effort" or, more colloquially, "Move your ass." Implemented by Macedonia's National Youth Council, the program provided grants between $1,500 and $5,000 for small projects such as renovating a school or constructing a rain shelter at a bus stop. The project, promoted through posts on Facebook, encouraged civic initiative—good for bus passengers today but potentially for political activism tomorrow.

All these activities had been aimed at boosting prosperity, democratic tendencies, and pro-Western feelings in Macedonia. The referendum would be a decisive test of what this work had wrought.

As the referendum neared, many civil society groups focused their efforts on getting people to the polls. Some NGO campaigners refrained from telling people how to vote, but their actions were implicitly pro-Zaev because government opponents were calling for a boycott. Other NGOs openly supported a "yes" vote and sponsored television advertisements to that end. Many mainstream media organizations in Macedonia, a focus of US effort for many years, called for a "yes" vote or presented news coverage that gave more time to pro-government voices. A study by the Organization for Security and Co-operation in Europe (OSCE) attributed the pro-"yes" imbalance in part to the pro-boycott side. It said media had trouble presenting balanced coverage because VMRO did not have an official position on the vote. Boycott campaigners had no single organization with a spokesperson who could be quoted. Only toward the end of the campaign did pro-boycott TV ads appear.[58]

Campaigners for a "yes" vote plastered cities with posters and billboards in the yellow and blue colors of the EU, knocked on doors, organized rallies and town hall meetings, and spun up their own efforts online. These included a colorful website, a Facebook page, and Instagram accounts. Slogans included, "Come out for a European Macedonia," "This is a historic opportunity," and "Yes to €260,000 in assistance from European funds every day."[59] Parliament spent €900,000 for pro-"yes" messages through 66 media outlets, mainly television networks. Some €400,000 remained unused because pro-boycott VMRO deputies refused to ask parliament to support messages in the other direction.[60]

All this activity in Macedonia caught the attention of the National Security Council (NSC) in Washington. The Skopje Embassy was concerned that Zaev's government had been slower in launching

---

[58] Organization for Security and Co-operation in Europe, "The Former Yugoslav Republic Of Macedonia, Referendum, 30 September 2018, ODIHR Referendum Observation Mission Final Report," January 21, 2019, https://www.osce.org/files/f/documents/6/1/409554.pdf
[59] See Facebook page at https://m.facebook.com/Izlezi.ZA?_rdr, campaign website as of Sept 2018 at https://web.archive.org/web/20180925101058/http://www.izlezi.mk/
[60] Apostolov, Vlado, "Macedonia Reveals Cost of Referendum Media Adverts," *BalkanInsight*, February 14, 2019, https://balkaninsight.com/2019/02/14/macedonia-reveals-cost-of-referendum-media-adverts

Macedonia: The Tank and the Lada | 257

its "yes" campaign than its opponents had been with their "I'm boycotting!" effort. To help the Macedonian government's campaign, Washington dispatched a team from the State Department's Global Engagement Center (GEC), the nation's official coordinator of counter-disinformation efforts. Working with Zaev's office from July 24 to August 17, the GEC's tasks included "providing the host nation with a snapshot of the social media environment, data on media outlets, training on data analysis tools, and building awareness on the disinformation tactics of our adversaries," GEC head Lea Gabrielle told Congress the following year. "We actually provided a people-on-the-ground [sic] there to support with insight reports, giving demographic and microtargeting information, really using data scientists to support that effort.[61]

US officials said the GEC devised ten "get out and vote" messages, suggested the best media outlets for advertising campaigns, and proposed tactics to reach rural populations. The US proposed that many public messages focus on economic issues. GEC analysts targeted in particular what they considered the "6-percenters"— Macedonians who were believed to be still undecided as the referendum neared. (The Macedonia operation was an early test of the GEC. It had been founded two years earlier and had spent much of its early energy struggling to receive operating funds through a government financial maze.)

Some US activity went beyond traditional diplomacy. Someone obtained wiretap evidence suggesting Savvidis was trying to undermine the Greece-Macedonia deal. The findings, turned over to Tsipras' government by the US, reportedly precipitated Greece's expulsion of the two Russian diplomats in July 2018. "We're pushing back and showing that we can play hardball, too,"

---

[61] Gabrielle, Lea, "United States Efforts to Counter Russian Disinformation and Malign Influence," (congressional testimony, July 10, 2019), https://docs.house.gov/meetings/AP/AP04/20190710/109748/HHRG-116-AP04-Wstate-GabrielleL-20190710.pdf

Christopher R. Hill, a former US ambassador to Macedonia, enthused in an interview with *The New York Times*.[62]

The US did not work alone. The UK Foreign Office reportedly funded a British PR firm to assist the Macedonian government.[63] Western nations rushed political star power to Skopje to praise Zaev's government and urge Macedonians to accept the name deal. Even before Prespa was signed, British Prime Minister Teresa May visited Skopje to say that an agreement with Greece on a new name for Macedonia would "bring clear benefits to both countries and also to the region as whole."[64] After Prespa, visitors with similar messages included NATO Secretary-General Jens Stoltenberg, Austrian Chancellor Sebastian Kurz, and German Chancellor Angela Merkel. (Opposition forces seemed to be watching closely; tweets calling for a "no" vote peaked the day Merkel arrived.[65]) French President Emmanuel Macron sent a video message.

Albania worked with Macedonia's ethnic Albanians to encourage them to vote "yes." Barely two weeks before the vote, US Defense Secretary James Mattis appeared in Skopje. He declared that by joining NATO, Macedonia would "gain an equal seat at the table of the most successful military alliance in history, alongside 29 other countries committed to protect you and your security, spurring economic prosperity and increased foreign investment, as well as

---

[62] Cooper, Helene, et al., "U.S. Spycraft and Stealthy Diplomacy Expose Russian Subversion in a Key Balkans Vote," *The New York Times*, October 9, 2018, https://www.nytimes.com/2018/10/09/us/politics/russia-macedonia-greece.html

[63] Purkiss, Jessica, "Russian warriors and British PR firms: Macedonia's information war," *The Bureau of Investigative Journalism*, September 28, 2018, https://www.thebureauinvestigates.com/stories/2018-09-28/russian-warriors-and-british-pr-firms-macedonias-information-war

[64] "Britain's May Pledges Support For Resolution on Macedonia Name Issue," *Radio Free Europe/Radio Liberty*, May 17, 2018, https://www.rferl.org/a/britain-macedonia-balkans-greece/29232876.html

[65] "Russian Narrative Proxies in the Western Balkans," op. cit.

strengthened security."[66] Addressing reporters on his plane, Mattis made clear that Russia was trying to swing the referendum's results. "We do not want to see Russia doing there [in Macedonia] what they have tried to do in so many other countries," he said. "No doubt they have transferred money and they are also conducting broader influence campaigns."[67]

In Moscow's view, it was quite rich for NATO nations to accuse Russia of interfering in the run-up to the referendum while a parade of Western leaders was marching through Skopje, openly appealing to Macedonians to vote "yes." As Russia declared on October 4 at a meeting of the OSCE:

> It is widely known that prominent political figures from the EU countries and NATO openly urged Macedonia's people to vote "yes." ... In our view, not only are such practices unacceptable but they are hypocritical, too, particularly given these countries' exaggerated "concern" over foreign intervention in any electoral or internal process.[68]

Referendum Day and the Constitution

Sunday, September 30, was a perfect day, cloudy in the capital with temperatures in the 60s and 70s. The polls for the referendum opened at 7:00 a.m. As befitted an event of such importance, the State Election Commission accredited 493 international observers. Thousands of local observers also were

---

[66] US Department of Defense press release at https://www.defense. gov/News/News-Stories/Article/Article/1636005/mattis-praises-macedonia-as-stabilizing-force

[67] Idress, Ali, "U.S. Defense Secretary warns of Russian meddling in Macedonia referendum," *Reuters*, September 17, 2018, https://www.reuters.com/article/us-macedonia-usa/u-s-defense-secretary-warns-of-russian-meddling-in-macedonia-referendum-idUSKCN1LX0ER

[68] Text at https://www.osce.org/files/f/documents/2/5/399632.pdf

260 | HOW RUSSIA LOSES

certified to oversee the vote, stationed at 90 percent of polling places.

What was missing was voters. By the time polls closed at 7:00 p.m., only 36.5 percent of those on the official voter rolls had shown up. The final tally was 609,427 for the government's proposal versus 37,687 against—a 94-percent result in favor. Most attention, however, focused on the turnout. "The world was hanging on this referendum," a US official said. "Only the Macedonians didn't seem to care that much."

Zaev made the best of the result. He declared that the name change had passed in a landslide, which was true if you ignored the turnout. "The will of those who voted now must be turned into political action inside parliament," he said. VMRO President Hristijan Mickoski also called the vote decisive, but in the other direction: "Those who voted against and those who decided to boycott showed that the vast majority of the people are against this agreement, and they are the ones who sent the strongest message today."[69] The Kremlin's new ambassador, Sergei Bazdnikin, agreed. He told *Sputnik* the low turnout made clear the referendum was void.[70]

In the case of a binding referendum in Macedonia, a question can legally pass only if a majority of all eligible voters approve it. On that basis, the State Electoral Commission declared that the question on the referendum had not been approved. Yet the law was unclear on whether the same standards applied to a consultative referendum, leaving Zaev free to claim that those Macedonians who chose to express an opinion had delivered a resounding verdict.

---

[69] Santora, Marc, "Both Sides Claim Victory in Macedonia's Vote on Changing Its Name," *The New York Times*, September 30, 2018, https://www.nytimes.com/2018/09/30/world/europe/macedonia-greece-referendum.html

[70] Sputnik interview cited in "Russian MFA: In the referendum, solutions imposed from the outside were boycotted," *Meta.mk*, October 2, 2018, https://meta.mk/en/russian-mfa-in-the-referendum-solutions-imposed-from-the-outside-were-boycotted

Macedonia: The Tank and the Lada | 261

What accounted for the low turnout? In the 2016 parliament elections, 66 percent of those on the voter rolls had shown up at the polls. The IRI poll in July 2018 had predicted that only 16 percent of voters would not vote in the referendum.[71] Was the boycott call successful, the weather too lovely for voting, or interest just not that high on any side? The 2016 parliamentary election had been followed by months of bitter political fighting and violence. Perhaps many people had decided that voting never decides matters anyhow. Some diplomats believed the official voter rolls themselves were out of date, loaded with hundreds of thousands of invalid names. If that were true, the turnout rate for people who were actually alive and eligible to vote could have been considerably higher.

Western media pulled no punches in concluding the vote was a clear loss for the "yes" forces. The turnout was "a setback for the government and for Western leaders," reported *The New York Times*, while *The Washington Post* called the outcome "a blow to the West."[72] *The Guardian* declared "a significant victory for Vladimir Putin, a setback for the EU and NATO, and another disturbing example of Russia's ability and willingness to influence the democratic process in Western countries."[73]

At the State Department, spokesperson Heather Nauert gamely stated that Macedonia's "citizens expressed their support for NATO and European Union (EU) membership by accepting the

---

[71] Another 13 percent refused to answer the question about how they would vote. IRI July 2017 poll, op. cit.

[72] "Both Sides Claim Victory in Macedonia's Vote on Changing Its Name," op. cit.; and Birnbaum, Michael, "In a blow to the West, most Macedonians sit out vote to unlock NATO and E.U. membership," *The Washington Post*, September 30, 2018, https://www.washingtonpost.com/world/in-a-blow-to-the-west-most-macedonians-sit-out-vote-to-unlock-nato-and-eu-membership/2018/09/30/2067b740-c4d6-11e8-9c0f-2ffaf6d422aa_story.html

[73] Tisdall, Simon, "Result of Macedonia's referendum is another victory for Russia," *The Guardian*, October 1, 2018, https://www.theguardian.com/world/2018/oct/01/result-of-macedonia-referendum-is-another-victory-for-russia

Prespa Agreement between Macedonia and Greece."[74] UK Foreign Secretary Jeremy Hunt said that, although turnout was below expectations, voters "showed their desire to resolve the long-standing dispute with neighbouring Greece over the country's name and take a positive step towards Euro-Atlantic integration."[75]

The US Embassy had tried to manage Washington's expectations in advance, explaining that robust approval of the proposal was not a sure thing. Nonetheless, within the US mission in Skopje, the turnout left staffers crestfallen, one official recalled. Staff members were disheartened that, despite all the aid dispensed to Macedonia, so few citizens showed up to support Western institutions. "Sometimes aid goes wide," an official said later, "but it doesn't go deep." Some at the mission wondered whether they could echo in good conscience the State Department's claim that the referendum was a decisive pro-Western statement.

Still, there was the fact that those who voted had overwhelmingly approved the name change. Just because voters did not show up on a gorgeous day did not mean they had expressly decided to boycott. "Yes" campaigners calculated that more people voted in favor of the referendum question than had voted for any single party in the 2016 parliament elections.[76] That suggested some momentum for a name change. Pro-Western forces now began to concentrate on constitutional amendments to make Macedonia's new name official.

Changing the constitution in Macedonia is not a simple matter. The procedure requires an elaborate sequence of proposals and drafts, with fixed time delays between steps and two parliament votes, each with a two-thirds majority. Zaev's coalition did not have enough votes to reach the two-thirds level. Therefore, it was essential to induce—by one means or another—deputies from

---

[74] Statement at https://2017-2021.state.gov/macedonias-referendum-on-the-prespa-agreement/index.html

[75] Statement at https://www.gov.uk/government/news/foreign-secretary-statement-on-macedonia-referendum

[76] "Yes" campaign Facebook page, op. cit.

Macedonia: The Tank and the Lada | 263

VMRO to vote for a name change their party had vehemently opposed. A number of prosecutions had been grinding forward against former Gruevski officials and VMRO MPs, some dating back to the release of the wiretap tapes. These cases would soon become highly relevant in Zaev's quest for the constitutional changes.

The prosecutions were wide-ranging. Eleven VMRO officials, including Gruevski, were accused of accepting illegal political contributions. Gruevski himself allegedly took €4.9 million between 2009 and 2015. The former minister of transport and communications was arrested for embezzling €2 million from the Spanish Steps project. (The steps were never built.) Two counterintelligence agents were accused of illegally using Interior Ministry equipment for wiretapping. Terrorism charges were filed against former Interior Minister Mitko Chavkov and more than 30 others, including five VMRO parliament deputies, for involvement in the April 2017 attack on parliament.

It was against this background of prosecutions that the campaign began for Macedonia's parliament to amend the constitution to change the country's name. Zaev's coalition needed at least eight votes from VMRO deputies for the required two-thirds margins. A Zaev official said 15 to 17 VMRO deputies, some of whom already had disputes with their party, were targeted for persuasion. The persuasion would be carried out by means ranging from political cajoling to what some saw as blatant pressure.

Pro-amendment officials laid out to the targeted VMRO deputies a series of strong political arguments for accepting the name change:

• Greece would never yield in its demand that Macedonia change its name. Athens had not hesitated to defy President Bush on the matter at the Bucharest summit; it would certainly not yield to entreaties from Macedonian politicians.

• The Prespa accord happened at a rare moment when flexibly minded leaders were in power simultaneously in Macedonia and Greece. With Tsipras on his way out politically, the circumstances

264 | HOW RUSSIA LOSES

in Greece for a new political accommodation might not recur for decades.

• Macedonia had other identities before and had survived them. Since World War II, it had been known as the Socialist Republic of Macedonia (within Yugoslavia), as the FYROM, and as Macedonia. There had never been a question about what geography and people these varied names referred to; the same would apply with the name North Macedonia. In addition, Greece had recognized in the Prespa accord Macedonia's understanding of its identity.

• NATO membership was a sure thing if Macedonia changed its name. All NATO members were ready to accept Macedonia as soon as the name issue was solved.

• Macedonia inhabited a dangerous neighborhood, where neighbors had had designs on its territory and identity for centuries. NATO offered an unparalleled security package. NATO membership would instantly turn three countries Macedonia had traditionally viewed as threats to its security—Greece, Bulgaria, and Albania—into allies.

• EU membership would weld Macedonia into Europe's most prosperous economic bloc. Full EU membership was not certain (as the country soon learned), but the name change would remove a critical obstacle.

Some VMRO deputies saw the strength of these arguments. They also wondered about VMRO's future after Gruevski's conviction for corruption and the Social Democrats' overwhelming victory in municipal elections in late 2017.

There were rumors that VMRO MPs who faced charges over corruption or involvement in the April attack on parliament had been given to understand that the cases against them might be dropped if they supported the name change. During the week of the first critical parliamentary vote in October 2018, three VMRO members who had been charged in the attack on parliament were released on bail from house arrest. They voted in favor of the government's proposal. Other VMRO deputies who voted "yes" included one who was facing corruption charges and another whose son had been convicted in a corruption case.[77]

The first vote on the name change passed on October 19 by a vote of 80-39—just meeting the two-thirds requirement. Zaev refused to say if the legislators allowed to leave their homes might eventually get amnesty. He also denied a charge by VMRO that the government had offered bribes for votes.[78] Whatever inducements might have been offered for the MPs' votes, it was still an act of courage to cast them; several had received threats, and police were sent to guard their homes.

The Russian Foreign Ministry insisted that the whole vote was the result of a conspiracy. The result, it charged, was obtained through "blackmail, threats and the buying of opposition deputies." A ministry statement said that, beyond the three parliament deputies who were allowed to leave their houses, two others were promised their freedom and "others, in return for 'the proper vote,' were given corrupt financial proposals." It claimed that "MPs were locked in their offices and their mobile phones were confiscated—obviously, in the spirit of European democratic practice."

The statement added, "It is notable that the US ambassador was in the parliament building right until the end of the session, which leaves no doubt as to who was running this process."[79] US

---

[77] Nikolovska-Rizvanovik, Galena, "Четворица обвинети пратеници од ВМРО-ДПМНЕ гласаа за уставните измени [Four accused deputies from VMRO-DPMNE voted for the constitutional amendments]," *Makfax*, October 19, 2018, https://makfax.com.mk/makedonija/владата-обезбеди-двотретинско-мнози

[78] "Macedonian Name Change Moves Ahead After Crucial Parliament Vote," *Radio Free Europe/Radio Liberty*, October 20, 2018, https://www.rferl.org/a/macedonian-name-changes-moves-ahead-after-crucial-vote-in-parliament/29554008.html

[79] "В МИД РФ рассказали о случаях шантажа депутатов в Македонии ради переименования страны [Russian Foreign Ministry tells of cases of blackmail against Macedonian deputies in order to rename the country]," *Interfax*, October 22, 2018, https://www.interfax.ru/world/634504

266 | HOW RUSSIA LOSES

Ambassador Jess Baily tweeted that his activity that night was hosting a Halloween party for the US Embassy community.

The second two-thirds vote needed to finally approve the country's name change was scheduled for January 2019. Immediately after the October vote, opposition deputies who had voted with Zaev's government conditioned their future support on an amnesty for non-violent participants in the parliament takeover—who included several of their number. Judicial and human rights activists protested that such a measure would undermine the very rule of law that the Social Democrats had promised to restore. Zaev, however, said, "I am willing to pay the political price." Social Democrats joined with VMRO deputies to approve the amnesty on December 18.[80]

With that, parliament voted to approve the name change on January 11, with 81 votes in favor. The remaining VMRO members boycotted. Several hundred demonstrators protested the vote in the streets outside parliament, and President Ivanov refused to sign off on the vote. Xhaferi certified it in Ivanov's place.

The actions by Macedonia's parliament checked all the boxes for a legally binding name change. Yet it raised the same kinds of concerns as the referendum. Did either truly represent the will of Macedonia's people? The maneuvering for votes was "not pretty," a senior foreign diplomat recalled. Zvonko Naumoski, who worked for a USAID-funded project at the time, said that the USAID staff in Skopje was split as to whether strong-arming of MPs was unacceptable, or unavoidable, to push the country forward.

Parliament President Xhaferi reacted mildly when asked two years later about whether VMRO deputies voted for the name change only to avoid prosecution. "I have no information there was any agreement on stopping prosecution. There was no official

---

[80] Marusic, Sinisa Jakov, "Macedonia MPs Approve Amnesty for Parliament Attackers," *BalkanInsight,* December 18, 2018, https://balkaninsight.com/2018/12/18/macedonia-passes-amnesty-for-parliament-attackers-12-18-2018

Macedonia: The Tank and the Lada | 267

who could guarantee that they would be free afterward," he said. But Xhaferi added: "From a philosophical and humanitarian standpoint, it is reasonable that people who acknowledge they made a mistake might be forgiven. If something is in the interests of the state, the payment of some price might be acceptable. The interests of the state always take priority over other priorities."[81]

Once the constitutional change was completed on January 11, the country's use of its new name was still contingent on Greece approving Prespa. All eyes turned to Athens. On January 25, Tspiras overcame opposition in the Greek parliament and won approval for the agreement by a vote of 153-146. NATO made good on its promise to admit the country quickly. On February 6, the alliance approved the accession protocol for North Macedonia to become the 30th member, and two days later, Greece gave its consent. Macedonia officially changed its name to North Macedonia on February 12. Even though all countries had not yet ratified its membership, North Macedonia was soon admitted to high-level NATO discussions. The US Senate ratified North Macedonia's accession in October. If conservative senators were still concerned about US policy in Macedonia, they put up little resistance to the further expansion of NATO. Only Mike Lee, along with libertarian Rand Paul of Kentucky, voted against the measure.

On May 6, Social Democrat Stevo Pendarovski was elected president of North Macedonia by a margin of 52 to 45 percent over his VMRO rival, Gordana Siljanovska-Davkova. (Ivanov was barred by term limits from running again.) Zaev's Social Democrats now held the premiership and presidency and led the ruling coalition in parliament. North Macedonia had clearly set out on a pro-Western course.

As for Gruevski, a court sentenced him in May 2018 to two years in prison for unlawfully influencing officials in the purchase of a €600,000 luxury limousine. The evidence included recordings from the opposition's wiretap "bombs" in 2015, which a judge ruled were admissible in court because of the public interest

---

[81] Talat Xhaferi, interview with author.

268 | HOW RUSSIA LOSES

involved. His sentence was to begin November 9, 2018, but shortly beforehand he fled to Hungary, where he still lives. Gruevski claimed he had intended to serve his jail term but received word the new government intended to assassinate him in prison. "I received information about my planned liquidation in jail, not immediately but after a certain period, so I changed my mind," he said.[82]

After Gruevski fled, authorities filed additional charges against him. They included the illegal acquisition of building lots and apartments, the use of money donated to VMRO for personal purposes, election violations, and abuse of office. He was sentenced in 2020 in absentia to an additional 18 months in prison over a violent protest in which his supporters disrupted an attempt by the Skopje municipality to block the "Skopje 2014" project.[83]

Russia's Loss in Macedonia

Competition between Russia and the West for influence in Macedonia moved into high gear with the political crisis in 2015, the Prespa accord, and the prospect that Macedonia would join NATO and the EU. Much depended on the image and authority each side had developed over the years—as well as the additional resources they could quickly bring to bear.

Russia worked hard with its Macedonian allies to convince the nation's citizens to boycott or vote "no" in the referendum and to

---

[82] Marusic, Sinisa Jakov, "Gruevski Fled Macedonia 'to Avoid Assassination'" *BalkanInsight*, February 2, 2019, https://balkaninsight.com/2019/02/02/macedonia-s-fugitive-gruevski-insists-his-life-was-in-danger-02-02-2019

[83] Testorides, Konstantin, "North Macedonia: Former PM sentenced to 1½ years in prison," *The Washington Post*, September 29, 2020, https://www.washingtonpost.com/national/former-pm-in-north-macedonia-sentenced-to-1-years-in-prison/2020/09/29/b4372288-0266-11eb-b92e-029676f9ebec_story.html

oppose the constitutional changes. But its efforts suffered from two important miscalculations:

• **The Kremlin pursued a top-down strategy in building its influence in Macedonia.** Russia, which under Putin became an increasingly dictatorial state, cast its lot with the Macedonian forces that most resembled its own power elite: Macedonia's strongmen in politics and business. Russia's strategy was to quickly turn the Macedonian economy toward Moscow through big deals in crucial sectors. It leveraged its traditional strengths in energy and mining, as well as connections with Russian oligarchs who had made it big in Macedonia. Gruevski's authoritarianism, and corruption in his government, were no barrier to cooperation with Moscow.

Russia engaged in some projects directed at ordinary Macedonians, such as setting up Russian-Macedonian friendship associations and building Orthodox churches. But it never made much effort. Naumoski said that, if Moscow had been more adept, it could have emphasized the creation of friendly civil society groups based on religious, cultural, and nationalistic themes. "If you compared the US projects to the Russian efforts, it was like comparing a tank to a Lada," he said, referring to the small Russian-built car. "Russia needs to learn more about organizing, not just appealing to emotions."

Russia and its allies would also have benefited from organizing protests that looked more like gatherings of ordinary people than of extremists and musclemen. Some diplomats felt pro-Russian actors could have "crossed the aisle" to build opposition to Prespa among Social Democratic and ethnic Albanian politicians, and within the Albanian community. Russia could also have made more efforts in Greece, where Tsipras faced significant domestic opposition over the deal and MPs also were subject to persuasive tactics.

The brunt of Russian efforts in Macedonia, however, was aimed at creating strong relationships with the country's big players. Russian involvement with the general population was small; the relationship was built on high-level deals and understandings.

270 | HOW RUSSIA LOSES

By contrast, the US and Western Europe, democracies with strong human rights interests as well as mercantile and military goals, concentrated on trade and aid. For political allies, they looked to Macedonia's public, seeking to rally them through civil society organizations that reflected the West's own political values. While Russia labored over mining and gas deals with top-level figures, it was Western products and culture that made the most consistent impact on Macedonian citizens. The EU's decision in 2009 to no longer require visas for Macedonian tourists further increased business and people-to-people contacts.

Politically, Western governments largely stuck by their principles in Macedonia. US and European governments openly criticized Gruevski's turn to authoritarianism, even at the risk of losing favor with his government (which they did). Whatever Gruevski thought of the Western powers, and however attracted he was to authoritarian models, the economic facts were that Macedonia needed trade with the West and the continuing economic support the EU provided.

The 2016 parliamentary elections were critical, especially to Russia. The US and EU had already played a key role in the run-up to the election, including overseeing the Pržino agreement. With so much of Moscow's influence concentrated on the Gruevski government and its business allies, a Social Democrat victory would risk overturning everything. A Zaev-led government could turn away from economic deals with Russia and orient the nation strongly toward the West—even if Greece continued to block NATO and EU membership. The mass public protests against Gruevski's government and the parliamentary crisis of 2017 evoked for Moscow the ghost of Ukraine's 2004–2005 Orange Revolution in Ukraine, if not Maidan in 2014. VMRO's failure to win a parliamentary majority was a true crisis for Russian interests.

The stakes were not quite as high for the West. If Gruevski had become prime minister again after the 2016 election, the EU and US would still have maintained their economic importance to Macedonian society. Public pressure on Gruevski would also have remained vigorous, restricting his freedom of maneuver.

Macedonia: The Tank and the Lada | 271

- **Russia's strategic disadvantage leading up to the referendum led it into aggressive actions that increased the likelihood of a strong Western response.** Moscow's public threats, and violent protests by VMRO supporters, alarmed the NSC, and sent top Western leaders rushing to a country that some might have had trouble finding on a map. In the words of Maxim Samorukov of the Carnegie Moscow Center:

> Amid so many complications, the [Prespa] settlement could have foundered many times and slipped down the West's list of priorities—if it hadn't been for the stubborn criticism coming from Russia. Moscow's ostentatious hostility meant the West blamed any difficulties over Macedonia on Kremlin machinations, and it resolved not to give up under any circumstances, because the stakes had suddenly grown from a small peripheral Balkans state to defeat in the geopolitical standoff with Russia. And it was Russia that raised these stakes.[84]

The West's actions in Macedonia were surprisingly assertive for that period. With the weak Western response to Russia's invasion of Ukraine in 2014 and American political disarray under Trump, the US and Europe seemed little equipped for dealing with a resurgent Russia. Macedonia was a place where the West could try to right the balance. Certainly, a Western victory in Macedonia would hardly be a mortal blow to the Kremlin. But the resources that NATO and the EU put into the contest—including the visits to Skopje by top NATO and EU leaders—showed that Western powers still knew how to exert influence, if they only would dare to do so. Western actions included actively coaching the Macedonian government on how to influence its own people, turning over wiretaps to Greece, publicly declaring the referendum had backed NATO and EU membership when it arguably had failed, and showing no public concern over the arm-

---

[84] Samorukov, Maxim, "Macedonia Joining NATO Is Self-Inflicted Defeat For Russia," Carnegie Endowment for International Peace," February 8, 2019, https://carnegiemoscow.org/commentary/78320

272 | HOW RUSSIA LOSES

twisting of MPs. US officials coordinated skillfully between Skopje and Athens, convincing politicians in both countries to discard generations of mistrust for a common benefit.

All this came as US officials, at least in some forums, baldly maintained they had interfered in no way in Macedonian politics. In November 2018, the US delegation to the OSCE issued a stiff statement denouncing "Russian disinformation" about US manipulation. Regarding the referendum, the statement said, "Simply because some parties do not like the outcome does not mean there was outside interference in the vote."[85]

Some US officials openly reveled in the use of American power. Word of the wiretapping of Savvidis crept into *The New York Times* just a week after the referendum. By the following year, GEC head Lea Gabrielle and the State Department's Jim Kulikowski were boasting to their funders from the House Committee on Appropriations how US agencies had helped obtain the outcome the West wanted. Asked at a hearing if US efforts to counter Russian malign influence were succeeding, Kulikowski, the coordinator for US assistance to Europe, Eurasia, and Central Asia, told lawmakers:

> You have to look at the results in North Macedonia, for instance, where a massive effort was put into place by Russia to make sure that the [Prespa] agreement was not accepted by either country. And through the combined efforts of all these agencies that we have talked about, we successfully battled that back and the people of North Macedonia and Greece gave us a huge victory, which is really an example that leads the rest of the West Balkans forward and gives them hope.[86]

---

[85] Statement at https://osce.usmission.gov/statement-on-the-macedonia-referendum-2

[86] Statement at https://www.govinfo.gov/content/pkg/CHRG-116hhrg39682/html/CHRG-116hhrg39682.htm

Could Russia have played its cards better? In the view of some, agitation against the name change was hopeless from the start. "Russia couldn't have won because the people were for democracy, economic benefit and security. Russia lost the battle because of weakness of their position," Aleksoska said. Geopolitically, Moscow could not offer membership in a significant military or economic bloc. Its vision for Macedonia was for it to remain without allies in a highly dangerous neighborhood while continuing to miss out on the benefits of EU membership. While Western powers worked tirelessly to end Macedonia's standoff with Greece, Russia offered no initiatives in that sphere. It simply whipped up nationalist opposition to the Prespa accord on both sides of the border. Moscow seemed content to let the dispute remain a running sore forever, much like the "frozen conflicts" the Kremlin finds so attractive elsewhere.

There are contrarian versions of the Macedonia story. In Nacev's view, the West fundamentally misread VMRO, seeing it as an opponent of NATO rather than as a potential ally in finding ways to make membership in the alliance compatible with nationalist public sentiment. "VMRO-DPMNE has never been pro-Russian. We never saw Russia as an alternative to the West," he said. "We still have hanging over our head the narrative that we were anti-NATO, but that doesn't make sense. We just wanted to solve the problem with Greece in a way that would be acceptable to the Macedonian people."

One could also argue that neither Russian nor Western efforts did much to change the outcomes at the ballot box or in parliament. In this view, most Macedonians were not driven by either pro-West or pro-Russian political feelings. Margarita Assenova, a Balkan scholar and senior fellow at The Jamestown Foundation, speculated that the NATO issue that so obsessed the great powers was a minor consideration for many. Those who voted "yes," she said, saw the referendum as just an incremental step in European integration—a process that could attract foreign investment and keep their children from leaving the country.[87] In an analysis for the German Marshall Fund, Asya Metodieva found "the boycott

---

[87] Margarita Assenova, interview with author, May 19, 2022

camp represented a very heterogenous group of people" and that not everyone using anti-Western rhetoric was actually pro-Russian.[88] Macedonians could oppose changing the country's name irrespective of whether they wanted to join NATO or the EU.

Petkovski of the Eurothink NGO said Macedonia's pro-Western elites inflated the level of Russian interference to attract more Western support. "The West was looking for a victory, and supposed Russian involvement was helpful to them, too," he said. The Western victory was a great story for US agencies to tell as they fought for bigger budgets. Within Macedonia, Petkovski said, fear of Russian influence "has become an industry, and [Western] donors are generous with those who see Russians under every bed."

For its part, Russia may not have made every possible effort in Macedonia because it thought the West's goals were so ambitious as to be impossible. The West needed Zaev to replace Gruevski, Macedonia to reach a name deal with Greece, a referendum result that was at least not negative, and victory in a parliament where opposition was strong. Amazingly, all four events transpired. Moscow might have also thought that, even if Macedonia joined NATO, the country could under some future leadership become a disruptive force within the alliance, just as Hungary had. Russia also knew EU membership for Macedonia was not a foregone conclusion. Indeed, Bulgaria continued to block Macedonia's admission because of its own ethnic and historical disputes with Skopje.

There seems little doubt that years of Western aid and democracy-building activity in Macedonia had their effect. Macedonia's history under the Ottomans and Tito had left little experience with democracy. The awareness of human rights and citizens' agency that Western efforts inculcated may well have contributed significantly to public resistance against Gruevski. A key role in that resistance was played by civil society organizations that EU and US agencies and foundations supported.

---

[88] "Russian narrative proxies in the Western Balkans, op. cit.

Some officials were downcast that their efforts did not bring a better result in the referendum. But beyond obvious VMRO supporters, no massive public protests took place over Zaev's decision to ignore the referendum and pursue constitutional amendments to accomplish the same goals. Broad masses of Macedonians seemed content to allow the country's name change and its movement toward NATO and the EU to proceed.

Both the West and Russia deployed aggressive tactics in the Macedonian contest. The kind of pressure Zaev put on parliament members might well have been condemned by the West had it happened in another situation. In this case, the West apparently decided the stakes were high enough in Macedonia to justify some forceful gamesmanship. The reward would be a new expansion of NATO, a further contraction of Russian influence in the Balkans, and an opportunity for North Macedonia to formally align itself with the Western world.

Epilogue: A Frustrated North Macedonia

The sense of excitement over what the country's name change would bring faded quickly in North Macedonia. The change immediately set in motion the country's accession to NATO, and it formally joined the alliance 15 months later. But the big prize in the view of most Macedonians—EU membership—remained out of reach.

The first obstacle was Bulgaria. Zaev's friendship agreement with Sofia in 2017 opened the way to negotiations on a series of disputes between the countries over Macedonians' national identity, interpretations of historical events dating to the Ottoman Empire, and current-day North Macedonian policies. Bulgaria insisted the Macedonian language is a dialect of Bulgarian, that Macedonian schoolbooks contain "hate speech" against Bulgaria, and that North Macedonia must recognize its Bulgarian minority in its constitution. Expert commissions were established to work on the historical and educational issues involved, but little progress followed.

276 | HOW RUSSIA LOSES

On October 10, 2019, Bulgaria issued a formal "Framework Position" setting out more than 20 demands of its neighbor. It approved the opening of talks on North Macedonia's accession to the EU but threatened to block further progress if the issues between the two countries were not resolved.[89]

A second major obstacle came that same month. On October 18, French President Emmanuel Macron vetoed the opening of accession talks with both North Macedonia and Albania, saying the EU needed to concentrate on internal reforms and re-evaluate its entire process for admitting new members.

Zaev, who had put his career on the line to pass the constitutional changes, was bitter. "We are still disappointed, angry and a little bit frustrated, because we got a promise from the European Union that when we deliver, they would deliver—and they failed," he said.[90] (The EU had not promised that the name change would automatically lead to full membership.)

With France and Bulgaria blocking EU accession, the public mood in Macedonia soured, depressed further by the COVID pandemic and an accompanying economic crisis. The percentage of Macedonians who said their country was heading in the right direction shrank from 37 to 14 percent from 2018 to mid-2023.[91] Many citizens complained that Zaev had failed to deliver administrative and judicial reforms and stem corruption.

President Pendarovski claimed Russia was working to manipulate the political situation, just as it had during the 2018

---

[89] For several of the demands, see Marusic, Sinisa Jakov, "Bulgaria Sets Tough Terms for North Macedonia's EU Progress," *BalkanInsight*, October 10, 2019, https://balkaninsight.com/2019/10/10/bulgaria-sets-tough-terms-for-north-macedonias-eu-progress

[90] Stamouli, Nektaria, "North Macedonia's post-Macron melancholy," *POLITICO*, November 12, 2019, "https://www.politico.eu/article/north-macedonia-eu-accession-post-emmanuel-macron-melancholy

[91] "National Survey of North Macedonia," April–May 2023, International Republican Institute, https://www.iri.org/resources/national-survey-of-north-macedonia-april-may-20232

referendum,[92] but there was much basis for discontent even without Russian interference. Elections for the assembly in 2020 left the Social Democrats in control with their Albanian partners, but Levica, an anti-NATO party that supported the Russian position on Ukraine, entered the assembly for the first time with three seats. After the Social Democrats performed poorly in local elections in 2021, Zaev resigned as prime minister and was replaced by another Social Democrat, Dimitar Kovachevski, who had been deputy finance minister.

A break in the standoff with France and Bulgaria seemed on the horizon in June 2022, when France proposed a compromise designed to satisfy Bulgaria's demands. Under the plan, North Macedonia would recognize the Bulgarian minority in its constitution, add provisions on hate speech to its criminal code, and take steps to protect minority rights. The accession talks would then move forward. Bulgaria's parliament endorsed the concept, leaving the next step to North Macedonia. On July 16, the Social Democrat–led assembly in Skopje approved the deal by a vote of 68 out of 120 members, with VMRO strongly opposed and its deputies walking out. Widespread demonstrations broke out against the proposal, but the population as a whole appeared fairly evenly split.[93]

Reasons for opposition to the French proposal varied. In principle, recognizing a Bulgarian minority in the constitution was not a big step; the document already recognized Turks, Vlach, Serbs, Roma and Bosniaks. However, some nationalists feared that reopening the constitution for amendments would lead to pressure for much larger changes, such as moves by Albanian parties to make Albanian an official language throughout the country.

---

[92] "President Stevo Pendarovski accuses Moscow for the third time for meddling in North Macedonia's internal affairs," *Meta.mk*, July 29, 2022, https://meta.mk/en/president-stevo-pendarovski-accuses-moscow-for-the-third-time-for-meddling-in-north-macedonias-internal-affairs
[93] "National Survey of North Macedonia," op. cit.

278 | HOW RUSSIA LOSES

Opponents of the French proposal also feared that, although the accession talks would open, Bulgaria would retain the ability to block the process again at any time. The Social Democrats saw no option other than to agree to the proposal and continue to try to mollify Bulgaria over its other concerns, benefiting from the EU's involvement in the negotiations. VMRO opposed the French package and called for early elections but offered no alternative strategy on entering the EU.

All this turmoil was not strong enough to turn North Macedonia's population against the EU-NATO project as a whole, though polls indicated some disenchantment. A 2023 survey found support for joining the EU was 79 percent compared to 83 percent in 2018, and for NATO membership 73 percent compared to 77 percent in 2018.[94] VMRO and other major parties continued their overall support for North Macedonia joining the EU and remaining a member of NATO. Russia also has remained active in North Macedonia, including in clandestine operations; the nation expelled at least 21 Russian diplomats between 2021 and 2023.

---

[94] Ibid.

6.

Ecuador: Who Played Whom?

It is unlikely that Ecuador has ever loomed very large in Kremlin strategic planning. But for a decade under Putin, the oil-producing nation of 17 million people became a useful partner for Russia in Latin America. Led by leftist President Rafael Correa, Ecuador became a fervent ideological member of the Bolivarian bloc that strongly opposed US interests in the Western Hemisphere and saw Russia as a supporter and ally. Correa visited Russian presidents in Moscow twice, establishing a "strategic partnership" between Quito and Moscow. Under Correa, Ecuador shut down a US military and drug interdiction facility, expelled the US ambassador and the US Agency for International Development, severed relations with the World Bank and International Monetary Fund, and forged strong ties with China and Iran.

The Andean country reputedly became a center for money-laundering and organized crime, including narcotics and human trafficking that principally targeted the United States and Western Europe. Correa became one of Moscow's leading allies in advocating for a world banking and money transfer system outside the reach of US monitoring and sanctions. Correa granted asylum at the Ecuadorian Embassy in London to WikiLeaks founder Julian Assange, who met at the embassy with Russian visitors at the height of WikiLeaks' interference in US politics. After Venezuelan leader Hugo Chávez died in 2013, some—including in Moscow—believed Correa had made himself the most important figure on the Latin left.

280 | HOW RUSSIA LOSES

Yet a decade after Correa took power in 2007, Ecuador's warm relationship with Russia suddenly evaporated. Correa decided not to run for re-election in 2017, endorsing as his successor former Vice President Lenín Moreno, who many believed would faithfully follow Correa's line. Within months, Moreno veered sharply away from the Latin left, quickly restoring relations with Washington and international financial institutions. He pulled Ecuador out of Latin American bodies where Russia had cultivated influence, expelled Assange from the embassy, and allowed US government aircraft to operate again from Ecuador.

Following an insurrection against his government that some suspected was encouraged from abroad, Moreno shut down Russia's RT television, which had devoted live coverage to the fighting in the streets. Correa denounced Moreno as a traitor and left for Belgium; seeking continued benefit from Correa's militant rhetoric, Russia gave him his own program on RT. But the Kremlin's top-level influence in Ecuador—and the country's value as a torchbearer for anti-US positions on the continent—had vanished.

What accounted for the dramatic reversal of Russian fortunes in Ecuador? Some believed the Kremlin misjudged Correa from the start, expecting him to become the kind of loyal asset who could turn Ecuador into another Cuba, Venezuela, or Nicaragua. Correa certainly talked the talk of "anti-imperialism," leftist social ideals, and a fondness for Moscow. Yet Correa seemed to be interested in Russia only to the degree that its interests aligned with his own and those of Ecuador.

Moscow also faced economic factors beyond its control. Correa extracted from China far more financial support than Russia could ever provide. Correa also could not ignore the immutable fact of Ecuador's economic dependence on the United States. However vitriolic Correa's denunciations of US "imperialism," trade with the US was essential to the Ecuadorian economy. Most significantly, Russia failed to build a positive profile of its own in Ecuador. Instead, it outsourced its interests to an authoritarian leader whose government was widely viewed as corrupt. When Ecuador ultimately turned away from Correa's path at home and abroad, the policies that had served Russia's interests well perished as collateral damage.

La Revolución Ciudadana

Correa was born to a mestizo family of modest means from Guayaquil, Ecuador's financial capital. When he was five years old, his father was imprisoned in the United States for smuggling drugs. The father later returned home and took his own life. The young Correa studied economics at a local university, taught impoverished indigenous students at a Catholic school in the Ecuadorian highlands, and studied economics in Europe and the United States. He received a PhD from the University of Illinois at Urbana–Champaign in 2001. After serving as an economic advisor to Ecuadorian government agencies and in an education post, he was named finance minister by President Alfredo Palacio in 2005.

By the time he took over Ecuador's finances, Correa's world view was fixed: the poor of Latin America were the victims of exploitation by local rightist elites, by the United States and its capitalist allies, and by institutions the West controlled, such as the International Monetary Fund. Correa lost no time putting his beliefs into action, convincing the National Congress to abolish a fund established to service foreign debt. In response, the World Bank canceled a $100 million loan. Palacio forced Correa to resign after less than a year in his post.

In 2006, Correa formed a political party, the Alianza PAIS ("Proud and Sovereign Homeland Alliance") and ran for the presidency. His platform promised more aid to the poor, justice for indigenous Ecuadorians, and an end to corruption and political instability. Correa's constant slogan was that Ecuador must protect its *soberanía* (sovereignty) from Western interference and *diktat*. He named his movement La Revolución Ciudadana, the "Citizens' Revolution." Correa's opponent was banana magnate Álvaro Noboa, Ecuador's richest man, who denounced Correa as a socialist who would bring economic catastrophe. Correa embraced the socialist label; he portrayed himself as the savior of the poor, called US President George W. Bush "dimwitted," and emphasized his friendship with Venezuela's Chávez.[1] Noboa won the most votes in the first round of the election, but Correa easily prevailed in the runoff. He became president in January 2007 at the age of 43.

At the time, the ascension of a leftist to a Latin American presidency was not an isolated event. Correa's election was the culmination of the so-called "pink tide"—a chain of leftist political victories that had started a decade before. The tide had already brought to power Chávez in Venezuela, Luiz Inácio Lula da Silva in Brazil, Evo Morales in Bolivia, and Nestor Kirchner in Argentina, as well as returning Daniel Ortega to the presidency of Nicaragua. These leaders not only established leftist policies in their own countries but also sought to build alliances with each other and more openly challenge US power.

Correa brought Ecuador into the Bolivarian Alliance of the Americas (ALBA), a Chávez-led trading bloc designed to compete with trade arrangements led by the US. Ecuador also joined the Community of Latin American and Caribbean States (CELAC), largely an attempt to create an Organization of American States without the United States and Canada, and PAIS joined the Sao Paulo Forum, a conference of "anti-imperialist" Latin American political parties. Correa provided a government building in Quito for the headquarters of the Union of South American Nations (UNASUR), aimed at creating a bloc of South American countries similar to the European Union. Importantly, UNASUR favored the creation of a "Bank of the South" for the continent, with a payments system that would bypass the Western-controlled SWIFT network.

Many Latin American leftists still espoused the principles of socialism, which Russia had dispensed with after its Soviet experience. But the Latin Americans' anti-US ideology was something Vladimir Putin could leverage in his mission to restore Russia's status as a geopolitical great power. Stung by the accession to NATO of East European countries that used to serve

---

[1] *The Associated Press*, "Ecuador presidential hopeful: Bush 'dimwitted,' " September 27, 2006, https://www.nbcnews.com/id/wbna15034597

as a security buffer for Russia, Putin saw an opportunity to even the score by building the Kremlin's own power in the Western Hemisphere. Russian efforts moved into particularly high gear when Moscow's relations with the US plummeted after Putin's 2008 invasion of Georgia. In 2008 alone, Russian warships and nuclear-capable bombers made showy visits to Venezuela, Nicaragua, and the Caribbean. Then-President Dmitry Medvedev traveled to Peru, Brazil, Venezuela, and Cuba.[2] Ortega directly backed Russia's dismemberment of Georgia by recognizing the independence of Abkhazia and South Ossetia.

Correa "truly thought China and Russia would change the world order, or at least counterbalance the hegemonic power of the United States," says Grace Jaramillo, an Ecuadorian scholar on international relations at The University of British Columbia.[3] Correa was also devoted to the unity and integration of Latin American nations. Although the newest of the pink tide leaders, his ambitions were great: to humble the United States in his own country, develop a wide-ranging relationship with other powers that opposed US hegemony, and build the unity of the Bolivarian world. Perhaps one day he might become its leader.

Correa and the United States

During his 2006 election campaign, Correa left open the possibility of maintaining some modicum of good relations with the US and world financial institutions. In the same interview in which he called Bush dimwitted (and compared him unfavorably to the devil), Correa stressed that his opinions were "personal." If elected, he said, "between states and at the level of leaders, the most absolute respect would be shown." He also had a friendly

---

[2] For a review of Russian activity in Latin America after the invasion of Georgia and of Ukraine, see Ellis, R. Evan, "The New Russian Engagement With Latin America: Strategic Position, Commerce, And Dreams Of The Past," US Army War College, June 2015, https://publications.armywarcollege.edu/wp-content/uploads/2022/11/2345.pdf

[3] Jaramillo, Grace, correspondence with author, November 2, 2021.

meeting ahead of the election with US Ambassador Linda Jewell. At the US Embassy, opinions were split on whether his anti-US rhetoric was just a prop for his election campaign, or if it would truly guide his actions in practice.

The answer became evident in Correa's first years as president. In 2008, he made clear that he would keep his campaign promise not to renew a lease, expiring in 2009, that allowed the US to run drug interdiction flights from a base at the Manta airport on the Pacific coast. Although the US delicately called the facility a "cooperative security location" in deference to Ecuadorian feelings, Correa said the US presence there was an affront to Ecuador's sovereignty. (He regularly joked that the base could stay if Ecuador could open its own air base in Miami.)

Correa also moved swiftly against international financial institutions. Three months into his presidency, he expelled the representative of the World Bank, Eduardo Somensatto, over the bank's cancellation of the $100 million loan when he was finance minister. In December 2008, Ecuador defaulted on a $30.6 million payment on its bonds. Correa said that the debt was illegitimate and that the international financial interests Ecuador faced were "real monsters."[4]

Correa purged, amid much publicity, a raft of senior Ecuadorian military and intelligence officials. Ecuador's intelligence community, he announced, was "totally infiltrated and subjugated to the CIA."[5] Further antagonizing the US, Correa began forging close relations with Iran. Iranian President Mahmoud Ahmadinejad had attended Correa's inauguration, and Correa visited Iran in December 2008.

---

[4] Mapstone, Naomi, "Ecuador defaults on sovereign bonds," *Financial Times*, December 12, 2008, https://www.ft.com/content/7170e224-c897-11dd-b86f-000077b07658

[5] Romero, Simon, "Ecuador's Leader Purges Military and Moves to Expel American Base," *The New York Times*, April 21, 2008, https://www.nytimes.com/2008/04/21/world/americas/21ecuador.html

Correa told one of his regular public rallies in November 2008:

> I don't have anything in particular against the US—in fact, I love the US—I even lived there, studied there. ... But our foreign policy must look to other places, countries like Russia, which is reassuming its position as superpower; it has an enormous market and the political will to get close to Latin America. Well, some are furious because we did not insist on the usual suspects: the US, Europe, Japan. ... Two hundred years of doing just that, and what have we gained? It was about time to look away. Even if we are wrong, we do not have much to lose; we have not obtained anything looking up to them.[6]

Correa said in a 2022 interview in exile in Belgium that it would have taken a sea change in US foreign policy, including an end to its backing of Latin American elites, for his administration to have had positive relations overall with Washington.[7]

Tension with the United States rose further after Colombian forces, pursuing guerrillas of the Revolutionary Armed Forces of Colombia (FARC), launched a bomb-and-commando attack on a FARC camp at Angostura, just inside Ecuador, on March 1, 2008. The FARC espoused a leftist ideology while financing itself through narcotics. The raid killed two dozen people, including Raúl Reyes, the FARC's second-in-command. An Ecuadorian investigation of the raid claimed the intelligence that supported the attack was processed at the Manta facility.[8]

---

[6] "Enlace Ciudadana [Citizen Link] 139," quoted in Jaramillo, Grace, "Rafael Correa's Foreign Policy Paradox: Discursive Sovereignty, Practical Dependency," in Sánchez, Francisco and Pachano, Simón, eds., *Assessing the Left Turn in Ecuador* (London: Palgrave Macmillan, 2020), p. 333.

[7] Rafael Correa, interview with author, March 24, 2022.

[8] Bronstein, Hugh, "Ecuador says U.S. helped Colombia plan '08 bombing," *Reuters*, December 10, 2009, https://www.reuters.com/article/idUSN10183171

286 | HOW RUSSIA LOSES

Correa was furious over the Angostura attack. He believed the US and Colombia, which were close allies, had personally humiliated him by conducting the raid, on his own territory, behind his back. "I was a new president, we were misled, my land was bombed," he recalled in the 2022 interview. "Imagine if it had been the other way around, with us attacking Colombia. It would have been a scandal."[9]

Opinions vary as to the impact of the Angostura attack on Correa personally. In Jaramillo's view, the raid changed Correa's "more nuanced approach to world politics into a radical, counter-hegemonic agenda."[10] Others believed that he was already well set on an anti-US course. In the 2022 interview, Correa said the raid had a significant impact on his view of the United States, making him even more mistrustful of Washington.

The replacement of George W. Bush by Barack Obama at the start of 2009 brought no sea change in Correa's view of the United States. In February, Correa ordered the expulsion of two US Embassy employees, Mark Sullivan, a first secretary who Correa claimed headed the CIA in Ecuador, and Armando Astorga, a Homeland Security attaché. Correa accused the two of trying to vet Ecuadorian personnel involved in US-funded anti-contraband operations. "Mr. Astorga, keep your dirty money," Correa asserted. "We don't need it. We have sovereignty and dignity here."[11]

Demonstrating that vetting can go two ways, Correa also said he would allow US Coast Guard planes to land on Ecuadorian soil only "on one condition: that we be allowed to vet the pilots of

---

[9] Rafael Correa, interview with author, March 24, 2022.
[10] Jaramillo, Grace, correspondence with author.
[11] "Ecuador expels 'insolent' U.S. diplomat," *United Press International*, February 7, 2009, https://www.upi.com/Top_News/2009/ 02/07/Ecuador-expels-insolent-US-diplomat/88901234056101

Ecuador: Who Played Whom? | 287

those planes, so that they don't sneak criminals into the country."[12]

Correa's fears that pro-US actors were active in Ecuador's security services gained new traction in 2010. In September of that year, a protest by police over pay and benefits spun into a violent rebellion. Correa tried to reason with angry officers, who shoved him and doused him with water. Correa took shelter in a police hospital, where he declared he was "practically captive." Security forces seized barracks in other cities, and sympathetic air force personnel blocked runways at Quito's Mariscal Sucre airport.

Although the military had its own disputes with Correa over pay and privileges, its troops rescued the president. Oswaldo Jarrín, a long-time military officer who served as defense minister before and after Correa, said the military's attitude toward Correa was one of "professional resistance"—it intended to wait him out, not overthrow him.[13]

Correa declared that the incident had been an attempted coup d'état. He told a US interviewer that while he thought the US had not directly fomented the rebellion, Ecuadorians involved might have had previous ties to the US embassy and CIA:

> It's clear, we can say, that extreme-right groups participated from the US who are no longer in government, but through their foundations and many other ways, they are always conspiring. We do have evidence that these groups finance the opposing groups, and they want to destabilize power in Ecuador. ... So I am certain that Barack Obama's government formally, regarding what President Obama feels, they had nothing to do with September 30. But I cannot exclude that some other instances from the US state, who act on their own

---

[12] "Ecuador expels US embassy official," *Al Jazeera*, February 8, 2009, https://www.aljazeera.com/news/2009/2/8/ecuador-expels-us-embassy-official

[13] Oswaldo Jarrín, interview with author, August 24, 2021.

inertia and their own agendas, and extreme-right groups did have something to do with September 30, and we have evidence, with account numbers, of how they finance opposing groups and destabilizing groups in Ecuador.[14]

Both Morales and Chávez said the US was involved in the "coup attempt."[15]

Seven months after the September violence, Correa expelled US Ambassador Heather Hodges. The reason ostensibly was a classified cable from the embassy, published by WikiLeaks, suggesting Correa was aware of corrupt conduct by Jaime Aquilino Hurtado, the national police chief. Like all cables from an embassy, it was signed with her name, and Correa held her personally responsible.

The most alarming thing about the cable, in Correa's view, seemed to be that the embassy had information about police activities. "The serious thing is that WikiLeaks said they have informants in the police and armed forces. ... This is espionage," Correa said in a radio interview.[16] By his action, Correa emulated Venezuela and Bolivia, which had expelled US ambassadors in 2008.

In June 2012, Correa granted political asylum at the Ecuadorian Embassy in London to WikiLeaks founder Julian Assange, who had published thousands of pages of classified US government

---

[14] "Ecuadoran President Rafael Correa on WikiLeaks, the September Coup, U.S. Denial of Climate Funding, and Controversial Forest Scheme REDD," *Democracy Now*, December 10, 2010, https://www.democracynow.org/2010/12/9/ecuadoran_president_rafa el_correa_on_the

[15] "Ecuador in state of siege, region supports Correa," *The Associated Press*, October 1, 2010, https://www.goshennews.com/news/ecuador-in-state-of-seige-region-supports-correa/article_4195340c-1a5e-5943-9cd5-195e2747069e.htm

[16] "Ecuador's Correa lashes out at U.S. embassy for spying," *Reuters*, April 8, 2011, https://www.reuters.com/article/us-ecuador-usa/ecuadors-correa-lashes-out-at-u-s-embassy-for-spying-idUSTRE7375UX20110408

documents. Correa said he did so because Assange would face death if he were extradited to the United States and because Ecuador had high respect for freedom of the press.

Correa continued to challenge the United States through his rhetoric as well as his actions. In 2013, he told *RT* that Obama's view of American exceptionalism reminded him of Nazi rhetoric. Improvising on Plato, he said that "justice is nothing other than the advantage of the stronger. They are the strongest, and will continue abusing and disrespecting the sovereignty of other countries and international law. One day this unjust world order will have to change."[17] In April 2014, Correa ordered out of Ecuador all 20 members of the Defense Department's Security Cooperation Office. Correa had warned previously that he planned to order the departure of US military officers who had been "infiltrated in all sectors" of Ecuador.[18]

However provoked it was by Correa, the United States maintained relations with Ecuador that were correct, even generous. It responded in kind to some of Correa's actions; it expelled the Ecuadorian ambassador from Washington when Correa ousted US Ambassador Hodges. But US government aid to Ecuador continued, totaling nearly $400 million under Correa. (The level declined in the second part of his reign.)[19] US-Ecuador travel, business, and cultural activities remained vibrant—to be expected, given the two countries' robust trade and the large number of Ecuadorians living in the US.

---

[17] "Correa a RT: "Que EE.UU. se crea un país excepcional es tremendamente peligroso [It is tremendously dangerous for the US to believe it is an exceptional country]," *RT*, October 4, 2013, https://actualidad.rt.com/actualidad/view/107495-correa-ecuador-eeuu-latinoamerica

[18] Solano, Gonzalo, "Ecuador orders US military group to leave," *The Associated Press*, April 25, 2014, https://apnews.com/article/9abfd2521f0f46549df811e57f7541f9

[19] https://foreignassistance.gov/cd/ecuador/2007/obligations/0

290 | HOW RUSSIA LOSES

Correa at Home

By some measures, Correa's policies at home did much to help Ecuador's people, especially early in his presidency. He was re-elected in 2009 and 2013, bringing rare stability to a country that ran through seven presidents in the decade before Correa came to power. Correa used income from the oil boom to improve healthcare, roads, and education; increase the minimum wage; and lower the cost of gasoline and natural gas. Poor citizens benefited from extra discounts on energy costs and direct cash transfers.

However, Correa's aspirations to turn Ecuador into an economic "jaguar"—an allusion to the economic "tigers" of Asia—never materialized. Except for extractive industries, the economy remained primarily agrarian. Many citizens' lives did not significantly improve. In return for some $6.5 billion in cash from China, Ecuador agreed to sell almost 90 percent of its oil, at a fixed price, to Beijing through 2024.[20] Indigenous peoples were outraged by new projects to extract oil, gold, copper, and water from their lands, with little attention paid to sacred areas or fragile ecosystems. Correa denounced indigenous activists trying to resist extractive projects as savages or "beggars sitting on gold."[21] He also proposed that, if other countries were worried about projects in Ecuador's Yasuni National Park in the Amazon, they should compensate Ecuador for not drilling there. Quito received few contributions.[22]

---

[20] Kraul, Chris, "Ecuador faces a huge budget deficit because of loans it received from China," *Los Angeles Times*, December 10, 2018, https://www.latimes.com/world/la-fg-ecuador-loans-china-20181210-story.html

[21] Picq, Manuela, "Ecuador's not-so-pink tide: a Citizen's Revolution against its citizens," *Democracy Now*, September 5, 2018, https://www.opendemocracy.net/en/democraciaabierta/ecuador-s-not-so-pink-tide-citizen-s-revolution-again

[22] "Ecuador To World: Pay Up To Save The Rainforest. World To Ecuador: Meh.," *NPR*, September 2, 2013, https://www.npr.org/sections/money/2013/09/02/216878935/ecuador-to-world-pay-up-to-save-the-rainforest-world-to-ecuador-meh

Ecuador: Who Played Whom? | 291

The oil boom ended in 2014, striking a blow to the government's finances. Spending on social programs had to be cut back; since Ecuador had adopted the US dollar as its currency in 2000, the government could not print money on its own. Correa's leftist foreign policy put no bread on the table, and some Ecuadorians feared he would make an enemy of the United States—where a half-million Ecuadorians worked, with many sending money home.

Meanwhile, Correa's critics claimed his government was involved in widespread corruption. Ecuador's big international deals, they asserted, funneled generous commissions to well-connected Ecuadorians and their foreign partners. Two journalists published a book claiming Fabricio Correa, the president's older brother, reaped $600 million in government contracts. (Correa canceled the contracts but sued the journalists for causing him "spiritual harm.") After Correa's presidency, a court ruled the former president had accepted bribes for public contracts from 2012 to 2016. The court also found that Correa had created a "criminal structure" that collected political contributions from companies and individuals.

In 2016, Transparency International gave Ecuador only 31 out of 90 points on its Corruption Perception Index, a measure of government honesty and judicial integrity.[23]

Ecuador under Correa also reputedly became a center for shady international financial dealings and organized crime. The dollarized economy enabled easy transactions between its banks and financial institutions of other countries. Ecuadorian banks became increasingly involved in payment and credit operations with banks in Russia, China, Belarus, and Iran—the latter despite US and UN sanctions. By 2011, some $3 billion a year was reportedly being laundered in Ecuador by a host of illicit actors. Abetting such activity were banking secrecy laws, as well as a regulation that hobbled prosecution when authorities seized

---

[23] Index at https://www.transparency.org/en/cpi/2016/index/nzl

292 | HOW RUSSIA LOSES

shipments of cash. To win a conviction, prosecutors had to prove exactly where the money originally came from.[24]

In 2012, the Financial Action Task Force (FATF), established by the G7 to monitor illicit currency flows, placed Ecuador on its "blacklist" of countries that winked at such activity. The FATF called on the government to take firmer steps to criminalize terrorist financing, identify and freeze terrorist assets, confiscate funds related to money laundering, and better coordinate supervision of the financial sector.[25] Correa denounced the FATF as "one of many tools of neo-colonialism." His government was able to win removal from the blacklist in 2015 with the understanding it would continue working on remaining deficiencies.[26]

Correa's term in power also reportedly saw a rise in the trafficking of weapons, human beings, and narcotics.[27] Ecuador produces almost no cocaine, but it is a popular drug shipment route from Bolivia, Peru, and Colombia to the United States. In 2014, Ecuador eased penalties for individuals transporting small amounts of drugs on the grounds that most "drug mules" were impoverished people simply trying to survive.[28]

---

[24] For details, see Wells, Miriam, "Ecuador Remains on International Money Laundering Blacklist," *InSight Crime*, February 27, 2013, https://insightcrime.org/news/brief/ecuador-remains-on-international-money-laundering-blacklist; and Bargent, James, "Ecuador Bulk Cash Smuggling Reflects New Laundering Trend," *InSight Crime*, April 11, 2013, https://insightcrime.org/news/analysis/rise-in-ecuador-cash-smuggling-reflects-wider-crime-trends
[25] FATF statement at https://www.fatf-gafi.org/countries/d-i/ecuador/documents/fatfpublicstatement22february2013.html#ecuador
[26] Rubenfeld, Samuel, "Ecuador, Sudan Removed From Money Laundering Blacklist," *The Wall Street Journal*, October 26, 2015, https://www.wsj.com/articles/BL-252B-8539
[27] "Ecuador at Risk: Drugs, Thugs, Guerillas and the Citizens Revolution," op. cit.
[28] Tegel, Simeon, "Ecuador is freeing thousands of convicted drug mules," *Global Post*, October 6, 2014, https://theworld.org/stories/2014-10-06/ecuador-freeing-thousands-convicted-drug-mules

Ecuador: Who Played Whom? | 293

Correa also canceled Ecuador's visa requirements, allowing almost anyone to enter the country for 90 days. The ideological basis for this, enshrined in Correa's 2008 constitution, was "the principle of universal citizenship, the free movement of all inhabitants of the planet, and the progressive end to the status of alien or foreigner as an element to transform the unequal relations between countries, especially north-south."[29] However, many saw the abolition of visas as a yawning opportunity for transnational criminal organizations and terrorists to open shop.

Ecuador's abolition of visas was a major sore point with the United States.[30] Soon after visa-free travel started, Russian, Colombian, and Chinese organized crime groups opened new routes for human trafficking through Ecuador, headed for the United States.[31] Correa acknowledged in the 2022 interview that "some not-so-good people," including human traffickers, entered Ecuador because of the visa-free regime. He noted that his government restored visa requirements for some countries.

As the oil boom faded and Correa's promises of economic revolution produced little for most people, protests began among students, trade unions, and indigenous activists. Protesters also denounced corruption, tariff increases on imported goods, a rise in inheritance taxes, and a proposal that would let the president be re-elected indefinitely.

Correa struck back at opposition to his rule. He was in a good position to do so with the enhanced powers he had gained from a new constitution in 2008. The new constitution not only increased the president's formal authority, but also allowed

---

[29] Text at https://www.asambleanacional.gob.ec/sites/default/files/documents/old/constitucion_de_bolsillo.pdf

[30] Reich, Otto J., et al., "How Ecuador's immigration policy helps al Qaeda," *Foreign Policy*, April 2, 2012, https://foreignpolicy.com/2012/04/02/how-ecuadors-immigration-policy-helps-al-qaeda

[31] Pachico, Elyssa, "Bin Laden's Cousin Arrested in Ecuador?" *InSight Crime*, May 5, 2011, https://insightcrime.org/news/analysis/bin-ladens-cousin-arrested-in-ecuador

Correa to rebuild, in the government's favor, the judiciary and other institutions of control and accountability.[32]

When resistance to Correa led to large-scale protests in the summer of 2015, his government responded vigorously. Correa had been elected on a platform strong on leftist principles and indigenous rights. However, he had warned as early as 2009 that "we have always said that the main dangers to our political project, after repeatedly defeating the right in elections, were leftism, environmentalism, and infantile indigenism."[33] The government broke up demonstrations, jailed dissident students and professors, and intimidated labor activists. The National Intelligence Secretariat, or SENAIN, hacked the computers of political opponents.[34] It also had access to video collected across the country by a Chinese-made system of more than 4,300 anti-crime surveillance cameras.[35]

The government reserved special wrath for news organizations—some of them owned by influential families whom Correa saw as potential political opponents. Authorities imprisoned reporters, filed multimillion-dollar lawsuits against news companies, and

---

[32] De La Torre, Carlos, "Populist Playbook: The Slow Death of Democracy in Correa's Ecuador," *World Politics Review*, March 19, 2015, https://www.worldpoliticsreview.com/populist-playbook-the-slow-death-of-democracy-in-correa-s-ecuador

[33] *El Universo*, " 'Infantilismo' tensa relación Correa-Acosta ['Infantilism' adds to tension between Correa and Acosta," January 21, 2009, https://www.eluniverso.com/2009/01/21/1/1355/51D051981FE44D54A46A35DBEFEC9037.html

[34] Bajak, Frank, et al., "Leaked emails suggest Hacking Team tailor-made malware used by Ecuador to illegally spy on opposition," *The Associated Press*, August 6, 2015, https://apnews.com/article/6f41d49888174b45857d34511fda1caf

[35] Mozur, Paul, et al., "Made in China, Exported to the World: The Surveillance State," *The New York Times*, April 24, 2019, https://www.nytimes.com/2019/04/24/technology/ecuador-surveillance-cameras-police-government.html

Ecuador: Who Played Whom? | 295

seized some outright. Some independent journalists were physically attacked or received death threats.[36]

"We won't tolerate abuses and crimes made every day in the name of freedom of speech. That is freedom of extortion and blackmail," Correa told *The Guardian*.[37] He told Julian Assange in a TV interview, "Let's stop portraying this image of poor and courageous journalists—saint-like media trying to tell the truth—and tyrants, autocrats, and dictators trying to hinder that. It isn't true. It's the other way around."[38] He declared that the protests against him were part of a coup plot with CIA connections.[39]

Correa's allies made heavy use of social networks to boost his policies and attack opponents. Bots flooded social media with pro-government messaging. In an angry three-hour address in 2015, Correa urged his followers to strike back at those who criticized him on Twitter. "For each tweet they'll send, we'll reply with 10,000," he declared.[40] To encourage that, the government set up a website called Somos+ ("We are more") that pointed out

---

[36] For general descriptions of Correa's crackdowns against critics, See "Ecuador's not-so-pink tide: a Citizen's Revolution against its citizens," op. cit.; "Populist Playbook: The Slow Death of Democracy in Correa's Ecuador," op. cit.; Nyst, Carly, et al., "State-Sponsored Trolling," Institute for the Future, July 2018, https://legacy.iftf.org/fileadmin/user_upload/images/DigIntel/IFTF_State_sponsored_trolling_report.pdf; and Human Rights Watch, "World Report 2012: Ecuador," https://www.hrw.org/world-report/2012/country-chapters/ecuador
[37] Watts, Jonathan, "Rafael Correa hits back over Ecuador's press freedom and charge of hypocrisy," *The Guardian*, August 24, 2012, https://www.theguardian.com/world/2012/aug/24/rafael-correa-assange-ecuador-press
[38] Video at https://www.youtube.com/watch?v=rW7edOQ3pCo
[39] Wyss, Jim, "As Ecuador protests, president warns of coup," *Miami Herald*, July 2, 2015, https://www.miamiherald.com/news/nation-world/world/americas/article26190235.html
[40] "Ecuador President Rafael Correa's troll warfare," *BBC*, January 30, 2015, https://www.bbc.com/news/blogs-trending-31057933

anti-government posts so Correa supporters could target those who posted them.[41]

Some saw a justification for Correa's hard line against his critics. A commentary published in 2013 by the US Council on Foreign Relations said:

> To be sure, this government is nationalistic, interventionist, and heavy-handed, and Correa is no conventional democrat, as his attack on the press so eloquently demonstrated. There is, however, a method to President Correa's heavy-handed tactics. They are arguably necessary in a country where few institutions work and vested interests, including foreign ones, regularly make use of raw power via marches, manipulation of the media, and corruption. Weak chief executives of any stripe would not survive in Ecuador. In fact, they haven't. U.S. officials are fretful of Correa who consistently resists closer ties with Washington. And in all fairness, it is easy to understand his mistrust given that the United States has demonstrated a willingness to stir up trouble for leftist governments in the region, both historically and in recent times.[42]

Correa was sensitive to any foreign involvement with his opponents. Ecuador had a large number of civil society organizations pursuing pro-democracy, press freedom, and anti-corruption agendas. As is common throughout the developing

---

[41] "Rafael Correa anuncia creación de sitio web Somos+ para combatir supuesta 'campaña de desprestigio' en redes [Rafael Correa announces the creation of the Somos+ website to combat supposed 'smear campaign' on social networks]," *El Comercio*, January 24, 2015, https://www.elcomercio.com/actualidad/politica/rafaelcorrea-web-redes-internet-crudoecuador.html
[42] O'Neil, Shannon K., "Guest Post: Ecuador's Military and Why Correa Will Be Reelected (Once)," Council on Foreign Relations, April 4, 2012, https://www.cfr.org/blog/guest-post-ecuadors-military-and-why-correa-will-be-reelected-once

world, many were funded by foreign governments and foundations. The US government contributed at least $8 million to civil society causes in Ecuador between 2007 and 2017.[43] "There was a lot of fear under Correa," said César Ricaurte of Fundamedios, a press freedom organization. "Civil society couldn't have survived without international support."[44]

Correa's government started to move against civil society NGOs in 2008. Presidential Decree 982 required them to identify their area of interest and register with the ministry responsible for those matters. By 2010, Correa was warning Ecuadorians to be "careful" of such groups and calling foreign assistance to them "imperialistic humanitarian" activity.[45] In 2013, Decree 16 barred civil society groups from deviating from their stated objectives, engaging in politics, threatening "internal or external security," or disturbing the peace. The government gained the right to veto who could serve as their top officers and to dissolve organizations that violated the law.

Significantly for the groups' international ties, they were required to report all foreign funding. Fundamedios, which received support from the United States, was ordered to shut down for allegedly engaging in "partisan political activities."[46]

"Officials can now essentially decide what groups may say or do, seriously undermining their role as a check on the government," said José Miguel Vivanco, Americas director at Human Rights Watch. He accused the government of "following the lead of countries such as Russia, Bahrain, Uganda, and Venezuela, which have imposed unjustified restrictions that violate fundamental

---

[43] Derived from https://foreignassistance.gov/cd/ecuador/2007/obligations/0

[44] César Ricaurte, interview with author, November 19, 2021.

[45] Appe, Susan, et al., "Organized Civil Society Under Authoritarian Populism: Cases from Ecuador," Nonprofit Policy Forum, October 9, 2019, https://www.degruyter.com/document/doi/10.1515/npf-2019-0039/html

[46] Hooper, Melissa "Russia's Bad Example," Free Russia Foundation and Human Rights First, February 2016, https://humanrightsfirst.org/wp-content/uploads/2022/10/Russias_Bad_Example.pdff

298 | HOW RUSSIA LOSES

rights and limit spaces that are critical to democratic society."[47] (Russia began imposing "foreign agent" laws against NGOs in 2012.)

Decree 16 and the subsequent suppression of a series of NGOs put a chill on foreign assistance to such organizations. The US Agency for International Development (USAID) closed its Ecuador office in September 2014 after Correa forced it to suspend operations pending a new bilateral agreement. He had demanded that USAID end support for civil society and press freedom organizations— about 10 percent of USAID's Ecuadorian operations. USAID financing for civil society NGOs "is a CIA strategy to finance the enemies of progressive countries," Correa said in the 2022 interview. USAID continued supporting civil society groups from outside the country.[48]

Germany's Konrad Adenauer Foundation, another supporter of democracy programs worldwide, shut down its office in Ecuador. It blamed increasing control over NGOs' work, including authorities reserving the right to change the programs these organizations conducted. "That was a condition we could no longer accept," said Director Winfried Weck."[49] A month earlier, Foreign Minister Ricardo Patiño had condemned the foundation, saying "let's not fool ourselves" about its true aims.[50]

---

[47] Human Rights Watch, "Ecuador: Clampdown on Civil Society," August 12, 2013, https://www.hrw.org/news/2013/08/12/ecuador-clampdown-civil-society

[48] Otis, John, "USAID is leaving Ecuador," *Global Post*, September 30, 2014, https://theworld.org/stories/2014-09-30/usaid-leaving-ecuador. USAID's work from outside after its expulsion was briefly mentioned by the agency's administrator when it returned in 2019. See Ordoñez, Franco, "U.S. and Ecuador sign new agreement after Assange expelled," McClatchyDC, May 15, 3019, https://www.mcclatchydc.com/news/politics-government/white-house/article230402254.html

[49] "Ecuador's Game," *Deutsche Welle*, August 20, 2014, https://www.dw.com/en/ecuadors-game-with-assange-and-free-speech/a-17864149

[50] "USAID is leaving Ecuador," op. cit.

Correa and Russia

While Correa fought critics at home and chipped away at relations with the United States, he sharply improved Ecuador's ties with Russia. In 2008, he traveled to Venezuela to meet Medvedev. Shortly afterward, Russian Foreign Minister Sergei Lavrov and Nikolai Patrushev, head of the Russian Security Council, visited Quito. In 2009, Correa flew to Moscow for another meeting with Medvedev. He signed with the then–Russian president a "Declaration of Strategic Partnership" that included cooperation on economic projects, trade, the environment, and culture, as well as security matters. On the latter point, the declaration said:

> Within the framework of strategic cooperation, the Sides will strengthen their cooperation in the area of security and defense, in particular by stepping up consultations between the appropriate organizations of the two countries. The strategic partnership between the Sides is not directed against any other state or group of states and it does not pursue the goal of creating a military-political union.[51]

Correa and Medvedev signed an agreement for peaceful cooperation in nuclear energy, and Correa agreed to buy two helicopters for the Ecuadorian military for $22 million. He said Ecuador would consider recognizing the independence of Abkhazia and South Ossetia, which Russia occupied after its 2008 invasion of Georgia.

---

[51] Document at http://www.kremlin.ru/supplement/356. A "strategic partnership" between Russia and a Latin American state is not unique. Russia has also established such relationships with Argentina, Brazil, Venezuela, Cuba, and Nicaragua. See Pyatakov, Andrey, "Russia and Latin America in the 21st Century," Institut français des relations internationales, July 2020, https://www.ifri.org/sites/default/files/atoms/files/pyatakov_latin_america_an_2020.pdf, p. 32.

300 | HOW RUSSIA LOSES

Trade between Ecuador and Russia doubled under Correa, with Ecuador enjoying a consistent trade surplus. Russia also began a series of direct investments in the country. In 2011, Russia's ambassador in Quito, Yan Burlyai, told journalists that Russia would invest nearly $1 billion in oil, energy, hydroelectric, transport, and other endeavors. Among them was a hydroelectric project in the Toachi and Pilatón river basins, financed by $153 million of Russian credit.[52]

In October 2013, Correa made his second visit to Moscow, meeting with Vladimir Putin, who had taken back the presidency after the Medvedev interregnum.

By this time, Correa's importance in the Bolivarian nations had grown. Chávez had died in March 2013, and Correa was a prime candidate for taking up his ideological mantle. By the end of 2014, the Strategic Culture Foundation, a website closely aligned with Russian officialdom, declared Correa to be Chávez's "political successor." A commentary on its site cast Correa as the leading figure at that year's 12-nation UNASUR conference in Quito and as the chief architect of a project to unite all South Americans:

> Together, we will be able to dictate the terms of international capital," said Rafael Correa. The concept of South American citizenship, which will give people the right to move around the region and get a job and an education anywhere on the continent, is an important achievement of the summit in Ecuador. Five hundred million people will receive such a "South American passport!" ... Correa's leadership qualities, as well as his perseverance in defending his position and the fact that he is a world-class economist, command deep respect.

The article also underscored Correa's geopolitical importance, cataloging in detail all of his actions against the United States.

---

[52] Arroyo, María Belén, "Luna de miel con el Kremlin [Honeymoon with the Kremlin]," *Vistazo*, November 22, 2013.

"Many in Latin America believe that following Hugo Chavez, Rafael Correa has become America's main target," the article said.[53]

Correa's importance as a carrier of the leftist torch grew further in 2015, when Dilma Rousseff was impeached in Brazil and Cristina Fernández de Kirchner's favored election candidate was defeated in Argentina. Had President Obama's rapprochement with Cuba in 2014 been more successful, Correa's significance might have been greater still.

It is not known what conversations Correa and Putin may have had in 2013 about Correa's role on the continent, or in long-term Ecuadorian-Russian strategy. To Moscow, Correa's significance may simply have been that he was one of the last Latin leftists standing. The main public takeaways from the meeting were additional economic projects, including $195 million in Russian financing for gas and steam turbines in Machala in Ecuador's southwest. The two presidents discussed $1.5 billion in other possible Russian projects, including an 1,800-mile railroad link between Quito and four Ecuadorian seaports.[54]

Following the meeting, Ecuador and Russia cultivated additional cultural and scientific relations. Russia's Skolkovo Innovation Center signed a cooperation agreement with Ecuador's Yachay Tech University, envisaging the construction of a vaccine factory at Yachay.[55] Scholarships for Ecuadorians to study in Moscow

---

[53] Nikandrov, Nil, "Rafael Correa – Hugo Chavez's Political Successor," Strategic Culture Foundation, December 18, 2014, https://strategic-culture.org/news/2014/12/18/rafael-correa-hugo-chavezs-political-successor

[54] "Correa pushing Ecuador cooperation with Russia," *EFE*, October 29, 2013, https://www.sandiegouniontribune.com/en-espanol/sdhoy-correa-pushing-ecuador-cooperation-with-russia-2013oct29-story.html. Text of Putin and Correa statements after their talks at http://www.kremlin.ru/events/president/transcripts/19505

[55] "Rusia construirá en Ecuador fábrica de vacunas y sueros para mercado regional [Russia will build a vaccine and serum factory in Ecuador for the regional market]," *Agence France-Presse*, November 13,

302 | HOW RUSSIA LOSES

were increased, and the Pushkin State Russian Language Institute and the Russkiy Mir ("Russian World") Foundation opened facilities in Ecuador.

Correa condemned Western trade sanctions against Russia after its first invasion of Ukraine in 2014 and said Ecuador would export more to Russia to help replace Western products.[56]

In 2015, Fernando Alvarado, Ecuador's national secretary for communications, visited *RT* in Moscow and signed an agreement to allow the Russian network to broadcast 24 hours a day in Ecuador. "What was the matter with that?" Correa said in the 2022 interview. "It's called pluralism." Correa's foreign minister, Ricardo Patiño, returned to Moscow that year for additional talks.

Correa was also helpful to Moscow as a leading advocate of a project of great importance both to Russia and China: the creation of a new international financial system. Such a system would challenge the dollar as the world's leading reserve currency and the SWIFT system as the most effective way to move money. Leveraging his training as an economist, Correa emerged as the project's top supporter in Latin America. ALBA countries experimented with an international payments system featuring a new virtual accounting unit, the Sucre. The idea was that imports and exports would be settled via the Sucre, whose value would be based not on the dollar, but on the strength of the currencies and economies of participating nations. It was used for about three years.

Correa also vocally supported Moscow's effort to expand its Eurasian Economic Union (EEU) beyond Russia, Armenia, Belarus, Kazakhstan, and Kyrgyzstan. Russia pushed for partnerships between the EEU and UNASUR, CELAC, and Mercosur economic bloc; Ecuador belonged to them all.

2016, https://www.elcomercio.com/actualidad/rusia-construira-ecuador-fabrica-vacunas.html

[56] "Ecuador to Boost Agricultural Exports to Russia," *Sputnik News*, December 1, 2015, https://sputniknews.com/business/201512011031079078-ecuador-boosts-russia-agricultural-exports/

Ecuador: Who Played Whom? | 303

Additionally, Correa was a leader in designing the Banco del Sur ("Bank of the South"). The bank, which was never funded, was to offer Latin nations an alternative to funding from the World Bank and IMF—and could have been used by Russia to evade Western economic sanctions.

Russia usually seeks strong intelligence cooperation with its allies. SENAIN agents reportedly received training in Moscow in 2015 and 2016 and obtained some Russian electronic espionage equipment.[57] However, SENAIN also spent millions on Israeli and Italian surveillance technology, a former Ecuadorian official said. The official speculated that Russian agencies may not have fully trusted SENAIN, as some of its operatives had past ties to the United States.

One possible nexus for Ecuadorian and Russian cooperation was Assange's refuge in the Ecuadorian Embassy in London. WikiLeaks' revelation of secret diplomatic cables had proven a huge embarrassment to the US in 2010, and Russia saw Assange's potential to bloody the United States further. In 2012, *RT* gave him an interview show, which he conducted from London while he battled in British courts to avoid extradition to Sweden for questioning in a rape case. Just two months before he fled to the embassy, Assange interviewed Correa on his *RT* program, which turned into a half-hour of mutual admiration. Correa praised WikiLeaks' work and told Assange, "Cheer up! Welcome to the club of the persecuted!"[58]

A senior Ecuadorian diplomat said Ecuador's decision to offer Assange asylum was made jointly with Russia, though no proof has ever been provided. Correa said in the 2022 interview that Assange had been "testing various embassies" and that "it wasn't a huge surprise" that he chose the Ecuadorian mission, where he had a good relationship with the consul, Fidel Narváez.

---

[57] Torres, Arturo, "El espionaje selló el nexo Correa-Putin [Espionage sealed the Correa-Putin nexus]," *Código Vidrio*, August 30, 2022, https://www.codigovidrio.com/code/el-espionaje-sello-el-nexo-corea-putin
[58] Video at https://www.youtube.com/watch?v=rW7edOQ3pCo

304 | HOW RUSSIA LOSES

To the mission's staff, Assange was hardly a model guest. They found him demanding and his conduct erratic, to the point that they hired security contractors to monitor him. The contractors reported that he continued to conduct WikiLeaks operations from the embassy, including during the period when the group released files stolen from John Podesta, chairman of Hillary Clinton's presidential campaign. The contractors said Assange received as many as 75 guests a month, among them Russian citizens and computer hackers. On one occasion, the London bureau chief of *RT* appeared on unusually short notice, handed Assange a USB drive, and departed within five minutes.[59] Assange also conducted from inside the embassy an interview for *RT* with the leader of Hezbollah.

As Assange's time at the embassy wore on, his presence became increasingly problematic for the United Kingdom as well. To enforce the Swedish extradition request, British officials had to maintain an army of police around the mission to capture Assange if he tried to leave. They asked Ecuador for options to end the situation. Ecuador contacted Russian officials and got their agreement to send Assange to Moscow. Ecuador even went so far as to announce that Assange would become an advisor at its Moscow embassy. But when the Ecuadorian consul in London asked the UK to give him diplomatic status so he could safely leave the embassy and head to Moscow, the UK refused.[60]

The standoff over Assange spawned other plans that were far more dramatic. One reportedly involved SENAIN agents sneaking Assange out of the embassy and transferring him to Russian agents using Russian or Ecuadorian diplomatic vehicles. The CIA reportedly picked up word of the plan and took it seriously enough to report it to the White House. Despite the boost that

---

[59] Cohen, Marshall, et al., "Exclusive: Security reports reveal how Assange turned an embassy into a command post for election meddling," *CNN*, July 15, 2019, https://www.cnn.com/2019/07/15/politics/assange-embassy-exclusive-documents/index.html

[60] Satter, Raphael, "Newly published files confirm plan to move Assange to Russia," *The Associated Press*, October 17, 2018, https://apnews.com/article/3728e1631d57454a9502dd51d1bf441b

Ecuador: Who Played Whom? | 305

WikiLeaks' revelations gave Donald Trump's election campaign—and Trump's own comments praising WikiLeaks—his administration remained intent on prosecuting Assange for exposing American secrets. By one account, the CIA was prepared to do whatever was necessary to block Assange, an Australian citizen, from making it to Russian protection—even if it meant ramming a Russian vehicle and shooting it out with Kremlin agents on the streets of London.[61]

The Ecuadorian mission in London was also involved in the case of Edward Snowden, who flew to Hong Kong after his revelations about the US National Security Agency in 2013. Narváez, the Ecuadorian consul who had tried unsuccessfully to win diplomatic status for Assange, sent a safe-conduct document to Snowden in Hong Kong stating he would receive political asylum in Ecuador. The document was enough for the Hong Kong authorities, who were eager to be done with Snowden, to let him board a plane to Moscow. Narváez then appeared in Moscow, where he met Snowden at the airport to clear the way for him to fly to Cuba and then Ecuador.[62] However, the journey to Ecuador was canceled after a call from then–Vice President Joe Biden to Correa. Snowden remains in Russia.

---

[61] Dorfman, Zack, et al., "Kidnapping, assassination and a London shoot-out: Inside the CIA's secret war plans against WikiLeaks," *Yahoo News*, September 26, 2021, https://news.yahoo.com/kidnapping-assassination-and-a-london-shoot-out-inside-the-ci-as-secret-war-plans-against-wiki-leaks-090057786.html. Other reported plans to get Assange out of the embassy included having him escape across rooftops, or be hefted out inside a diplomatic pouch. See Ball, James et al., "Secret Memos Reveal Julian Assange's Escape Plans From Ecuador's Embassy," *BuzzFeed News*, September 1, 2015, https://www.buzzfeed.com/jamesball/mr-white-and-mr-blue

[62] Torres, Arturo, "Fotos confirman cita Assange-Vallejo, 72 horas antes de fallida extracción [Photos confirm Assange-Vallejo meeting, 72 hours before failed extraction]," *Código Vidrio*, September 21, 2018, https://www.codigovidrio.com/code/vallejo-y-assange-una-cita-en-el-corazon-de-londres

306 | HOW RUSSIA LOSES

Ecuador Reverses Course

As Ecuador's 2017 presidential elections approached, the public enthusiasm that had initially buoyed Correa and his Revolución Ciudadana had declined precipitously. The government's finances were weighed down by the end of the oil boom, interest payments on big loans from China, and an obligation to keep selling oil to Beijing at below-market prices. Many Ecuadorians were angered by the government's suppression of domestic critics, including workers, journalists, civil society, and indigenous activists.

Faced with growing opposition, Correa decided not to run again for president. (Constitutional term limits blocked him from running, but his allies had proposed a referendum to change that.) Many analysts saw Correa's move as a calculated stratagem. He would allow Lenín Moreno, who had been his vice president until 2013, to win the presidency and rule under Correa's instructions. If Moreno proved troublesome, he could be replaced by Jorge Glas, Correa's most recent vice president, who also became vice president under Moreno. Once public dislike for Correa had cooled down, according to the purported strategy, Correa would then run for a new term in 2021. The maneuver would be similar to how Putin and Medvedev had exchanged jobs in 2008–2012 to let Putin continue to control Russia without violating the constitution.

With Correa's endorsement, Moreno became president in May 2017, defeating conservative banker Guillermo Lasso by only 3 percent of the vote. To all outside appearances, Moreno was Correa's man. Correa retained a strong political machine, and the sharply divided legislature seemed to offer Moreno little room for maneuver. *The Wall Street Journal* said, "Critics say the new leader, an ally of his predecessor, will likely not change things much."[63]

---

[63] Dube, Ryan, "Ecuador Swears in Moreno as President to Succeed Correa," *The Wall Street Journal*, May 24, 2017, https://www.wsj.com/articles/ecuador-swears-in-moreno-as-president-to-succeed-correa-1495659294?mod=article_inline

Ecuador: Who Played Whom? | 307

If that was what Correa expected, it was a spectacular miscalculation. Moreno had been active in the Alianza PAIS party, but his personality was far different from that of the combative Correa. Moreno had a business background and first joined the government as a tourism official. "He was the good cop, even when Correa was being his toughest," recalls María Paula Romo, who served as Moreno's interior minister.[64] In 1998, Moreno was shot in the back in a robbery and lost the use of his legs. He became devoted to humor as a remedy for illness and depression, writing several books on the subject and establishing the Eventa Foundation to promote humor in everyday life. He sharply improved services to Ecuador's disabled during his vice presidency, then left government to become a UN special envoy on disability.

With Moreno in charge, Ecuador's direction changed swiftly. From his first days in office, the new president set a tone of conciliation and compromise. He reached out to Correa's bitterest opponents, including indigenous activists, civil society, and the private sector. When Correa denounced Moreno for welcoming tribal leaders who had clashed with Correa over water and land rights, Moreno tweeted back, "If it's hatred you want, don't look to me."[65]

Moreno was still loyal to the Alianza PAIS goals of social justice and fighting corruption but said he was shocked by what he found when he became president—especially the degree of corruption and the sheer unreliability of government information. He said that it was hard to determine just how big Ecuador's debt really was and that government statistics had been manipulated to exaggerate the progress made against poverty. He told an American audience that "Ecuador was becoming Venezuela."[66]

---

[64] María Paula Romo, interview with author, September 15, 2021.
[65] Solano, Gonzalo, "As Correa leaves Ecuador, a rift opens with his successor," *The Associated Press*, July 11, 2017, https://apnews.com/article/9a5e5053005d4ec6a447beb37ed7c1c7
[66] Video at https://www.atlanticcouncil.org/news/event-recaps/the-new-ecuador-a-conversation-with-h-e-lenin-moreno-president-of-ecuador

308 | HOW RUSSIA LOSES

Moreno ousted Correa appointees from critical ministries overseeing defense, foreign affairs, and the economy, replacing them with professionals who were well known to the West. He also eased restrictions on civil society organizations.

In February 2018, Moreno organized and decisively won a referendum that limited presidents to a total of two terms, blocking Correa from becoming president again. The referendum also gave Moreno the power to replace many of the judges whom Correa had appointed. Civil society groups were invited to nominate candidates for judicial positions. Moreno also dissolved SENAIN, Correa's security service, and Supercom, a state body that had investigated and sanctioned journalists.

Internationally, Moreno's government quickly distanced itself from Correa's leftist associations on the continent. Ecuador pulled out of the Bolivarian ALBA alliance in August 2018. Foreign Minister Jose Valencia said Ecuador did not want to be part of organizations that were trying to impose "specific views" on social and political issues.[67] Ecuador withdrew from UNASUR in 2019, joining several other nations that had left the body, and evicted it from the building in Quito that Correa had provided for its headquarters. In perhaps Moreno's most dramatic break with the Latin left, he recognized Juan Guaidó as the legitimate president of Venezuela, withdrawing Correa's support for Chávez heir Nicolás Maduro. Meeting personally with Guaidó in March 2019, Moreno described Maduro's Venezuela as a "completely failed state."[68]

Relations with Russia collapsed. "In Ecuador, in the last four years of Lenín Moreno's government, our relations unfortunately chilled. They froze," Ambassador Vladimir Sprinchan told an Ecuadorian journalist in 2021. "Projects were paralyzed, like the

---

[67] *The Associated Press*, "Ecuador leaves Venezuelan-run regional alliance," August 23, 2018, https://apnews.com/article/6a7d8ed8738a475d8b6c276ffa0b761e

[68] *TASS*, "Президент Эквадора назвал Венесуэлу несостоявшимся государством [Ecuador president calls Venezuela a failed state]," March 2, 2019, https://tass.ru/mezhdunarodnaya-panorama/6179371

use of space for scientific purposes, the peaceful use of nuclear energy, and the recognition of credentials of Ecuadorians who graduated from Russian universities, among others." Russia tried to resurrect with Moreno the railroad project between Quito and Ecuadorian ports that Putin and Correa had imagined. But Moreno showed no interest, Sprinchan said.[69]

Russia could have done little to prevent Moreno's decision to suddenly switch Ecuador's political loyalties back to the United States, said Romo. "He turned against Correa because of corruption and authoritarianism," she said, "things not connected to Russia's relationship with Ecuador."[70]

Moreno quickly restored Ecuador's relations with the United States and international financial institutions. Ecuador renewed military and law enforcement cooperation with Washington. It allowed the US to operate aircraft from the Ecuadorian mainland and the Galápagos Islands to monitor drug traffic. It further tightened visa requirements and recalled its defense attachés from Iran, Cuba, Belarus, and Venezuela. Jaramillo said Moreno feared the Latin left and, more importantly, Correa's supporters inside and outside Ecuador. He thought the US could afford him protection, she said. A senior Ecuadorian diplomat added: "Moreno was afraid of Russia. They had a dangerous intelligence agency."

With Moreno steadily reversing Correa's policies, US government assistance to Ecuador shot up from $18 million in 2017 to $79 million in 2018.[71] Vice President Mike Pence visited the country in June 2018 as his first stop on a Latin American tour. Ecuador received an IMF loan of $4.2 billion in March 2019, and Moreno won support from the US International Development Finance Corporation to escape Ecuador's loan deals with China. "The US

---

[69] Torres, Arturo, "Rusia y Ecuador afinan acuerdo nuclear pacífico," *Código Vidrio*, September 14, 2021, https://www.codigovidrio.com/code/rusia-y-ecuador-afinan-acuerdo-nuclear-pacifico/
[70] María Paula Romo, interview with author.
[71] Derived from https://foreignassistance.gov/cd/ecuador/2021/obligations/0

310 | HOW RUSSIA LOSES

got it right," said Evan Ellis, a professor at the US Army War College and a former State Department specialist on Latin America. "We saw Ecuador not as a US puppet, but we wanted it to succeed."[72]

Moreno also thrust Ecuador into world headlines by terminating Assange's embassy asylum in April 2019. A throng of British plainclothes police hustled him out of the building, handcuffed and shouting. Since the Swedish extradition request had been dropped, Assange was detained on an American arrest warrant. Moreno said the Australian was "a stone in the shoe" and an "inherited problem."[73]

A month after Assange's expulsion, USAID signed a memorandum of understanding with Ecuador on economic development, environmental cooperation, responses to natural disasters, and democracy initiatives.[74] Nine months later, Moreno was received by President Trump in Washington.

Had Moreno taken a true intellectual journey from leftist politics to conservative, pro-American views? Or had he simply been appalled by what he discovered after becoming president and felt Ecuador needed to reverse course both nationally and internationally? After Moreno's first year as president, Ellis wrote:

> Even beyond President Moreno's actions [to replace Correa loyalists in] key cabinet posts, much of the President's focus, and his most significant choices since taking office have been driven less by the desire to change Ecuador's

---

[72] Evan Ellis, interview with author, July 21, 2021.

[73] Sieff, Kevin et al., "In Ecuador, Assange's expulsion reflects desire for better relations with the U.S.," *The Washington Post*, April 11, 2019, https://www.washingtonpost.com/world/in-ecuador-assanges-expulsion-reflects-a-shifting-political-tide/2019/04/11/7b50e852-5c66-11e9-98d4-844088d135f2_story.html

[74] "U.S. and Ecuador sign new agreement after Assange expelled," op. cit.

> ideology, than a courageous and necessary effort to confront the significant corruption and cronyism that appears to have been left behind by his predecessor.[75]

It is easy to believe that, returning to Ecuador from his UN post in Geneva, Moreno was stunned by what Correísmo had wrought: little progress in ending poverty, heavy foreign debts, repression of human rights, and a foreign policy that seemed to value leftist rhetoric over concrete results. Surely Moreno was aware that rightist rule in Latin America and an alliance with the United States had their downsides. But he may have felt he had no alternative. When Correa turned Ecuador's orientation toward allies such as Russia, he argued, "Even if we are wrong, we don't have much to lose." In his first months in the Carondelet Presidential Palace, Moreno may have felt similarly about moving Ecuador in the opposite direction.

Whatever Moreno's personal convictions, leftists inside and outside the country were furious at his sweeping reversal of Correísmo. A livid Patiño declared on *RT* that, undoubtedly, Moreno was in league with the CIA because he lacked "the intelligence, the head, to carry out something of this nature unless it was organized from the American Embassy."[76] Correa, who like Assange had received his own talk show on *RT*, continued to attack Moreno from his new base in Belgium. He tweeted that Moreno's expulsion of Assange was "a crime that humanity will never forget" and that his former vice president was "the greatest

---

[75] Ellis, Evan, "Lenín Moreno and the struggle for the soul of Ecuador's (and Latin America's) left," *Global Americans*, August 2, 2018, https://theglobalamericans.org/2018/08/lenin-moreno-and-the-struggle-for-the-soul-of-ecuadors-and-latin-americas-left

[76] *RT*, "Ricardo Patiño: "Lenín Moreno es un impostor profesional; todo lo que hace fue programado con la CIA [Ricardo Patiño: Lenín Moreno is a profesional impostor; everything he does was directed by the CIA]," April 20, 2019, https://actualidad.rt.com/actualidad/312311-ricardo-patrino-lenin-moreno-impostor-profesional

312 | HOW RUSSIA LOSES

traitor in Ecuadorian and Latin American history."[77] He said he wanted to return to Ecuador and run for vice president.

Pro-Correa activists, some still organized through Somos+, claimed the new presidential term limit was a desperate effort by Moreno to block the return of a popular leader. Moreno, they said, was a lapdog of the United States, willing to barter away Ecuador's principles for financial aid and political protection. They charged that Ecuador recognized Guaidó and expelled Assange from its embassy because Pence demanded it during his visit.

Moreno's replacements of judges and election officials, his critics asserted, were aimed at imposing dictatorship—the same charge Correa's opponents had leveled at him. Moreno's opponents also said the corruption charges against Correa were flimsy, that judges had rushed to reject his appeals, and that Moreno used legal maneuvers to block Correa from registering to run as a candidate of a new party.

There were also claims that Moreno was corrupt himself. Days before he expelled Assange from the embassy, Moreno had been accused by WikiLeaks of being behind allegations that he profited off a tax haven in Belize—charges that Moreno denied.[78]

In 2020, an Ecuadorian court sentenced Correa in absentia to eight years' imprisonment and banned him from politics for 25 years. Glas, whom Moreno had suspended from the vice presidency in 2017 amid claims of corruption, was sentenced to six years in prison. He had allegedly received more than $13 million in bribes from Brazilian construction company Odebrecht

---

[77] Rafael Correa, Twitter, April 11, 2019, https://twitter.com/Mashi Rafael/status/1116289091061075968?lang=en

[78] Many of the accusations against Moreno by Correa's allies are laid out in an article by a former foreign minister under Correa. See Long, Guillaume, "Political trials and electoral bans: the battle for democracy in Ecuador," *openDemocracy*, September 18, 2020, https://www.open democracy.net/en/democraciaabierta/political-tirals-electoral-bans-battle-ecuador-democracy

Ecuador: Who Played Whom? | 313

in return for public contracts. Eighteen other Correa associates were convicted of bribery.

Moscow and Quito: The Limits of Solidarity

From the moment Correa became president, a strong basis materialized for a mutually advantageous relationship between him and Russia. But multiple factors, including Russian miscalculations, Correa's nature, and Ecuador's dependence on the United States, severely limited what Russia could accomplish.

On the plus side for Moscow. Correa's militant, anti-US ideology served the Kremlin geopolitically. Correa was an increasingly important figure in leftist Latin circles and, as an economist, was particularly devoted to undermining US economic power—a priority for Russia.

Correa's new administration was consolidating itself just as Russia, stung by the Western reaction to its invasion of Georgia, was looking for ways to strike back in the Western Hemisphere. Correa was a comparatively minor figure in the pink tide, had little political experience, and led one of South America's smallest countries. Yet he was skilled at crowd-pleasing rhetoric and was prepared to follow up his anti-US ideology with concrete actions. He was also dedicated to the Bolivarian bloc, Russia's most loyal contingent of Latin American countries.

The Bolivarians badly needed shoring up: Nicaragua was tiny and isolated in Central America, Cuba was needy, Venezuela was a monument to socialist economic failure, and Bolivia was far geographically from the continent's mainstream. Ecuador had more people than Bolivia, Cuba, or Nicaragua, and Correa looked to be an ambitious, charismatic figure who could bring new excitement to the Bolivarian enterprise. Later, as the pink tide receded, Correa took on even more importance. With leftists losing elections and Chávez's death, Correa appeared to be one of the most important remaining agitators against the US in Latin America.

314 | HOW RUSSIA LOSES

Russia also could hope to make some money in Ecuador. Small as the country is, it has been among Moscow's top-four trading partners in Latin America.[79] Ecuador mined oil, copper, and gold, and its energy needs were growing. Russia had expertise in mining and energy. Moscow's efforts to secure an atomic energy agreement with Ecuador in 2009 signaled Russian interest in a possible deal for nuclear power plants.

Some Russians gained at least tangentially from Ecuador's illegal economy. Organized crime in Ecuador created opportunities for criminal groups from many countries, including Russia, that laundered money, smuggled drugs, and engaged in human trafficking. Beyond full-time criminals, more upscale Russians may have benefited in some way. Maria-Laura Patiño, an advisor to the Ecuadorian Ministry of Finance, said she had learned that, between 2010 and 2014, streams of private Russian yachts dropped anchor in the Galápagos Islands, exchanging unknown cargo with people who flew in from the Ecuadorian mainland.[80]

Even if organized crime in Ecuador did not directly enrich the Russian state, the Kremlin benefits from illegal actors at all levels who can occasionally be useful to state interests. Drug addiction and political polarization over migrants help weaken the United States, and the permissiveness of Correa's regime made a contribution in both areas. In every major case in which people from countries other than Mexico and Central America entered the US illegally in 2009, the migrants had traveled through Ecuador.[81]

---

[79] Shkolyar, Nikolai, "Торговля России со странами Латинской Америки: ориентиры на третье десятилетие [Russian trade with Latin American countries: landmarks for the third decade]," Russian Council for International Affairs, February 3, 2021, https://russian council.ru/analytics-and-comments/analytics/torgovlya-rossii-so-stranami-latinskoy-ameriki-orientiry-na-trete-desyatiletie
[80] Maria-Laura Patiño, interview with author, August 21, 2021.
[81] "Ecuador at Risk: Drugs, Thugs, Guerillas and the Citizens Revolution," op. cit.

Ecuador: Who Played Whom? | 315

Yet by other measures, Russia's attempts to build real influence in Ecuador was an impossible quest.

Russia's limited economic power could not make a dent in the trading patterns of a country even as small as Ecuador. Trade between the two countries doubled under Correa, but never surpassed $2 billion a year.[82] Moscow never even achieved a trade surplus in goods. The bananas and flowers Ecuador shipped to Russia, it seemed, were more valuable than anything that all of Russia could summon up to sell in the other direction.

Russia simply did not have the financial strength to offer the massive investments and long-term contracts that China could. Correa said in 2022 that China and Ecuador had a mutually beneficial relationship, since Beijing needed energy and Quito needed financial support. Russia did not need any hydrocarbons and had little money to offer. "China materialized its relations with Ecuador," said a former Ecuadorian diplomat. "Russia didn't provide us resources in a committed way." The Russian ambassador visited the Ecuadorian Foreign Ministry rarely, he said; the Chinese were there constantly. "The Russian relationship with us was more rhetorical, symbolic, based on pre-1990 ties with people in Ecuador who had studied in Russia," the diplomat said. Ecuador, meanwhile, lacked the economic weight to make a significant monetary contribution to projects like the Bank of the South.

Russian investments that looked impressive at the start did not always go smoothly. The Toachi-Pilatón hydroelectric project fell victim to delays and a long dispute between a Russian contractor and Ecuador's electric utility company. The railroad Putin and Correa envisaged from Quito to the coast was never built. The vaccine plant at Yachay never appeared. (If it had, foreign companies might have vied to use it during the COVID pandemic.) Russian oil drilling projects failed to get underway. The 2009 atomic energy agreement with Moscow, whose provisions were initially kept secret, caused a scandal in the Ecuadorian National

---

[82] Statistics from https://en.ru-stat.com/date-Y2013-2020/RU/trade/EC

316 | HOW RUSSIA LOSES

Assembly when it became public two years later. A provision in the document appeared to allow Russia to ship nuclear waste to Ecuador from other countries. Russia denied any such intention, but legislators were outraged.[83]

To some degree, prospects for big deals with Russia may have been simply drowned out by Ecuador's galloping trade with China. Moscow did not hide its disappointment over Beijing's economic power. Ambassador Burlyai said in 2013 that, while Russian investments in Ecuador had totaled $500 million since 2008, "I'm not happy. The Chinese have signed $10 billion in the same period."[84]

Beyond trade issues, Correa conducted a foreign policy that did not always comply with Moscow's needs. Although the two countries were aligned on many issues, Correa failed to come through on key Russian priorities. Although he had said he was considering doing so, Correa never recognized the independence of Abkhazia or South Ossetia. He also declined to join Venezuela, Bolivia, and other Bolivarian countries in voting against a 2014 UN resolution that called Russia's annexation of Crimea illegal. Ecuador abstained, though it made a bow to Russia by declaring that the Ukrainian government resulting from the Maidan revolution was illegal.

The vote on Crimea suggested that Correa had a rather transactional view of his relationship with Russia; he would do what was useful to him and Ecuador, but not necessarily go further. In the 2022 interview, Correa said that Ecuador's policy was to oppose offensive wars and that Russia's invasion of Ukraine in 2014 was just that. However, he added, there was no reason not to take the opportunity to sell Russia food when Western countries imposed trade sanctions on Moscow after the invasion. "What was wrong with exporting food? It was a sale for

---

[83] The agreement was published by the Supreme Court. Link to full text at https://portal.corteconstitucional.gob.ec/FichaCausa.aspx?numcausa=0048-10-TI

[84] Arroyo, María Belén, "Luna de miel con el Kremlin [Honeymoon with the Kremlin]," op. cit.

the well-being of our people," he said. He added that it was not constructive "to divide the world between good guys and bad guys."

The same focus on Ecuador's needs applied to military deals, usually a lively activity between the Kremlin and its allies. Russian Ambassador Burlyai told journalists in 2011 that Correa's purchase of the two helicopters in 2009 was likely just the start of many more deals, possibly including armored vehicles and portable bridges. Another report speculated about purchases of SU-30 fighters and anti-aircraft systems.[85] Yet little was actually purchased. In 2013 Burlyai acknowledged to an Ecuadorian reporter that a $200 million line of credit offered for military purchases had not been used.[86]

Jarrín, the former defense minister, suspected that Correa was never serious about buying Russian weapons. He called the president's occasional public comments about impending deals "simply a protocol thing."[87] "Russia was always eager to sell us military equipment, mainly trucks and armored vehicles," another former government official recalled. "But we did not need them because we weren't involved in any conflict."[88]

---

[85] "Российские миллиарды будут вложены в развитие Эквадора [Russian billions will be invested in the development of Ecuador]," *Ekvador Segodnya*, October 11, 2011, https://rusecuador.ru/ecuador-novedades/politica/8525-rossijskie-milliardy-budut-vlozheny-v-razvitie-ekvadora.html

[86] Arroyo, María Belén, "Luna de miel con el Kremlin [Honeymoon with the Kremlin]," op. cit.

[87] Oswaldo Jarrín, interview with author.

[88] Russian officialdom itself seemed lukewarm about military deals with Ecuador. Ahead of Correa's 2013 talks with Putin, a newspaper close to the Russian government suggested that any deals with Ecuador should be based solely on their economic profitability for Moscow. The commentary noted that Ecuador had previously defaulted on its debts and that Quito's trade with Russia—based on "bananas and Ecuador's famous roses"—was tiny compared to Russia's dealings with larger Latin American nations. Bratersky, Alexander, "Не бананом единым [Not by bananas alone]," *Gazeta.ru*, October 28, 2013, https://www.gazeta.ru/politics/2013/10/28_a_5726833.shtml

318 | HOW RUSSIA LOSES

Correa's understanding of *soberanía*, then, included protecting Ecuador's sovereignty even from ideological allies such as Russia. There was a limit to how much the two countries could truly be comrades. Even so, Moscow complicated its relationship with Ecuador through miscalculations of its own:

• **Moscow may have badly misread Correa from the start.** An Ecuadorian diplomat who had occasion to meet with senior Russian officials said Russia expected Ecuador to be a solid and reliable ally. Another diplomat said, "Russia thought Correa could be a regional leader. But he was arrogant. The Cubans never trusted him. They saw him as an impostor." Some believe Correa saw himself as a wheeler-dealer, constantly searching for advantage with Washington, Moscow, Beijing, and even Tehran by never giving any of them everything they wanted.

"Correa's interest in Russia was not bilateral. It was a function of politics, about the degree to which Russia could help him become the regional leader," Jarrín said. Ecuador had been a member of the Non-Aligned Movement since the 1980s; Correa may have felt that, in that spirit, he could accomplish his goals without having to wholly commit himself to any outside bloc.

Moscow would have been wrong to imagine that under any leader, Ecuador could become another Cuba or Nicaragua. Ecuador is a country of rambunctious politics. People value their right to demonstrate against unpopular leaders, and soldiers and parliaments have a history of throwing out presidents they find unsatisfactory. The result has been decades of political turbulence, coupled with a firm sense that leaders must constantly prove their value. Ecuador was ill-suited for the heavy-handed *caudillismo* that has served Moscow's interests in other Bolivarian countries. If Correa had tried to imitate Cuba or Nicaragua too closely, the army's willingness to wait him out might have changed

• **Russia seemed confident that Correa could handle his domestic opposition.** While Correa enjoyed broad public support early in his presidency, he eventually faced increasing protests over corruption and repression. Since both are in the Putin

Ecuador: Who Played Whom? | 319

regime's DNA, it is unlikely Russia would have advised Correa against either. In fact, the Strategic Culture Foundation exulted in Correa's crackdown on independent media: "The president has beaten back the attacks of Ecuadorian media groups that reflect the positions of pro-American elements. Today in Ecuador all owners of mass media know they will have to answer in court for slander and participating in subversive campaigns."[89] The phrasing suggested Russia was complacent about Correa's hold on power and did not prepare a back-up plan for his fall.

Such a plan might have involved shoring up Russia's own visibility in Ecuador to build a relationship with the Ecuadorian people that could outlast Correa.

Russia had *RT's* Spanish service as a possible tool, but that network normally spends its time bashing the West, not emphasizing Russian benevolence. Many listeners do not even know *RT* is Russian, which is handy for spreading disinformation but limits its ability to promote Russia as a brand. Ecuadorian newspapers carried routine stories when Russian scientific and education projects were announced, but Moscow conducted no publicity campaigns around them. In truth, there was little of substance to promote, but Russia has experience in positioning itself as a benefactor of countries even when its actual contribution is small. (Many Serbs, for instance, firmly believe Russia gives them more aid than the European Union.)

Ecuador's small Russian diaspora could have helped with such an effort. Instead, Russia settled for a minimal public profile in Ecuador, mainly that of Correa's distant ideological partner. When Ecuador's population and new administration turned against Correa, Russia could count on no reserve of public affection.

Some Russian officials have long been aware of the need for their country to build connections with foreign populations that can survive leadership changes. Russia has become proficient in spreading broad messages about the supposed evils of Western

---

[89] "Rafael Correa – Hugo Chavez's Political Successor," op. cit.

countries, and in promoting Russia's conservative social values. But successful public diplomacy also means searching for issues important to the host country and designing meaningful programs around them, a former Western diplomat said. "The Russians don't think, 'How can I be of service to this country? How can I help them?' " he said. "If roses are the big thing, then design an agricultural program around roses." Tatyana Poloskova, an advisor to Rossotrudnichestvo, a Russian aid and "humanitarian influence"[90] organization, said in 2019 that Russia needs to work with Latin America systematically, not just from revolution to revolution or coup to coup. "It is essential that in Ecuador, in addition to the Russian Embassy, other structures be present," she said. "Not only commercial ones, but public organizations."[91] In March 2023, a Russian public diplomacy organization inaugurated a program called Hablemos con Rusia ("Let's Talk With Russia"), aimed at promoting "a productive dialogue of new generation leaders from Russia and Latin America."[92]

There were moments after Moreno's rise to power when Russia's fortunes might have surged back—during a 2019 rebellion against Moreno's austerity program and the 2021 election, in which Guillermo Lasso narrowly won the presidency over leftist economist Andrés Arauz. (Arauz spent part of his youth living in Moscow and openly favored Correa's eventual return to the presidency.) If robust Russian-controlled "public organizations" had existed at those points, with propaganda skills learned from Moscow, they might have had some impact on events.

- **Russia failed to give Correa prestige that could have strengthened him at home.** Given its modest financial capabilities compared to those of China, Moscow was not in a position to deliver much aid or investment to Ecuador. But it

---

[90] The organization describes itself thus on its website at https://rs.gov.ru/about-foiv

[91] Gasanov, Kamran, "Проклятие Ассанжа. Эквадор Свергает Ленина [The Curse of Assange: Ecuador Overthrows Lenin]," *Tsargrad TV*, October 9, 2019, https://tsargrad.tv/articles/prokljatie-assanzha-jekvador-svergaet-lenina_220821

[92] https://www.picreadi.com/hablemos_video

Ecuador: Who Played Whom? | 321

might have given Correa more of the political recognition he craved, both internationally and domestically. Yet neither Putin nor Medvedev ever visited Ecuador, despite multiple trips to Latin America. "Russia could have helped itself by paying more attention to Correa's ego, elevating him, visiting the country," said Romo. "They could have seduced him."[93]

In the 2022 interview, Correa recalled with pleasure the elegant Kremlin apartment he was given on his first visit to Moscow (vodka was available even at breakfast) and made a point of the fall in status he felt on his second visit, when he was lodged at a hotel. He also said Putin seemed to him stiff and enigmatic. "Putin is a smart guy but it's difficult to know what he's thinking," Correa said. "With some people you feel to have a real personal empathy. With Putin, it was just a formal meeting."

Correa said he felt strong personal rapport with Belarusian President Alyaksandr Lukashenka, who visited Ecuador in 2016. A visit by a Russian leader, with an effort to be more comradely, might have paid off significantly. "Russia had all the conditions for a closer relationship: past connections, the narrative about independence from the United States," said a former senior official in Correa's government.

- **Russia failed to maximize Correa's value in terms of its broader political goals.** Hostility to the United States was one thing, but overt demonstrations of the "strategic partnership" with Russia would have been even more impressive. Moscow could have gained significantly if it had been able to induce Correa to recognize the annexation of Crimea, accept visits by Russian warships and bombers as Venezuela did, or use the Kremlin's proffered credits to buy and display some Russian weaponry.

However, even if Russia had managed to make any of this happen, there were limits to what could be accomplished. Correa could never evade the reality of Ecuador's economic dependence on the United States. Ecuador's trade with the US under Correa soared as

---

[93] María Paula Romo, interview with author.

322 | HOW RUSSIA LOSES

high as $18 billion,[94] nine times its trade with Russia. (Beijing, too, was a much more significant trading partner than Moscow.) Remittances from Ecuadorians working in the United States brought critically needed income to Ecuador; to the families that received this income, the US was a source of support, not an enemy.

A former Ecuadorian diplomat dismissed Correa's jabs at the United States, despite the drama involved, as simply "part of the political discourse." Exports and remittances, the diplomat said, were simply too important to jeopardize. Actions like recognizing Russia's annexation of Crimea, purchases of Russian weaponry, or allowing Russian warplanes to land in Ecuador would have worried many Ecuadorians, as well as provoked the United States. Correa said in the 2022 interview that he would not have allowed Russia to use Ecuador for a demonstration of its military might.

Ecuador even tried to soften some of the actions it did take against the United States. After the expulsion of the US ambassador in 2011, the Ecuadorian Embassy in Washington stated that the expulsion was "aimed solely at the individual involved" and "not toward the United States government or the Obama administration."[95] In 2013, when Ecuador was preparing to give asylum to Snowden, Correa said then–Vice President Biden called to warn him that relations would "strongly deteriorate" if that happened. Correa said Biden's comments were worth considering, and Ecuador never received Snowden. At the time, Ecuador was lobbying for US duty-free waivers for its roses, broccoli, and artichokes, which supported tens of thousands of jobs.[96]

---

[94] https://www.census.gov/foreign-trade/balance/c3310.html#2007

[95] Lakshmanan, Indira A.R., et al., "U.S. Expels Envoy From Ecuador, President Correa Slams U.S.," *Bloomberg*, April 7, 2011, https://www.bloomberg.com/news/articles/2011-04-07/u-s-expels-ecuadorian-ambassador-to-washington-in-retaliation?sref=Y2tgfPTW

[96] Forero, Juan, "Ecuador's strange journey from embracing Snowden to turning him away," *The Washington Post*, July 2, 2013, https://www.washingtonpost.com/news/worldviews/wp/2013/07/02/ecuadors-strange-journey-from-embracing-snowden-to-turning-him-away

Ecuador: Who Played Whom? | 323

In another likely effort to avoid an all-out clash with the United States, Ecuador cut off Julian Assange's internet access in its London embassy in 2016 after WikiLeaks published John Podesta's emails. Explaining the action, Ecuador said it "respects the principle of nonintervention in the affairs of other countries."[97] Ecuador also had disconnected Assange's internet for a time in 2012 over fear he was damaging relations with Britain and other European nations.

For its part, the United States sought to maintain the best relations it could with Correa despite his verbal hostility. At the US Embassy, his relationship with Russia was little discussed, a former diplomat said; the US was more concerned with his ties to Cuba, other Latin leftists, and Iran. American policymakers decided not to overreact to Correa's provocative statements. It is certainly annoying to give aid with a hand that is being bitten. Yet while the United States reduced its assistance to Ecuador, it never stopped it.

In 2010, when Correa was captured for ten hours by police demanding more pay, Secretary of State Hillary Clinton called him personally to declare US support for Ecuador's constitutional order. Correa and his allies still suggested that pro-US interests had a hand in the uprising, but Clinton's call signaled that the United States ranked the fact that Correa was the legally elected president above the two countries' tattered relations.

In February 2016, the new US ambassador, Todd Chapman, praised Correa's social and infrastructure initiatives in an interview with state television.[98] After an earthquake in April, the United States sent more than $5 million in aid.[99]

---

[97] Erlander, Steven, et al., "Ecuador Cuts Internet of Julian Assange, WikiLeaks' Founder," *The New York Times*, October 18, 2016, https://www.nytimes.com/2016/10/19/world/europe/julian-assange-embassy.html
[98] Interview at https://www.youtube.com/watch?v=YfxDXnRwuGc
[99] US Embassy press release at https://ec.usembassy.gov/united-states-earthquake-assistance-reaches-5-45-million

324 | HOW RUSSIA LOSES

Most important, the US continued to nourish its "other structures" with the Ecuadorian people in a way that Rossotrudnichestvo's Poloskova could only have envied. Even when it was forced to close its office, USAID never gave up supporting Ecuador's civil society. When Correa's war on NGOs had reached a peak in 2016, the congressionally funded National Endowment for Democracy contributed more than $1.3 million to Ecuadorian projects.[100]

The United States had plenty of reasons to be confident about its long-term position in Ecuador. Washington likely considered that Ecuador was so solidly bolted into the US-dominated Latin American economy that neither Correa's radicalism nor Russian geopolitical fantasies could disrupt that. "Ecuador is too deeply linked to the US, not only because of the huge amount of Ecuadorian migrants in the UN but also because Ecuador's currency is dollars," said Romo. "Dollarization turned out to be the toughest democratic institution." Ecuador's vibrant (if disorderly) democratic tendencies also pointed to it ultimately remaining in the Western camp.

Russia's vision for Ecuador took into account only Moscow's own interests. It was eager for Ecuador to be hostile to the United States but offered the nation nothing of significance to replace the benefits it derived from the US relationship. Looking back from 2022 on the strategic partnership between Quito and Moscow, Correa said, "We got nothing out of it. They could have given us technology support but it didn't happen. Perhaps I visited a second time because the first time there was no result." He added, "Maybe the Russian leaders didn't visit Ecuador because it's not important. Maybe they were right."

Given the speed at which world events now move, and the disruption of traditional assumptions, Russia might have imagined that Ecuador could become a key asset in Latin America. Moscow needed friends, and its options were few. Kremlin policymakers could have hoped that a charismatic leftist in Ecuador, friendly to Russia, hostile to the US, backed by Chinese

---

[100] Derived from https://www.ned.org/wpcontent/themes/ned/search/grant-search.php

Ecuador: Who Played Whom? | 325

money, and riding a pink tide could make his country into a compact, reliable ally of some sort in a region where Russian projects badly needed new blood.

Ultimately, however, if Russia expected a strong, unquestioning ally or another Cuba, it misjudged Correa and Ecuador from the start. Russia may have anticipated a relationship in which each country was regularly doing favors for the other. Yet Correa seemed to view his ties with Russia as, at best, a marriage of convenience. Russia bet its fortunes almost entirely on one politician, neglected opportunities to bring him closer, and failed to prepare a proper back-up plan.

Russia took Ecuador's change of direction under Moreno badly. In its current era of diplomacy, the Kremlin tries to maintain positive relations whenever possible with governments of the Global South. Yet Moscow apparently considered Ecuador under Moreno a lost cause. Just 13 months after the start of his term, *RT* gave Correa a talk show on its Spanish-language service. Since Correa could be expected to devote generous airtime to blasting Moreno, Moscow apparently felt that maintaining Correa's militant voice in Latin America still had value and was more important than its relations with the new regime in Ecuador.

Correa said in 2022 that *RT* gave him the show because he could win interviews with political heavyweights: "They paid me well. It helped me pay my lawyers in Ecuador, and lawyers here [in Belgium] to avoid extradition."

By 2019, the trend of events across Latin America had shifted significantly from the "pink tide" period. A downbeat commentary by the Strategic Culture Foundation described the change of power in Ecuador as a key component of a US resurgence:

> The whole Venezuelan crisis, the Ecuadorian political shift that crushed Assange and the possibly (probably) [US-]aided rise of Bolsonaro in Brazil ousting the previous Russia-friendly president are all signs that the shift [of US attention] to Latin America is really happening.

326 | HOW RUSSIA LOSES

> We may be seeing an actual move back to some sort of Monroe Doctrine 2.0 where Washington focuses on controlling the satellites that it knows that it can control. Dealing with a rising Russia and a risen China is much easier in one's own hemisphere, where not only are the distances massive for China and Russia, but also the political will from them is not strong enough to do anything in particular other that [sic] try to maintain the status quo in Venezuela and maybe Cuba.[101]

Epilogue: New Crises for Ecuador

For ordinary Ecuadorians, Moreno's foreign policy turnabout was far less important than their own economic welfare. Moreno faced a desperate financial situation. Alarmed at the size of the nation's obligations to China and eager to secure IMF loans, he began in 2018 to introduce austerity measures, including tax hikes and cuts in public spending. Resentment over these measures led to sporadic demonstrations, but exploded on October 1, 2019, after his government ended subsidies on the most popular grade of gasoline. The price was meant to rise from $1.85 to $2.39 a gallon, but panic and speculation drove prices in some places to double the intended rate.

Business, union, and student protesters were soon joined by indigenous Ecuadorians, who poured into the capital from the Amazon and the Andes. Protesters set fire to government buildings and overran Carondelet Palace. Moreno fled with his government to Guayaquil. Other demonstrators blocked roads throughout the country and forced television stations to broadcast statements threatening more violence. Between eight and ten people reportedly died. A former Western diplomat noted

---

[101] Kirby, Tim, "Assange Arrest Impossible Without Trump Foreign Policy," Strategic Culture Foundation, April 12, 2019, https://www.strategic-culture.org/news/2019/04/12/assange-arrest-impossible-without-trump-foreign-policy

that the protesters' actions—especially attacks on cell phone towers and the blocking of oil production—seemed more organized than what might have been expected of ordinary Ecuadorians angry at price increases.

On October 13, after Moreno had deployed the army to restore order, he reached a compromise with the protesters under which the gasoline subsidies would be restored and other means would be found to reduce debt. The protests caused hundreds of millions of dollars in losses to oil production, flower-growing, and other key industries.

Now it was Moreno's turn to claim he had been the victim of an attempted coup. Government officials blamed Correa, Maduro, and Russia. A 14-point "Quito Manifesto," purportedly prepared by the plotters, surfaced on Facebook. It contained a series of demands consistent with Correa's policies and called for Moreno to be put on trial. The charges at trial would include violating international asylum rights—a clear reference to Assange's expulsion from the London embassy.[102] Correa said claims of a coup plot were "nonsense" but called for a new presidential election.[103]

The authorities were particularly concerned by live coverage of the demonstrations by *RT*. "The intensity and violence in the streets of the country existed similarly in the area of communication," Interior Minister Romo told a news conference. She cited "a great amount of false information, in which it is notable that one protest was broadcast live by the public network of the Russian government."[104] The National Telecommunications

---

[102] For the supposed manifesto, see Romo, María Paula and Ribadeneira, Amelia, *Octubre: La Democracia Bajo Ataque* [October: Democracy Under Attack] (Quito: Poligráfica C.A.), 2nd Ed., p. 113.
[103] Petrequin, Samuel, "Ex-Ecuador president wants new vote, denies planning coup," *The Associated Press*, October 19, 2019, https://apnews.com/article/2ba31ddc50854e93af2b356a771efe79
[104] Alandete, David, "Ecuador y Bolivia tratan de frenar la propaganda rusa [Ecuador and Bolivia try to rein in Russian propaganda]," *ABC International*, January 12, 2019, https://www.abc.es/internacional/abci-ecuador-y-bolivia-tratan-frenar-propaganda-rusa-

328 | HOW RUSSIA LOSES

Corporation removed *RT* from its television channels in November. Romo also said anti-government posts on social networks during the protests originated from Venezuela and from IP addresses in Russia.[105] (Several months earlier, Romo had told a news conference that two Russian hackers and a WikiLeaks activist inside Ecuador had been working to destabilize the government.[106])

The US State Department accused Russia of social posts encouraging the protests in Ecuador, as well as protests that same autumn in Chile, Peru, Bolivia, Columbia, and Chile—all of which had governments hostile to Maduro.[107] In November, Moreno's government closed down the rebroadcasting of *RT* in Ecuador.

Moreno, his poll numbers in the single digits because of his austerity programs and the government's poor showing against COVID, chose not to run for re-election in 2021. His successor was Guillermo Lasso, whose victory over Andrés Arauz, many said, reflected continued popular opposition to a return of Correísmo.

201912010204_noticia.html?ref=https%3A%2F%2Fwww.google.com%2F

[105] Imbaquingo, Jorge R., "María Paula Romo: 'La inteligencia falló, debió entregar alarmas más claras' [María Paula Romo: The intelligence failed. There should have been clearer warnings]," *El Comercio*, October 17, 2019, https://www.elcomercio.com/actualidad/ministra-romo-inteligencia-fallo-protestas.html

[106] "Hackers rusos y un miembro de Wikileaks viven en Ecuador, revela María Paula Romo [Russian hackers and a Wikileaks member are living in Ecuador, María Paula Romo reveals]," *El Universo*, April 11, 2019, https://www.eluniverso.com/noticias/2019/04/11/nota/7279946/jackers-rusos-miembro-wikileaks-viven-ecuador-denuncia-maria-paula. Top Ecuadorian officials reportedly accused the two Russians and a Swedish national of threatening to release compromising documents about Moreno. See Goodman, Joshua et al., "Sources: US to question Assange pal jailed in Ecuador," *The Associated Press*, June 17, 2019, https://apnews.com/article/europe-ecuador-ap-top-news-bogota-london-09ac93b95bbe46d7b90a73c73fda6389

[107] Jakes, Lara, "As Protests in South America Surged, So Did Russian Trolls on Twitter, U.S. Finds," *The New York Times*, January 19, 2020, https://www.nytimes.com/2020/01/19/us/politics/south-america-russian-twitter.html

Ecuador: Who Played Whom? | 329

Lasso, who became president in May 2021, continued Moreno's conservative style of government and his friendship with the West.

When Russia invaded Ukraine, Ecuador condemned the action at the United Nations and voted for Russia's expulsion from the global body's Human Rights Council. For Ecuador, "there will never be a factor more important than the protection of human rights," Foreign Minister Juan Carlos Holguín said. Although Ecuador's trade with Russia was worth more than $1 billion per year, Holguín added, "trade can never be more important than the most fundamental values of our society."[108]

Russia continued to try to restore its relationship with Ecuador. In June 2022, Russian representatives reportedly visited Ecuador's Center for Strategic Intelligence, the successor to SENAIN, in an effort to establish contacts, but left empty-handed. Russian Ambassador Sprinchan tried to revive projects discussed under Correa, including cooperation on nuclear energy, but with no success.[109]

In December 2022, Lasso spent an hour talking with Biden at the White House. They were aligned on issues of democracy and Ukraine, but Lasso was seeking urgent US economic help. Six months earlier, the Ecuadorian president had faced 18 days of strikes and violent protests that recalled the massive 2019 demonstrations against Moreno. Led by indigenous people but soon joined by others, the protests forced Lasso to accept demands regarding fuel prices, protection of sensitive lands from

---

[108] Loaiza, Yalilé, "El canciller de Ecuador sobre la relación con Rusia: "Nunca lo comercial podrá ser más importante que los valores más estructurados de nuestra sociedad [Ecuador foreign minister on relations with Russia: 'Nothing commercial can be more important than the most basic values of our society']," *Infobae*, April 12, 2022, https://www.infobae.com/america/america-latina/2022/04/12/el-canciller-de-ecuador-sobre-la-relacion-con-rusia-nunca-lo-comercial-podra-ser-mas-importante-que-los-valores-mas-estructurados-de-nuestra-sociedad

[109] "El espionaje selló el nexo Correa-Putin [Espionage sealed the Correa-Putin nexus]," op. cit.

330 | HOW RUSSIA LOSES

mining, improvement of public health services, and other issues. Substantial public discontent remained in the country over economic issues, violence, and drug trafficking, and a poll showed two-thirds of Ecuadorians would trade away elections for a guarantee of basic income and services.[110] In June 2023, after opposition deputies began efforts to impeach Lasso, he triggered the constitution's "mutual death" clause requiring elections for both the National Assembly and the presidency.

Lasso decided not to run again. The first round of elections for a successor took place on August 20, 2023, just days after the assassination of candidate Fernando Villavicencio, who had campaigned against corruption and any restoration of Correa's power. The two candidates who emerged for the second round were Luisa González, a leftist lawyer and former National Assembly member who promised to bring Correa back as her "main advisor," and Daniel Noboa, the pro-free-market son of the banana tycoon Correa defeated in 2006. Noboa, 35 years old, won the runoff October 15 to become Ecuador's youngest president.

More political instability lay ahead, however, for the crime-ridden country. Noboa was elected only to complete the rest of Lasso's term, meaning a new election battle would have to be fought in 2024.

---

[110] See Vigers, Benedict, "Ecuador: The Most Dangerous Country in Latin America?" Gallup, January 20, 2023, https://news.gallup.com/poll/468227/ecuador-dangerous-country-latin-america.aspx; and Oung, Katherine, "Who Is Willing to Trade Away Elections for Material Guarantees?" LAPOP Lab, Sept. 13, 2022, https://www.vanderbilt.edu/lapop/insights/IO953en-1.pdf

7.

How Russia Loses

Each of the six case studies in this book describes miscalculations or weaknesses that undermined the Kremlin's goals. This chapter synthesizes the failings in these cases in an effort to identify systemic faults in Russian influence efforts. It also draws in examples from cases beyond those detailed in the book.

The chapter after this one will offer recommendations as to how a knowledge of systemic Russian weaknesses can be used to predict and counter Russian behavior.

To be sure, the Kremlin has sometimes triumphed over these failings. But they are frequent and significant enough to create opportunities for astute Western statecraft:

• **Russia yokes its fortunes to the strength and durability of a thin layer of top political and business figures.** All countries curry favor with powerful individuals in the countries and issues they interact with, but Russia makes this almost its exclusive strategy. Moscow's attitude reflects the workings of its own society. Almost all power is vested in Vladimir Putin and his inner circle. Thus, it expects small elites elsewhere to wield similar authority. The Kremlin looked to Nikola Gruevski in Macedonia, Jacob Zuma in South Africa, and Rafael Correa in Ecuador to reliably advance its interests. Russia was confident that Angela Merkel and Germany's big industrialists would guarantee the success of the Nord Stream 2 pipeline. In Ukraine, Russia expected

331

332 | HOW RUSSIA LOSES

Viktor Yanukovych and oligarchs like Viktor Medvedchuk to put the country firmly under Moscow's sway.

This elite capture strategy can be successful. Russia, with its weak economy, can do little to make other countries more prosperous as a whole. However, in any country it can make a few people rich, or help them with political survival.

Moscow uses local elites to advance its commercial interests, which can also pay geopolitical benefits. The Kremlin sought to turn the Macedonian and South African economies toward Moscow through big deals in crucial sectors. It sought to do the same in Ecuador with energy and mining projects and even laid the foundation for a possible nuclear power plant contract. Locking in big deals with Russia may make little sense for a country's overall interests, but it makes eminent sense for Russia and the target country's elite.

Joseph Siegle of the Africa Center for Strategic Studies notes that Russia has signed agreements with at least 17 African nations to construct nuclear power plants. "Given their costs, these nuclear deals are not seen as viable for most African countries," Siegle wrote. "However, the enormous expenditures of these projects create ample opportunities for graft, generating political incentives for well-placed Kremlin and African government officials."[1] Given these circumstances, Russia's relationships with its elite partners frequently involve secrecy. The nuclear agreements with South Africa and Ecuador were not initially published and almost nothing was revealed about Putin's meetings with Yanukovych before the Ukrainian leader suspended Ukraine's trade deal with the European Union.

Beyond offering business deals, Russia can also promise to make its favored elites more secure in power. Moscow's intelligence capabilities and mercenaries are attractive to repressive leaders who worry that their hold on power is shaky. The imperative of

---

[1] Siegle, Joseph, "Decoding Russia's Economic Engagements in Africa," Africa Center for Strategic Studies, January 6, 2023, https://africa center.org/spotlight/decoding-russia-economic-engagements-africa

How Russia Loses | 333

regime protection led the leaders of the Central African Republic and Mali in recent years to bank heavily on support from Wagner Group mercenaries. Russia provided training to intelligence operatives working for Zuma's and Correa's governments. Today, Russia helps authoritarian regimes replicate the repressive laws and surveillance systems that Moscow uses to control its own population.

There are downsides to Russia's elite capture strategies. First, few national leaders control their countries as tightly as Putin has controlled Russia. Therefore, they cannot always deliver what Moscow wants. Leaders with whom Moscow aligns itself may be popular at first but find their support beginning to slip because of poor governance or corruption. Such was the case with Zuma, Correa, and Gruevski. Leaders on the defensive are less able to guide policies to the Kremlin's advantage.

A second downside is that, when the local leaders fall from power, Russian influence can evaporate. When Gruevski lost his premiership, Zuma was forced to resign, and Correa decided not to run again, Russia suffered clear reversals of fortune— temporary in South Africa but severe and longer lasting in North Macedonia. As Vladimir Shubin, the Russian expert on South Africa, noted, "The friendly relations established between Russia's leadership and Zuma turned into a brake on bilateral cooperation since the overall negative feelings about Zuma carried over onto our country [Russia] and its president." When Yanukovych fled Ukraine, Russian influence went with him. In Germany, Nord Stream 2 had seemed secure so long as the "grand coalition" of political parties that supported it remained in power. The coalition fell in the 2021 elections, making Nord Stream 2 a less certain prospect.

Russia caught a lucky break in Belarus when President Lukashenka managed to subdue demonstrations that nearly forced him from power in 2020. The mutual dependence of Putin and Lukashenka was the cornerstone of the ties between their countries. If Lukashenka had fallen, Russian influence would have been deeply threatened. Putin would have needed either to invade the country, or potentially accept another democratic "anti-Russia" on his doorstep.

Another downside to attempts at elite capture is that the targeted elite may see their relationship with Russia as mainly transactional, to be used when convenient and ignored when not. Many believed Correa saw his ties with Russia as useful to the degree they helped his country and burnished his leftist credentials in Latin America. He declined to endorse Russian land grabs in Ukraine, Abkhazia, and South Ossetia, and ignored offers (and financing) to buy Russian military hardware. In Ukraine, Putin reportedly was furious when Yanukovych, after all the help Putin had given him, vacillated over accepting Russia's proffered trade deal.

Ironically, for a country that relies so much on top-level allies, Russia fails to get the most benefit from them. Neither Putin nor Medvedev visited Ecuador during Correa's entire presidency, though they found time to visit nearby countries. Medvedev, as president, failed to visit South Africa in 2009, though he was just two countries away in Angola. Russia might have gotten more from Correa by elevating his international visibility and reinforcing his own sense of importance. Correa noted that he was disappointed by the less prestigious housing he received on his second visit to Moscow and by how hard-to-read he found Putin in their private meeting.

The same transactional considerations apply to the lobbyists, oligarchs, organized crime figures, and hackers Russia deals with. Such actors tend not to be sentimental about their attachments. Unless they are incentivized regularly to remain Moscow's ally, they can be bought off by competing parties or simply decide by themselves to head in other directions.

• **Russia focuses on advantages to itself.** Altruism is sorely lacking in most of Russia's foreign influence efforts. Russia's goals are usually focused on advantages for the Kremlin. The Kremlin's apparent vision for Macedonia was for it never to enter the EU or NATO and perpetually be at odds with Bulgaria and Greece. This would have served Moscow's interests by maintaining tension in

How Russia Loses | 335

the Balkans, but it clearly was not sustainable for Macedonia. The Kremlin promoted Correa's anti-American positions while knowing it could offer Ecuador no real economic benefit or alternative to its dependence on Washington. "We got nothing out of it," Correa said. The Kremlin's intent for South Africa was for the country to be eternally dependent on Russia, regularly having to ask Moscow to restructure a huge debt.

Similarly, Russia was intent on isolating Ukraine from the economic benefits of the West and luring Europe into continued energy dependence. With Nord Stream 2, it even enlisted Europe's energy giants in backing its obsession with marginalizing Ukraine.

All countries try to gain advantage from their influence and business deals, but Russia's efforts stand out for a frequent lack of benefit to the other party. Even in the case of life-saving Sputnik, Russia positioned it almost entirely as a product to be sold, not donated.

• **Russia fails to prioritize public diplomacy and aid.** Russia far prefers making deals with a country's elite to the harder and more expensive task of winning favor with local populations. The focus on people-to-people projects that comes naturally to Western nations (along with America's constant concern over whether foreign populations "like us") are alien to Russia's strategy for accomplishing its goals.

Where necessary, Russian "political technologists" and their allies do try to manipulate public opinion, as several of the case studies in this book show. To support its nuclear hopes in South Africa, Rosatom hired a PR firm to build its public image. The online campaign before the Macedonian referendum, Russia's promotion of the Sputnik vaccine and Nord Stream 2, and Yevgeny Prigozhin's reported plan to swing South Africa's 2019 election, are all examples

However, such operations are usually focused on a specific goal within the target country, or the general denigration of Western countries, rather than building a positive image of how Russia can make the country in question more successful in the long term. This was true before its 2022 invasion of Ukraine; building a positive image is increasingly difficult goal now because of Russian brutality and the vicious tone of its officials and media. As Foreign Minister Sergei Lavrov said, "Russia is not white and fluffy. Russia is what it is. And we are not ashamed of showing who we are."[2] The antithesis of a successful PR campaign was Putin's two decades of behavior in Ukraine leading up to the 2022 invasion. Putin effectively ran a reverse influence operation, turning a country where he had high popularity into an implacable enemy.

Although Russia publishes little data on its foreign assistance, its programs are a shadow of the massive international aid and public diplomacy establishments run by the United States, Britain, Germany, and other Western nations. Even in the case of the Sputnik vaccine, where millions in poor countries were desperate for supplies, Russia gave away relatively few doses as free donations. The Kremlin engages in little on-the-ground activity with local populations. It does not even have a central foreign aid organization, or a people-to-people effort on the scale of the Peace Corps or Britain's VSO International.

Most Russian foreign aid, estimated at about $1 billion a year, goes to Central Asia and to geopolitically important countries like Cuba, Nicaragua, Guinea, Serbia and Syria, according to the fragmentary information available.[3] Even on that basis, there is not much to go around, even to hotspots of political competition.

---

[2] Rosenberg, Steve, "Russia is not squeaky clean and not ashamed," *BBC*, June 17, 2022, https://www.bbc.com/news/world-europe-61825525

[3] See OECD, "The Russian Federation's Official Development Assistance (ODA)," https://www.oecd.org/dac/dac-global-relations/russias-official-development-assistance.htm; Asmus, Gerda, et al., "Russia's foreign aid re-emerges," AidData, April 9, 2018, https://www.aiddata.org/blog/russias-foreign-aid-re-emerges; and Yaicev, Y., "New Challenges for Russia's Foreign Aid and Its Contribution to the Sustainable Development Goals," *International Organisations Research Journal*, May 2020, http://dx.doi.org/10.17323/1996-7845-2020-01-03

On a 2023 trip to Moldova, where Russian and Western interests are competing fiercely, this author saw many projects bearing EU logos. (Moldova is a candidate member.) Many other projects and facilities bore plaques commemorating direct donations by the US, UK, Sweden, Slovakia, and even Liechtenstein. No Russian projects were prominent.

Western aid programs commonly cast a wide net, supporting agriculture, technology, schools, museums, cultural activities and services for the disabled, as well as governance and legal reforms. Comparing Western and Russian aid projects in Macedonia in the years before the 2018 referendum was like comparing a tank to a Lada, as media consultant Zvonko Naumoski put it. Russia's strategy "doesn't demand long term investments and relationship-building across multiple sectors of shared interests, as do traditional bilateral relations," wrote Siegle. "It certainly doesn't involve broad-based popular engagement."[4] It is difficult to imagine Russia launching a Global Music Diplomacy Initiative, as the United States did in September 2023.

Skipping large-scale public activities in favor of cultivating small elites is economical for Russia. While elite decision-makers may need to be compensated for their cooperation, the sums involved are far smaller than the cost of big aid or infrastructure projects. As a result, however, Russia becomes known to the public mainly through its links to those elites. Some Russian commentators have been aware of this problem for years, arguing that the Kremlin must systematically build a national image that can outlast individual local allies.

This would not be an impossible task. The fact that people in many countries know little about Russia means they also know little negative information. Some still remember the Soviet bloc's strong backing of anti-colonialist movements and new leftist governments during the Cold War—not only military aid but also

---

[4] Siegle, Joe, "Russia in Africa – Undermining democracy through elite capture," Democracy in Africa, September 23, 2021, http://democracyinafrica.org/russia-in-africa-undermining-democracy-through-elite-capture

doctors from Cuba and engineers from East Germany. Russia tries to exploit this reservoir of historic gratitude, even as it disclaims responsibility for many other acts of Soviet communism. However, local populations are focused above all on what countries can offer them in the present day. In the words of former Russian diplomat Boris Bondarev, "Few emerging economies are prepared to openly stand under Russian banners and confront the West for free. Such a scenario would only be successful with a substantial injection of Russian cash." He adds:

> The Russian leadership is still unable and unwilling to work within the paradigm of soft power, believing only in armed force and a hard, extremely inflexible political approach. Therefore, the enormous potential of Russia's soft power cannot be used to its fullest potential and likely will not lead to serious progress.[5]

• **Russia overestimates its own strength.** Putin's regime often acts as if its power is overwhelming. This could be the result of Russia intentionally exaggerating its capabilities to intimidate its adversaries; a belief that anything can be accomplished with enough resources and force (as with Russia's war against Ukraine); or a lack of accurate information within Russia's highest councils. (This can be due to poor intelligence or over-optimistic promises by lower-ranking officials seeking favor.)

Whatever the cause, the results of such confidence can be unfortunate for the Kremlin. Russia claimed its vaccine could immunize 700 million people in 2021; by late in the year, it was clear that Sputnik production would hit nothing near that target. Moscow never made any effort to produce and distribute Sputnik in partnership with a Western pharmaceutical giant, remaining convinced it could successfully control the whole production and distribution chain itself. An alliance with more experienced

---

[5] Bondarev, Boris, "Russia 'Recruits' Allies and Partners in the Global South," *Eurasia Daily Monitor*, April 26, 2023, https://jamestown.org/program/russia-recruits-allies-and-partners-in-the-global-south

companies could have helped with WHO and EMA approval and made Sputnik a much more important vaccine.

Russian arrogance toward Ukraine was founded on a belief, repeatedly disproved, that Moscow could always bend Kyiv to its will. The Kremlin repeatedly turned away from opportunities to build a respectful relationship with Ukraine, under which its neighbor would have enjoyed strong economic ties to both Russia and the West while remaining outside NATO. (Such opportunities existed right up to, and reportedly even immediately after, the 2022 invasion.) In another example of hubris, Putin announced the annexation of Ukraine's Luhansk, Donetsk, Zaporizhzhia, and Kherson oblasts seven months into the invasion, when Russia fully controlled none of those territories.

Russia's overconfidence merges with its taste for threats and bluster. Ahead of the 2018 referendum in Macedonia, Russia's ambassador warned that NATO membership could make Macedonia a "target of retaliation from Russia." When NATO considered extending membership to Ukraine in 2008, Putin made a point of mentioning how frightening it was "even to think" that Russia might have to target Ukraine with nuclear weapons. Neither threat made much of an impact on the countries threatened. (Oddly, Russian threats of nuclear attack seem to resonate most in well-defended NATO nations, such as Germany and the United States.)

Other examples of Russia flexing its muscles were the dispatch of nuclear-capable bombers to Venezuela in 2018 as a sign of support for President Nicolás Maduro and to South Africa on the opening day of the 2019 Russia-Africa Summit. The flights were strategically insignificant but Russia apparently assumed they would demonstrate its forces' globe-girdling capabilities.

One reason for Russia's overconfidence in foreign affairs may be uneven analytical abilities. Although Russia is famous for its skill in parsing the internal politics of major NATO nations, it is not expert everywhere. Moscow failed to anticipate that the multiple complicated steps to implement the Prespa agreement in Macedonia could actually be accomplished, or that the nuclear

340 | HOW RUSSIA LOSES

deal would be the straw that broke Jacob Zuma's leadership. After the 2022 invasion of Ukraine, it did not expect Kyiv to mount a powerful response, the West to send a steady stream of lethal weapons, or Western Europe to survive even one winter without Russian gas. After Germany suspended approval of Nord Stream 2, Dmitry Medvedev, who presumably had access to top-level commercial intelligence, predicted the cost of gas would jump by 250 percent. In actuality, the price plunged.

Russia's lack of engagement with local populations is part of its analytical problem. When local elites make a claim or prediction, Russian diplomats and intelligence officers often lack street-level contacts for a reality check. Russian embassies tend to be closed worlds. Western embassies and aid organizations hold frequent public events and make a point of interacting with as many levels of society as possible. This gives them regular access to local citizens who can be quizzed for information and sounded out on the local mood.

- **Russia underestimates the strength of democratic institutions, civil society activists, and Western nations.** In Ecuador, South Africa, Macedonia, and Ukraine, Russia saw the peril that democratic institutions and activists posed to its favored actors. Journalists and civil society groups relentlessly catalogued and publicized corruption in the Correa, Zuma, Gruevski, and Yanukovych regimes. Civil society in South Africa sank the nuclear deal with Russia. Environmental groups and political activists dogged the Nord Stream 2 project.

In Russia's view, self-appointed members of the public are the last people who should determine state policy. In Macedonia, the Russian Foreign Ministry said claims that the Gruevski regime was authoritarian and corrupt were not a subject for civil society protests but should be worked out "strictly in an institutional and legal framework"—in other words, through mechanisms the government could control. A well-organized regime, the Kremlin believes, should be more than equal to inconvenient activists and journalists, and to conscientious civil servants. Putin's state offers a master class in how to address such threats: jailing or expelling anyone who publicly criticizes the state and transforming all branches of government into extensions of executive power.

Russia has difficulty understanding that such tactics do not work everywhere. Some populations expect to be heard. The governments of Zuma, Correa, and Gruevski got away with some spying, harassment, and prosecution against their opponents but ran into resistance when they went too far. Ecuador's people and parliament had brought down a string of leaders before Correa; South Africa's robust media and courts had maintained their strength even under the repression of the apartheid regime. As Barbara Groeblinghoff of the Naumann Foundation said of Zuma's animus toward opposition journalists and NGOs, "South Africa isn't North Korea. They couldn't just go out and destroy them."

This does not mean, however, that democratic institutions and activists have permanent immunity from repression, however positive a country's traditions may be. In recent years, Russia has been developing and sharing with its allies new tactics to suppress pro-democracy activism. These include "foreign agent" laws, digital spying, and normalizing the intimidation of journalists. However, Russia continues to underestimate the local, organic nature of pro-democracy activity, seeing it mainly as created and controlled by its geopolitical rivals.

Russia and its allies occasionally attempt to recruit local citizens to advance their policies. But too often these are sports teams, motorcycle clubs, and the like, who easily come across as heavies and thugs. Some shade into neo-Nazis. Moscow devotes less attention to establishing reputable-looking organizations that can argue Russia's case in a more sophisticated way. However, Moscow is learning. The public foundation Gazprom set up in Mecklenburg-Western Pomerania was respectable on its face—if the source of its funding was disregarded—and portrayed Nord Stream 2 as a boon for the environment. (If Rosatom had tried more such tactics in South Africa, it might have helped the nuclear deal there.) The Kremlin created Russian-Macedonian "friendship associations" to build its image in that country. Creative Diplomacy, a Russian government–funded public diplomacy group, has organized academic debates and people-to-people

342 | HOW RUSSIA LOSES

exchanges. Russia will host a World Youth Festival near Sochi in March 2024. Such initiatives are more difficult for Russia since the invasion of Ukraine, however. Another Russian public diplomacy venture, the EU-sanctioned Gorchakov Fund, appears to have reduced its activities sharply since the invasion of Ukraine.[6]

As for Russia's view of Western nations' power, most Kremlin propaganda suggests that the West is coiled at every moment to attack Russia and its interests. However, Russian actions suggest quite the opposite: that Moscow's leadership actually believes a different strand of Russian propaganda, which depicts the West as weak and indecisive.

When the West acts otherwise, Russia is surprised. The West's feeble response to Russia's invasion of Georgia, and to its seizure of Ukrainian territory in 2014, gave Russia no reason to expect a strong reaction to its invasion of Ukraine in 2022. Similarly, Trump's mild comments about Nord Stream 2 at his 2018 news conference with Putin hardly signaled he would stop the project dead in its tracks a year later. Given Denmark's small size and dependence on Germany, it seemed inconceivable it would block Nord Stream 2's construction for more than two years. Decades of weak Western public diplomacy in the Balkans never hinted that, in a geopolitical backwater like Macedonia, major Western countries would mobilize every asset. (Indeed, as the case study indicates, the US might have paid little attention to Macedonia if Russian activities there had not been so visible.) The West's capability to surprise Russia at critical moments is an important consideration for the recommendations in the next chapter.

• **Russia is contemptuous of international organizations, independent regulators, and legal processes.** The issuance of an arrest warrant for Putin in March 2023 by the International Criminal Court outraged the Kremlin, not only because of the war crimes charges against him but also because it was issued by an international body with considerable legitimacy, including in the Global South. In a major humiliation for Putin, the ICC indictment forced him to skip the 2023 BRICS summit in South Africa, lest he

---

[6] https://gorchakovfund.com

be arrested. Putin believes in the nation-state as the only legitimate building block of society and has little patience for multinational organizations that Russia cannot control.

Russia also questions the entire rules-based international order, which it describes as a perversion of international law by "a narrow group of states" aimed at "the imposition of rules, standards and norms created without the equal participation of all interested states."[7] Gazprom sought full control of the Nord Stream 2 pipeline and its redistribution networks, ignoring the anti-monopoly policies of European regulators. Russia openly conspired with Germany to keep the project away from EU institutions. When the EU inevitably became involved, Moscow seemed convinced that Germany could use its power to keep Brussels at bay. (No international body, Russia must have reasoned, can defy its wealthiest funder.) Only in the last months of the project, as time ran out before its invasion of Ukraine, did Moscow realize that EU councils, courts, and regulators had their own integrity and could not be ignored.

In the case of the Sputnik vaccine, Russia so persistently ignored the requirements of the World Health Organization, the European Medicines Agency, and the world scientific community that one wondered if stonewalling them was an intentional strategy. Instead of following established WHO and EMA procedures to prove that Sputnik was safe and effective, Russia circumvented the two agencies to sell Sputnik directly to countries willing to take it. Putin also proposed that all countries recognize vaccines certified by any country, a measure that would have sidelined international regulators entirely.

Russian propaganda is full of praise for international bodies and agreements when they serve Kremlin interests. The Ecuador case study notes Russia's warmth toward Latin American regional groupings like ALBA, UNASUR, and CELAC. But Russia never subordinates its sovereignty to any international body, as shown

---

[7] "Foreign Policy concept of the Russian Federation," March 31, 2023, http://kremlin.ru/acts/news/70811

344 | HOW RUSSIA LOSES

dramatically by its continued war in Ukraine in the face of overwhelming UN condemnation.

The ideal international grouping in Russia's eyes is the BRICS alliance, historically dominated by Russia and China. BRICS has no permanent leader or system of unanimous voting that restricts its members' freedom of action. The downside is that BRICS is more of a forum for rhetoric than action. The bloc's members did not act on Putin's urging that they work jointly to produce Sputnik.

• **Russian goals conflict.** Kremlin strategy is complicated by multiple Russian organizations and individuals that pursue conflicting objectives. Many believe Putin encourages rivalry among Russian power centers so that he can preserve his position by alternately backing various factions. However, this can lead to policy confusion. Anyone trying to design Russian policy toward a given country or issue must try to balance Putin's conception of Russia's grandeur, more concrete geopolitical objectives, private and state companies pursuing lucrative contracts, individual oligarchs hatching their own deals, private military companies looking for business, Russia-linked cybercriminals searching for targets and profits, security services bent on espionage and assassinations, and state and private propaganda shops.

When the interests of multiple Russian actors align, the syzygy can pay off for Moscow. For instance, Russian businessmen can finance popular, glitzy television channels that spread pro-Kremlin narratives on their newscasts—yielding a monetary profit to the businessmen and a propaganda dividend to Moscow.

However, the interests of all Russian parties may clash. Perhaps no one but Putin can give orders to every Russian actor, meaning their agendas are frequently left to collide from country to country, and even within Russia.[8] These collisions can have high stakes, as shown by the Prigozhin rebellion.

---

[8] In March 2023, Foreign Ministry spokesperson Maria Zakharova said a "battle of elites" was complicating Russia's ability to propagate coherent messaging about the war. See "Захарова и Игорь Ашманов

In the case of Nord Stream 2, the best way to assure the pipeline's opening would have been for relations between Germany and Russia to be as placid as possible. However, the desire of various Russian actors to assassinate Zelimkhan Khangoshvili, hack the Bundestag, and boost far-right German politicians had the opposite effect. Similarly, the developers of Russia's COVID vaccine might have hoped that Sputnik's simplicity and effectiveness would bring a fair-and-square victory over Western competitors (assuring the $100 billion in business that Putin once spoke of). But such hopes were upended by the Russian leadership's headlong rush for a "first-in-the-world" propaganda victory. This crippled the vaccine's scientific credibility, and conscripted Sputnik's social media boosters into the anti-Western nastiness of Russian geopolitical propaganda.

Putin's obsession with politically dominating Ukraine clashed with prospects for a stable trade relationship that could have benefited the Russian economy. In the case of Nord Stream 2, Russian financial analysts felt the project was a bad deal for Gazprom, a state-controlled company. But Gazprom's corporate interests fell victim to Putin's fixation on routing gas around Ukraine and to the eagerness of Kremlin-connected contractors to profit from the project. In South Africa, Rosatom's nuclear deal, personally promoted by Putin, was a major factor in the fall of Zuma, a major geopolitical ally.

Russia had trouble building a strong relationship with former Sudanese leader Omar al-Bashir, aimed at establishing a naval base in Sudan, because Russian military companies were supporting Libyan warlord Khalifa Haftar, an enemy of al-Bashir. The Russian government and the Wagner Group have been associated with different sides in the current Sudan conflict.[9] In

---

поспорили о нужности Росинформбюро: 'Нет единой информационной картины' [Zakharova and Igor Ashmanov argue over the need for a Russian Information Bureau: 'There is no united information picture']," *Biznesonline*, March 11, 2023, https://www.business-gazeta.ru/news/586371

[9] Dubow, Ben, "Sands of Time Running Out for Russia's Sudanese Gambit," Center for European Policy Analysis, September 12, 2023,

346 | HOW RUSSIA LOSES

the wake of the Ukraine invasion, the Kremlin has tried hard to maintain strong relations with Serbian President Aleksandar Vucic, while Russian radicals with access to Russian state media have condemned him for being too liberal.[10]

Western countries, too, suffer from conflicting goals. Often, for example, the United States must figure out how to deal with a regime that is geopolitically useful but tramples on human rights. These conflicts, however, pose less of a structural problem for the US, as—for better or worse—the nation's foreign policy, business, media, and cultural institutions are well understood to operate independently. The US military can train a foreign country's armed forces while the State Department expresses concern about the fairness of its elections. American businesses can flatter its government, American media can criticize it, and US-based exiles can plot against it—with no expectation that someone should pull all these actors into line. In some cases, pro-democracy groups in a country, financed through congressional grants, organize anti-government protests at the same time the State Department is seeking the government's cooperation.

In Russia, however, all institutions ultimately report to the same place. Visible clashes may occur as various sides compete to prioritize their own goals. In the meantime, Russia's image and effectiveness suffer.

• **Russian policy is constricted by a new wave of ideology and Putin's personal beliefs.** It is questionable whether, in the last years of the Soviet Union, anyone still cared about communist ideology. But obligatory ideology has reasserted itself under Putin. Today's official Russian belief system reflects almost exactly the creed of "orthodoxy, autocracy, and nationality" established under Nicholas I in the 19th century. Putin's regime

---

https://cepa.org/article/sands-of-time-running-out-for-russias-sudanese-gambit

[10] $$Kirillova, Ksenia, ""Radical 'Diplomacy' Harms Moscow's Allies," *Eurasia Daily Monitor*, September 27, 2023, https://jamestown.org/program/radical-diplomacy-harms-moscows-allies

identifies heavily with the Russian Orthodox Church. It has become as autocratic as an industrialized society can be. Nicholas' concept of nationality has been scaled up by Putin to see Russians as a civilization of their own, a branch of humanity separate from the decadent, declining West. Putin's ideology even flirts with radical pan-Slavist beliefs of the 19th and early 20th centuries— that Russia's destiny is to lead all of Christianity, perhaps after a catastrophic world war of purification.

Ahead of his invasion of Ukraine, Putin had access to well-based, professional military advice about the dangers of the operation. This advice clashed, however, with his apparent personal faith that Ukraine and Russia were destined again to become one country, based on Slavic messianism and his view of himself as a new Peter the Great. Putin knew NATO was arming Ukrainian forces, but he could hope this would be for naught if Ukrainians refused to fire on their Russian brothers. There is no sign the Kremlin engaged in "red-teaming" to test Putin's assumptions. In a system as autocratic as Putin's, there can be no questioning of what is ordained from on high.

This was pitifully clear from Putin's televised meeting with his Security Council two days before the invasion, where every speaker wholeheartedly supported a proposal to recognize the independence of Ukraine's Donetsk and Luhansk provinces. Foreign intelligence chief Sergei Naryshkin flubbed his lines. He was sharply interrogated by Putin until, shaken, he properly recited and endorsed the proposal.

Putin's personal belief system even dictated Russian military preparations. Russia's invasion force was equipped only for the short campaign Putin expected. By one account, Defense Minister Sergei Shoigu had little idea whether his military was truly ready to invade Ukraine in 2022 but trusted that Putin had reliable information that it was.[11]

---

[11] Zheguyov, Ilya, "Как Путин возненавидел Украину [How Putin came to hate Ukraine]," *Vyorstka*, April 25, 2023, https://verstka. media/kak-putin-pridumal-voynu

348 | HOW RUSSIA LOSES

The ascendant ideology within the Kremlin vis-à-vis the West may change again. If Russian decision-making has been based up to now on the idea that the West is a spent force running on fumes, Putin may need to change the basis for Russian decision-making. The West cannot be an existential threat and a walking corpse at the same time. The Russian president may need to impose a new ideology for his top lieutenants to learn and loyally enunciate.

8.

Strategies for the West

The fact that Russia's influence failings repeat themselves creates opportunities for Western governments and activists. By being aware of how the Kremlin has miscalculated in the past, the West can construct strategies for the future.

In constructing such strategies, however, it is important to remember that the West does not face Russia in a vacuum. China plays a key role in several of the case studies in this book. When it is allied with Russia, its wealth can make up for Russia's economic weakness. It can also conceivably function as a brake on Moscow's disruptive behavior. China benefits from political conditions that keep markets calm, and from rule of law (at least regarding commercial transactions); Russia sees its advantage in sowing chaos and in contempt for international practices.

The West must also consider that countries in the Global South have much more agency than they have in years past. The map of the world is no longer the zero-sum game of Cold War times, in which almost every country fell into the Western or Soviet camp. Countries today can embrace the "anti-colonialist" rhetoric fostered by Russia and China, deeply resent Western behavior in Iraq or Palestine, and yet vie for investment from the United States, the United Kingdom, or France. Nations speak increasingly of non-alignment, refusing to be any side's total satellite and basing their policies on what is most advantageous to them.

349

350 | HOW RUSSIA LOSES

This can be maddening to the West when such long-term allies as Saudi Arabia decide to reinforce their ties with Russia and China, or democracies like Brazil and India take a nonchalant attitude toward the invasion of Ukraine. But national agency can hurt Russia, too, when nations use it to demand tangible benefits from a relationship.

In contrast to Soviet Marxism of the past, which purportedly had universal application, the Kremlin's current ideology of nationalism and religion is too Russia-centered to be a useful export. For countries not dependent on its mining expertise, grain, or fertilizer, Moscow's ability to ingratiate itself with other nations rests mainly on anti-colonialist sloganeering, mercenaries, intelligence cooperation, and elite capture. This works best in poor, unstable countries. The more promising a country's future, the more difficult it is for Russia to make it a true client state. Russia's main "equalizer" in this situation is its experience in information operations, which will be considered below.

The strategies proposed in this chapter are designed with an eye to these considerations. Russian influence must be opposed to the degree it presents a threat, but with respect for the agency and dignity of the countries where competition takes place. Not every deal a country makes with Russia is unacceptable. The recommendations call for restraint in cases where anti-Western positions taken by national leaders are mainly rhetorical; for prioritizing aid, trade, public diplomacy, and information tactics; and for encouraging local actors as the most authentic and effective force for democracy and progress.

The strategies do call for aggressive action by Western countries when their interests are truly threatened. They also emphasize the importance of promoting the rule of law, for its own sake and because of the obstacles that laws and international procedures have posed to Russian ambitions. The strategies include highlighting the Kremlin's contradictory statements and goals.

Western powers should:

- **Judiciously assess Russia's alliances with top power brokers.** Some leaders' support for Moscow is mainly rhetorical, perhaps just incidental to a more important agenda. Other leaders' closeness to Russia presents a greater threat. In every case, the West needs to consider thoughtfully where its long-term interests lie and what that means in dealing with leaders who espouse anti-Western positions.

No one likes the idea of "doing nothing" when a national leader denigrates Western nations and makes common cause with Russia. However, if the threat posed by a regime is mainly nasty comments, the best approach may be to avoid being baited. Experience shows that Russian alliances with national leaders can be short-lived or simply transactional. They do not always require a maximalist response.

In Ecuador and South Africa, successive American ambassadors chose not to pick public fights with Rafael Correa and Jacob Zuma. The two presidents' rhetoric was insulting; one can imagine the temptation to react by slowing the issuance of visas, discouraging investors, or curtailing aid. However, Zuma's and Correa's verbiage did not create a broad threat to US interests. (Their UN votes were sometimes annoying but not game-changers.) Zuma and Correa would have posed a more substantive threat to Western security and values if they had allowed Russia to set up military bases or filled jails with political prisoners. As it happened, Ecuador's economic dependence on the US was an immutable fact, and its population had no taste for Russian-style repression. South Africa, too, was heavily dependent on trade with the West, and Zuma's regime was far from a police state.

Both Correa and Zuma likely hoped their anti-US posturing would help them politically at home. The chances for that would have greatly increased if it looked like the US Embassy considered their comments important enough to constantly rebut. The US missions in Ecuador and South Africa chose to play a long game by avoiding angry exchanges. Instead, the embassies offered bland statements and interviews emphasizing the benefits of

352 | HOW RUSSIA LOSES

American aid and trade. Even after Correa expelled the US ambassador, Washington's aid to Ecuador continued, totaling nearly $400 million under Correa. This meant that, when Correa left power and Julian Assange was expelled from the London embassy, a structure was intact to rapidly restore the US-Ecuador relationship. USAID quickly signed an agreement on new projects, Vice President Mike Pence visited Quito, and nine months later, Trump received Lenín Moreno in Washington.

Public spats between the embassies and the two leaders would probably not have ended well. Citizens have a natural tendency to sympathize with their own leaders, even flawed ones, in the face of attacks from a foreign power. Actions such as delaying visas and stopping aid antagonize ordinary people and validate their leaders' anti-American attitudes. The US view of Zuma and Correa was that "this too shall pass." America's focus was on preparing for the day when those regimes either disappeared or changed policy.

In recent years, Western nations have taken a similar attitude toward President Aleksandar Vučić's government in Serbia, on the theory that he has no long-term alternative other than bringing Serbia closer to the European Union. The United States has also largely ignored India's extensive deals with Russia and its democratic backsliding, recognizing the large scale of US-India trade and the nation's value as an ally against China.

At the same time, Western countries must continue to support local pro-democracy groups, as described below. The support need not come from the local embassy; it may be better if it does not. It can come from a semi-governmental foundation like the National Endowment for Democracy, or a US or UK government program based outside the country. If authorities are adapt at crushing anti-government activities, covert strategies may be appropriate. Playing a long game with undemocratic authorities does not mean retreating from the promotion of democracy.

Western powers should avoid humiliating foreign leaders unless they present a clear danger. Presidents and prime ministers, like all humans, hold grudges and have long memories. Correa said the

2008 raid on a FARC guerrilla camp inside Ecuador by US-backed Colombian forces significantly affected his view of the United States. Gruevski was furious when Macedonia's bid to join NATO was vetoed by Greece. Correa remembered, even a decade later, the fall in status he felt over his Moscow lodgings. Obviously, the ruler of any country will be disappointed from time to time, but it is prudent to make some effort to soften the blow or provide a compensating benefit.

It is true that a this-too-shall-pass attitude, applied on too large a scale, can transform itself from prudent restraint to dangerous complacency. If the chief business of the American people is business, as Calvin Coolidge asserted, the keep-cool approach largely works, so long as advantageous trade continues. Most experts, however, would now add to America's chief business the preservation of some modicum of democracy and free speech in other nations. Without them there can be no resistance to the bribes and malign ideologies of authoritarian countries. By this measure, democratic backsliding and the growth of Russian influence in the Global South cannot long be ignored.

Russia offers struggling nations security assistance, including brutal mercenaries, with no questions asked about human rights. Its goal is not so much to create direct military allies, but to encourage broad "anti-colonialist" sentiment that, bit by bit, will undermine the US-dominated financial system, the West's access to raw materials, and ultimately Western security. Anti-colonialism is an attractive concept in developing nations because it attributes much of the blame for poverty and instability, past and present, to Western actors.[1] People may know little about life in Russia or China, but the fact that they did not have colonial empires in the Global South evokes positive feelings in itself.

The newly expanded[2] BRICS alliance, dominated by Russia and China, is a key device in transforming historical anti-colonialist

---

[1] This is not to dismiss the pernicious aspects of colonialism.
[2] BRICS announced at its 2023 summit that, beginning in January 2024, the bloc would expand beyond its original members—Brazil, Russia,

354 | HOW RUSSIA LOSES

attitudes into modern-day rewards for Russia and China. There is little in common among the BRICS nations; joining the bloc may look simply like a low-risk way to signal anti-colonialist virtue and win more money from China. However, if the organization manages to impose foreign policy discipline on its members, it could become a coordinated bloc of large, populous, resource-rich countries—increasingly authoritarian at home and so imbued with antipathy toward colonizers of the past that they support hegemonists of the modern day.

Still, the West should initially try high-level bargaining in a calm atmosphere when governments present a true challenge, emphasizing the importance of its aid and trade, and engaging in large-scale information and democracy-promotion efforts with their populations.

• **Use aggressive tactics when warranted.** Sometimes the threat to Western interests is not just rhetorical but has clear security implications. The case studies show that assertive Western action in such situations can have a significant effect.

A small model of such a situation was Macedonia's drift toward Russia after Gruevski's humiliation in 2008. In that case, the West's response was not "this too shall pass," but an aggressive increase in activity of its own to pull the country into NATO and the EU. This effort carried the day.

The United States has adopted aggressive tactics elsewhere. US Ambassador Reuben Brigety dropped his usual emphasis on friendly US–South Africa relations to accuse South Africa of sending arms to Russia in mid-2023. The claim sent shockwaves through South Africa, where the government had insisted it was neutral on the Ukraine conflict. US sanctions at the end of 2019 against pipe-laying for Nord Stream 2 stopped the work in a surgical legal move that only affected a single essential contractor; if not for that action, the pipeline might have been in full operation well ahead of Russia's invasion of Ukraine. That

---

India, China, and South Africa—to include Saudi Arabia, the United Arab Emirates, Argentina, Ethiopia, Egypt, and Iran.

Strategies for the West | 355

would have left Russia free to destroy the Ukrainian pipeline network that had carried Russian gas to Europe, depriving Ukraine of transit revenues as well as heat and power for many of its citizens.

Germany and the European Union were indignant over Congress' threats in 2020 to impose sanctions on EU companies involved with the pipeline. The sanctions did not materialize, but the aggressiveness of Capitol Hill and Trump administration figures created an opportunity for Joe Biden to play the "good cop" by waiving the sanctions in return for a tougher German position on Russia.

The West was assertive, too, in spreading its influence in Ukraine. Western governments and foundations funded Ukrainian pro-democracy NGOs for years after its independence, including during the Orange Revolution. Their involvement reached a peak when demonstrators massed on Maidan Square in 2013. A dozen Western governments and Western-leaning international bodies demanded that Yanukovych not attack the demonstrators. Two US senators and an assistant secretary of state made personal appearances on the square to encourage the protests. All this was very different from the "Ukraine fatigue" of the past. Despite Russia's claims, the United States and its allies did not create Ukraine's democracy movement, but they recognized the importance of supporting it.

After Russia's 2014 invasion, NATO nations pursued their activity by pouring arms and trainers into Ukraine, enabling it to resist the 2022 invasion with a strength Russia had never expected. After the invasion, EU countries moved swiftly to block their own citizens from accessing propaganda on TV channels and websites from Russia. (Although the West's anger at such propaganda is understandable, censorship is not a good look for supposedly democratic countries. It would have been better to effectively contest the Kremlin's narratives, rather than implicitly validate their effectiveness by trying to suppress them.)

In another assertive action, in early 2023, the European Union denied candidate status to Georgia. (It bestowed that status on

Ukraine, despite the ongoing war, and on Moldova, despite its political instability.) The EU decision on Georgia followed measures by the ruling Georgian Dream party that were widely viewed as serving the interests of Russia and corrupt local figures. The EU action triggered anti-government protests in a country whose citizens overwhelmingly favor EU membership.

Happily, assertive action by the West in the present era usually involves strengthening pro-democracy forces; thus, it can be seen as morally right as well as effective. It also, interestingly, can challenge the countries the West engages with to take assertive stands themselves on critical issues. Large regional powers, including Brazil, India, South Africa, and prosperous Middle Eastern states, aspire to a bigger role on the world stage, often including permanent UN Security Council membership. However, it is hard to be a respected world power while taking refuge in neutrality on the most consequential issues of the day. It is a potentially dangerous game, especially if BRICS attempts to align all its members' foreign policies. But if Russia's power continues to decline, the West may be able to induce such countries to declare a stance against Moscow's adventurism for their own diplomatic prestige and self-respect.

If the opposite should happen, however—for instance, key countries increasingly line up with Russia and China in ways that affect US security—Washington's response must be more assertive.

In this, Congress is likely to play an important role. Congress forced the Reagan administration to impose sanctions on South Africa's apartheid government, ending a US policy that was gravely out of step with morality and world opinion. Many believe congressional pressure was the main reason for the US sanctions that stopped the Nord Stream 2 pipeline in 2019.

US diplomats, and even the president, can point to Congress as the final decision-maker on many issues and as the body that unhelpful foreign leaders will ultimately have to deal with. In 2022, the House of Representatives, angry at African states that continued to trade with Russia after its invasion of Ukraine, overwhelmingly passed legislation that demanded to know how US officials were was holding to account governments and individuals in Africa "complicit in violating or facilitating the evasion of" US sanctions.[3]

Although the bill did not become law, the African Growth and Opportunity Act (AGOA), which provides African nations with duty-free access to the US market, is up for renewal by Congress in 2025. It requires participating nations to be making progress on human rights and fighting corruption.[4] One can imagine Congress adding provisions that nations must not take actions or join blocs opposed to US commercial and security interests. Some believed that fear of losing AGOA benefits figured in South Africa's agreement with Russia that Putin would not attend the 2023 BRICS summit. In 2023, the danger of jeopardizing massive military aid from the US was believed to have weighed heavily in Egypt's consideration of whether to send arms to Russia for use in Ukraine.

Of course, congressional intervention can also undermine good policy. George Soros is a perpetual bugbear of US conservatives. But when Republican senators denounced cooperation between the US Embassy in Macedonia and Soros-sponsored civil society groups, they showed ignorance of overall US needs in that country. America's overriding interest there was to make

---

[3] Text at https://www.congress.gov/117/bills/hr7311/BILLS-117hr7311rfs.pdf. The measure failed to win Senate approval, but the House vote—419-9—signaled the depth of US concern over the issue. Reacting to the legislation, Ramaphosa said, "Both the US and Russia are strategic partners for South Africa. As a sovereign country that pursues an independent foreign policy, the bill seems to punish those who hold independent views." See Nemakonde, Vhahangwele, "US bill to counter 'malign' Russian activities could badly affect Africa, says Ramaphosa," *The Citizen*, September 16, 2022, https://www.citizen.co.za/news/us-bill-to-counter-malign-russian-activities-affect-africa-ramaphosa

[4] Executive Office of the President, "African Growth and Opportunity Act (AGOA)," https://ustr.gov/issue-areas/trade-development/preference-programs/african-growth-and-opportunity-act-agoa

common cause with all those opposing VMRO policies, including Soros-founded activists. In the current Ukraine conflict, if Congress forces a reduction in US aid to Kyiv, it will hand a gift to Putin.

As noted previously, one advantage of aggressive Western action is that Russia does not expect it. It expects a disorganized West to put up feeble resistance to its influence, or to leap to heavy-handed sanctions or military action that make it look like a bully. When the West takes action that is perfectly calibrated to the moment, be it in Macedonia, in pipeline-laying or by rushing weapons to Ukrainians, Russian assumptions are upended.

• **Prioritize aid, trade, and public diplomacy.** Russian public diplomacy that failed to connect with the concrete needs of local populations played a role in almost every case study in this book. Despite its skill in anti-Western propaganda, Russia has no inspiring economic or governance model to offer the world, and its foreign aid and trade are far less than what Western countries and China offer. These are enduring, systemic weaknesses in Russian influence that the West should exploit aggressively.

Some countries once looked at democracy practically as a cargo cult, in which simply imitating an alien culture's practices (in this case representative government and a market system) would cause the spirits to deliver the riches of that culture. This has not always worked out, but the technology and living conditions of the EU and North America are still the standard most hope to achieve. By some accounts, the EU's economy was so attractive to some East European nations that they joined NATO not primarily for military protection, but because membership was easy to obtain, and NATO endorsement of their democratic credentials could help them join the EU.[5] (Many admire China's dramatic progress and are happy to accept its investments and aid, but find its methods difficult to replicate in their own cultures.)

---

[5] For such an argument see Selden, Zachary, "Will Finland and Sweden joining NATO deepen the alliance's problem?" *War on the Rocks*, May 31, 2022, https://warontherocks.com/2022/05/will-finland-and-sweden-joining-nato-deepen-the-alliances-problems

Strategies for the West | 359

For all these reasons, it is difficult to overestimate the importance of the investments, trade, and aid that the EU and US offer struggling economies. This is especially true because of China's growing position in world trade; South Africa's trade with China, for instance, was twice its trade with the US in 2022. (In contrast, the biggest investors in South Africa remain Western countries.) Enormous goodwill flows from on-the-ground investments and aid projects that employ local workers and create products and services that people need.

Comments by Correa and Zuma in the case studies highlight the extreme sensitivity of Global South nations to economic *diktat* from wealthy countries and the international financial organizations they control. Wealthy entities with money to lend and invest feel they are in the right by ensuring that projects are economically sensible and that funds go where they are intended. National leaders intent on projects that are grandiose but uneconomical, or that mainly benefit their inner circle, will obviously look to authoritarian countries as less finicky sources of loans. Local pro-democracy actors are the best voices to oppose such loans and deals since they can more genuinely position themselves as defending their own countries' interests.

Public diplomacy sometimes fails to adequately promote the benefits of Western investments and aid. The US was well known in South Africa for the millions it spent helping combat AIDS. A massive US communication effort immediately after Zuma's fall might have leveraged new aid, cultural ties, and the anti-Russian feelings of the moment to solidify the decline in Russian influence. The EU is often weak in conveying how much aid it provides around the world. Russia's tendency to focus its international business and influence efforts on its own advantage is also a worthy subject to highlight.

Western diplomats often embark on the political side of public diplomacy with trepidation. They face persistent anti-Western narratives, especially in the Global South where many strongly disapprove of US foreign policy. Populations are also well aware of racism in Western countries, and many find Western sexual freedom sinful.

360 | HOW RUSSIA LOSES

However, surveys in developing nations do not reflect across-the-board anti-Western attitudes, nor do they show much admiration of Russia.[6] The US and its allies may be disliked for their foreign policy, but their prosperity is well known and their culture and products are familiar. Almost every nation has a significant diaspora in the West, whose members presumably tell their relatives at home that they are content to remain where they are. Millions seek visas to emigrate to Western countries. Surveys repeatedly find support for democracy, even if citizens are skeptical whether their political systems can deliver it.

Despite Western actions that have been unwise, deadly, contradictory, and tone-deaf, the power and authority of Western nations and citizens remains overwhelming. Activists against trans people in Kenya and Uganda sought to bolster their cause in 2023 by circulating a fake speech by Biden denouncing people who change their gender identification; they chose the American president rather than Vladimir Putin or Xi Jinping. After the military seized control of Burkina Faso in 2022, a fabricated video circulated there of American "pan-Africans" praising the new rulers.[7] Even after Trump had become a subject of disgust and ridicule worldwide, Zaev invited him to Macedonia to help campaign for a "yes" vote in the referendum. "The United States—still—is the huge example of democratic institutions, [rule] of law, free speech, and free media," Zaev said. "It's a huge model for us and good example around the world."

---

[6] For results of surveys in 34 countries in 2019-2021, see "Africans welcome China's influence but maintain democratic aspirations," Afrobarometer, Nov. 15, 2021, https://www.afrobarometer.org/wp-content/uploads/2022/02/ad489-pap3-africans_welcome_chinas_influence_maintain_democratic_aspirations-afrobarometer_dispatch-15nov21.pdf

[7] See "Clip of US President Joe Biden vilifying gay people was digitally manipulated," *Agence-France Presse,* March 7, 2023, https://factcheck.afp.com/doc.afp.com.33AN8U7; and *France 24,* "Deepfakes circulate of AI 'pan-Africans' backing Burkina Faso's military junta," January 27, 2023, https://www.france24.com/en/tv-shows/truth-or-fake/20230127-deepfakes-circulate-of-ai-pan-africans-backing-burkina-faso-s-military-junta

However, in its public communication, Western public diplomacy must resist spreading a message—mainly its own creation—that democracy is a Western product that people should buy because it works so well in the West. Since declining numbers of people abroad admire the US democratic model, such arguments set up the US and its allies for accusations of lying and hypocrisy.[8] It is far more effective to talk not about the uprightness of Western countries but about what people want for their own countries, in their own context. America's founders never saw democracy as something they invented, but as a right that all people are entitled to by nature.

Indeed, few people anywhere dream of living in a corrupt state where criticizing the government can lead to prison. Coups d'état and other unrest in the Global South these days usually involve at least some aspiration for democratic government and an end to corruption.[9] Understandings of freedom cannot live in total isolation from a country's religious, nationalistic, or cultural traditions. However, most people accept that some level of political participation and respect for human rights is essential for stability, progress, and renewal. Dictatorships rarely become more liberal; they typically become only more rigid, autocratic, and corrupt.

As for America itself, Jessica Brandt of the Brookings Institution recommends that US public diplomacy "focus on themes that continue to attract global audiences, including the United States' capacity for innovation and entrepreneurship, its technological and scientific achievements, and its support for freedom of expression."[10]

---

[8] Pew Research Center, "Global Public Opinion in an Era of Democratic Anxiety," December 7, 2021, https://www.pewresearch.org/global/2021/12/07/global-public-opinion-in-an-era-of-democratic-anxiety
[9] See Mbulle-Nziege et al., "Coups in Africa: Why they don't spell the end of democracy," *BBC*, February 8, 2022, https://www.bbc.com/news/world-africa-60289571
[10] Brandt, Jessica, "An information strategy for the United States," Brookings Institution, May 5, 2023, https://www.brookings.edu/testimonies/an-information-strategy-for-the-united-states

362 | HOW RUSSIA LOSES

In some places, the very word "democracy" is of fading value. Authoritarian regimes have tarnished the term by arguing that democracy requires all the liberal social values of Western countries, or counterfeit the word to claim their own states are democratic. America's founders managed to get through the entire Declaration of Independence and Constitution without using the word "democracy"; they simply enumerated the specifics of what they saw as a just society. We should follow the same approach. It is better to promote specific, easily understood rights, such as freedom of speech and a real choice among political candidates, than to build campaigns on a political science term whose meaning has become increasingly controversial.

The West should also humbly acknowledge that free societies are always evolving. Democracy is not a sealed system that requires no maintenance. Established democratic states, we should acknowledge, may be able to learn something from newer ones.

Information operations by Russia and its allies were active in each case study in this book. Russia's *RT* television network praised Zuma and Correa during their terms in office, and its Spanish service gave Correa his own talk show after he left power. *RT*'s German service endorsed right-wing politicians ahead of the 2021 German elections. Macedonian social networks were bombarded by postings, turbocharged by bots, opposing the Prespa agreement. Russia launched a large-scale campaign to promote the Sputnik vaccine, and targeted Ukraine with non-stop propaganda about the failings of Ukrainian leaders and the corruption of the state. Russian campaigns take on any tone that works. Gazprom's in Germany was sugar-coated, featuring generous gifts to schools and sports teams to promote the Nord Stream 2 pipeline. The pro-Sputnik campaign veered regularly into aggressiveness and snark.

At present, *RT*'s English, Russian, Spanish, German, French, and Serbo-Croatian services continue to blanket critical parts of the world with pro-Moscow programming, while the *Sputnik* news agency operates in 30 languages. Messaging on social networks adds to Russia's information power.

Strategies for the West | 363

In contrast, ever since the end of the Cold War, Western officials have been loath to conduct large-scale information operations. The reasons include insecurity about the story the West has to tell, and a revulsion toward engaging in "propaganda from our side"—which, some believe, would inevitably turn into disinformation. It is not an option, however, to simply ignore the impact of Russian information operations, or to exhaustively catalogue them (as is often done) but not respond. There is no need to lie in defense of Western interests, but we should be willing to vigorously argue our beliefs and hold Russia publicly accountable for its actions.

Western messaging has become slightly more effective since the start of the Ukraine war. The US and its allies have been successful in "prebunking"—anticipating, and publicly warning about, actions that Russia might take. When the Kremlin was vociferously denying that it intended to invade Ukraine, the US declared that it would—and predicted the timing almost to the day. This tactic often requires declassifying sensitive information, but it is worthwhile in terms of the information effect.

In 2023, the US State Department began to produce a stream of videos, aimed at Russian speakers worldwide and marked as official US products. They directly accused Putin of lying about the war, implicitly endorsed anti-war demonstrations in Russia, and contained grisly descriptions of what Russian soldiers faced in Ukraine.[11]

International media based in the West—the *BBC, Deutsche Welle, Radio France Internationale, CNN, CNN en Español,* and America's five government-owned international broadcasters operating in 60 languages[12]—have enormous audiences. Viewed from Moscow, they form an intimidating array of information power.

---

[11] Kent, Thomas, "US Messages to Russians Anger Kremlin," Center for European Policy Analysis, April 17, 2023, https://cepa.org/article/us-messages-to-russians-anger-kremlin

[12] The networks are the *Voice of America, Radio Free Europe/Radio Liberty, Middle East Broadcasting Networks, Radio Free Asia,* and *Radio-TV Martí,* aimed at Cuba.

364 | HOW RUSSIA LOSES

However, in the spirit of Western editorial independence, all these outlets are either private companies, or government-owned entities with independent editorial boards. The US government cannot instruct the *Voice of America*, much less *CNN*, to cover a certain story or turn up the heat on a foreign politician. Their freedom from government control is critical to their journalistic credibility. That leaves Western governments with few communications channels—mainly a few social media accounts—that they can calibrate to a sudden crisis or opportunity. These governments need an ability to generate intense, targeted messaging at a key moment and punch those messages through radio jamming and internet blocks.

For instance, Russian claims that Western COVID vaccines were dangerous were mentioned and appropriately debunked by the *Voice of America* and *CNN*. But given all the other events in the world, the coverage was necessarily fleeting. Yet suppose these Russian messages were resonating in a specific region of the world, scaring people away from lifesaving vaccines or even provoking them to attack vaccine clinics? Western governments lack an always-on-standby capability to immediately launch high-volume messaging campaigns—on social networks, on radio, and with posters and stickers—in specific geographies where such needs might suddenly arise. It is not even clear what components of the US government have the skills for such an operation and who would take operational charge of it.

Similarly, suppose Prigozhin's rebellion had led to chaos across Russia, with rumors flying that a US invasion was imminent? Washington would have needed a capability for intense messaging to make clear to Russians that it had no such intention.

• **Encourage local pro-democracy actors and independent journalism.** Messaging by Western countries, important as it is, can only accomplish so much. There is no way that communication from abroad can match the authenticity of local activists and journalists. The attacks on pro-democracy NGOs and journalists by Gruevski, Zuma, and Correa reflected their fear of any force that can rally public opinion and inspire protests. We can anticipate that Russia and its allies will always view such

Strategies for the West | 365

actors as dangerous, and a highly effective way to advance Western goals.

Just in Russia's neighborhood, popular movements helped bring down Serbia's Slobodan Milošević in 2000, Eduard Shevardnadze in Georgia in 2003, Askar Akayev in Kyrgyzstan in 2005, Viktor Yanukovych in Ukraine in 2005 and 2014, Gruevski in 2017 and Armenia's Serzh Sargsyan in 2018. Further afield, popular movements for democracy and against corruption triumphed (for a time) during the Arab Spring and have a long history in Latin America and Africa. Some of the most aggressive campaigning against Russia's war in Ukraine has come from activists in Eastern Europe.

Sometimes these groups are aided from the West—not usually by the CIA, as authoritarians dramatically claim—but through quite overt programs run by embassies, aid agencies, and private foundations. Unfortunately, the structure that provides this aid is far from the precisely honed influence machine that authoritarians imagine.

It would not be difficult for Western countries and foundations to create resource centers that would help such groups launch fast, effective responses to disinformation and fill media spaces with convincing pro-democracy content. However, in many countries, pro-democracy NGOs and free media struggle to fund their operations, recruit new members, and reach a broad audience. To address such problems, these actors and their Western supporters must come to grips with issues that have hampered their work for decades.

Democracy advocates are often well-educated, English-speaking, and city-raised. They lack the perspective of less worldly, less-educated citizens, especially from rural areas, who constitute important voting blocs. These citizens read and travel little, have quite different frames of reference, and often speak in a way immediately distinguishable from city-dwellers. Religion may be a big part of their lives. Disinformation actors target these populations with messages that are simplistic and populist, sometimes involving religious imagery. In Macedonia, Russia

366 | HOW RUSSIA LOSES

built Orthodox crosses and churches. To win the trust of such citizens, civil society must recruit allies who can speak to them in an equally credible way.

Civil society groups and independent news outlets must also become financially sustainable.[13] Pro-Russian media are often sensational in tone, filled with sports and entertainment stories along with political messages. Democracy activists are loathe to engage in anything that smacks of tabloid journalism, even if creating such outlets would also be a way to convey useful political content. Democracy-oriented information products tend to concentrate on politics, with little to attract ordinary people who are cynical about the political world. However, some are learning to build financial stability, gain trust, and broaden their audiences.[14]

Foreign donors frequently scatter their funds among a variety of recipients, who compete for grants and may be jealous of each other. Donors may not coordinate their actions. Some give small sums to so many recipients that they are hard-pressed to say what exactly each is doing. Donors also commonly provide grants for only six months to a year for specific short-term projects. This makes it hard for recipients to cover the ongoing running costs of an organization and to recruit permanent staff.

To address these issues, donors should concentrate their funding on a small number of recipients, requiring them to work together if they wish support. Funding should be bigger, longer-term, and take running costs into consideration. Effective democracy campaigners have lightened up their approaches, using humor and popular cultural references and working to reach citizens of all backgrounds. They should seek intersections with environmental, women's, and workers' rights groups; any organization that believes in civic activism is a potential ally.

---

[13] Perpetual foreign funding leave them open to claims they are "foreign agents."

[14] See White, Jessica, "Reviving News Media in an Embattled Europe," Freedom House, June 2023, https://freedomhouse.org/sites/default/files/2023-06/MD_Report_62823_Digital_GW.pdf

(Conservative anti-Kremlin politicians and environmental activists were unlikely allies in opposing Nord Stream 2, but their interests coincided.)

Volunteer online campaigners who battle trolls and disrupt online conspiracy groups have been effective in some East European countries.[15]

Democracy advocates must also prepare for new challenges authoritarian rulers are devising. They need to be able to respond to the suppression of campaigning and demonstrations, slowdowns and blockages of the internet, as well as legal harassment. Such tactics are beyond the scope of this book, but have been detailed elsewhere.[16]

An important focus for NGOs and journalists is to hold Russia to account when it, or its allies, play fast and loose with facts. What would have been the real cost to South Africa of the nuclear deal? (Zuma's attitude was that it made no difference because Russia would keep restructuring the debt.) Was Sputnik really safe and effective? (To this day, Russia has not satisfied scientists and regulators.) Was Nord Stream 2 so essential to Europe as to justify the huge investments by the continent's biggest energy companies? (It seemed to be mainly about punishing Ukraine.)

Assertions by Russia and its allies that its influence projects are simply "business deals" should be subjected to rigorous scrutiny. Russia made such claims about Nord Stream 2 and the South

---

[15] See Kent, Thomas, "In the global meme wars, it's time to side with the elves against the trolls," *The Washington Post*, November 16, 2022, https://www.washingtonpost.com/opinions/2022/11/16/support-elves-trolls-disinformation-wars

[16] For longer discussions of the strengths and weaknesses of pro-democracy groups and tactics for their survival on repressive conditions, see Kent, Thomas, *Striking Back: Overt and Covert Options to Combat Russian Disinformation* (Washington: Jamestown Foundation, 2020); and Adams, Laura, et al., "How civic mobilizations grow in authoritarian contexts," Freedom House, December 8, 2022, https://freedomhouse.org/sites/default/files/2022-11/FHPrecursorsFinal_11152022.pdf

368 | HOW RUSSIA LOSES

African nuclear program. Its Czech ally, President Miloš Zeman, said the same about the Sputnik vaccine. Russia's penchant for secrecy should be catnip to investigative reporters, who revel in obtaining documents and information that governments try to hide.

Finally, many democracy advocates seek to solve the problem of disinformation through pressure on social networks. There is no doubt that these networks are prime distributors of malign content; anything they can be forced to do to counter the tide is welcome. However, pro-democracy groups will have more success in the short term by learning to use the networks' algorithms to distribute their own messages. There is no reason to let hostile actors monopolize the use of social channels. Artificial intelligence can also be used to construct and distribute messages; if pro-democracy actors do not take advantage of this capability, hostile forces will certainly use it to geometrically increase their effectiveness.

• **Leverage the power of laws, courts, legislative bodies, and international organizations.** In almost every case study in this book, laws, courts, procedures, and referendums helped foil the efforts of Russia and its allies. Pro-democracy forces should use these institutions, even if results take time. A South African court blocked the nuclear deal with Russia. The Nord Stream 2 pipeline was delayed at critical moments by Danish legal deliberations and European and German regulators. The Sputnik vaccine's failure to win WHO and EMA approval sharply limited its distribution. President Gjorge Ivanov, Russia's Macedonian ally, tried to ignore his legal obligation to allow Zoran Zaev to form a government, but failed. When Zaev finally came to power, he used a referendum and constitutional amendments to accomplish his goals.

Since Russia does not operate by rule of law, Russian influence operators are not attuned to legal issues. When faced with legal and regulatory barriers, they project onto them the politicization of such institutions in Russia; it is hard for the Kremlin to understand what an independent judiciary or regulator is. As the case studies show, even powerful lobbyists in the West cannot guarantee to make legal issues "disappear." Russia's team of high-

Strategies for the West | 369

paid former politicians failed to get Denmark to speed up its decision on Nord Stream 2, or to keep EU regulators from becoming involved in the project.

Russia's contempt for international organizations has only grown as it has become increasingly repressive and aggressive under Putin. In recent years, the Kremlin has run afoul of the International Criminal Court, the European Court of Human Rights, the International Court of Justice, the EU Court of Justice, the International Olympic Committee, the World Anti-Doping Agency, the Court of Arbitration for Sport, and multiple sports federations. Although Russia occasionally wins appeals, or simply ignores the rulings, the drumbeat of verdicts by prestigious bodies corrodes Moscow's reputation.

Democratic governments and activists should take every opportunity to subject Russian personnel and actions to legal consequences. They are not always hopeless efforts. Such actions can impede the Kremlin's influence operations while demonstrating the power of the rule of law.

• **Profit from Russia's conflicting goals.** It is only due to Russian bluster, and inattentiveness by pro-democracy actors, that Moscow gets away with pursuing so many contradictory goals at the same time. Vigilant monitoring of activity by different Russian actors can identify contradictions to exploit. In Germany, during the years before the invasion of Ukraine, Russia blatantly interfered with domestic politics and carried out an assassination within two miles of the chancellery, all while smilingly funding sports and cultural enterprises to promote Nord Stream 2. Moscow purports to promote international legislation against cybercriminals, while hackers linked to Russian intelligence agencies rampage worldwide. Russia has tried to build brotherly relations with countries in southern Africa while suggesting, in TV programs for its domestic audience, that Black governments there are terrorizing Whites through "reverse apartheid."[17]

---

[17] See Sukhanin, Sergey, "The Kremlin's Controversial 'Soft Power' in Africa (Part Two)," *Eurasia Daily Monitor*, December 10, 2019,

370 | HOW RUSSIA LOSES

Russia's "Foreign Policy Concept" adopted in March 2023 is piously worded but stunningly contradicts Russia's actual behavior. Published 14 months into the invasion of Ukraine, it says Russian policy will give priority attention to "the territorial integrity of states." The document, issued the same month that Putin was indicted for war crimes, declares that the Russian Armed Forces will be used "in accordance with the generally recognized principles and norms of international law." It said Russia would work to prevent military conflicts that could escalate to the use of nuclear weapons—even as Putin continued to threaten that the war he started could turn into a nuclear conflict.[18]

The contradictions and hypocrisy in Russian policy are ripe for exposure by democratic forces. They often focus only on what Russia is saying to their populations; they need to know what Russian assets are saying elsewhere as well. Democracy activists in Africa, for example, may not be aware what television inside Russia is saying about "reverse apartheid." Contradictions such as those in the "Foreign Policy Concept," however, are so blatant that, properly publicized, they should be effective if exposed anywhere.

It is dangerous when democratic leaders and media, inured to Russian hypocrisy, simply stop highlighting it. This creates the risk that new generations of citizens will be unaware of Russian prevarications, or not realize Russia is telling different stories to different audiences.

• **Do not panic.** Russian influence success is not inevitable. The case studies in this book are all about surprises and miscalculations, usually to the Kremlin's disadvantage. The cases also cite many incorrect predictions by Western analysts that events would unfold in Russia's favor.

---

https://jamestown.org/program/the-kremlinscontroversial-soft-power-in-africa-part-two

[18] "Foreign Policy concept of the Russian Federation," op. cit.

The Wall Street Journal quoted critics as predicting that Moreno, who completely reversed Correa's foreign policy, "will likely not change things much." *The Guardian* wrote that the outcome of Macedonia's 2018 referendum was "a significant victory for Vladimir Putin"—four months before Russia's efforts in Macedonia collapsed entirely. *The Economist* said the West's reputation for COVID vaccines would be "hard to repair" because of early deliveries from Russia and China; Western vaccines became the world standard. On Zuma's political future, the *Mail & Guardian* opined during his rape trial in 2006 that, whatever the verdict, he "cannot now be president." He won the presidency in 2009.

These errors are cited not to demonstrate that some predictions can be wrong, but to argue that the prediction enterprise itself is fundamentally hazardous. Most major events in the world begin as surprises, or take surprising turns once they are underway. Confident predictions always risk igniting false hopes or unwarranted despair. Analysts do best when they develop a variety of possible outcomes. They may rank the scenarios in terms of likelihood, but rigorous thinking requires recognizing that a range of possibilities exist.

These include the possibility that Russian influence operations will fail. Much of the power of the Kremlin's influence comes from people believing its influence is powerful. As the case studies in this book show, Russia does not always succeed. The myth that Russia is invincible is a Russian asset in itself.

This is the key message of the book. Although Putin's Russia has often accomplished its goals, other outcomes are possible. Western actors can learn to recognize the kinds of Russian behavior that have led to the Kremlin's failures. They then can exploit that knowledge to counter Russian influence and advance the cause of liberty—if they have the courage to do so.

372

Chronology

A chronology of key events in the case studies in this book:

1991
>December 1 – Ukraine becomes independent, with Leonid Kravchuk as first president
>December 25 – Mikhail Gorbachev resigns; Boris Yeltsin becomes president of Russia

1993
>January 20 – Bill Clinton becomes US president, succeeding George H.W. Bush

1994
>July 19 - Leonid Kuchma becomes president of Ukraine
>December 5 – Budapest memorandum on Ukrainian security signed

1999
>March 12 - NATO expansion begins with Poland, Hungary, and the Czech Republic
>June 16 - Thabo Mbeki becomes South African president, succeeding Nelson Mandela
>December 31 – Vladimir Putin becomes acting president of Russia

2000
>May 7 – Putin's first official presidential term begins after he wins election

2001
>January 20 – George W. Bush becomes US president

2004
>November 21 –Viktor Yanukovych's election triggers Orange Revolution in Ukraine

374 | HOW RUSSIA LOSES

2005

January 10 – Viktor Yushchenko declared president of Ukraine after new vote
September 8 – Letter of intent signed for Nord Stream 1 pipeline
November 22 – Angela Merkel replaces Gerhard Schröder as German chancellor

2006

August 27 – Nicola Gruevski becomes prime minister of Macedonia
September 5 – Putin makes his first visit to South Africa

2007

January 15 – Rafael Correa becomes president of Ecuador
February 10 - Putin denounces West at Munich security conference

2008

April 2-4 – Bucharest NATO summit denies entry to Macedonia, defers plan for Ukraine
May 7 – Putin turns presidency over to Dmitry Medvedev; becomes prime minister
August 8 – Russian troops enter Georgia

2009

January 20 – Barack Obama becomes US president
May 9 – Jacob Zuma becomes president of South Africa

2010

February 25 – Viktor Yanukovych becomes Ukrainian president
December 24 – South Africa joins the BRICS bloc

2011

April 5 – Ecuador expels US ambassador Heather Hodges
November 8 - First conduit of Nord Stream 1 goes into operation

Chronology | 375

2012

    May 8 – Putin reclaims presidency from Medvedev
    June 18 – Gruevski begins five-day visit to Russia
    June 19 – Julian Assange enters Ecuadorian Embassy in London

2013

    November 21 – Yanukovych suspends trade pact talks with EU; Maidan protests begin

2014

    February 22 – Yanukovych flees Kyiv
    March 16 – Officials announce that Crimea referendum approves union with Russia
    June 7 - Petro Poroshenko becomes Ukrainian president
    August 24 – Regular Russian troops enter Donbas
    September 22 – Russia and South Africa sign framework nuclear agreement

2015

    June 8 – Large demonstrations begin against Correa's policies
    September 4 – Shareholders' agreement signed for Nord Stream 2

2016

    January 1 – Ukrainian trade agreement with EU goes into effect
    October 16 – Coup attempt in Montenegro

2017

    January 15 – Nikola Gruevski steps down as Macedonian premier
    January 20 – Donald Trump becomes US president
    April 3 – Gazprom applies to route Nord Stream 2 through Danish waters
    April 26 – South African High Court invalidates nuclear deal with Russia
    April 27 – Nationalists storm Macedonian assembly
    May 24 – Lenín Moreno becomes president of Ecuador
    May 31 – Zoran Zaev becomes Macedonian premier

July 11 – Correa leaves Ecuador for Belgium

2018

February 14 – Zuma resigns presidency; succeeded by Cyril Ramaphosa

June 27 – Greece and Macedonia sign the Prespa agreement

September 30 – Macedonian referendum on the Prespa agreement

November 13 – Gruevski says he is in Budapest after fleeing Macedonia

2019

January 11 – Constitutional change adopts name North Macedonia, effective February 1

April 11 – Assange expelled from Ecuadorian Embassy in London

May 20 – Volodymyr Zelenskyy becomes Ukrainian president

October 10 – Bulgaria issues new conditions for North Macedonia to join EU

Oct 19 – France vetoes start of EU accession talks for North Macedonia

October 21 – Large protests break out against Moreno in Ecuador

October 30 – Denmark approves Nord Stream 2 route through its economic zone

December 20 – Trump signs sanctions that stop Nord Stream 2 pipe-laying

December 30 – Russia signs new agreement for gas transit through Ukraine

December 31 – Original target date for opening of Nord Stream 2

2020

February 12 – Moreno meets with Trump in Washington

March 27 – North Macedonia formally joins NATO

April 7 – Correa sentenced in absentia on corruption charges

August 11 – Russia announces Sputnik vaccine

Chronology | 377

August 20 - Russian agents poison Alexei Navalny

2021

January 20 – Joe Biden becomes US president
February 2 – Russian study and editorials in *The Lancet* say Sputnik is safe and effective
May 19 – Biden waives sanctions on Nord Stream 2
May 24 – Guillermo Lasso becomes president of Ecuador
July 9 – Riots break out in South Africa after Zuma is jailed
September 10 – Nord Stream 2 construction completed
December 8 – Olaf Scholz becomes German chancellor

2022

February 22 – Germany suspends regulatory review of Nord Stream 2
February 24 – Russia launches full-scale invasion of Ukraine
June 13 – Protests break out against Lasso's government in Ecuador
June 30 – France presents proposal for North Macedonia to join the EU
September 2 – Gazprom stops all gas flowing through Nord Stream 1
September 26 – Explosions strike Nord Stream 1 and 2
September 30 – Putin annexes four Ukrainian oblasts he does not fully control
December 19 – Ramaphosa re-elected as ANC leader

2023

August 30 – Pro-free-market and pro-Correa candidates emerge from first-round presidential election in Ecuador

Acknowledgments

The case studies in this book cover a broad range of subjects and geography. More than 80 subject matter experts were kind enough to grant me interviews. Several of them reviewed drafts of the case studies and made valuable suggestions.

I would like to acknowledge in particular the help I received on Ukraine from Elise Giuliano of Columbia University and John Herbst of the Atlantic Council; on South Africa from Barbara Groeblinghoff of the Friedrich Naumann Foundation and Joseph Siegle of the Africa Center for Strategic Studies; on the Sputnik vaccine from J. Stephen Morrison, director of the Global Health Policy Center of the Center for Strategic & International Studies, and Enrico Bucci of the Department of Biology at Temple University; on Nord Stream 2 from Jeffrey Rathke, president of the American Institute for Contemporary German Studies at Johns Hopkins University, and from energy consultant Bartosz Bieliszczuk, formerly of the Polish Institute for International Affairs; on Macedonia from media and community development consultant Zvonko Naumoski and from Martin Pechijareski; and on Ecuador from journalist Arturo Torres Ramírez and R. Evan Ellis, Latin America research professor at the US War College.

Several government officials and diplomats who were intimately involved in the events described talked to me at length about their experiences. Some of these declined to be quoted by name because of their positions.

Research for the book was generously supported the Smith Richardson Foundation through The Jamestown Foundation. Glen Howard, president of Jamestown, provided valuable advice throughout. Joseph Bebel was my patient and careful editor.

I am deeply grateful to all those who gave me assistance. Any errors are, of course, my responsibility.

T. J. K.

About the Author

Thomas Kent is a specialist on influence operations, Russian affairs, and journalistic ethics. Until September 2018, he was president and CEO of US-funded Radio Free Europe/Radio Liberty. He now teaches at Columbia University and consults for governments, media, NGOs, corporations, and news media in the United States and Europe. He is a senior fellow of The Jamestown Foundation in Washington and an associate fellow of the GLOBSEC think tank in Slovakia.

His first book, *Striking Back: Overt and Covert Options to Combat Russian Disinformation*, was published by Jamestown in 2020.

Prior to heading RFE/RL, Kent was a correspondent and news executive at The Associated Press. Among other assignments, he was bureau chief in Moscow, chief of AP operations in Tehran during the Iranian revolution, EU correspondent in Brussels, head of AP's international news coverage, and standards editor, responsible for the credibility and ethics of AP's content.

Kent has spoken at professional forums in 24 countries, lectured to students of 29 universities, and has written for *The New York Times, The Washington Post*, the Atlantic Council, Jamestown, *The Hill*, the Center for European Policy Analysis, *The American Interest*, and others.

He has served twice as a juror for the Pulitzer Prizes in international reporting and has held board or advisory positions with the Online News Association, Ethical Journalism Network, Society of Professional Journalists, and Organization of News Ombudsmen and Standards Editors.

He was raised in Shaker Heights, Ohio, holds a degree in Russian and East European Studies from Yale University, and speaks Russian, French, and Spanish.